ADMINISTRATIVE BEHAVIOR

ADMINISTRATIVE BEHAVIOR

A Study of Decision-Making Processes in Administrative Organization

HERBERT A. SIMON

With a foreword by
Chester I. Barnard

Third Edition
With New Introduction

FP

THE FREE PRESS
A Division of Macmillan Publishing Co., Inc.
NEW YORK

Collier Macmillan Publishers
LONDON

The Free Press
A Division of Macmillan Publishing Co., Inc.
866 Third Avenue, New York, N.Y. 10022

Collier Macmillan Canada, Ltd.

Library of Congress Catalog Card Number: 75-18009

Printed in the United States of America

Hardcover printing number
6 7 8 9 10

Paperback printing number
10

Library of Congress Cataloging in Publication Data

Simon, Herbert Alexander
   Administrative behavior

   Includes bibliographical references and index.
   1. Management. 2. Decision-making. I. Title.
HD31.S55 1976   658.4   75-18009
ISBN 0-02-928971-8
ISBN 0-02-929000-7 pbk.

TO D. P. S.

CONTENTS

INTRODUCTION TO THE THIRD EDITION

Administrative Behavior is basically a book for organization watchers and for organization designers. As the preface to the original edition explains, the book's aim is to show how organizations can be understood in terms of their decision processes. Almost all of us qualify as organization watchers, since we spend most of our waking lives in organizational environments. Many of us qualify also as organization designers, since we have managerial responsibilities of greater or lesser scope for maintaining and modifying organizations. We are organization watchers, too, all of us, in our role as citizens. Increasing attention has been fixed in recent years upon the functioning of our society's organizations: its large corporations and its governments. Hence, this could also be described as a book for Everyman—for it proposes a way of thinking about organizational issues that concern all of us.

In this third edition, as in the second, the text of the original work (Chapters I through XI) is kept intact, for there is essentially nothing in it that I wish to retract. *Administrative Behavior* has served me as a useful and reliable port of embarkation for voyages of discovery into human decision-making: the relation of organization structure to decision-making, the formalized decision-making of operations research and management science, and in more recent years, the thinking and problem-solving activities of individual human beings.

But although I have no urge to recant, I do wish to augment the text with considerable additional material that develops and illustrates some of the important themes of the first edition. Accordingly, six new chapters (Chapters XII through XVII) have been added to this edition, each of them based on a previously published article that either elucidates an issue treated more

ix

briefly in the earlier chapters or applies the analytic scheme of those chapters to concrete organizational problems.

In the present edition as in the second one, I will use this Introduction to clarify and elaborate upon some of the central ideas with which the book deals, in the light of what organization theorists have learned in the generation since it was first published. This will permit me to supply added emphasis to the propositions in the original text that now, by hindsight, appear to me the most significant for the science of organization and its application to practice; and to discuss the relation of the book to some of the important contemporary developments in theory.

The subject matter of organization theory is of considerable interest, as I have already suggested, both to practitioners—administrators and executives in business, government, and education—and to behavioral scientists—economists, political scientists, sociologists, social psychologists, and cognitive psychologists. When a practitioner picks up a copy of this book, he will be searching for other things than will a scientist; and even among social scientists, interests and vocabularies are sufficiently diverse that all parts of the book will not be of equal interest to all readers. In the first section of this Introduction I shall comment on the structure and organization of the book so that the reader, whatever his special interest, can more readily find his way through it.

The second section of the Introduction is addressed particularly to executives—it tries to show how the decision-making theory set forth in the book can be applied to practical organization problems. The third section undertakes a corresponding orientation for behavioral scientists by discussing the relation of organization theory in general, and the theory proposed here in particular, to other frames of reference in the social sciences.

STRUCTURE OF THE BOOK

Anyone who tries to write a book soon learns that there is a fundamental incompatibility between the simple linear sequence of words that he has to set down and the complex web of his thoughts. To meet this difficulty, he combs out his thoughts as best he can into long strands and ties them together in as orderly a manner as possible. While preserving the most important relations in the pattern of his ideas, he sacrifices others.

The present edition of *Administrative Behavior* consists of two parts. Part I is the text of the first edition; Part II contains the six new chapters that have been added. The basic plan of the two parts is described in the paragraphs that follow.

Plan of Part I

Chapter I is a general introduction and summary.

Chapters II and III (together with the Appendix) seek to clear out some methodological underbrush so that the task of constructing the theory can begin.

Chapters IV and V represent the core of the book. These chapters propose a theory of human choice or decision-making that aims to accommodate both those rational aspects of choice that have been the principal concern of the economists and those properties and limitations of the human decision-making mechanisms that have attracted the attention of psychologists and practical decision-makers. Because these chapters are so central to the whole argument of the book, I shall pay particular attention to them in this Introduction.

Chapter VI is in the nature of a diversion—a necessary diversion, but a diversion nonetheless. Whereas the rest of the book is concerned largely with what goes on "inside" administrative organizations, Chapter VI discusses what takes place at their boundaries—the decisions that human beings make to join organizations or to leave them. This chapter is largely a restatement of the ideas of Chester Barnard, who first provided a systematic framework for discussing the human motivations that are involved in the "decision to belong."

Chapters VII through X return to the main theme—the decision-making processes that are internal to organizations. These chapters describe how organizations influence the decisions of their members, bring about consistency among those decisions, and guarantee that the decisions will be compatible with over-all organization goals.

The material of these later chapters rests squarely upon the structure of theory erected in Chapters IV andV, and one technical innovation introduced in those chapters proves to be of crucial importance. Instead of taking decisions as basic unanalyzable units, we regard human choice as a process of "drawing conclusions from premises." It is therefore the *premise* (and a large number of these are combined in every decision) rather than the whole *decision* that serves as the smallest unit of analysis.

The importance of breaking decisions into their component premises can be illustrated in many ways, of which I shall mention one. Discussions of administrative centralization and decentralization often bog down on the question: "Who *really* makes the decisions?" Such a question is meaningless—a complex decision is like a great river, drawing from its many tributaries the innumerable component premises of which it is constituted. Many individuals and organization units contribute to every large decision, and the problem of centralization and decentralization is a problem of arranging this complex system into an effective scheme.

These four chapters (VII to X) are concerned, then, with the study of the streams of decision premises and the ways in which these premises converge to influence the decision-making of organization members. (See also pages 11–16.) Chapter VII is devoted to the *authority* mechanism, and Chapter VIII to the *communication processes* that are used in organizations to influence and link together the component choice processes of their members.

Chapters IX and X deal with the two most important special classes of decision premises included in this stream. The *criterion of efficiency* considered in Chapter IX, is important for conserving the scarce resources the organization has at its disposal for accomplishing its tasks. The loyalties to goals and groups (*identifications*) described in Chapter X bring about a meshing of the subgoals of components of an organization with the goals of the whole organization.

In Chapter XI these several elements in the process of composite decision are brought together again in a description of the process as a whole. Here the method of analysis developed in the previous chapters is brought to bear, by way of application and illustration, upon the planning and control processes in organization and upon the problem of centralization and decentralization.

Plan of Part II

The new chapters (XII through XVII), which build upon Chapters VI through XI, have all been published previously. I have selected them, from among my papers on administration written since *Administrative Behavior* appeared, either because they clarify and amplify an important idea in the original text (Chapters XII and XV), because they discuss an aspect of organization theory that has undergone important development in the past twenty years (Chapters XIII and XIV), or because they provide useful examples of how the theory presented in the book can be applied (Chapters XVI and XVII). These chapters are reproduced in essentially their published form. Chapter XIII, based on a talk to the 1967 Mexico City meeting of the Institute of Management Sciences, is written somewhat less formally than the other chapters, but perhaps the reader will be ready for a bit of relaxation when he reaches that point in the text. Let me say a word about the content of each of the new chapters.

Chapter XII, an analysis of the concept of "organizational goal," clarifies the relation of the individual motives underlying the "decision to belong" (Chapter VI) with the goal premises stemming from the organization's formal authority structure (Chapter VII) and from the efficiency criterion (Chapter IX).

Chapters XIII and XIV reexamine communication (Chapter VIII) in the light of the new information processing technology that has been introduced with the electronic digital computer. The first of these two chapters explains what it means to do business in an information-rich world; the second inquires into the implications of the new information technology for the design of organizations.

The brief Chapter XV provides an empirical demonstration of a point that is central to Chapter X: Members of organizations identify with particular subgoals not merely (or mainly) because of the reward structure, but because these subgoals are closest to their daily activities, hence are perceived most clearly. Thus, subgoal identification has deep roots in the limits of rationality discussed in Chapter V and in the selectivity with which the individual perceives his environment.

The final two chapters, XVI and XVII, show how the decision-making analysis of *Administrative Behavior* can help to explain the evolution of an organization structure or to design such a structure. Chapter XVI provides further evidence for the cognitive bases of organizational identification (Chapter X), whereas Chapter XVII builds upon the discussion of organizational design in Chapter XI.

Overview of the Book

The basic structure of the book, then, may be outlined quite simply as follows: It consists of five strata of topics, each of which has to be discussed in order to provide a basis for dealing with the next.

1. In Chapters II and III we deal with certain methodological issues in order to be able to analyze the structure of human rational choice.

2. In Chapters IV and V we construct a theory of rational choice in order to be able to understand the influences that come to bear upon decision-making in an organizational environment.

3. In Chapters VII through X, we examine these influence processes in detail in order to discuss the effects of organization itself on the decision-making process.

4. In Chapter XI, we illustrate how the analysis can be used to deal with questions of organization structure.

5. In Chapters XII through XVII, which constitute Part II, we expand upon a number of topics that have been introduced in the chapters of the third and fourth strata, with particular emphasis upon questions of organization design.

Chapter VI is inserted along the way to provide a motivational link between the individual and the organization—to explain, that is, why organizational influences, and particularly the influence of authority, are such effective forces in molding human behavior.

In its genesis the book developed in reverse order—from the higher strata (i.e., strata 3 and 4) down. When I tried, beginning forty years ago, to find answers to some questions of municipal organization—e.g., whether a recreation department should be administered by the school board or the city government, or how the city planning function should be organized (see pages 212 and 244)—I discovered that no existing theory could provide the answers, and I was forced into an analysis of the ways in which organization affects human choice. Finding no better answers to this new stratum of questions, I began to reexamine the theory of rational decision-making. The latter task required me, in turn, to settle in my own mind some basic problems of logic. At this point the regress came temporarily to an end—partly, I hope, because the foundations were now firmer. *Administrative Behavior* records the answers I found to these successive layers of questions about administrative organization and about the nature of rational human choice.

LESSONS FOR ORGANIZATION

In recent years, organizations have not had a good press. Large organizations, especially international corporations and Big Government, have been blamed for all manner of social ills, including widespread "alienation" of both workers and executives from their work and from society. The empirical evidence that alienation is more widespread than it has been in previous ages and in other societies is nonexistent, as is the evidence that alienation is to be attributed to organizations. However, this kind of criticism has one merit: It takes organizations seriously and recognizes that they do influence the behavior of the people who inhabit them.

A rather different view of organizations, often expressed by managers, is that it is the *man* who matters, not the organization.

I am sure you have heard it many times: "I used to think that organization was important, but now I think it is much more a matter of personality. The important thing is the man. If he has drive, ability, imagination, he can work in almost any organization." To be sure, "personality" is a useful concept. Human beings differ along all sorts of dimensions, many of them influencing their behavior in organizations. But the importance of personal characteristics for organizational performance does not imply the unimportance of organizational characteristics. The complex world of human affairs does not operate in such simple-minded single-variable ways.

Moreover, personality is not formed in a vacuum. A man's language is not independent of the language of his fathers, nor his attitudes divorced from those of his associates and his teachers. A man does not live for months or years in a particular position in an organization, exposed to some streams of communication, shielded from others, without the most profound effects upon what he knows, believes, attends to, hopes, wishes, emphasizes, fears, and proposes.

If organization is inessential, if all we need is the man, why do we insist on creating a position for the man? Why not let each create his own position, appropriate to his personal abilities and qualities? Why does the boss have to be called the boss before his creative energies can be amplified by the organization? And finally, if we have to give a man some measure of authority before his personal qualities can be transformed into effective influence, in what ways may his effectiveness depend on the manner in which others are organized around him?

The answers are simple. Organization is important, first, because organizational environments provide much of the force that molds and develops personal qualities and habits (see especially Chapters V, X, and XV). Organization is important, second, because it provides those in responsible positions the means for exercising authority and influence over others (see especially Chapters VII and VIII). Organization is important, third, because, by structuring communications, it determines the environments of information in which decisions are taken (see especially Chapters

VIII, XIII, and XIV). We cannot understand either the "input" or the "output" of the executive without understanding the organization in which he works. His behavior and its effect on others are functions of his organizational situation.

The Meaning of Organization

Part of the resistance to attending to the organizational factors in executive behavior stems from misunderstanding of the term "organization." To many persons, an organization is something that is drawn on charts or recorded in elaborate manuals of job descriptions. In such charts and manuals the organization takes on more the appearance of a series of orderly cubicles contrived according to an abstract architectural logic than of a house designed to be inhabited by human beings. And the charting and manual-writing activities of the departments of organization that one finds in large corporations and governmental agencies more often reinforce than dispel this stereotype of what is involved in "organization."

In the pages of this book, the term *organization* refers to the complex pattern of communication and relationships in a group of human beings. This pattern provides to each member of the group much of the information and many of the assumptions, goals, and attitudes that enter into his decisions, and provides him also with a set of stable and comprehensible expectations as to what the other members of the group are doing and how they will react to what he says and does. The sociologist calls this pattern a "role system"; to most of us it is known as an "organization."

Much of what an executive does has its principal short-run effect on day-to-day operations. He makes a decision about a product price, a contract for materials, the location of a plant, an employee's grievance. Each of these has an immediate effect in settling the specific question before him. But the most important cumulative effect of this stream of decisions and refusals to decide—like the erosion caused by a small but steady trickle of water—is upon the patterns of action in the organization around him. How will the next contract be made? Will it be brought to him at all, or handled by his subordinates? What preparatory work will have been done before it reaches him, and what policies will guide those who handle it? And after the next contract, what about the next ten, and the next hundred?

Every executive makes his decisions and takes his actions with one eye on the matter before him and one eye on the effect of *this* decision upon the future pattern—that is to say, upon its organizational consequences (see page 144). When he pays attention to these indirect consequences, he is concerning himself with *organization*.

Understanding Organizations: Identifications

A good place to start one's thinking about organization is with one's own job. What identifications do I have (Chapters X and XV)? What are my attachments to goals and to organization units? What are the important situations in my work where I have to choose between competing goals and loyalties? What do my choices in such situations show about my values and the values that others in the organization will impute to me?

A next step consists in finding how these goals and loyalties have come to be and what maintains them. In speaking to groups of executives, I have sometimes constructed an imaginary conversation among a sales manager, a production scheduler, a factory department head, and a product design engineer. The four are discussing mutual problems that have arisen in the course of designing, producing, and selling the company's product. Each, of course, is trying to induce the others to change their methods of operation to make his own job easier. I put together this conversation as an exercise in the predictive value of organization theory—I simply assumed that each actor in the drama would respond to a particular problem in proportion to the volume and vigor of the communications he received about it. Starting from this obvious premise, it was easy to predict that the sales manager would be most concerned with customers' wishes for low price, prompt delivery, and product quality; that the scheduler would want predictability of sales; that the factory man would urge longer lead times and less reckless promises to customers; that the design engineer would complain about the inflexibility of the factory in introducing design improvements; and so on. The stereotyped reactions in my scenario are stereotypes of roles, not of personalities.

Am I describing your company? I am describing Everyman's company. A sales manager reacts like a sales manager because he occupies a particular organizational position, receives particular kinds of communications, is responsible for particular subgoals, and experiences particular kinds of pressure. And similarly for the other characters in my drama.

Understanding Organizations: Authority

An executive who can construct such an imaginary conversation is well on his way to understanding how organizational position molds beliefs and attitudes. He has taken the first step also toward analyzing how to modify beliefs and attitudes by changing the flow of communications. He can turn his attention next to the authority he exercises and the authority that is exercised by those around him (Chapter VII).

How far can I take for granted the authority I employ in getting my job done, and under what particular circumstances must I concern myself with it? Do people do what I want done (or better, what needs to be done) because I have the power to fire and promote? Do the attitudes of fellow employees support or undermine the ready acceptance of authority? Is authority a yoke or a more or less accepted procedure for the orderly conduct of business?

Asking these questions seriously—and with a determination to avoid gross self-deception—brings one to consider the motivations of people for accepting or rejecting authority or for remaining in the organization at all (Chapter VI). And this raises a new set of questions: What conditions do we have to create and maintain in this organization so that authority will become one of the effective instruments for getting our job done? How can we supplement the obvious sanctions that every employer has with the even more powerful sanctions of legitimacy and confidence?

No question has excited more controversy during the past generation than the proper scope and use of authority in organization and management. On the one side, we have classical organization theory, stressing formal lines of authority in a hierarchical organization and implying that legitimate commands are always carried out. On the other side, we have the research and writings of the "human relations" school, pointing up the value of broad participation in decision-making, demonstrating the importance of informal organization and the consequent limits on formal authority, and raising difficult questions about the human costs of excessively authoritarian environments. At the fringe of the human relations school we even have writers who regard all exercise of authority as antithetical to human freedom and "self-actualization," and who imagine a future in which organizations will operate in a completely egalitarian way without using formal authority.

Chapters VI and VII take a middle ground on these questions of authority—not to avoid controversy, but because this middle ground provides the best explanation of how authority actually operates in organizations, its limits, and the consequences of its exercise. To understand where this middle ground lies, the reader must be careful not to interpret the term "authority" too narrowly. Following Chester Barnard, I see an exercise of authority in an organization whenever a person allows his decisions to be guided by decision premises provided to him by some other person. Authority, interpreted in this way, is not the limited formal authority of the classical theorists, nor does it fit the stereotype of authority relations drawn by the writers of the human relations school.

To be effective in an organization, one must be able to observe when authority (in its broader definition) is being exercised and to judge when it will be effective and what its limits are. Chapters VI and VII are aimed at aiding these judgments. These chapters have little to say about the broader moral or social issues of the proper role of authority in society. That is not to say that those issues are unimportant—on the contrary, they are of the greatest significance. But they lie largely outside the scope of this book. I will merely record here my view that there is nothing intrinsically immoral or demeaning in the existence of authority relations between human beings. The genuine moral questions are all relative: questions of how much authority, based on what rewards or sanctions, employed toward what goals, and in what social context. The business, governmental, and educational organizations I see about me today are substantially less "authoritarian" (use formal authority more sparingly) than the organizations of a generation ago. Being a creature of my times, I view that shift as generally beneficial, but I do not draw the conclusion that a further dilution of the authority relation would be equally desirable, or that it is inevitable.

Organization Structure: The Big Questions

Up to this point I have deliberately avoided the big and dramatic questions of departmental reorganization: Shall we centralize or decentralize, strengthen the line or the staff, organize by product or by process? I have avoided them because these large issues are often discussed in a wholly formal and dehumanized way, as though they had nothing to do with human behavior and as though they were something apart from the everyday concerns of the executive.

The point of view of this book is that reorganization—reshuffling departments, or what not—derives its importance from its effects on the behaviors of individual executives and groups of executives. That is to say, it works through the mechanisms we have already been considering—identifications and loyalties, authority, communications. (See the introductory description of these influences on pages 11–16, and the retrospective summary on pages 221–228.) An executive who wants to understand the issues of large-scale organization may well begin with the organization immediately around him. When he has done that, he will have some basis for visualizing in terms of actual human behaviors the possible effects and consequences of reorganization on a larger scale. He will be immunized against the most virulent strains of chartism and directivitis.

Organization design is not unlike architectural design. It involves creating large, complex systems having multiple goals. It is illusory to suppose that good designs can be created by using the so-called "principles" of classical organization theory (Chapter II, pages 20–36). Although these "principles" still occupy a prominent place in the textbooks, their nature and limitations appear to be better understood today than when the first edition of *Administrative Behavior* appeared.

To design an organization requires balancing competing and conflicting considerations and desiderata. No single design principle can be applied without taking account of the consequences of the numerous alternative principles that are also applicable. The examples provided in this book show how attention to the decision-making and communication processes provides a viable alternative approach to organization design, which dispenses with the classical "principles."[1]

The final pages of Chapter II (pages 41–44) now seem to me to give an inadequate account of the kind of empirical investigation that is needed for organization design. Many studies over the past twenty years have shown how the design of an organization must adapt to its environment and its technology. Since we can hardly hope to find a set of invariant "weights" that apply to all organizations under all circumstances, research in administration needs to be more concerned with identifying and understanding the basic mechanisms that are present in systems of organizational behavior than with assigning numbers to specific design features.

Two brief examples will illustrate how the theory of this book can be used to approach organization design in business. Two additional examples of design—one drawn from government, the other from educational administration—are developed at length in Chapters XVI and XVII.

---

[1] On the theory of the design process, and recent progress toward a technology of design, see Chapter 3, "The Science of Design," in my *The Sciences of the Artificial* (Cambridge, Mass.: M.I.T. Press, 1969).

Example 1 : *Accounting organization.* Here is how the methods of this book were applied in an investigation of accounting departments in large business firms.[2]

The question, was this : How should a company's accounting department be organized in order that the data it assembles be of the greatest usefulness to the operating executives of the business in making decisions and solving problems?

To answer this question, it was necessary, first, to determine what important kinds of decisions are made by operating executives, how accounting data might be useful in making these decisions, and at what point in the decision-making process the data could most usefully be injected. By observing the actual decision-making process, specific data needs were identified at particular organizational levels—the vice presidential level, the level of the factory manager, and the level of the factory department head, for example—each involving quite distinct problems of communication for the accounting department.

Out of the analysis of data requirements at specific locations, a pattern of accounting department organization was developed that would be effective in providing data for operating executives. For example, it was proposed to establish at the factory department level one or more accounting analysts, thoroughly conversant with operations, to help department heads interpret and trace costs through the monthly and other periodic cost statements. At higher levels, on the other hand, it was proposed to create a small number of strategically placed groups of analysts largely occupied with special studies rather than periodic reports—analyzing the costs and savings associated with possible changes in operating methods and equipment.

These brief statements only sketch the analysis of accounting organization problems that was carried out in this particular research study. Our present interest lies in the study's implications

[2] This discussion is based on a report of a study carried out in collaboration with Harold Guetzkow, George Kozmetsky, and Gordon Tyndall: *Centralization v. Decentralization in Organizing the Controller's Department* (New York: Controllership Foundation, Inc., 1954).

for the *technique* of organizational design and reorganization. (1) The core of the study was an analysis of the way in which decisions actually were made and the locations of important decision functions. (2) The recommended organizational pattern for the accounting department was built around its task of informing and influencing these operating decisions. (3) The recommendations for organizational change were to be implemented by bringing about changes in the communication patterns—in the patterns of who-talks-to-whom-how-often-about-what—rather than by formal changes in organization charts.

Example 2: Product development. Industries that are based initially on a radically new technology typically go through several stages with respect to product development and improvement. In the first phase, the principal source of product improvement is usually in the new technology itself and the sciences underlying it. Thus, when the computer industry was at this stage, technical leadership depended heavily on basic improvements in computer memories and switching circuits, improvements that stemmed, in turn, from advances in solid state physics and fundamental inquiry into the organization of computer systems. At a later stage, product improvement became considerably more a matter of adaptation to end use—for example, providing appropriate software packages for customer applications.

An analysis of new-idea sources in these two phases would show that different types of research and development skills were needed, and that different communications patterns existed between the engineering departments and their environments. In the long run, events forced the appropriate organizational changes on most companies, but systematic organizational analysis of the product development process could often have brought these changes about more promptly and profitably.

More generally, the main problems in organizing research and development activities lie in bringing together information from two distinct sources: from the scientific disciplines that underlie the basic technologies being used, and from the environments that define the requirements for products in their end use. As will be shown in Chapter XVII, organizing a professional school poses almost identical problems of information flow and organization.

These two examples may serve to indicate how the methods of analysis proposed in this book can be applied to specific situations.[3] The key to the process is to develop a careful and realistic picture of the decisions that are required for the organization's activity, and of the flow of premises that contribute to these decisions. To do this, one needs a vocabulary and concepts that focus upon the significant and dismiss the irrelevant. The vocabulary and concepts described here deal with organizational problems in a more fundamental way than does the homely wisdom that has passed for organizational analysis in the past.

Decision Making and the Computer

The first edition of this book was published shortly after the first modern digital computer came into the world and some years before the computer found even the most prosaic applications in management. In spite of the extensive use of computers in organizations today, we still live pretty much in the horseless carriage stage of computer development. That is, we use computers to perform, more rapidly and cheaply, functions that we formerly carried out by adding machine and typewriter. Apart from some areas of middle-management decision, where operations research techniques like linear programming are now widely employed, computers have changed only modestly executive decision-making processes or the shapes of organization designs. We must be cautious, however, about extrapolating from past to future. The automobile, when it first appeared on the scene, also had a modest impact: It took over transportation tasks formerly performed by horse and wagon. It gave few hints of its future enormous effects on our whole transportation system and, indeed, on our whole society. There is every reason to think that the computer, too,

---

[3] In *Public Administration* (New York: Alfred A. Knopf, 1950), my colleagues, Don Smithburg and Victor Thompson, and I discuss a number of issues of organization design in Big Government. Although some of the examples in that volume will seem a bit prehistoric to readers who do not remember World War II, there is little else in the text that now seems outdated. The adaptation of organization to environment and task is discussed particularly in Chapter 7 and Chapters 12 through 15.

is something far different from an oversize adding machine, and far more significant for our society.[4]

The central lesson for organization design that stems from the new technology of the computer is that information is no longer scarce: We now live in an information-rich world. Two new chapters, XIII and XIV, explore the problems of communication and organization design in such a world. The second of these chapters explains why management information systems have generally been something less than a great success and sketches the form that more effective information systems may be expected to take in the future.

ADMINISTRATIVE BEHAVIOR AND CONTEMPORARY BEHAVIORAL SCIENCE

Up to this point, we have been discussing primarily Chapters VII to XVII, which I described earlier as the topmost strata of the book. I should like to excavate a little deeper now, down to the third stratum, consisting of Chapters IV and V. These chapters treat of rational human decision-making. Perhaps the simplest way to explain their organization is to answer the following two questions:

1. Why are these chapters preoccupied with *rational* behavior?
2. Why do they emphasize the *limits* of rationality?

I shall try to answer these questions in the next two sections and then proceed in subsequent sections to relate this theory of behavior to others now current in the behavioral sciences.

Rational Behavior and Administration

The social sciences suffer from acute schizophrenia in their treatment of rationality. At one extreme, the economists attribute

---

[4] Elsewhere, in my lectures entitled *The New Science of Management Decision* (New York: Harper & Row, 1960), also published as a part of *The Shape of Automation* (New York: Harper & Row, 1965), I have examined these developments in the computer and in operations research, as well as their implications—both present and prospective—for management and organization. A revised edition of these lectures, bearing the original (1960) title will be published by Prentice-Hall in 1976.

to economic man a preposterously omniscient rationality. Economic man has a complete and consistent system of preferences that allows him always to choose among the alternatives open to him; he is always completely aware of what these alternatives are; there are no limits on the complexity of the computations he can perform in order to determine which alternatives are best; probability calculations are neither frightening nor mysterious to him. Within the past generation, in its extension to competitive game situations and to decision-making under uncertainty, this body of theory has reached a state of Thomistic refinement having great intellectual and esthetic appeal but little discernible relation to the actual or possible behavior of flesh-and-blood human beings.

At the other extreme, are those tendencies in social psychology traceable to Freud that try to reduce all cognition to affect. Thus, we show that coins look larger to poor children than to rich (Bruner and Postman), that the pressures of a social group can persuade a man he sees spots that are not there (Asch), that the process of group problem-solving involves accumulating and discharging tensions (Bales), and so on. The past generation of behavioral scientists has been busy, following Freud, showing that people are not nearly as rational as they thought they were. Perhaps the next generation will have to show that they are far more rational than we now describe them as being—but with a rationality less grandiose than that proclaimed by economists.

This schizophrenia is reflected in Chapters IV and V. The first of these two chapters undertakes to clarify the concept of rationality as it has been developed in economics and formal decision theory. The second chapter discusses the boundaries that man's limited cognitive capabilities place on the exercise of rationality. Hence, it is Chapter V and not Chapter IV that describes rationality as we should expect actually to see it in real life.[5]

[5] I now feel that in Chapter IX, "Efficiency," too much ground is yielded to the omniscient rationality of economic man. The absence of a "common numerator," discussed on pages 178–180, makes the criterion of efficiency, in the form it assumes in this chapter, applicable largely to rather low-level decisions. My present views are reflected more fully in the chapter on efficiency (Chapter 23) in *Public Administration* (*op. cit.*), and in my paper, "A Behavioral Model of Rational Choice," *Quarterly Journal of Economics,* February, 1955, reprinted in *Models of Man* (New York: Wiley, 1956).

To anyone who has observed administrative organizations or has concerned himself with their theory, it seems obvious enough that human behavior in organizations is, if not wholly rational, at least in good part *intendedly* so. Much behavior in organizations is, or seems to be, task-oriented—and sometimes efficacious in attaining its goals. Hence, if we are to give a psychological account of human behavior in organizations, the psychological theory we employ must have room in it for rational behavior.

It seems equally apparent to one who observes behavior in organizations that the rationality exhibited there has none of the global omniscience that is attributed to economic man. Hence, we cannot simply chuck psychology overboard and place the theory of organization on an economic foundation. Indeed—and I shall elaborate on this point in the next section—it is precisely in the realm where human behavior is *intendedly* rational, but only *limited* so, that there is room for a genuine theory of organization and administration.

The Limits of Rationality

In one sentence, the thesis of Chapters IV and V is this: *The central concern of administrative theory is with the boundary between the rational and the nonrational aspects of human social behavior.* Administrative theory is peculiarly the theory of intended and bounded rationality—of the behavior of human beings who *satisfice* because they have not the wits to *maximize*.

This thesis is discussed explicitly at three points in the book: in an introductory way on pages 38–41, in relation to the psychology of decision-making on pages 80–81, and in its implications for administration on pages 240–244. An examination of these pages will provide useful guidelines for reading and interpreting Chapters IV and V.

Chapter IV prepares the way for the description of human rationality in organizations by depicting the more global rationality of economic man, and by showing what conditions a man would have to meet to make his choices in the manner assumed by economic theory. Chapter V then undertakes to specify how actual behavior deviates from the economic model, and the role that the organizational environment plays in such behavior.

At the time these chapters were written, the model of economic man was far more completely and formally developed than the model of administrative man (partly because of the preoccupation of psychologists with the nonrational). Consequently, the limits of rationality were defined in the book largely as residual categories, and the positive characterization of the process of choice is very incomplete.

In psychology during the past twenty years, there has been a great renaissance of interest in human rationality—in the whole range of matters that goes under the label of "cognitive psychology." As a result, it is more feasible now than when *Administrative Behavior* was first published to construct a model of rational choice that incorporates the actual properties of human beings and at the same time retains some of the formal clarity of the economic model. As it has turned out, two crucial alterations are needed to transmute the economic man of Chapter IV into the man of limited rationality, the administrative man, of Chapter V whom we recognize from everyday life.[6]

(1) Whereas economic man maximizes—selects the best alternative from among all those available to him, his cousin, administrative man, satisfices—looks for a course of action that is satisfactory or "good enough." Examples of satisficing criteria, familiar enough to businessmen if unfamiliar to most economists, are "share of market," "adequate profit," "fair price."[7]

(2) Economic man deals with the "real world" in all its complexity. Administrative man recognizes that the world he perceives is a drastically simplified model of the buzzing, blooming confusion that constitutes the real world. He is content with this gross simplification because he believes that the real world is mostly empty—that most of the facts of the real world have no

---

[6] See my "A Behavioral Model of Rational Choice," *op. cit.;* and "Rational Choice and the Structure of the Environment," in the *Psychological Review,* April, 1956, both of which were reprinted in *Models of Man, op. cit.*
[7] See, for example, R. M. Cyert and J. G. March, "Organizational Factors in the Theory of Oligopoly," *Quarterly Journal of Economics,* 70:44–64 (February, 1956).

great relevance to any particular situation he is facing and that most significant chains of causes and consequences are short and simple (see pages 68–70). Hence, he is content to leave out of account those aspects of reality—and that means *most* aspects—that appear irrelevant at a given time. He makes his choices using a simple picture of the situation that takes into account just a few of the factors that he regards as most relevant and crucial.

What is the significance of these two characteristics of administrative man? First, because he satisfices rather than maximizes, administrative man can make his choices without first examining all possible behavior alternatives and without ascertaining that these *are* in fact all the alternatives. Second, because he treats the world as rather empty and ignores the interrelatedness of all things (so stupefying to thought and action), administrative man can make his decisions with relatively simple rules of thumb that do not make impossible demands upon his capacity for thought.

This description of administrative man is essentially a development and formalization of the description in pages 81–84 of *Administrative Behavior*. But how do we know that it is a *correct* description—more accurate, for example, than the model of economic man? The first test, and perhaps not the least important, is the test of common sense. It is not difficult to imagine the decision-making mechanisms that administrative man would use. Our picture of him fits pretty well our introspective knowledge of our own judgmental processes as well as the more formal descriptions of those processes made by the psychologists who have studied them.

The past twenty years has seen enormous progress in what has come to be called "information processing psychology." Human thought processes in difficult problem-solving, concept-attainment, and decision-making tasks have been successfully described in terms of programs of basic symbol-manipulating processes. These explanations have been carried out in sufficient detail so that actual computer programs have been written for simulating the human behavior, and close matches have been obtained between the outputs of the computer programs and the thinkingaloud protocols of human subjects engaged in the same tasks.[8]

This is not the place to describe these developments in psychology in detail. What is important for our purposes is that the basic postulates about human rationality built into these simulations of behavior are essentially the postulates of satisficing man, described above. Nor have the tests of these new psychological theories been limited to laboratory tasks. As examples, the decision-making of a bank trust officer choosing investment portfolios has been simulated successfully, and a detailed analysis has been carried out, in information-processing terms, of how students completing a graduate program in business made their first job selections.[9]

In view of the substantial body of evidence now available in support of the concept of bounded rationality, of satisficing, and of the limited rationality of administrative man, I do not regard the description of human rationality in Chapters IV and V as hypothetical but as now having been verified in its main features.

Relation to Current Developments in Formal Decision Theory

It is interesting and even a bit ironical that at the very time when we have learned to build reasonably precise and empirically verified theories of rational human decision-making, there should

---

[8] For an introduction to these developments in psychology, see Herbert A. Simon, *The Sciences of the Artificial* (*op. cit.*, Chapter 2). A more complete account of the research on problem-solving will be found in Allen Newell and Herbert A. Simon, *Human Problem Solving* (Englewood Cliffs, N.J.: Prentice-Hall, 1972), which also contains an extensive bibliography.

[9] The simulation of the bank trust officer is reported in G. P. E. Clarkson, *Portfolio Selection: A Simulation of Trust Investment* (Englewood Cliffs, N.J.: Prentice-Hall, 1962). The job choice study is described briefly in Peer Soelberg, "Unprogrammed Decision Making," in J. H. Turner, A. C. Filley, and Robert J. House, eds., *Studies in Managerial Process and Organizational Behavior* (Glenview, Ill.: Scott Foresman, 1972). Several empirical studies on organizational decision making are included in R. Cyert and J. G. March, *Behavioral Theory of the Firm* (Englewood Cliffs, N.J.: Prentice-Hall, 1963). A substantial number of additional studies of decision-making in the business firm have been published during the past two decades, almost all confirming the picture of administrative man that is drawn in *Administrative Behavior*. Regrettably, there is no single place where these studies or the references to them have been drawn together.

be a vigorous renaissance of theorizing about economic man. The renaissance can be dated from the remarkable progress in game theory, owing to von Neumann and Morgenstern, on the one hand, and the equally remarkable and closely related progress in statistical decision theory, owing to Neyman and Pearson, to Wald, and to Savage, on the other.[10]

These developments tend often to be treated as a single package; the various individual parts are not aways fully dissected. At least five separate and distinct concepts, all of them important, are built into the von Neumann and Morgenstern game theory.

(1) The idea of representing possibe future behavior as a "tree," with branches radiating from each choice point, so that the individual must select at each such point the appropriate branch to follow (see page 67 below). This concept is much older than the modern theory of games, being traceable back to at least 1893. It is intuitively familiar to most chess players and to psychologists who have run rats through mazes.

(2) The idea of taking the minimax (selecting the branch that will give the best result in the face of a malevolent opponent) as the definition of rational choice in a competitive situation (see pages 71–72 below). This concept, too, has a long history. It is known intuitively to chess players and was formally described as early as 1912 by the logician Ernst Zermelo.[11]

(3) The idea of using a mixed strategy (e.g., bluffing) in a competitive situation to prevent one's move from being found out by the opponent. In 1928, von Neumann proved that there always exists a "best" strategy in this sense.

(4) The idea of defining rational choice in competitive situations with more than two players in terms of the possibilities of forming coalitions. This was the important new idea proposed in

[10] On game theory, see J. von Neumann and O. Morgenstern, *Theory of Games and Economic Behavior* (Princeton: Princeton University Press, 1947), and R. D. Luce and H. Raiffa, *Games and Decisions* (New York: Wiley, 1957). On statistical decision theory see L. J. Savage, *The Foundations of Statistics* (New York: Wiley, 1954), and the references to Neyman and Wald in Savage's bibliography.

[11] On the history of game theory, see Denes König, *Theorie der Endlichen und Unendlichen Graphen* (Leipzig: Akademische Verlogsgesellschaft, 1936), Chap. 8.

1945 with the publication of *The Theory of Games and Economic Behavior*. Up to the present time, this idea has had some application in political science but little in economics or organization theory.

(5) The demonstration that, in the face of uncertain choices, where only the probability distribution of outcomes is known, an assumption of consistent choice is tantamount to the assumption that the decision-maker has a cardinal utility function and is choosing so as to maximize its expected value. This idea can be traced back to the English philosopher Frank Ramsey (1926) but was brought back to attention by game theory.

The theory of bounded rationality in *Administrative Behavior* incorporates item (1) of this list and is not incompatible with item (3), but the remaining items characterize economic man rather than administrative man and are not part of the model used here. This vital distinction has sometimes been overlooked by commentators, who have mistakenly supposed that the term "rational" in *Administrative Behavior* has essentially the same meaning as it has for classical economists, game theorists, and statistical decision theorists.

One cannot help being impressed by the virtuosity that has been exhibited in formal decision theory during the past generation, the beauty of some of the results, and the applicability of these results as normative rules for decision-making under certain rather restricted circumstances.[12] What needs to be made clear, however, is that the theories of human choice and of organization developed in this volume rest on a very different description of rational man than do game theory and statistical decision theory.

If we are to find a common conceptual roof under which both economic man and administrative man can live, that roof can include only item (1) of the above list—the "tree" of possible future behaviors. Remarkably enough, this tree provides also the central concept for another theoretical development of the past generation that has attracted wide attention—the theory, owing to Shannon,

---

[12] Most of the management science research on normative rules for production and inventory control belongs to this line of development, as do the important advances that have taken place in linear programming. This matter is discussed further in *Models of Man, op. cit.*, Part IV.

Wiener, and others; of selective information.[13] In psychology, the so-called stochastic learning theories, in turn, make use of this very same notion, probably derived by way of the Shannon theory. The fact that this concept has been seized upon independently in such a variety of contexts to provide a framework for a theory of behavior suggests that it represents the real core of the new behavioral *Zeitgeist*.[14]

Psychological Roots of Organizational Identification

Chapter X discusses briefly (pages 208–212) the psychological bases for organizational identification. My present inclination would be to stress the cognitive factors (see the discussion of "focus of attention," pages 210–212) a good deal more than the chapter now does. This was, indeed, my original intention, but I was swayed by the then-current fashion in social psychology of always preferring affective to cognitive explanatory mechanisms. Thus, too little emphasis was placed in Chapter X on the limits of rationality as an explanation for subgoal formation and loyalties to subgoals, and as a result the close dependence of this chapter upon Chapter V was obscured. This gap is now somewhat repaired by the new Chapter XV, which provides empirical evidence that selective attention causes subgoal identification.

The mechanism of identification—or at least its cognitive aspect—might be described thus:

(1) High-level goals provide little guide for action because it is difficult to measure their attainment and difficult to measure the effects of concrete actions upon them. The broad goals (e.g., "long-term profit," "public welfare," and so on) are thus not *operative*—nor do they provide the "common numerator" discussed in Chapter 9 on efficiency as essential to a choice among alternatives.

(2) Decisions tend to be made, consequently, in terms of the

[13] See N. Wiener, *Cybernetics* (New York: Wiley, 1948).
[14] I have cited only a few of the most striking instances in which this idea of a behavior tree has cropped up in recent years. Its emergence can be traced back to the early development of Boolean algebra, symbolic logic, and set theory. For further comments on the history of this notion, see *Human Problem Solving, op. cit.,* pp. 874–888.

highest-level goals that are operative—the most general goals to which action can be related in a fairly definite way and those that provide some basis for assessing accomplishment. The operative goals provide the seed around which the administrator's simplified model of the world crystallizes. He takes into account those matters that are reasonably directly related to these goals and discounts or ignores others.

(3) Not only do his subgoals cause the administrator to attend selectively to his environment, but the administrative structures and communication channels he erects to attain those goals expose him to particular kinds of information and shield him from others. Yet, because of the complexity of the information that does reach him, even this selected information is analyzed only partially and incompletely.

Relations to Sociological Theory

The question is sometimes asked whether an analysis of organizations in terms of their decision-making processes is "sociological" or whether it is "psychological." The question is a bit odd; it is like asking whether molecular biology is biology or chemistry. The correct answer in either case is "both." *Administrative Behavior* analyzes organizations in terms of the decision-making behavior of their participants, but it is precisely the organizational *system* surrounding this behavior that gives it its special character. The roles of organization members are shaped by their goal identifications, and goal identifications, in turn, are a product of location in the organization.

Of course, decision-making analysis is not the only approach to the study of organizations, any more than biochemistry is the only approach to the study of organisms. A number of investigators, particularly sociologists, prefer to look at more global characteristics of organizations and to relate these to variables like organization size or organizational environment. Such studies have an important place in research on organizations; but ultimately, of course, we wish to find the connections between the various levels of inquiry. If organizations that operate in different industries (e.g., steel companies as compared with advertising agencies) typically take on different structural characteristics, we will want to explain these differences in terms of underlying differences in decision-making processes.

Decision-making in organizations does not go on in isolated human heads. Instead, one member's outputs become the inputs of another. Because of this interrelatedness, supported by a rich network of partially formalized communications, decision-making is an organized system of relations, and organizing is a problem in system design. This point of view toward organization design is perhaps best illustrated in this volume by the new Chapter XVII. The reader who turns to this chapter can decide for himself whether he is reading "psychology" or "sociology," or he can simply dismiss the whole issue as unimportant. I confess that my own inclination is to do just that.

Role Theory. The concept of *role* provides the standard "sociological" explanation of behavior—the captain goes down with his ship because he has accepted the role of captain, and that is what captains do in our culture. The term is not much used in *Administrative Behavior,* but it might easily have been if my linguistic habits had been formed in sociology instead of political science (see, e.g., pages 100–102). The utility of the term is limited, however, because it has never been given a sufficiently precise definition.

In its original connotation of a dramatic part, "role" implies too specific a pattern of behavior. A mother does not speak set lines; her role behavior adapts to and depends upon the situation in which she finds herself. Moreover, there is room for all sorts of idiosyncratic variation in the enactment of a social role. Now the sociologists who employ the concept of role point out these qualifications but do not tell us how to incorporate them in a role definition, and hence they fail to indicate just how role theory should be used for the prediction of behavior.

Herein lies the significance of my earlier comment that the decision is too gross a unit of analysis and must be dissected into its component premises. The difficulties in role theory drop away if we view social influence as influence upon decision *premises.*

A role is a specification of some, but not all, of the premises that underlie an individual's decisions (cf. pages 221–228). Many other premises also enter into the same decisions, including informational premises and idiosyncratic premises that are expressive of personality differences. Behavior can be predicted, then, when the premises of decision are known (or can be predicted) in sufficient detail. For some purposes, it may be enough to know the role premises (e.g., to predict the behavior of a policeman who sees you go through a stop sign); for other purposes, the informational premises or others may be the crucial ones.

Unless the premise is taken as the unit, role theory commits an error that is just the opposite of the one committed by economic theory—it does not leave any room for rationality in behavior. If a role is a pattern of behavior, the role may be functional from a social standpoint, but the performer of the role cannot be a rational actor—he simply acts his part. On the other hand, if a role consists in the specification of certain value and factual premises, then the enactor of the role will ordinarily have to think and solve problems in order to attain these values. A role defined in terms of premises leaves room for rational calculation in behavior.

Action theory, as it has been developed by Talcott Parsons and his followers, faces the same difficulty as role theory but perhaps in a less acute form. The "action" is a unit less gross than the "role," but comparable to the "decision." For this and other reasons, the categories of Parsonian action theory seem to me insufficiently subtle and flexible for the description of behavior. The orientation of the actor to the world almost certainly admits of a much wider variety than is provided by Parsons' dichotomous pattern variables.

Thus we draw the same conclusions about role theory and action theory: It is not possible to build an adequate theory of human behavior without an appropriate unit of analysis. The role is too gross a unit; so is the unit act. The decision *premise* is a much smaller unit than either of these—for many premises are involved in any specific decision or action, and many premises are incorporated in the definition of a single role. It is a unit, moreover, that is fully compatible with the description of behavior in terms of the decision tree. In all respects the decision premise seems to me now, as it did when I wrote the first edition of this book, to be the appropriate unit for the study of human behavior.

The Organization's Environment

As is shown in Chapter II of this book, classical organization theory mistakenly sought to discover categorical and invariant "principles" of organization, applicable unqualifiedly to all organizations at all times. The "principles" have gradually been yielding to a vigorous stream of criticism and empirical research that has shown that an organization can be effective only if its design is appropriate to its functions and to its social and technical environment. As William Dill showed in an early study of this kind, a company that manufactures a wide range of diverse products for customers in several industries is bound to organize differently, if it wishes to survive, from a company manufacturing a single line of products for a homogeneous group of customers.[15]

Additional studies, which now provide a wealth of information on the nature of the adaptations of organization to environment, have been carried out by Joan Woodward, Tom Burns and G. M. Stalker, Charles Perrow, James D. Thompson, P. R. Lawrence and J. W. Lorsch, and a number of others.[16]

Chapters XVI and XVII of the present volume both address themselves to the issue of how organizational form relates to environment and task. The first of these chapters is a case study of the Economic Cooperation Administration, the Federal agency organized in 1948 to administer the Marshall Plan of aid to Western European nations. The second is a normative discussion, drawing heavily upon my own experience in the Graduate School

---

[15] See W. R. Dill, "Environment as an Influence on Managerial Autonomy," *Administrative Science Quarterly*, 2:409–443 (1958).

[16] An excellent introduction to this literature is provided by W. H. Starbuck, ed., *Organizational Growth and Development* (Harmondsworth, Middlesex, England: Penguin Books, 1971), especially Starbuck's introductory essay, "Organizational Growth and Development," Chapter 9 by D. S. Pugh, D. J. Hickson, C. R. Hinings and C. Turner, "The Context of Organization Structures" (published originally in *Administrative Science Quarterly*, 14:91–114, 1969), and the bibliography at the end of Starbuck's volume.

of Industrial Administration at Carnegie-Mellon University, of the organizational problems of business schools.

The ECA study emphasizes an aspect of organization that has not been prominent in the literature of administration but that is closely bound to the so-called "representation issue" now widely discussed and studied in cognitive psychology. In contemporary theories of problem-solving, two stages in the problem-solving process are distinguished: an initial stage of problem formulation, during which the problem solver arrives at a way of representing the problem situation, and a subsequent stage during which he manipulates the problem situation, within the representation he has adopted, in a succession of efforts to find a solution. The temporal separation between these two stages is not usually sharp—there is much overlap—but, unless the solver comes to the problem with a ready-made representation (i.e., the problem is of a kind he has faced many times before), his initial preoccupation is with finding such a representation, and only gradually does he shift to attempts at problem-solving.[17]

The ECA study describes a very similar representation-seeking process in the initial stages of forming a new organization. Only as alternative representations were tested against the requirements of the agency's task, and a consensus reached on a suitable representation, did the organization of the Economic Cooperation Administration take definite form. The case study shows that to stabilize the decision-making pattern in an organization requires that more or less congruent pictures of that pattern be stored in the memories of many of its members.

Just as anatomy and physiology provide complementary approaches to the study of organisms, so structure and process provide complementary approaches to the study of organizations. Most of the contemporary research that relates organization to environment places its emphasis on aggregate structural charac-

---

[17] Representation in problem-solving and other cognitive tasks is discussed in Chapter 3 of *Human Problem Solving, op. cit.,* in H. A. Simon and L. Siklossy, eds., *Representation and Meaning* (Englewood Cliffs, N.J.: Prentice-Hall, 1972), and in J. R. Hayes and H. A. Simon, "Understanding Written Problem Instructions," in L. W. Gregg, ed., *Knowledge and Cognition* (Potomac, Md.: Erlbaum Associates, 1974).

teristics of organizations. In this volume we look more closely at the mechanisms of adaptation: how the decision-making process and the system of communications mediate between the organization and its environment.

CONCLUSION

As this Introduction suggests, a good deal has happened in organizational studies since the first edition of *Administrative Behavior* appeared. There has been a great outpouring of writing and research on human relations and a persistent questioning of classical views about the exercise of authority in organizations. The study of human thinking and decision processes has been pursued vigorously, with the result that the theory of bounded rationality has been placed on firm empirical foundations. The computer has appeared and multiplied in the world of business, introducing new concepts of communication and information processing. The dependence of organization structure and processes upon environment and technology is now being explored from many standpoints.

Administrative Behavior was written on the assumption that decision-making processes hold the key to the understanding of organizational phenomena. The developments summarized above make this assumption even more tenable today than it was twenty-five years ago. It is my hope that this book, augmented by its new chapters, will continue to help those who would like to understand better, and manage more effectively, these complex social systems, the organizations in which we do our work.

ACKNOWLEDGMENTS

I am especially grateful to DeWitt C. Dearborn for his kind permission to use our joint piece of work on identifications as Chapter XV of this third edition.

Over the past twenty years, numerous colleagues, DeWitt among them, have contributed to my continuing education on matters administrative and organizational. The identities of many

of these associates are revealed by the footnotes to this new Introduction, but I should like to single out some with whom I was
most closely associated and who therefore are most responsible
for what I learned. At Illinois Institute of Technology, there
were Donald Smithburg and Victor Thompson, with whom I col-
laborated in writing *Public Administration.* In the early 1950s,
at what was then Carnegie Institute of Technology, my main
partners in organizational studies were, at first, Harold Guetzkow,
George Kozmetsky, and Gordon Tyndall; subsequently, Richard
Cyert, James March, and William Dill. I am deeply indebted to
all of them, as well as to at least two dozen other faculty colleagues
and able graduate students who populated the halls of the Graduate School of Industrial Administration in the 1950s.

Permission for reprinting Chapter XII has been kindly granted
by the editors of the *Administrative Science Quarterly;* for Chapter XIII, by the editors of *Management Science;* for Chapters
XIV and XVI, by the editors of the *Public Administrative Review;* for Chapter XV, by the editors of *Sociometry;* and for
Chapter XVII, by the editors of the *Journal of Management
Studies.* To all of these journals, my thanks.

As I reread the names of those whose help I acknowledged in
the first edition, I find two people whose lifelong friendship I
count among my special blessings. No young man could have
been more fortunate in his first boss than I. I marvel, in retro-
spect, at Clarence E. Ridley's combination of theoretical insight
and practical astuteness, at his ability both to plan and to see that
the plans happened, and at his talent for causing his associates to
play way over their heads. I am especially grateful to him for his
tolerance of youthful brashness, his almost reckless willingness to
delegate responsibility to the young, and his warm friendship.

My friendship with Harold Guetzkow began on a train that
carried us both to Chicago in 1933 to become freshmen at the
University. It was Harold who first interested me in cognitive
psychology when we were still undergraduates. Although that
interest incubated for two decades, during which we were im-
mersed in our joint and separate organizational studies, it has
been my major preoccupation, if not obsession, since the middle

1950s. I owe to Harold, among many other things, much of the deep intellectual pleasure that these years have brought me.

And what shall I say of my wife, Dorothea, to whom this edition of *Administrative Behavior,* as well as the two previous editions, is dedicated? Claude Bernard once said, "If I had to define life in a word, it would be: Life is creation." To which I would add: And it takes two people to create. At least that has been my experience in the full partnership Dot and I have shared through all our adult lives.

Herbert A. Simon
Pittsburgh, Pennsylvania
January 7, 1975

FOREWORD

IN THIS book Professor Simon gives us an important contribution to the social science of formal organization and administration. His objective, as he says in the Preface, is to construct a set of tools—a set of concepts and a vocabulary—suitable for describing an organization and the way an administrative organization works. His interest has been primarily in the field of public administration; but to achieve his purpose adequately he has taken into account experience in other kinds of formal organizations such as military, commercial, and industrial and private non-profit organizations. This makes his conclusions generally applicable and his work useful for describing administrative behavior in all types of organizations.

However useful this set of tools may be for scientific purposes, the chief value of Professor Simon's exposition for the general reader and for men of affairs lies in the clarity, comprehensiveness, and generality of his description of organization, of the administrative process, of the nature of decision, and of the elements of value and fact entering into decisions. His success in this respect is outstanding. I have had extensive experience as an executive in business, governmental, and private non-profit service organizaions. This book conveys what I have experienced as common to all and what is in this sense essential in all organization and administration. It has the right "feel." This means that I find Professor Simon's apprehension of the structure of organized action consonant with my experience. It therefore appeals to me as sound. Even though it is not final or exhaustive, I believe those who grasp this structure will find it helpful and not misleading. For those who have little experience and knowledge of organization, Professor Simon's treatment of the subject will prove illuminating, and it should protect them from many current false notions, e.g., about "power," authority, incentives. This in itself is an important service.

But the generality achieved implies that the conclusions are highly abstract. Even though Professor Simon's style is simple and he gives many concrete examples, the necessarily abstract character of the treatise leads me to add a few remarks on the function of this kind of work for men of affairs, men who are actually dealing day in and day out with concrete situations.

I have found it convenient to recognize three quite different levels of experience and knowledge of organizations. The first is the level of concrete behavior in specific situations. Here much of the behavior is habitual and unconsciously responsive and adaptive. Indeed, much of such behavior would change and would be ineffective if it were not unconscious. At this level experience is the teacher, and what we acquire is "know-how" rather than knowledge. Moreover, we can as little expect to govern such behavior by book knowledge as we would expect to control our bodily functions by reading physiology. What takes place at this level of experience is, to be sure, a proper field of study, and such study is useful for scientific purposes and for diagnosis, therapy, and prevention. Professor Simon indicates this in his discussion of informal organization—one example of this level of organization experience.

The second level of experience is that of specific organization practice. By this I mean the lines of organization, the governing policies, the rules and regulations, the patterns of behavior, of a specific organization. Though much of this is recorded in writing in any organization and can be studied, much is "unwritten law" and can chiefly be learned by intimate observation and experience. There is no doubt that general experience and general knowledge sometimes enables some men to behave effectively in such specific organizations, especially if they are supported by men having long specific experience of the organization. But broadly, an effective working knowledge of a specific organization can be acquired only by working in it. We do not expect men to have a competent behavioral understanding of these specific organizations except as they spend their careers in them.

Two general observations are here pertinent. One is that each organization has a language or organization jargon of its own. The use and meaning of each has to be learned. The second is that behavior is often inconsistent with the language used to describe it. For example, I believe that in most good organizations administrative behavior is consonant with the theory of authority as set forth by Professor Simon; but principles of authority as expressed in such organizations are usually rather legalistic and not consistent with the behavior. The harm that arises from this state of affairs results less from misunderstanding because of misstatement than from the not infrequent attempt to govern behavior on the basis of a false philosophy.

Knowledge of a science of organization and administration can never be a substitute for specific experience in a specific organization. The usefulness of the more general knowledge to the administrators of organization comes from the rational understanding it gives of behavior that is largely based on trial and error or repetitive experience. Its immediate practical use is limited. Its ultimate practical value is great, sharpening observation, preventing the neglect of important factors, giving the advantages of a more general language, and reducing the inconsistencies between behavior and its verbal description.

The third level of knowledge is, of course, the one exemplified in this book. I shall say no more of it. But what justifies the belief that general knowledge of administrative behavior or organization is attainable? Professor Simon has not demonstrated this, nor have others who have been working in this field. We merely assert or assume it. I can only give the grounds for my belief briefly. Professor Simon's abstractions seemed sound to me because they express aspects of my experience under a wide variety of conditions. A university president tells me that his principal organization difficulty is the "following which, of course, is peculiar to universities." He then describes a problem I have encountered a hundred times, but never in a university. I listen to the Commanding General of the Air Transport Corps lecturing on organization problems of that

Corps. I have never had military experience, I have read little of military organization, yet I think I understand him almost perfectly. I give a lecture mistitled "The Principles of Organization" at the Air War College. The questions and discussion in the hour following indicate that I have made myself fairly well understood. Such experience forms the ground for the belief that abstract principles of structure may be discerned in organizations of great variety, and that ultimately it may be possible to state principles of general organization.

CHESTER I. BARNARD

PREFACE TO THE FIRST EDITION

THIS STUDY represents an attempt to construct tools useful in my own research in the field of public administration. It derived from my conviction that we do not yet have, in this field, adequate linguistic and conceptual tools for realistically and significantly describing even a simple administrative organization—describing it, that is, in a way that will provide the basis for scientific analysis of the effectiveness of its structure and operation. Among the studies of administrative organizations that I have read, few have caught and set down in words the real flesh and bones of an organization; even fewer have convinced me that their conclusions as to the effectiveness of the organization or the recommendations for its improvement could properly be deduced from the evidence presented.

The response to the preliminary edition of this book and to several published articles drawn from it shows that these doubts are not peculiar to me but are shared by many practitioners and researchers in the field of administration. This state of affairs constitutes a serious indictment of our science, and of ourselves as scientists. An experiment in chemistry derives its validity—its scientific authority—from its reproducibility; and unless it is described in sufficient detail to be repeated it is useless. In administration we have as yet only a very imperfect ability to tell what has happened in our administrative "experiments"—much less to insure their reproducibility.

Before we can establish any immutable "principles" of administration, we must be able to describe, in words, exactly how an administrative organization looks and exactly how it works. As a basis for my own studies in administration, I have attempted to construct a vocabulary which will permit such description;

and this volume records the conclusions I have reached. These conclusions do not constitute a "theory" of administration, for except for a few dicta offered by way of hypothesis, no principles of administration are laid down. If any "theory" is involved, it is that decision-making is the heart of administration, and that the vocabulary of administrative theory must be derived from the logic and psychology of human choice.

I hope that this volume may be of some use to three groups of persons : first, to individuals concerned with the science of administration, who may find in it some applicable methods of description and analysis of organization; second, to practical administrators who may find it helpful sometimes to think of administration at that third level of generalization of which Mr. Barnard speaks in his Foreword; third, to graduate and undergraduate students who may wish to supplement their textbooks with a closer study of the behavioral processes that go to make the real warp and woof of administration.

HERBERT A. SIMON

December, 1946

ACKNOWLEDGMENTS TO THE FIRST EDITION

> "And certainly there were many others . . . from whom I had assimilated a word, a glance, but of whom as individual beings I remembered nothing; a book is a great cemetery in which, for the most part, the names upon the tombs are effaced."
>
> MARCEL PROUST, *Time Regained*

IN THE eight years that this book, or portions of it, has been in preparation, the list of persons to whom I am indebted for assistance, criticism, and encouragement has grown to unmanageable proportions. I hope I will be pardoned for singling out a few upon whom I have called most frequently for help, and failing to name many others who have aided me.

I am indebted, first, to the Faculty of the University of Chicago which made of its campus when I studied there a nettle-field of intellectual stimulation, but in particular to Mr. Clarence E. Ridley, the late Professor Henry Schultz, and Professor Leonard D. White. Among colleagues and others who have read and criticized earlier drafts or the published preliminary edition of the book I must mention Messrs. Lyndon E. Abbott, Herbert Bohnert, Milton Chernin, William R. Divine, Herbert Emmerich, Victor Jones, Albert Lepawsky, Lyman S. Moore, Richard O. Niehoff, Charner Marquis Perry, C. Herman Pritchett, Kenneth J. Seigworth, Edwin O. Stene, John A. Vieg, William L. C. Wheaton, and the members of the Public Administration Discussion Group. Mr. Harold Guetzkow proved, as always, my exceptionally severe and helpful critic.

To Mr. Chester I. Barnard I owe a special debt: first, for his own book, *The Functions of the Executive,* which has been a major influence upon my thinking about administration; secondly, for the extremely careful critical review he gave the preliminary version of this book; and finally for his Foreword to the present edition.

Several chapters of this book have been published in whole or part as separate articles. Chapters I and II are largely drawn from articles in the *Public Administration Review,* while certain portions of Chapter IX were first published in *Public Management.*

I hasten to pronounce the customary absolution, relieving all the persons mentioned above of responsibility for what I have written; but I cannot absolve them of responsibility for providing the sources of inspiration from which the book was drawn.

H. A. S.

Part I

Chapter I

DECISION-MAKING AND ADMINISTRATIVE ORGANIZATION

ADMINISTRATION is ordinarily discussed as the art of "getting things done." Emphasis is placed upon processes and methods for insuring incisive action. Principles are set forth for securing concerted action from groups of men. In all this discussion, however, not very much attention is paid to the choice which prefaces all action—to the determining of what is to be done rather than to the actual doing. It is with this problem—the process of choice which leads to action—that the present study is concerned. In this introductory chapter the problem will be posed and a survey made of the topics to be taken up in the remaining chapters.

Although any practical activity involves both "deciding" and "doing," it has not commonly been recognized that a theory of administration should be concerned with the processes of decision as well as with the processes of action.[1] This neglect perhaps stems from the notion that decision-making is confined to the formulation of over-all policy. On the contrary, the process of decision does not come to an end when the general purpose of an organization has been determined. The task of "deciding" pervades the entire administrative organization quite as much as does the task of "doing"—indeed, it is integrally tied up with the latter. A general theory of administration must include principles of organization that will insure correct decision-making, just as it must include principles that will insure effective action.

[1] For two notable exceptions to the general neglect of decision-making see C. I. Barnard, *The Functions of the Executive* (Cambridge: Harvard University Press, 1938), and Edwin O. Stene, "An Approach to a Science of Administration," *American Political Science Review*, 34:1124–1137 (Dec., 1940).

DECISION-MAKING AND THE EXECUTION OF DECISIONS

It is clear that the actual physical task of carrying out an organization's objectives falls to the persons at the lowest level of the administrative hierarchy. The automobile, as a physical object, is built not by the engineer or the executive, but by the mechanic on the assembly line. The fire is extinguished, not by the fire chief or the captain, but by the team of firemen who play a hose on the blaze.

It is equally clear that the persons above this lowest or operative level in the administrative hierarchy are not mere surplus baggage, and that they too must have an essential role to play in the accomplishment of the agency's objectives. Even though, as far as physical cause and effect are concerned, it is the machine gunner and not the major who fights battles, the major is likely to have a greater influence upon the outcome of a battle than any single machine gunner.

How, then, do the administrative and supervisory staff of an organization affect that organization's work? The nonoperative staff of an administrative organization participate in the accomplishment of the objectives of that organization to the extent that they influence the decisions of the operatives—the persons at the lowest level of the administrative hierarchy. The major can influence the battle to the extent that his head is able to direct the machine gunner's hand. By deploying his forces in the battle area and assigning specific tasks to subordinate units he determines for the machine gunner where he will take his stand and what his objective will be. In very small organizations the influence of all supervisory employees upon the operative employees may be direct, but in units of any size there are interposed between the top supervisors and the operative employees several levels of intermediate supervisors who are themselves subject to influences from above, and who transmit, elaborate, and modify these influences before they reach the operatives.

If this is a correct description of the administrative process, then the construction of an efficient administrative organization is a problem in social psychology. It is a task of setting up an operative staff and superimposing on that staff a supervisory staff capable of influencing the operative group toward a pattern of coordinated and effective behavior. The term "influencing" rather than "directing" is used here, for direction—that is, the use of administrative authority—is only one of several ways in which the administrative staff may affect the decisions of the operative staff; and, consequently, the construction of an administrative organization involves more than a mere assignment of functions and allocation of authority.

In the study of organization, the operative employee must be at the focus of attention, for the success of the structure will be judged by his performance within it. Insight into the structure and function of an organization can best be gained by analyzing the manner in which the decisions and behavior of such employees are influenced within and by the organization.

CHOICE AND BEHAVIOR

All behavior involves conscious or unconscious selection of particular actions out of all those which are physically possible to the actor and to those persons over whom he exercises influence and authority. The term "selection" is used here without any implication of a conscious or deliberate process. It refers simply to the fact that, if the individual follows one particular course of action, there are other courses of action that he thereby forgoes. In many cases the selection process consists simply in an established reflex action—a typist hits a particular key with a finger because a reflex has been established between a letter on a printed page and this particular key. Here the action is, in some sense at least, rational (i.e. goal-oriented), yet no element of consciousness or deliberation is involved.

In other cases the selection is itself the product of a complex chain of activities called "planning" or "design" activities. An engineer, for example, may decide upon the basis of extensive analysis that a particular bridge should be of cantilever design. His design, further implemented by detailed plans for the structure, will lead to a whole chain of behaviors by the individuals constructing the bridge.

In this volume many examples will be given of all varieties of selection process. All these examples have in common the following characteristics: At any moment there are a multitude of alternative (physically) possible actions, any one of which a given individual may undertake; by some process these numerous alternatives are narrowed down to that one which is in fact acted out. The words "choice" and "decision" will be used interchangeably in this study to refer to this process. Since these terms as ordinarily used carry connotations of self-conscious, deliberate, rational selection, it should be emphasized that as used here they include any process of selection, regardless of whether the above elements are present to any degree.

VALUE AND FACT IN DECISION

A great deal of behavior, and particularly the behavior of individuals within administrative organizations, is purposive—oriented toward goals or objectives. This purposiveness brings about an integration in the pattern of behavior, in the absence of which adminstration would be meaningless; for, if administration consists in "getting things done" by groups of people, purpose provides a principal criterion in determining what things are to be done.

The minute decisions that govern specific actions are inevitably instances of the application of broader decisions relative to purpose and to method. The walker contracts his leg muscles in order to take a step; he takes a step in order to proceed toward his destination; he is going to the destination, a mail box, in order to mail a letter; he is sending a letter in order to transmit certain information to another person, and so forth. Each decision involves the selection of a goal, and a behavior relevant to it; this goal may in turn be mediate to a somewhat more distant goal; and so on, until a relatively final aim is reached.[2] In so far as decisions lead toward the

---

[2] In chap. iv, this distinction between mediate and final goals will be elaborated, and its necessity shown.

selection of final goals, they will be called "value judgments"; so far as they involve the implementation of such goals they will be called "factual judgments." [3]

Unfortunately, problems do not come to the administrator carefully wrapped in bundles with the value elements and the factual elements neatly sorted. For one thing, goals or final objectives of governmental organization and activity are usually formulated in very general and ambiguous terms—"justice," "the general welfare," or "liberty." Then, too, the objectives as defined may be merely intermediate to the attainment of more final aims. For example, in certain spheres of action, the behavior of men is generally oriented around the "economic motive." Yet, for most men, economic gain is not usually an end in itself, but a means for attaining more final ends: security, comfort, and prestige.

Finally, the value and factual elements may be combined, in some cases, in a single objective. The apprehension of criminals is commonly set up as an objective of a municipal police department. To a certain extent this objective is conceived as an end in itself, that is, as aimed toward the apprehension and punishment of offenders against the law; but from another point of view apprehension is considered a means for protecting citizens, for rehabilitating offenders, and for discouraging potential offenders.

The Hierarchy of Decisions. The concept of *purposiveness* involves a notion of a hierarchy of decisions—each step downward in the hierarchy consisting in an implementation of the goals set forth in the step immediately above. Behavior is purposive in so far as it is guided by general goals or objectives; it is rational in so far as it selects alternatives which are conducive to the achievement of the previously selected goals.[4]

It should not be inferred that this hierarchy or pyramid of goals

[3] The word "factual," though possibly misleading, is used for lack of a better term. It is clear that the "facts" on which practical decisions are based are usually estimates or judgments, rather than positive and certain items of fact. To add to the confusion, the term "valuation" is often applied by writers to refer to this process of judging or estimating facts. The reader will avoid confusion if he remembers that "value" in this study refers to *ought*'s, however certain, "fact" to *is*'es, however conjectural.

[4] This definition of "rational" is not exact, and will be further elaborated in chap. iv.

is perfectly organized or integrated in any actual behavior. A governmental agency, for instance, may be directed simultaneously toward several distinct objectives: a recreation department may seek to improve the health of children, to provide them with good uses for their leisure time, and to prevent juvenile delinquency, as well as to achieve similar goals for the adults in the community.

Even when no conscious or deliberate integration of these goals takes place in decision, it should be noted that an integration generally takes place in fact. Although in making decisions for his agency, the recreation administrator may fail to weigh the diverse and sometimes conflicting objectives against one another in terms of their relative importance, yet his actual decisions, and the direction which he gives to the policy of his agency will amount in practice to a particular set of weights for these objectives. If the program emphasizes athletics for adolescent boys, then this objective is given an actual weight in practice which it may, or may not, have had in the consciousness of the administrator planning the program. Hence, although the administrator may refuse the task, or be unable to perform it, of consciously and deliberately integrating his system of objectives, he cannot avoid the implications of his actual decisions, which achieve such a synthesis in fact.

The Relative Element in Decision. In an important sense, all decision is a matter of compromise. The alternative that is finally selected never permits a complete or perfect achievement of objectives, but is merely the best solution that is available under the circumstances. The environmental situation inevitably limits the alternatives that are available, and hence sets a maximum to the level of attainment of purpose that is possible.

This relative element in achievement—this element of compromise—makes even more inescapable the necessity of finding a common denominator when behavior is aimed simultaneously at several objectives. For instance, if experience showed that an organization like the Work Projects Administration could at one and the same time dispense relief and construct public works without handicapping either objective, then the agency might attempt to attain at the same time both of these objectives. If, on the other hand, experience showed that the accomplishment of either of these objectives through the organization seriously impeded the accomplishment of the other, one would have to be selected as the objective of the agency, and the other sacrificed. In balancing the one aim against the other, and in attempting to find a common denominator, it would be necessary to cease thinking of the two aims as ends in themselves, and instead to conceive them as means to some more general end.[5]

An Illustration of the Process of Decision. In order to understand more clearly the intimate relationships that exist in any practical administrative problem between judgments of value and fact, it will be helpful to study an example from the field of municipal government.

What questions of value and fact arise in the opening and improvement of a new street? It is necessary to determine: (1) the design of the street, (2) the proper relationship of the street to the master plan, (3) means of financing the project, (4) whether the project should be let on contract or done by force account, (5) the relation of this project to construction that may be required subsequent to the improvement (e.g., utility cuts in this particular street), and (6) numerous other questions of like nature. These are questions for which answers must be found—each one combining value and factual elements. A partial separation of the two elements can be achieved by distinguishing the purposes of the project from its procedures.

On the one hand, decisions regarding these questions must be based upon the purposes for which the street is intended, and the social values affected by its construction—among them, (1) speed and convenience in transportation, (2) traffic safety, (3) effect of street layout on property values, (4) construction costs, and (5) distribution of cost among taxpayers.

On the other hand, the decisions must be made in the light of scientific and practical knowledge as to the effect particular meas-

[5] From the description by MacMahon, Millett, and Ogden of the WPA during its planning stage, it would appear that thinking about this integration was at a rather primitive level in the organization at the time the basic decisions were made. Arthur W. MacMahon, John D. Millett, and Gladys Ogden, *The Administration of Federal Work Relief* (Chicago: Public Administration Service, 1941), pp. 17–42.

ures will have in realizing these values. Included here are (1) the relative smoothness, permanence, and cost of each type of pavement, (2) relative advantages of alternate routes from the standpoint of cost and convenience to traffic, and (3) the total cost and distribution of cost for alternative methods of financing.

The final decision, then, will depend both on the relative weight that is given to the different objectives and on judgment as to the extent to which any given plan will attain each objective.

This brief account will serve to indicate some of the basic features of the process of decision—features that will be further elaborated in this study.

DECISION-MAKING IN THE ADMINISTRATIVE PROCESS

Administrative activity is group activity. Simple situations are familiar where a man plans and executes his own work; but as soon as a task grows to the point where the efforts of several persons are required to accomplish it this is no longer possible, and it becomes necessary to develop processes for the application of organized effort to the group task. The techniques which facilitate this application are the administrative processes.

It should be noted that the administrative processes are decisional processes: they consist in segregating certain elements in the decisions of members of the organization, and establishing regular organizational procedures to select and determine these elements and to communicate them to the members concerned. If the task of the group is to build a ship, a design for the ship is drawn and adopted by the organization, and this design limits and guides the activities of the persons who actually construct the ship.

The organization, then, takes from the individual some of his decisional autonomy, and substitutes for it an organization decision-making process. The decisions which the organization makes for the individual ordinarily (1) specify his function, that is, the general scope and nature of his duties; (2) allocate authority, that is, determine who in the organization is to have power to make further decisions for the individual; and (3) set such other limits to his choice as are needed to coordinate the activities of several individuals in the organization.

The administrative organization is characterized by specialization—particular tasks are delegated to particular parts of the organization. It has already been noted above that this specialization may take the form of "vertical" division of labor. A pyramid or hierarchy of authority may be established, with greater or less formality, and decision-making functions may be specialized among the members of this hierarchy.

Most analyses of organization have emphasized "horizontal" specialization—the division of work—as the basic characteristic of organized activity. Luther Gulick, for example, in his "Notes on the Theory of Organization," says: "Work division is the foundation of organization; indeed, the reason for organization." [6] In this study we shall be primarily concerned with "vertical" specialization—the division of decision-making duties between operative and supervisory personnel. One inquiry will be into the reasons why the operative employees are deprived of a portion of their autonomy in the making of decisions and subjected to the authority and influence of supervisors.

There would seem to be at least three reasons for vertical specialization in organization. First, if there is any horizontal specialization, vertical specialization is absolutely essential to achieve coordination among the operative employees. Second, just as horizontal specialization permits greater skill and expertise to be developed by the operative group in the performance of their tasks, so vertical specialization permits greater expertise in the making of decisions. Third, vertical specialization permits the operative personnel to be held accountable for their decisions: to the board of directors in the case of a business organization; to the legislative body in the case of a public agency.

Coordination. Group behavior requires not only the adoption of correct decisions, but also the adoption by all members of the group of the same decisions. Suppose ten persons decide to cooperate in building a boat. If each has his own plan, and they do not communi-

---

[6] Luther Gulick and L. Urwick, eds., *Papers on the Science of Administration* (New York: Institute of Public Administration, 1937), p. 3.

cate their plans, the chances are that the resulting craft will not be very seaworthy; they would probably meet with better success if they adopted even a very mediocre design, and if then all followed this same design.

By the exercise of authority or other forms of influence, it is possible to centralize the function of deciding so that a general plan of operations will govern the activities of all members of the organization. This coordination may be either procedural or substantive in nature: by procedural coordination is meant the specification of the organization itself—that is, the generalized description of the behaviors and relationships of the members of the organization. Procedural coordination establishes the lines of authority and outlines the sphere of activity of each organization member, while substantive coordination specifies the content of his work. In an automobile factory, an organization chart is an aspect of procedural coordination; blueprints for the engine block of the car being manufactured are an aspect of substantive coordination.

Expertise. To gain the advantages of specialized skill at the operative level, the work of an organization must be so subdivided that all processes requiring a particular skill can be performed by persons possessing that skill. Likewise, to gain the advantages of expertise in decision-making, the responsibility for decisions must be so allocated that all decisions requiring a particular skill can be made by persons possessing that skill.

To subdivide decisions is rather more complicated than to subdivide performance; for, while it is not usually possible to combine the sharp eye of one workman with the steady hand of another to secure greater precision in a particular operation, it is often possible to add the knowledge of a lawyer to that of an engineer in order to improve the quality of a particular decision.

Responsibility. Writers on the political and legal aspects of authority have emphasized that a primary function of organization is to enforce the conformity of the individual to norms laid down by the group, or by its authority-wielding members. The discretion of subordinate personnel is limited by policies determined near the top of the administrative hierarchy. When the maintenance of responsibility is a central concern, the purpose of vertical specialization is to assure legislative control over the administrator, leaving to the administrative staff adequate discretion to deal with technical matters which a legislative body composed of laymen would not be competent to decide.

MODES OF ORGANIZATIONAL INFLUENCE

Decisions reached in the higher ranks of the organization hierarchy will have no effect upon the activities of operative employees unless they are communicated downward. Consideration of the process requires an examination of the ways in which the behavior of the operative employee can be influenced. These influences fall roughly into two categories: (1) establishing in the operative employee *himself* attitudes, habits, and a state of mind which lead him to reach that decision which is advantageous to the organization, and (2) imposing on the operative employee decisions reached elsewhere in the organization. The first type of influence operates by inculcating in the employee organizational loyalties and a concern with efficiency, and more generally by training him. The second type of influence depends primarily upon authority and upon advisory and informational services. It is not insisted that these categories are either exhaustive or mutually exclusive, but they will serve the purposes of this introductory discussion.

As a matter of fact, the present discussion is somewhat more general than the preceding paragraph suggests, for it is concerned with organizational influences not only upon operative employees but upon all individuals making decisions within the organization.

Authority. The concept of authority has been analyzed at length by students of administration. We shall employ here a definition substantially equivalent to that put forth by C. I. Barnard.[7] A subordinate is said to accept authority whenever he permits his behavior to be guided by the decision of a superior, without independently examining the merits of that decision. When exercising authority, the superior does not seek to convince the subordinate, but only to obtain his acquiescence. In actual practice, of course,

[7] Chester I. Barnard, *The Functions of the Executive* (Cambridge: Harvard University Press, 1938), pp. 163 ff.

authority is usually liberally admixed with suggestion and persuasion.

Although it is an important function of authority to permit a decision to be made and carried out even when agreement cannot be reached, perhaps this arbitrary aspect of authority has been overemphasized. In any event, if it is attempted to carry authority beyond a certain point, which may be described as the subordinate's "zone of acceptance," disobedience will follow.[8] The magnitude of the zone of acceptance depends upon the sanctions which authority has available to enforce its commands. The term "sanctions" must be interpreted broadly in this connection, for positive and neutral stimuli—such as community of purpose, habit, and leadership—are at least as important in securing acceptance of authority as the threat of physical or economic punishment.

It follows that authority, in the sense here defined, can operate "upward" and "sidewise" as well as "downward" in the organization. If an executive delegates to his secretary a decision about file cabinets and accepts her recommendation without reexamination of its merits, he is accepting her authority. The "lines of authority" represented on organization charts do have a special significance, however, for they are commonly resorted to in order to terminate debate when it proves impossible to reach a consensus on a particular decision. Since this appellate use of authority generally requires sanctions to be effective, the structure of formal authority in an organization usually is related to the appointment, disciplining, and dismissal of personnel. These formal lines of authority are commonly supplemented by informal authority relations in the day-to-day work of the organization, while the formal hierarchy is largely reserved for the settlement of disputes.

Organizational Loyalties. It is a prevalent characteristic of human behavior that members of an organized group tend to identify with that group. In making decisions their organizational loyalty leads them to evaluate alternative courses of action in terms of the consequences of their action for the group. When a person prefers a particular course of action because it is "good for America," he

[8] Barnard (*op. cit.,* p. 169) calls this the "zone of indifference"; but I prefer the term "acceptance."

identifies himself with Americans, when he prefers it because it will "boost business in Berkeley," he identifies himself with Berkeleyans. National and class loyalties are examples of identifications which are of fundamental importance in the structure of modern society.

The loyalties that are of particular interest in the study of administration are those which attach to administrative organizations or segments of such organizations. The regimental battle flag is the traditional symbol of this identification in military administration; in civil administration, a frequently encountered evidence of loyalty is the cry, "Our Bureau needs more funds!"

This phenomenon of identification, or organizational loyalty, performs one very important function in administration. If an administrator, each time he is faced with a decision, must perforce evaluate that decision in terms of the whole range of human values, rationality in administration is impossible. If he need consider the decision only in the light of limited organizational aims, his task is more nearly within the range of human powers. The fireman can concentrate on the problem of fires, the health officer on problems of disease, without irrelevant considerations entering in.

Furthermore, this concentration on a limited range of values is almost essential if the administrator is to be held accountable for his decisions. When the organization's objectives are specified by some higher authority, the major value-premise of the administrator's decisions is thereby given him, leaving to him only the implementation of these objectives. If the fire chief were permitted to roam over the whole field of human values—to decide that parks were more important than fire trucks, and consequently to remake his fire department into a recreation department—chaos would displace organization, and responsibility would disappear.

Organizational loyalties lead also, however, to certain difficulties which should not be underestimated. The principal undesirable effect of identification is that it prevents the institutionalized individual from making correct decisions in cases where the restricted area of values with which he identifies himself must be weighed against other values outside that area. This is a principal cause of the interbureau competition and wrangling which characterize any large administrative organization. The organization members, identifying themselves with the bureau instead of with the over-all organization, believe the bureau's welfare more important than the general welfare when the two conflict. This problem is frequently evident in the case of "housekeeping" agencies, where the facilitative and auxiliary nature of the agency is lost sight of in the effort to force the line agencies to follow standard procedures.

Organizational loyalties also result in incapacitating almost any department head for the task of balancing the financial needs of his department against the financial needs of other departments—whence the need for a centrally located budget agency that is free from these psychological biases. The higher we go in the administrative hierarchy, and the broader becomes the range of social values that must come within the administrator's purview, the more harmful is the effect of valuational bias, and the more important is it that the administrator be freed from his narrower identifications.

The Criterion of Efficiency. We have seen that the exercise of authority and the development of organizational loyalties are two principal means whereby the individual's value-premises are influenced by the organization. What about the issues of fact that underlie his decisions? These are largely determined by a principle that is implied in all rational behavior: the criterion of efficiency. In its broadest sense, to be efficient simply means to take the shortest path, the cheapest means, toward the attainment of the desired goals. The efficiency criterion is completely neutral as to what goals are to be attained. The commandment, "Be efficient!" is a major organizational influence over the decisions of the members of any administrative agency; and a determination whether this commandment has been obeyed is a major function of the review process.[9]

Advice and Information. Many of the influences the organization exercises over its members are of a less formal nature than those we have been discussing. These influences are perhaps most realistically viewed as a form of internal public relations, for there is nothing to guarantee that advice produced at one point in an organization will have any effect at another point in the organiza-

[9] For further discussion of the efficiency concept, see Clarence E. Ridley and Herbert A. Simon, *Measuring Municipal Activities* (Chicago: International City Managers' Association, 1943).

tion unless the lines of communication are adequate to its transmission, and unless it is transmitted in such form as to be persuasive. It is a prevalent misconception in headquarters offices that the internal advisory function consists in preparing precisely worded explanatory bulletins and making certain that the proper number of these are prepared, and that they are placed in the proper compartment of the "router." No plague has produced a rate of mortality higher than the rate that customarily afflicts central-office communications between the time they leave the issuing office and the moment when they are assumed to be effected in the revised practice of the operative employees.

Information and advice flow in all directions through the organization—not merely from the top downward. Many of the facts that are relevant to decision are of a rapidly changing nature, ascertainable only at the moment of decision, and often ascertainable only by operative employees. For instance, in military operations knowledge of the disposition of the enemy's forces is of crucial importance, and military organization has developed elaborate procedures for transmitting to a person who is to make a decision all relevant facts that he is not in a position to ascertain personally.

Training. Like organizational loyalties and the efficiency criterion, and unlike the other modes of influence we have been discussing, training influences decisions "from the inside out." That is, training prepares the organization member to reach satisfactory decisions himself, without the need for the constant exercise of authority or advice. In this sense, training procedures are alternatives to the exercise of authority or advice as means of control over the subordinate's decisions.

Training may be of an in-service or a pre-service nature. When persons with particular educational qualifications are recruited for certain jobs, the organization is depending upon this pre-training as a principal means of assuring correct decisions in their work. The mutual relation between training and the range of discretion that may be permitted an employee is an important factor to be taken into consideration in designing the administrative organization. That is, it may often be possible to minimize, or even dispense with, certain review processes by giving the subordinates training that enables them to perform their work with less supervision. Similarly, in drafting the qualifications required of applicants for particular positions, the possibility should be considered of lowering personnel costs by drafting semi-skilled employees and training them for particular jobs.

Training is applicable to the process of decision whenever the same elements are involved in a large number of decisions. Training may supply the trainee with the facts necessary in dealing with these decisions; it may provide him a frame of reference for his thinking; it may teach him "approved" solutions; or it may indoctrinate him with the values in terms of which his decisions are to be made.

THE EQUILIBRIUM OF THE ORGANIZATION

The question may next be raised why the individual *accepts* these organizational influences—why he accommodates his behavior to the demands the organization makes upon him. To understand how the behavior of the individual becomes a part of the system of behavior of the organization, it is necessary to study the relation between the personal motivation of the individual and the objectives toward which the activity of the organization is oriented.

If a business organization be taken, for the moment, as the type, three kinds of participants can be distinguished: entrepreneurs, employees, and customers.[10] Entrepreneurs are distinguished by the fact that their decisions ultimately control the activities of employees; employees, by the fact that they contribute their (undifferentiated) time and efforts to the organization in return for wages; customers, by the fact that they contribute money to the organization in return for its products. (Any actual human being can, of course, stand in more than one of these relations to an organization, e.g. a Red Cross volunteer, who is really a composite customer and employee.)

Each of these participants has his own personal motives for en-

[10] We follow Barnard (*op. cit.*) here in insisting that customers are an integral part of the system of organization behavior. Whether they are "members" or not is a terminological question of no particular importance. Suppliers of materials might have been added, above, as a fourth class of participants; but they would not add any essentially new element to the picture.

gaging in these organizational activities. Simplifying the motives and adopting the standpoint of economic theory, we may say that the entrepreneur seeks profit (i.e. an excess of revenues over expenditures), the employees seek wages, and the customers find (at certain prices) the exchange of money for products attractive. The entrepreneur gains the right to dispose of the employees' time by entering into employment contracts with them; he obtains funds to pay wages by entering into sales contracts with the customers. If these two sets of contracts are sufficiently advantageous, the entrepreneur makes a profit and, what is perhaps more important for our purposes, the organization remains in existence. If the contracts are not sufficiently advantageous, the entrepreneur becomes unable to maintain inducements to keep others in organized activity with him, and may even lose his own inducement to continue his organizational efforts. In either event, the organization disappears unless an equilibrium can be reached at some level of activity. In any actual organization, of course, the entrepreneur will depend upon many inducements other than the purely economic ones mentioned above: prestige, "good will," loyalty, and others.

In an organization such as that just described, there appears, in addition to the personal aims of the participants, an *organization* objective, or objectives. If the organization is a shoe factory, for example, it assumes the objective of making shoes. Whose objective is this—the entrepreneur's, the customers', or the employees'? To deny that it belongs to any of these would seem to posit some "group mind," some organismic entity which is over and above its human components. The true explanation is simpler: the organization objective is, indirectly, a personal objective of *all* the participants. It is the means whereby their organizational activity is bound together to achieve a satisfaction of their own diverse personal motives. It is by employing workers to make shoes and by selling them that the entrepreneur makes his profit; it is by accepting the direction of the entrepreneur in the making of shoes that the employee earns his wage; and it is by buying the finished shoes that the customer obtains his satisfaction from the organization. Since the entrepreneur wishes a profit, and since he controls the behavior of the employees (within their respective areas of acceptance), it behooves him to guide the behavior of the employees by the criterion of "making shoes as efficiently as possible." In so far, then, as he can control behavior in the organization, he establishes this as the objective of the behavior.

It is to be noted that the objectives of the customer are very closely, and rather directly, related to the *objectives* of the organization; the objectives of the entrepreneur are closely related to the *survival* of the organization; while the objectives of the employee are directly related to neither of these, but are brought into the organization scheme by the existence of his area of acceptance. Granted that pure "entrepreneurs," "customers," and "employees" do not exist; granted further that this scheme needs to be modified somewhat to fit voluntary, religious, and governmental organizations, still it is the existence of these three type roles which gives behavior in administrative organizations the particular character that we recognize.

ORGANIZATION OF THIS VOLUME

The framework of the investigation that is to be undertaken in subsequent chapters has now been set forth. We may conclude the present chapter by outlining briefly the order in which the various topics will be taken up.

Chapter II is also, in a sense, prefatory. The present work was undertaken partly as a result of the author's dissatisfaction with the so-called "principles of administration" that are to be found in the current literature of administrative theory. In Chapter II these principles are subjected to critical analysis with a view to showing their inadequacy and the need for their development along the lines suggested here.

In Chapter III, the exposition, properly speaking, begins with an analysis of the role played by value questions and questions of fact in administrative decision. This is followed, in Chapter IV, by a description of the conceptual apparatus that will be used throughout the volume for the description and analysis of social behavior systems, including behavior in administrative organizations.

Chapter V will consider the psychology of the individual in the organization and the ways in which the organization modifies his behavior. In Chapter VI the organization will be viewed as a system of individuals whose behavior maintains some sort of equilibrium—along lines suggested above. Chapter VII will analyze in detail the role of authority and vertical specialization in organization, and the organizational processes through which such specialization is effectuated. Chapter VIII is concerned with the process of communication whereby organizational influences are transmitted. In Chapter IX the concept of efficiency will be examined in detail, and in Chapter X, organizational loyalty, or identifications.

Chapter XI brings the volume to a close with a survey of the structure of administrative organizations and a discussion of the problems faced by research in administrative theory.

Chapter II

SOME PROBLEMS OF ADMINISTRATIVE
THEORY

SINCE the present volume departs rather widely from the usual presentation of the "principles of administration," [1] some explanation should perhaps be given for this deviation, and some description of the defects in the current theory which made this deviation necessary. The present chapter will first undertake a critical examination of the "principles," and then will turn to a discussion of how a sound theory of administrative behavior can be constructed. It builds, therefore, the methodological foundations for the later chapters.

It is a fatal defect of the current principles of administration that, like proverbs, they occur in pairs. For almost every principle one can find an equally plausible and acceptable contradictory principle. Although the two principles of the pair will lead to exactly opposite organizational recommendations, there is nothing in the theory to indicate which is the proper one to apply. To substantiate this criticism, it is necessary to examine briefly some of the leading principles.

SOME ACCEPTED ADMINISTRATIVE PRINCIPLES

Among the more common "principles" that occur in the literature of administration are these:

1. Administrative efficiency is increased by a specialization of the task among the group.

[1] For a systematic exposition of the currently accepted "principles" see Gulick and Urwick, *op. cit.*, or L. Urwick, *The Elements of Administration* (New York: Harper & Brothers, 1945).

2. Administrative efficiency is increased by arranging the members of the group in a determinate hierarchy of authority.

3. Administrative efficiency is increased by limiting the span of control at any point in the hierarchy to a small number.

4. Administrative efficiency is increased by grouping the workers, for purposes of control, according to (a) purpose, (b) process, (c) clientele, or (d) place. (This is really an elaboration of the first principle, but deserves separate discussion.)

Since these principles appear relatively simple and clear, it would seem that their application to concrete problems of administrative organization would be unambiguous, and that their validity would be easily submitted to empirical test. Such, however, seems not to be the case.

Specialization

Administrative efficiency is supposed to increase with an increase in specialization. But is this intended to mean that *any* increase in specialization will increase efficiency? If so, which of the following alternatives is the correct application of the principle?

(A) A plan of nursing should be put into effect by which nurses will be assigned to districts and do all nursing within that district, including school examinations, visits to homes or school children, and tuberculosis nursing.

(B) A functional plan of nursing should be put into effect by which different nurses will be assigned to school examinations, visits to homes of school children and tuberculosis nursing. The present method of generalized nursing by districts impedes the development of specialized skills in the three very diverse programs.

Both of these administrative arrangements satisfy the requirement of specialization: the first provides specialization by place; the second, specialization by function. The principle of specialization is of no help at all in choosing between the two alternatives.

It appears that the simplicity of the principle of specialization is a deceptive simplicity—a simplicity that conceals fundamental ambiguities. For "specialization" is not a condition of efficient administration: it is an inevitable characteristic of all group effort, however efficient or inefficient that effort may be. Specialization merely means that different persons are doing different things— and since it is physically impossible for two persons to be doing the same thing in the same place at the same time two persons are always doing different things.

The real problem of administration, then, is not to "specialize," but to specialize in that particular manner, and along those particular lines, which will lead to administrative efficiency. But, in thus rephrasing this "principle" of administration, there has been brought clearly into the open its fundamental ambiguity: "Administrative efficiency is increased by a specialization of the task among the group in the direction that will lead to greater efficiency."

Further discussion of the choice between competing bases of specialization will be undertaken later, but must be postponed momentarily until two other principles of administration have been examined.

Unity of Command

Administrative efficiency is supposed to be enhanced by arranging the members of the organization in a determinate hierarchy of authority in order to preserve "unity of command."

Analysis of this "principle" requires a clear understanding of what is meant by the term "authority." A subordinate may be said to accept authority whenever he permits his behavior to be guided by a decision reached by another, irrespective of his own judgment as to the merits of that decision.

In one sense the principle of unity of command, like the principle of specialization, cannot be violated; for it is physically impossible for a man to obey two contradictory commands. Presumably, if unity of command is a principle of administration, it must assert something more than this physical impossibility. Perhaps it asserts this: that it is undesirable to place a member of an organization in a position where he receives orders from more than one superior. This is evidently the meaning that Gulick attaches to the principle when he says:

The significance of this principle in the process of coordination and organization must not be lost sight of. In building a structure of coordination, it is often tempting to set up more than one boss for a man who is doing work which has more than one relationship. Even as great a philosopher of management as Taylor fell into this error in setting up separate foremen to deal with machinery, with materials, with speed, etc., each with the power of giving orders directly to the individual workman. The rigid adherence to the principle of unity of command may have its absurdities; these are, however, unimportant in comparison with the certainty of confusion, inefficiency and irresponsibility which arises from the violation of the principle.[2]

Certainly the principle of unity of command, thus interpreted, cannot be criticized for any lack of clarity or for ambiguity. The definition of "authority" given above should provide a clear test whether, in any concrete situation, the principle is observed. The real fault that must be found with this principle is that it is incompatible with the principle of specialization. One of the most important uses to which authority is put in organization is to bring about specialization in the work of making decisions, so that each decision is made at the point in the organization where it can be made most expertly. As a result, the use of authority permits a greater degree of expertness to be achieved in decision-making than would be possible if each operative employee had to make all the decisions upon which his activity is predicated. The individual fireman does not decide whether to use a two-inch hose or a fire extinguisher; that is decided for him by his officers, and the decision communicated to him in the form of a command.

However, if unity of command, in Gulick's sense, is observed, the decisions of a person at any point in the administrative hierarchy are subject to influence through only one channel of authority; and if his decisions are of a kind that requires expertise in more than one field of knowledge, then advisory and informational services must be relied upon to supply those premises which lie in a field not recognized by the mode of specialization in the organization. For example, if an accountant in a school department is subordinate to an educator, and if unity of command is observed, then the finance department cannot issue direct orders to him regarding

[2] L. Gulick, "Notes on the Theory of Organization," in Gulick and Urwick, *op. cit.*, p. 9.

the technical, accounting aspects of his work. Similarly, the director of motor vehicles in the public works department will be unable to issue direct orders on care of motor equipment to the fire-truck driver.[3]

Gulick, in the statement quoted above, clearly indicates the difficulties to be faced if unity of command is not observed. A certain amount of irresponsibility and confusion is almost certain to ensue. But perhaps this is not too great a price to pay for the increased expertise that can be applied to decisions. What is needed to decide the issue is a principle of administration that will enable one to weigh the relative advantages of the two courses of action. But neither the principle of unity of command nor the principle of specialization is helpful in adjudicating the controversy. They merely contradict each other without indicating any procedure for resolving the contradiction.

If this were merely an academic controversy—if it were generally agreed and had been generally demonstrated that unity of command must be preserved in all cases, even with a loss in expertise—one could assert that in case of conflict between the two principles, unity of command should prevail. But the issue is far from clear, and experts can be ranged on both sides of the controversy. On the side of unity of command there may be cited the dicta of Gulick and others.[4] On the side of specialization there are Taylor's theory of functional supervision, MacMahon and Millett's idea of "dual supervision," and the practice of technical supervision in military organization.[5]

It may be, as Gulick asserts, that the notion of Taylor and these others is an "error." If so, the evidence that it is an error has never been marshaled or published—apart from loose heuristic argu-

[3] This point is discussed by Herbert A. Simon in "Decision-Making and Administrative Organization," *Public Administration Review* 4:20–21 (Winter, 1944).

[4] Gulick, "Notes on the Theory of Organization," p. 9; L. D. White, *Introduction to the Study of Public Administration* (New York: Macmillan Company, 1939), p. 45.

[5] Frederick W. Taylor, *Shop Management* (New York: Harper & Bros., 1911), p. 99; MacMahon, Millett, and Ogden, *The Administration of Federal Work Relief* (Chicago: Public Administration Service, 1941), pp. 265–268, and L. Urwick, who describes British army practice in "Organization as a Technical Problem," Gulick and Urwick, eds., *op. cit.*, pp. 67–69.

ments like that quoted above. One is left with a choice between equally eminent theorists of administration, and without any evidential basis for making that choice.

What evidence there is of actual administrative practice would seem to indicate that the need for specialization is to a very large degree given priority over the need for unity of command. As a matter of fact, it does not go too far to say that unity of command, in Gulick's sense, never has existed in any administrative organization. If a line officer accepts the regulations of an accounting department with regard to the procedure for making requisitions, can it be said that, in this sphere, he is not subject to the authority of the accounting department? In any actual administrative situation authority is zoned, and to maintain that this zoning does not contradict the principle of unity of command requires a very different definition of "authority" from that used here. This subjection of the line officer to the accounting department is no different, in principle, from Taylor's recommendation that a workman be subject in the matter of work programming to one foreman, in the matter of machine operation to another.

The principle of unity of command is perhaps more defensible if narrowed down to the following: In case two authoritative commands conflict, there should be a single determinate person whom the subordinate is expected to obey; and the sanctions of authority should be applied against the subordinate only to enforce his obedience to that one person.

If the principle of unity of command is more defensible when stated in this limited form it also solves fewer problems. In the first place, it no longer requires, except for settling conflicts of authority, a single hierarchy of authority. Consequently, it leaves unsettled the very important question of how authority should be zoned in a particular organization (i.e. the modes of specialization), and through what channels it should be exercised. Finally, even this narrower concept of unity of command conflicts with the principle of specialization, for whenever disagreement does occur and the organization members revert to the formal lines of authority, then only those types of specialization which are represented in the hierarchy of authority can impress themselves on decision. If the training officer of a city exercises only functional supervision over the police training officer, then in case of disagreement with the police chief specialized knowledge of police problems will determine the outcome while specialized knowledge of training problems will be subordinated or ignored. That this actually occurs is shown by the frustration so commonly expressed by functional supervisors at their lack of authority to apply sanctions.

Span of Control

Administrative efficiency is supposed to be enhanced by limiting the number of subordinates who report directly to any one administrator to a small number—say six. This notion that the "span of control" should be narrow is confidently asserted as a third incontrovertible principle of administration. The usual common-sense arguments for restricting the span of control are familiar and need not be repeated here. What is not so generally recognized is that a contradictory proverb of administration can be stated which, though it is not so familiar as the principle of span of control, can be supported by arguments of equal plausibility. The proverb in question is the following:

Administrative efficiency is enhanced by keeping at a minimum the number of organizational levels through which a matter must pass before it is acted upon.

This latter proverb is one of the fundamental criteria that guide administrative analysts in simplifying procedures. Yet in many situations the results to which this principle leads are in direct contradiction to the requirements of the principle of span of control, the principle of unity of command, and the principle of specialization. The present discussion is concerned with the first of these conflicts. To illustrate the difficulty, two alternative proposals for the organization of a small health department will be presented— one based on the restriction of span of control, the other on the limitation of number of organization levels:

(A) The present organization of the department places an administrative overload on the Health Officer by reason of the fact that all eleven employees of the department report directly to him and the further fact that some of the staff lack adequate technical training. Consequently, venereal disease clinic treatments and other details require an undue amount of the Health Officer's personal attention.

It has previously been recommended that the proposed Medical Officer be placed in charge of the venereal disease and chest clinics and all child hygiene work. It is further recommended that one of the inspectors be designated chief inspector and placed in charge of all the department's inspectional activities; and that one of the nurses be designated as head nurse. This will relieve the Health Commissioner of considerable detail and will leave him greater freedom to plan and supervise the health program as a whole, to conduct health education, and to coordinate the work of the department with that of other community agencies. If the department were thus organized, the effectiveness of all employees could be substantially increased.

(B) The present organization of the department leads to inefficiency and excessive red tape by reason of the fact that an unnecessary supervisory level intervenes between the Health Officer and the operative employees, and that those four of the twelve employees who are best trained technically are engaged largely in "overhead" administrative duties. Consequently, unnecessary delays occur in securing the approval of the Health Officer on matters requiring his attention, and too many matters require review and re-review.

The Medical Officer should be left in charge of the venereal disease and chest clinics and child hygiene work. It is recommended, however, that the position of chief inspector and head nurse be abolished, and that the employees now filling these positions perform regular inspectional and nursing duties. The details of work scheduling now handled by these two employees can be taken care of more economically by the Secretary to the Health Officer, and, since broader matters of policy have, in any event, always required the personal attention of the Health Officer, the abolition of these two positions will eliminate a wholly unnecessary step in review, will allow an expansion of inspectional and nursing services, and will permit at least a beginning to be made in the recommended program of health education. The number of persons reporting directly to the Health Officer will be increased to nine, but since there are few matters requiring the coordination of these employees, other than the work schedules and policy questions referred to above, this change will not materially increase his work load.

The dilemma is this: in a large organization with interrelations between members, a restricted span of control inevitably produces excessive red tape, for each contact between organization members must be carried upward until a common superior is found. If the organization is at all large, this will involve carrying all such matters upward through several levels of officials for decision, and then downward again in the form of orders and instructions—a cumbersome and time-consuming process.

The alternative is to increase the number of persons who are under the command of each officer, so that the pyramid will come more rapidly to a peak, with fewer intervening levels. But this, too, leads to difficulty, for if an officer is required to supervise too many employees, his control over them is weakened.[6]

Granted, then, that both the increase and the decrease in span of control have some undesirable consequences, what is the optimum point? Proponents of a restricted span of control have suggested three, five, even eleven, as suitable numbers, but nowhere have they explained the reasoning which led them to the particular number they selected. The principle as stated casts no light on this very crucial question.

Organization by Purpose, Process, Clientele, Place [7]

Administrative efficiency is supposed to be increased by grouping workers according to (a) purpose, (b) process, (c) clientele, or (d) place. But from the discussion of specialization it is clear that this principle is internally inconsistent; for purpose, process, clientele, and place are competing bases of organization, and at any given point of division the advantages of three must be sacrificed to secure the advantages of the fourth. If the major departments of a city, for example, are organized on the basis of major purpose, then it follows that all the physicians, all the lawyers, all the engineers, or all the statisticians will not be located in a single department exclusively composed of members of their profession, but will be distributed among the various city departments need-

[6] A typical justification for limiting the span of control is given by L. Urwick, *op. cit.,* pp. 52–54.
[7] Cf. Schuyler Wallace, *Federal Departmentalization* (New York: Columbia University Press, 1941), pp. 91–146.

ing their services. The advantages of organization by process will thereby be partly lost.

Some of these advantages can be regained by organizing on the basis of process *within* the major departments. Thus there may be an engineering bureau within the public works department, or the board of education may have a school health service as a major division of its work. Similarly, within smaller units there may be division by area or by clientele; e.g., a fire department will have separate companies located throughout the city, while a welfare bureau will have intake and case-work offices in various locations. Again, however, these major types of specialization cannot be simultaneously achieved, for at any point in the organization it must be decided whether specialization at the next level will be accomplished by distinction of major purpose, major process, clientele, or area.

Competition Between Purpose and Clientele. The conflict may be illustrated by showing how the principle of specialization according to purpose would lead to a different result from specialization according to clientele in the organization of a health department.

(A) Public health administration consists of the following activities for the prevention of disease and the maintenance of healthful conditions: (1) vital statistics; (2) child hygiene—prenatal, maternity, postnatal, infant, pre-school, and school health programs; (3) communicable disease control; (4) inspection of milk, foods, and drugs; (5) sanitary inspection; (6) laboratory service; (7) health education.

One of the handicaps under which the health department labors is the fact that the department has no control over school health, which is an activity of the county board of education, and there is little or no coordination between that highly important part of the community health program and the rest of the program, which is conducted by the city-county health unit. It is recommended that the city and county open negotiations with the board of education for the transfer of all school health work and the appropriation therefor to the joint health unit.

(B) To the modern school department is entrusted the care of children during almost the entire period that they are absent from the parental home. It has three principal responsibilities toward them: (1) to provide for their education in useful skills and knowledge, and in character; (2) to provide them with wholesome play activities outside school hours; (3) to care for their health and to assure the attainment of minimum standards of nutrition.

One of the handicaps under which the school board labors is the fact that, except for school lunches, the board has no control over child health and nutrition, and there is little or no coordination between that highly important part of the child development program and the rest of the program, which is conducted by the board of education. It is recommended that the city and county open negotiations for the transfer of all health work for children of school age to the board of education.

Here again is posed the dilemma of choosing between alternative, equally plausible, administrative principles. But this is not the only difficulty in the present case, for a closer study of the situation shows there are fundamental ambiguities in the meanings of the key terms: "purpose," "process," "clientele," and "place."

Ambiguities in Key Terms. "Purpose" may be roughly defined as the objective or end for which an activity is carried on; "process," as a means of accomplishing a purpose. Processes, then, are carried on in order to achieve purposes. But purposes themselves may generally be arranged in some sort of hierarchy. A typist moves her fingers in order to type; types in order to reproduce a letter; reproduces a letter in order that an inquiry may be answered. Writing a letter is then the purpose for which the typing is performed; while writing a letter is also the process whereby the purpose of replying to an inquiry is achieved. It follows that the same activity may be described as purpose or as process.

This ambiguity is easily illustrated for the case of an administrative organization. A health department conceived as a unit whose task it is to care for the health of the community is a purpose organization; the same department conceived as a unit which makes use of the medical arts to carry on its work is a process organization. In the same way, an education department may be viewed as a purpose (to educate) organization, or a clientele (children) organization; the Forest Service as a purpose (forest conservation), process (forest management), clientele (lumbermen and cattlemen utilizing public forests), or area (publicly owned forest lands) organization. When concrete illustrations of this sort are selected, the lines of demarcation between these categories become very hazy and unclear indeed.

"Organization by major purpose," says Gulick,[8] "serves to bring together in a single large department all of those who are at work endeavoring to render a particular service." But what is a particular service? Is fire protection a single purpose, or is it merely a part of the purpose of public safety? Or is it a combination of purposes including fire prevention and fire fighting? It must be concluded that there is no such a thing as a purpose, or a *unifunctional* (single-purpose) organization. What is to be considered as *a* single function depends entirely on language and techniques.[9] If the English language has a comprehensive term which covers both of two sub-purposes it is natural to think of the two together as a single purpose. If such a term is lacking, the two sub-purposes become purposes in their own right. On the other hand, a single activity may contribute to several objectives; but since they are technically (procedurally) inseparable the activity is considered as a single function or purpose.

The fact mentioned previously that purposes form a hierarchy, each sub-purpose contributing to some more final and comprehensive end, helps to make clear the relation between purpose and process. "Organization by major process," says Gulick,[10] ". . . tends to bring together in a single department all of those who are at work making use of a given skill or technology, or are members of a given profession." Consider a simple skill of this kind—typing. Typing is a skill that brings about a means-end coordination of muscular movements, but brings it about at a very low level in the means-end hierarchy. The content of the type-written letter is indifferent to the skill that produces it. The skill consists merely in the ability to hit the letter *t* quickly whenever *t*

---

[8] *Op. cit.,* p. 21.
[9] If this is correct, then any attempt to prove that certain activities belong in a single department because they relate to a single purpose is doomed to fail. See, for example, John M. Gaus and Leon Wolcott, *Public Administration and the U. S. Department of Agriculture* (Chicago: Public Administrative Service, 1941).
[10] *Op. cit.,* p. 23.

is required by the content, and to hit the letter *a* whenever *a* is required by the content.

There is, then, no essential difference between a "purpose" and a "process," but only a distinction of degree. A "process" is an activity whose immediate purpose is at a low level in the hierarchy of means and ends, while a "purpose" is a collection of activities whose orienting value or aim is at a high level in the means-end hierarchy.

Next consider "clientele" and "place" as bases of organization. These categories are really not separate from purpose, but a part of it. A complete statement of the purpose of a fire department would have to include the area served by it; "to reduce fire losses on property in the city of X." Objectives of an administrative organization are phrased in terms of a service to be provided and an area for which it is provided. Usually, the term "purpose" is meant to refer only to the first element; but the second is just as legitimately an aspect of purpose. Area of service, of course, may be a specified clientele quite as well as a geographical area. In the case of an agency which works on "shifts," time will be a third dimension of purpose—to provide a given service in a given area (or to a given clientele) during a given time period.

With this terminology, the next task is to reconsider the problem of specializing the work of an organization. It is no longer legitimate to speak of a "purpose" organization, or a "process" organization, a "clientele" organization, or an "area" organization. The same unit might fall into any one of these four categories, depending on the nature of the larger organizational unit of which it was a part. A unit providing public health and medical services for school-age children in Multnomah County might be considered as (1) an "area" organization if it were part of a unit providing the same service for the state of Oregon; (2) a "clientele" organization if it were part of a unit providing similar services for children of all ages; (3) a "purpose" or a "process" organization (it would be impossible to say which) if it were part of an education department.

It is incorrect to say that Bureau A is a process bureau; the correct statement is that Bureau A is a process bureau *within* Department X.[11] This latter statement would mean that Bureau A incorporated all the processes of a certain kind in Department X, without reference to any special sub-purposes, sub-areas, or sub-clienteles of Department X. Now it is conceivable that a particular unit might incorporate all processes of a certain kind, but that these processes might relate only to certain particular sub-purposes of the department purpose. In this case, which corresponds to the health unit in an education department mentioned above, the unit would be specialized by both purpose and process. The health unit would be the only one in the education department using the medical art (process) and concerned with health (sub-purpose).

Lack of Criteria for Specialization. Even when the problem is solved of proper usage for the terms "purpose," "process," "clientele," and "area," the principles of administration give no guide as to which of these four competing bases of specialization is applicable in any particular situation. The British Machinery of Government Committee had no doubts about the matter. It considered purpose and clientele as the two possible bases of organization and put its faith entirely in the former. Others have had equal assurance in choosing between purpose and process. The reasoning which leads to these unequivocal conclusions leaves something to be desired. The Machinery of Government Committee gives this sole argument for its choice:

Now the inevitable outcome of this method of organization [by clientele] is a tendency to Lilliputian administration. It is impossible that the specialized service which each Department has to render to the community can be of as high a standard when its work is at the same time limited to a particular class of persons and extended to every variety of provision for them, as when the Department concentrates itself on the provision of the particular service only, by whomsoever required, and looks beyond the interest of comparatively small classes.[12]

[11] It should be noted that this distinction is implicit in most of Gulick's analysis of specialization (*op. cit.*, pp. 15–30). However, since he cites as examples single departments within a city, and since he usually speaks of "grouping activities" rather than "dividing work," the relative character of these categories is not always apparent in this discussion.

[12] *Report of the Machinery of Government Committee* (London: His Majesty's Stationery Office, 1918), p. 7.

The faults in this analysis are clearly obvious. First, there is no attempt to determine how *a* service is to be recognized. Second, there is a bald assumption, absolutely without proof, that a child health unit, for example, in a department of child welfare could not offer services of "as high a standard" as the same unit if it were located in a department of health. Just how the shifting of the unit from one department to another would improve or damage the quality of its work is not explained. Third, no basis is set forth for adjudicating the competing claims of purpose and process— the two are merged in the ambiguous term "service." It is not necessary here to decide whether the committee was right or wrong in its recommendation; the important point is that the recommendation represented a choice, without any apparent logical or empirical grounds, between contradictory principles of administration.

Even more remarkable illustrations of illogic can be found in most discussions of purpose *vs.* process. They would be too ridiculous to cite if they were not commonly used in serious political and administrative debate.

For instance, where should agricultural education come: in the Ministry of Education, or of Agriculture? That depends on whether we want to see the best farming taught, though possibly by old methods, or a possibly out-of-date style of farming, taught in the most modern and compelling manner. The question answers itself.[18]

But does the question really answer itself? Suppose a bureau of agricultural education were set up, headed, for example, by a man who had had extensive experience in agricultural research or as administrator of an agricultural school, and staffed by men of similarly appropriate background. What reason is there to believe that if attached to a Ministry of Education they would teach old-fashioned farming by new-fashioned methods, while if attached to a Ministry of Agriculture they would teach new-fashioned farming by old-fashioned methods? The administrative problem of such a bureau would be to teach new-fashioned farming by new-fashioned methods, and it is a little difficult to see how the depart-

[18] Sir Charles Harris, "Decentralization," *Journal of Public Administration,* 3:117–133 (Apr., 1925).

mental location of the unit would affect this result. "The question answers itself" only if one has a rather mystical faith in the potency of bureau shuffling as a means of redirecting the activities of an agency.

These contradictions and competitions have received increasing attention from students of administration during the past few years. For example, Gulick, Wallace, and Benson have stated certain advantages and disadvantages of the several modes of specialization, and have considered the conditions under which one or the other mode might best be adopted.[14] All this analysis has been at a theoretical level—in the sense that data have not been employed to demonstrate the superior effectiveness claimed for the different modes. But, though theoretical, the analysis has lacked a theory. Since no comprehensive framework has been constructed within which the discussion could take place, the analysis has tended either to the logical one-sidedness which characterizes the examples quoted above or to inconclusiveness.

The Impasse of Administrative Theory

The four "principles of administration" that were set forth at the beginning of this paper have now been subjected to critical analysis. None of the four survived in very good shape, for in each case there was found, instead of a univocal principle, a set of two or more mutually incompatible principles apparently equally applicable to the administrative situation.

Moreover, the reader will see that the very same objections can be urged against the customary discussions of "centralization" vs. "decentralization," which usually conclude, in effect, that "on the one hand, centralization of decision-making function is desirable; on the other hand, there are definite advantages in decentralization."

Can anything be salvaged which will be useful in the construction of an administrative theory? As a matter of fact, almost everything can be salvaged. The difficulty has arisen from treating as

[14] Gulick, "Notes on the Theory of Organization," in Gulick and Urwick, *op. cit.*, pp. 21–30; Schuyler Wallace, *op. cit.;* George C. S. Benson, "Internal Administrative Organization," *Public Administration Review,* 1:473–486 (Autumn, 1941).

"principles of administration" what are really only criteria for describing and diagnosing administrative situations. Closet space is certainly an important item in the design of a successful house; yet, a house designed entirely with a view to securing a maximum of closet space—all other considerations being forgotten—would be considered, to say the least, as somewhat unbalanced. Similarly, unity of command, specialization by purpose, decentralization, all are items to be considered in the design of an efficient administrative organization. No single one of these items is of sufficient importance to suffice as a guiding principle for the administrative analyst. In the design of administrative organizations, as in their operation, over-all efficiency must be the guiding criterion. Mutually incompatible advantages must be balanced against each other, just as an architect weighs the advantages of additional closet space against the advantages of a larger living room.

This position, if it is a valid one, constitutes an indictment of much current writing about administrative matters. As the examples cited in this chapter amply demonstrate, much administrative analysis proceeds by selecting a single criterion, and applying it to an administrative situation to reach a recommendation; while the fact that equally valid, but contradictory, criteria exist which could be applied with equal reason, but with a different result, is conveniently ignored. A valid approach to the study of administration requires that *all* the relevant diagnostic criteria be identified; that each administrative situation be analyzed in terms of the entire set of criteria; and that research be instituted to determine how weights can be assigned to the several criteria when they are, as they usually will be, mutually incompatible.

AN APPROACH TO ADMINISTRATIVE THEORY

This program needs to be considered step by step. First, what is included in the description of administrative situations for purposes of such an analysis? Second, how can weights be assigned to the various criteria to give them their proper place in the total picture?

The Description of Administrative Situations

Before a science can develop principles, it must possess concepts. Before a law of gravitation could be formulated, it was necessary to have the notions of "acceleration" and "weight." The first task of administrative theory is to develop a set of concepts that will permit the description, in terms relevant to the theory, of administrative situations. These concepts, to be scientifically useful, must be operational; that is, their meanings must correspond to empirically observable facts or situations. The definition of "authority" given earlier in this chapter is an example of an operational definition.

What is a scientifically relevant description of an organization? It is a description that, so far as possible, designates for each person in the organization what decisions that person makes, and the influences to which he is subject in making each of these decisions. Current descriptions of administrative organizations fall far short of this standard. For the most part, they confine themselves to the allocation of *functions,* and the formal structure of *authority.* They give little attention to the other types of organizational influence or to the system of communication.[15]

What does it mean, for example to say: "The Department is made up of three Bureaus. The first has the function of ———, the second the function of ———, and the third the function of ———?" What can be learned from such a description about the workability of the organizational arrangement? Very little, indeed. For, from the description, there is obtained no idea of the degree to which decisions are centralized at the bureau level or at the departmental level. No notion is given of the extent to which the (presumably unlimited) authority of the department over the bureau is actually exercised, nor by what mechanisms. There is no indication of the extent to which systems of communication assist the coordination of the three bureaus, nor, for that matter to what extent coordination is required by the nature of their work.

[15] The monograph by MacMahon, Millett, and Ogden (*op. cit.*) perhaps approaches nearer than any other published administrative study to the sophistication required in administrative description. See, for example, the discussion on pp. 233–236 of headquarters-field relationships.

There is no description of the kinds of training the members of the bureau have undergone, nor the extent to which this training permits decentralization at the bureau level. In sum, a description of administrative organizations in terms almost exclusively of functions and lines of authority is completely inadequate for purposes of administrative analysis.

Consider the term "centralization." How is it determined whether the operations of a particular organization are "centralized" or "decentralized"? Does the fact that field offices exist prove anything about decentralization? Might not the same decentralization take place in the bureaus of a centrally located office? A realistic analysis of centralization must include a study of the allocation of decisions in the organization, and the methods of influence that are employed by the higher levels to affect the decisions at the lower levels. Such an analysis would reveal a much more complex picture of the decision-making process than any enumeration of the geographical locations of organizational units at the different levels.

Administrative description suffers currently from superficiality, oversimplification, lack of realism. It has confined itself too closely to the mechanism of authority, and has failed to bring within its orbit the other, equally important, modes of influence on organizational behavior. It has refused to undertake the tiresome task of studying the actual allocations of decision-making functions. It has been satisfied to speak of "authority," "centralization," "span of control," "function," without seeking operational definitions of these terms. Until administrative description reaches a higher level of sophistication, there is little reason to hope that rapid progress will be made toward the identification and verification of valid administrative principles.

The Diagnosis of Administrative Situations

Before any positive suggestions can be made, it is necessary to digress a bit, and to consider more closely the exact nature of the propositions of administrative theory. The theory of administration is concerned with how an organization should be constructed and operated in order to accomplish its work efficiently. A fundamental principle of administration, which follows almost immediately from the rational character of "good" administration, is that among several alternatives involving the same expenditure the one should always be selected which leads to the greatest accomplishment of administrative objectives; and among several alternatives that lead to the same accomplishment the one should be selected which involves the least expenditure. Since this "principle of efficiency" is characteristic of any activity that attempts rationally to maximize the attainment of certain ends with the use of scarce means, it is as characteristic of economic theory as it is of administrative theory. The "administrative man" takes his place alongside the classical "economic man." [16]

Actually, the "principle" of efficiency should be considered as a definition rather than a principle: it is a definition of what is meant by "good" or "correct" administrative behavior. It does not tell *how* accomplishments are to be maximized, but merely states that this maximization is the aim of administrative activity, and that administrative theory must disclose under what conditions the maximization takes place.

Now what are the factors that determine the level of efficiency which is achieved by an administrative organization? It is not possible to make an exhaustive list of these, but the principal categories can be enumerated. Perhaps the simplest method of approach is to consider the single member of the administrative organization, and ask what the limits are to the quantity and quality of his output. These limits include (a) limits on his ability to *perform,* and (b) limits on his ability to *make correct decisions.* To the extent that these limits are removed, the administrative organization approaches its goal of high efficiency. Two persons, given the same skills, the same objectives and values, the same knowledge and information, can rationally decide only upon the same course of action. Hence, administrative theory must be interested in the factors that will determine with what skills, values, and knowledge the organization member undertakes his work. These are the

---

[16] For an elaboration of the principle of efficiency and its place in administrative theory see Clarence E. Ridley and Herbert A. Simon, *Measuring Municipal Activities* (Chicago: International City Managers' Ass., 2nd ed., 1943), particularly chap. I and the preface to the second edition.

"limits" to rationality with which the principles of administration must deal.

On one side, the individual is limited by those skills, habits, and reflexes which are no longer in the realm of the conscious. His performance, for example, may be limited by his manual dexterity or his reaction time or his strength. His decision-making processes may be limited by the speed of his mental processes, his skill in elementary arithmetic, and so forth. In this area, the principles of administration must be concerned with the physiology of the human body, the laws of skill-training, and of habit. This is the field that has been most successfully cultivated by the followers of Taylor, and in which has been developed time-and-motion study and the therblig.

On a second side, the individual is limited by his values and those conceptions of purpose which influence him in making his decisions. If his loyalty to the organization is high, his decisions may evidence sincere acceptance of the objectives set for the organization; if that loyalty is lacking, personal motives may interfere with his administrative efficiency. If his loyalties are attached to the bureau by which he is employed, he may sometimes make decisions that are inimical to the larger unit of which the bureau is a part. In this area the principles of administration must be concerned with the determinants of loyalty and morale, with leadership and initiative, and with the influences that determine where the individual's organizational loyalties will be attached.

On a third side, the individual is limited by the extent of his knowledge of things relevant to his job. This applies both to the basic knowledge required in decision-making—a bridge designer must know the fundamentals of mechanics—and to the information that is required to make his decisions appropriate to the given situation. In this area, administrative theory is concerned with such fundamental questions as these: what the limits are on the mass of knowledge that human minds can accumulate and apply; how rapidly knowledge can be assimilated; how specialization in the administrative organization is to be related to the specializations of knowledge that are prevalent in the community's occupational structure; how the system of communication is to channel knowledge and information to the appropriate decision-points; what types of knowledge can, and what types cannot, be easily transmitted; how the need for intercommunication of information is affected by the modes of specialization in the organization? This is perhaps the *terra incognita* of administrative theory, and undoubtedly its careful exploration will cast great light on the proper application of the proverbs of administration.

Perhaps this triangle of limits does not completely bound the area of rationality, and other sides need to be added to the figure In any case, the enumeration will serve to indicate the kinds of considerations that must go into the construction of valid and non-contradictory principles of administration.

An important fact to be kept in mind is that the limits of rationality are variable limits. Most important of all, consciousness of the limits may in itself alter them. Suppose it were discovered in a particular organization, for example, that organizational loyalties attached to small units had frequently led to a harmful degree of intra-organizational competition. Then, a program which trained members of the organization to be conscious of their loyalties, and to subordinate loyalties toward the smaller group to those toward the larger, might lead to a very considerable alteration of the limits in that organization.[17]

A related point is that the term "rational behavior," as employed here, refers to rationality when that behavior is evaluated in terms of the objectives of the larger organization; for, as it has just been pointed out, the difference in direction of the individual's aims from those of the larger organization is just one of those elements of nonrationality with which the theory must deal.

Assigning Weights to the Criteria

A first step, then, in the overhauling of the proverbs of administration is to develop a vocabulary, along the lines just suggested, for the description of administrative organization. A second step, which has also been outlined, is to study the limits of rationality in

[17] For an example of the use of such training, see Herbert A. Simon and William Divine, "Controlling Human Factors in an Administrative Experiment," *Public Administration Review*, 1:487–492 (Autumn, 1941).

order to develop a complete and comprehensive enumeration of the criteria that must be weighed in evaluating an administrative organization. The current proverbs represent only a fragmentary and unsystematized portion of these criteria.

When these two tasks have been carried out, it remains to assign weights to the criteria. Since the criteria, or "proverbs," are often mutually competitive or contradictory, it is not sufficient merely to identify them. Merely to know, for example, that a specified change in organization will reduce the span of control is not enough to justify the change. This gain must be balanced against the possible resulting loss of contact between the higher and lower ranks of the hierarchy.

Hence, administrative theory must also be concerned with the question of the weights that are to be applied to these criteria—to the problems of their relative importance in any concrete situation. This question is an empirical one, and its solution cannot even be attempted in a volume like this one. What is needed is empirical research and experimentation to determine the relative desirability of alternative administrative arrangements. The methodological framework for this research is already at hand in the principle of efficiency. If an administrative organization whose activities are susceptible to objective evaluation be studied, then the actual change in accomplishment that results from modifying administrative arrangements in these organizations can be observed and analyzed.

There are two indispensable conditions to successful research along these lines. First, it is necessary that the objectives of the administrative organization under study be defined in concrete terms so that results, expressed in terms of these objectives, may be accurately measured. Second, it is necessary that sufficient experimental control be exercised to make possible the isolation of the particular effect under study from other disturbing factors that might be operating on the organization at the same time.

These two conditions have seldom been even partially fulfilled in so-called "administrative experiments." The mere fact that a legislature passes a law creating an administrative agency, that the agency operates for five years, that it is finally abolished, and that an historical study is then made of its operations is not sufficient to

make of that agency's history an "administrative experiment."
Modern American legislation is full of such "experiments" which
furnish orators in neighboring states with abundant ammunition
when similar issues arise in their bailiwicks, but which provide the
scientific investigator with little or nothing in the way of objective
evidence, one way or the other.

In the literature of administration, only a handful of research
studies satisfy these fundamental conditions of methodology—and
they are, for the most part, on the periphery of the problem of organization. There are, first of all, the studies of the Taylor group which
sought to determine the technological conditions of efficiency. Perhaps none of these is a better example of the painstaking methods
of science than Taylor's own studies of the cutting of metals.[18]

Studies dealing with the human and social aspects of administration are even rarer than the technological studies. Among the more
important are the whole series of studies on fatigue, starting in
Great Britain during the First World War, and culminating in the
Western Electric experiments.[19]

In the field of public administration, almost the sole example of
such experimentation is the series of studies that have been conducted in the public welfare field to determine the proper case loads
for social workers.[20]

Because, apart from these scattered examples, studies of administrative agencies have been carried out without benefit of control
or objective measurements of results, they have had to depend for

[18] F. W. Taylor, *On the Art of Cutting Metals* (New York: American Society
of Mechanical Engineers, 1907).
[19] Great Britain, Ministry of Munitions, Health of Munitions Workers Committee, *Final Report* (London: H.M. Stationery Office, 1918); F. J. Roethlisberger and William J. Dickson, *Management and the Worker* (Cambridge:
Harvard University Press, 1939).
[20] Ellery F. Reed, *An Experiment in Reducing the Cost of Relief* (Chicago:
American Public Welfare Assn., 1937); Rebecca Staman, "What Is the Most
Economical Case Load in Public Relief Administration?" *Social Work Technique,*
4:117–121 (May–June, 1938); Chicago Relief Administration, *Adequate Staff
Brings Economy* (Chicago: American Public Welfare Assn., 1939); Constance
Hastings and Saya S. Schwartz, *Size of Visitor's Caseload as a Factor in Ef-
ficient Administration of Public Assistance* (Philadelphia; Philadelphia County
Board of Assistance, 1939); H. A. Simon et al., *Determining Work Loads for
Professional Staff in a Public Welfare Agency* (Berkeley: University of Cali-
fornia, Bureau of Public Administration, 1941).

their recommendations and conclusions upon *a priori* reasoning proceeding from "principles of administration." The reasons have already been stated in this chapter why the "principles" derived in this way cannot be more than "proverbs."

Perhaps the program outlined here will appear an ambitious or even a quixotic one. There should certainly be no illusions, in undertaking it, as to the length and deviousness of the path. It is hard to see, however, what alternative remains open. Certainly neither the practitioner of administration nor the theoretician can be satisfied with the poor analytic tools that the proverbs provide him. Nor is there any reason to believe that a less drastic reconversion than that outlined here will rebuild those tools to usefulness.

It may be objected that administration cannot aspire to be a "science," that by the nature of its subject it cannot be more than an "art." Whether true or false, this objection is irrelevant to the present discussion. The question of how "exact" the principles of administration can be made is one that only experience can answer. But as to whether they should be logical or illogical there can be no debate. Even an "art" cannot be founded on proverbs.

As already indicated, the present volume will attempt only the first step in the reconstruction of administrative theory—the construction of an adequate vocabulary and analytic scheme. In saying that other steps must follow, one must be careful not to underestimate the importance or necessity of this first one. To be sure, the literature of administration has not been lacking in "theory," any more than it has in descriptive and empirical studies. What has been lacking has been a bridge between these two, so that theory could provide a guide to the design of "critical" experiments and studies, while experimental studies could provide a sharp test and corrective of theory. If this volume is successful, it will contribute toward the construction of such a bridge.

Chapter III

FACT AND VALUE IN DECISION-MAKING

IN CHAPTER I it was pointed out that every decision involves elements of two kinds, which were called "factual" and "value" elements respectively. This distinction proves to be a very fundamental one for administration. It leads first of all to an understanding of what is meant by a "correct" administrative decision. Secondly, it clarifies the distinction, so often made in the literature of administration, between policy questions and questions of administration. These important issues will be the subject matter of the present chapter.

To ground an answer to these questions on first principles would require that this volume on administration be prefaced by an even longer philosophical treatise. The necessary ideas are already accessible in the literature of philosophy. Hence, the conclusions reached by a particular school of modern philosophy—logical positivism—will be accepted as a starting point, and their implications for the theory of decisions examined. The reader who is interested in examining the reasoning upon which these doctrines are based will find references to the literature in the footnotes to this chapter.

DISTINCTION BETWEEN FACTUAL AND ETHICAL MEANING

Factual propositions are statements about the observable world and the way in which it operates.[1] In principle, factual propositions

[1] The positivist theory as to the nature of scientific propositions is discussed at length by Charles W. Morris, *Foundations of the Theory of Signs,* and Rudolf Carnap, *Foundations of Logic and Mathematics,* in International Encyclopedia of Unified Science, vol. I, nos. 2 and 3 (Chicago: University of Chicago Press, 1937 and 1938) ; P. W. Bridgman, *The Logic of Modern Physics* (New York: Macmillan Co., 1937) ; Rudolf Carnap, "Testability and Meaning," *Philosophy*

may be tested to determine whether they are *true* or *false*—whether what they say about the world actually occurs, or whether it does not.

Decisions are something more than factual propositions. To be sure, they are descriptive of a future state of affairs, and this description can be true or false in a strictly empirical sense; but they possess, in addition, an imperative quality—they select one future state of affairs in preference to another and direct behavior toward the chosen alternative. In short, they have an *ethical* as well as a factual content.

The question of whether decisions can be correct and incorrect resolves itself, then, into the question of whether ethical terms like "ought," "good," and "preferable" have a purely empirical meaning. It is a fundamental premise of this study that ethical terms are not completely reducible to factual terms. No attempt will be made here to demonstrate conclusively the correctness of this view toward ethical propositions; the justification has been set forth at length by logical positivists and others.[2]

The argument, briefly, runs as follows. To determine whether a proposition is correct, it must be compared directly with experience—with the facts—or it must lead by logical reasoning to other propositions that can be compared with experience. But factual propositions cannot be derived from ethical ones by any process of reasoning, nor can ethical propositions be compared directly with the facts—since they assert "oughts" rather than facts. Hence, there is no way in which the correctness of ethical propositions can be empirically or rationally tested.

From this viewpoint, if a sentence declares that some particular state of affairs "ought to be," or that it is "preferable" or "desirable," then the sentence performs an imperative function, and is neither true nor false, correct nor incorrect. Since decisions involve valuation of this kind, they too cannot be objectively described as correct or incorrect.

---

of *Science*, 3: 420–471 (Oct., 1936), and 4: 2–40 (Jan., 1937); Rudolf Carnap, *The Logical Syntax of Language* (New York: Harcourt, Brace & Co., 1937); Alfred J. Ayer, *Language, Truth, and Logic* (London: Victor Gollancz, 1936).
[2] Two recent treatments are Ayer, *op. cit.*, and T. V. Smith, *Beyond Conscience* (New York: McGraw-Hill Book Co., 1934).

The search for the philosopher's stone and the squaring of the circle have not been more popular pursuits among philosophers than the attempt to derive ethical sentences, as consequences of purely factual ones. To mention a relatively modern example— Bentham defined the term "good" as equivalent with "conducive to happiness," defining "happiness" in psychological terms.[3] He then considered whether or not particular states of affairs were conducive to happiness, and hence good. Of course, no logical objection can be raised against this procedure: it is here rejected because the word "good" thus defined by Bentham cannot perform the function required of the word "good" in ethics—that of expressing moral preference for one alternative over another. It may be possible by such a process to derive the conclusion that people will be happier under one set of circumstances than under another, but this does not prove that they *ought* to be happier. The Aristotelian definition— that something is good for man which makes him correspond more closely with his essential nature as a rational animal [4]—suffers from the same limitation.

Thus, by appropriate definitions of the word "good" it may be possible to construct sentences of the form: "Such a state of affairs *is good.*" But from "good" defined in this way it is impossible to deduce "Such a state of affairs *ought to be.*" The task of ethics is to select imperatives—ought-sentences; and this task cannot be accomplished if the term "good" is defined in such a way that it merely designates existents. In this study, therefore, words like "good" and "ought" will be reserved for their ethical functions, and will not be predicated of any state of affairs in a purely factual sense. It follows that decisions may be "good," but they cannot, in an unqualified sense, be "correct," or "true."

The Evaluation of Decisions

We see that, in a strict sense, the administrator's decisions cannot be evaluated by scientific means. Is there no scientific content, then, to administrative problems? Are they purely questions of

---

[3] Jeremy Bentham, *An Introduction to the Principles of Morals and Legislation* (Oxford: Clarendon Press, 1907), p. 1.
[4] Aristotle, "Nicomachean Ethics," bk. I, chap. vii, 12–18, in *The Basic Works of Aristotle*, ed. by Richard McKeon (New York: Random House, 1941).

ethics? Quite the contrary: to assert that there is an ethical element involved in every decision is not to assert that decisions involve only ethical elements.

Consider the following passage from the *Infantry Field Manual* of the United States Army:

> Surprise is an essential element of a successful attack. Its effects should be striven for in small as well as in large operations. Infantry effects surprise by concealment of the time and place of the attack, screening of its dispositions, rapidity of maneuver, deception, and the avoidance of stereotyped procedures.[5]

It is difficult to say to what extent these three sentences are meant as factual propositions, and to what extent they are intended as imperatives, that is, as decisions. The first may be read purely as a statement about the conditions for a successful attack; the third may be interpreted as a listing of the conditions under which a state of surprise is achieved. But binding together these factual sentences —providing them with connective tissue, so to speak—is a set of expressed and implied imperatives, which may be paraphrased thus: "Attack successfully!" "Employ surprise!" and "Conceal the time and place of attack, screen dispositions, move rapidly, deceive the enemy, and avoid stereotyped procedures!"

In fact, the paragraph can be rephrased in another way, separating it into three sentences, the first ethical, the others purely factual:

1. Attack successfully!
2. An attack is successful only when carried out under conditions of surprise.
3. The conditions of surprise are concealment of the time and place of attack, etc.

It follows that the decisions that a military commander makes to screen the dispositions of his troops contain both factual and ethical elements, for he screens the dispositions *in order* to effect "surprise," and this *in order* to attack successfully. Hence, there is one sense in which the correctness of his decisions can be judged: it is a purely factual question whether the measures he takes *in order* to accomplish his aim are appropriate measures. It is not a factual

[5] *Complete Tactics, Infantry Rifle Battalion* (Washington: Infantry Journal, 1940), p. 20.

question whether the aim itself is correct or not, except in so far as this aim is connected, by an "in order," to further aims.

Decisions can always be evaluated in this relative sense—it can be determined whether they are correct, given the objective at which they are aimed—but a change in objectives implies a change in evaluation. Strictly speaking, it is not the decision itself which is evaluated, but the purely factual relationship that is asserted between the decision and its aims.[6] The commander's decision to take particular measures in order to attain surprise is not evaluated; what is evaluated is his factual judgment that the measures he takes will, in fact, attain surprise.

This argument may be presented in a slightly different way. Consider the two sentences: "Achieve surprise!" and "The conditions of surprise are concealment of the time and place of attack, etc." While the first sentence contains an imperative, or ethical, element, and hence is neither true nor false, the second sentence is purely factual. If the notion of logical inference be extended so as to apply to the ethical as well as the factual element in sentences, then from these two sentences a third may be deduced: "Conceal the time and place of attack, etc.!" Thus, with the mediation of a factual premise (the second sentence), one imperative can be deduced from another.[7]

The Mixed Character of Ethical Statements

It should be clear from the illustrations already put forth that most ethical propositions have admixed with them factual elements.

[6] This point of view is developed by Jorgen Jorgensen in "Imperatives and Logic," *Erkenntnis*, 7:288–296 (1938).

[7] In fact the usual laws of inference do not appear to hold strictly in deducing one imperative from another. For a number of discussions of the possibility of a logical calculus for imperatives and attempts to construct a rigorous calculus, see the following: Karl Menger, "A Logic of the Doubtful: On Optative and Imperative Logic," *Reports of a Mathematical Colloquium* (Notre Dame, Indiana, 1939), series 2, No. 1, pp. 53–64; K. Grue-Sörensen, "Imperativsätze und Logik: Begegnung einer Kritik," *Theoria*, 5:195–202 (1939); Albert Hofstadter and J. C. C. McKinsey, "On the Logic of Imperatives," *Philosophy of Science*, 6:446–457 (1939); Kurt Grelling, "Zur Logik der Sollsätze," *Unity of Science Forum*, Jan., 1939, pp. 44–47; K. Reach, "Some Comments on Grelling's Paper," *Ibid.*, Apr., 1939, p. 72; Kalle Sorainen, "Der Modus und die Logik," *Theoria*, 5:202–204 (1939); Rose Rand, "Logik der Forderungssätze," *Revue internationale de la Theorie du droit* (Zurich), New Series. 5:308–322 (1939).

Since most imperatives are not ends-in-themselves but intermediate ends, the question of their appropriateness to the more final ends at which they are aimed remains a factual question. Whether it is ever possible to trace the chain of implementation far enough to isolate a "pure" value—an end that is desired purely for itself—is a question that need not be settled here. The important point for the present discussion is that any statement that contains an ethical element, intermediate or final, cannot be described as correct or incorrect, and that the decision-making process must start with some ethical premise that is taken as "given." This ethical premise describes the objective of the organization in question.

In administration, the mixed character of the ethical "givens" is usually fairly obvious. A municipal department may take as its objective the providing of recreation to the city's inhabitants. This aim may then be further analyzed as a means toward "building healthier bodies," "using leisure time constructively," "preventing juvenile delinquency," and a host of others, until the chain of means and ends is traced into a vague realm labeled "the good life." At this point the means-ends connections become so conjectural (e.g. the relation between recreation and character), and the content of the values so ill defined (e.g. "happiness"), that the analysis becomes valueless for administrative purposes.[8]

The last point may be stated in a more positive way. In order for an ethical proposition to be useful for rational decision-making, (a) the values taken as organizational objectives must be definite, so that their degree of realization in any situation can be assessed, and (b) it must be possible to form judgments as to the probability that particular actions will implement these objectives.

The Role of Judgment in Decision

The division of the premises of decision into those that are ethical and those that are factual might appear to leave no room for judgment in decision-making. This difficulty is avoided by the very broad meaning that has been given to the word "factual": a statement about the observable world is factual if, in principle, its truth

<hr>

[8] See the excellent discussion of this point by Wayne A. R. Leys in "Ethics and Administrative Discretion," *Public Administration Review*, 3:19 (Winter, 1943).

or falsity may be tested. That is, if certain events occur, we say the statement was true; if other events occur, we say that it was false.

This does not by any means imply that we are able to determine in advance whether it is true or false. It is here that judgment enters. In making administrative decisions it is continually necessary to choose factual premises whose truth or falsehood is not definitely known and cannot be determined with certainty with the information and time available for reaching the decision.

It is a purely factual question whether a particular infantry attack will take its objective or fail. It is, nevertheless, a question involving judgment, since the success or failure will depend upon the disposition of the enemy, the accuracy and strength of artillery support, the topography, the morale of the attacking and defending troops, and a host of other factors that cannot be completely known or assessed by the commander who has to order the attack.

In ordinary speech there is often confusion between the element of judgment in decision and the ethical element. This confusion is enhanced by the fact that the further the means-end chain is followed, i.e. the greater the ethical element, the more doubtful are the steps in the chain, and the greater is the element of judgment involved in determining what means will contribute to what ends.[9]

The process by which judgments are formed has been very imperfectly studied. In practical administration it may be feared that confidence in the correctness of judgments sometimes takes the place of any serious attempt to evaluate them systematically on the basis of subsequent results. But further consideration of the psychology of decision-making will have to be postponed to a later chapter.[10]

Value Judgments in Private Management

The illustrations used thus far in this chapter have been drawn largely from the field of public administration. One reason for this is that the problem of value judgments has been more fully explored

[9] Leys, *op. cit.*, p. 18, points out that this confusion has been present in most of the literature on administrative discretion.
[10] Barnard, *op. cit.*, presents an interesting, but perhaps too optimistic, view of the "intuitive" element in administrative decision, in an Appendix, "Mind in Everyday Affairs," pp. 299–322.

—particularly in relation to administrative discretion and administrative regulation—in the public than in the private field. There is, in fact, no essential difference on this topic between the two. Decisions in private management, like decisions in public management, must take as their ethical premises the objectives that have been set for the organization.

There are important differences between public and private management, of course, in the types of organizational objectives that are set up and in the procedures and mechanisms for establishing them. In public administration final responsibility for determining objectives rests with a legislative body; in private management, with the board of directors, and ultimately with the stockholders.[11] In both fields serious problems have arisen as to the means to be used in implementing the responsibility of these control bodies.[12] It is to this problem that we turn next—again directing our attention particularly to the field of public administration. A little translation of terms should suffice to make most of the discussion applicable to the stockholder-management relationship.

POLICY AND ADMINISTRATION

In practice, the separation between the ethical and the factual elements in judgment can usually be carried only a short distance. The values involved in administrative decisions are seldom final values in any psychological or philosophical sense. Most objectives and activities derive their value from the means-ends relationships which connect them with objectives or activities that are valued in themselves. By a process of anticipation, the value inhering in the desired end is transferred to the means. The product of a manufacturing process is valued by its producers for its convertibility into money (which in turn has value only in exchange) and by its pur-

---

[11] In chap. vi arguments will be presented that the true analogue of the legislative body is the customer rather than the stockholder.

[12] The private-management literature on this topic, while for the most part relatively recent, is growing rapidly. See for example Beardsley Ruml, *Tomorrow's Business* (New York: Farrar & Rinehart, 1945) ; Robert A. Brady, *Business as a System of Power* (New York: Columbia University Press, 1943); or Robert Aaron Gordon, *Business Leadership in the Large Corporation* (Washington: Brookings Institution, 1945).

chasers for the values to be derived from its consumption. Just so, the activities of a fire department, or a school system, are valued ultimately for their contribution to human and social life, and they retain their value only so long as they serve those more final ends.

To the extent that these intermediate values are involved, valuation includes important factual as well as ethical elements. Since the results of administrative activity can be considered as ends only in an intermediate sense, the values that will be attached to these results depend on the empirical connections that are believed to exist between them and the more final goals. To weight properly these intermediate values, it is necessary to understand their objective consequences.

At best it might be hoped that the process of decision could be subdivided into two major segments. The first would involve the development of a system of intermediate values, and an appraisal of their relative weights. The second would consist in a comparison of the possible lines of action in terms of this value system. The first segment would obviously involve both ethical and factual considerations; the second segment could be pretty well restricted to factual problems.

As already pointed out, the reason for making a division of this sort lies in the different criteria of "correctness" that must be applied to the ethical and factual elements in a decision. "Correctness" as applied to imperatives has meaning only in terms of subjective human values. "Correctness" as applied to factual propositions means objective, empirical truth. If two persons give different answers to a factual problem, both cannot be right. Not so with ethical questions.

Vagueness of the "Policy and Administration" Distinction

Recognition of this distinction in the meanings of "correctness" would lend clarity to the distinction that is commonly made in the literature of political science between "policy questions" and "administrative questions." These latter terms were given currency by Goodnow's classical treatise, *Politics and Administration*,[18] pub-

---

[18] Frank J. Goodnow, *Politics and Administration* (New York: Macmillan Company, 1900).

lished in 1900. Yet, neither in Goodnow's study nor in any of the innumerable discussions that have followed it have any clear-cut criteria or marks of identification been suggested that would enable one to recognize a "policy question" on sight, or to distinguish it from an "administrative question." Apparently, it has been assumed that the distinction is self-evident—so self-evident as hardly to require discussion.

In *The New Democracy and the New Despotism,* Charles E. Merriam sets forth as one of the five principal assumptions of democracy "the desirability of popular decision in the last analysis on basic questions of social direction and policy, and of recognized procedures for the expression of such decisions and their validation in policy." [14] As to the exact scope and nature of these "basic questions," he is less explicit:

> It may be asked, Who shall decide what are "basic questions," and who shall determine whether the ways and means of expressing the mass will are appropriate and effective? We cannot go farther back than the "general understandings" of the community, always the judge of the form and functioning of the legal order in which the system is set.[15]

Similarly, Goodnow, in the original statement of the roles of politics and administration in government, fails to draw a careful line between the two. In fact, he comes perilously close to identifying "policy" with "deciding," and "administration" with "doing." For example:

> . . . political functions group themselves naturally under two heads, which are equally applicable to the mental operations and the actions of self-conscious personalities. That is, the action of the state as a political entity consists either in operations necessary to the expression of its will, or in operations necessary to the execution of that will.[16]

And again:

> These two functions of government may for purposes of convenience be designated respectively as Politics and Administration. Politics has

---

[14] Charles E. Merriam, *The New Democracy and the New Despotism* (New York: McGraw-Hill Book Co., 1939), p. 11.
[15] *Ibid.,* p. 39.   [16] Goodnow, *op. cit.,* p. 9.

to do with policies or expressions of the state will. Administration has to do with the execution of these policies.[17]

At a later point in his discussion, however, Goodnow retreats from this extreme position, and recognizes that certain decisional elements are included in the administrative function:

The fact is, then, that there is a large part of administration which is unconnected with politics, which should therefore be relieved very largely, if not altogether, from the control of political bodies. It is unconnected with politics because it embraces fields of semi-scientific, *quasi*-judicial and *quasi*-business or commercial activity—work which has little if any influence on the expression of the true state will.[18]

Without embracing Goodnow's conclusion regarding the desirability of removing some portions of administration from political control, we may recognize in this third statement an attempt on his part to segregate a class of decisions which do not require external control because they possess an internal criterion of correctness. The epistemological position of the present volume leads us to identify this internal criterion with the criterion of factual correctness, and the group of decisions possessing this criterion with those that are factual in nature.

In discussions of administrative discretion from the point of view of administrative law there has sometimes been a tendency to deny that there exists any class of factual questions which possess a unique epistemological status. Neither Freund nor Dickinson is able to find a justification for administrative discretion except as an application of decisions to concrete instances, or as a transitory phenomenon confined to a sphere of uncertainty within which the rule of law has not yet penetrated.[19]

To be sure, the two men offer different suggestions for the gradual elimination of this area of uncertainty. Freund relies upon the legislature to restrict discretion by the exercise of its function of policy determination.[20] Dickinson thinks that administrative discretion can gradually be replaced by general rules to be formu-

---

[17] *Ibid.*, p. 18. [18] *Ibid.*, p. 85.
[19] Ernst Freund, *Administrative Powers over Persons and Property* (Chicago: University of Chicago Press, 1928), pp. 97–103; John Dickinson, *Administrative Justice and the Supremacy of Law in the United States* (Cambridge: Harvard University Press, 1927), *passim*.
[20] Freund, *op. cit.*, pp. 98–99.

lated by the courts, as principles gradually emerge to view from a given set of problems.[21] Neither is willing to admit any fundamental difference between the factual and normative elements involved in law-finding, or to see in that difference a justification for discretionary action.

The courts have come somewhat closer to a recognition of this distinction, though their separation of "questions of fact" from "questions of law" places in the latter category a great many factual issues—especially when "jurisdictional facts" and "constitutional facts" become "questions of law." [22] This is not the place, however, to discuss the whole problem of judicial review. These brief comments serve merely to illustrate the lack of any general agreement as to the fundamental difference between factual and value questions in the field of administrative law.

Opposed to the view that discretion is inherently undesirable, is the equally extreme view that *all* administrative decisions can safely be guided by the internal criteria of correctness, and that legislative control can be supplanted by the control which is exercised by the fellowship of science.[23] Our own analysis exposes the fallacy of an argument that declares decisions to be all factual as clearly as it refutes an argument that declares them to be all ethical.

The position to which the methodological assumptions of the present study lead us is this: The process of validating a factual proposition is quite distinct from the process of validating a value judgment. The former is validated by its agreement with the facts, the latter by human fiat.

Legislator and Administrator

Democratic institutions find their principal justification as a procedure for the validation of value judgments. There is no "scien-

---

[21] Dickinson, *op. cit.*, pp. 105–156.
[22] Freund, *op. cit.*, pp. 289–299; Dickinson, *op. cit.*, pp. 307–313.
[23] C. J. Friedrich stresses the value of the "fellowship of science" in enforcing responsibility. He does not propose, however, to dispense with the device of legislative control. See "Public Policy and the Nature of Administrative Responsibility," in *Public Policy, 1940* (Cambridge: Harvard University Press, 1940), pp. 3–24. Cf. John M. Gaus, "The Responsibility of Public Administration," in *The Frontiers of Public Administration*, ed. Gaus, White, and Dimock (Chicago: University of Chicago Press, 1936), pp. 26–44.

tific" or "expert" way of making such judgments, hence expertise of whatever kind is no qualification for the performance of this function. If the factual elements in decision could be strictly sepa-rated, in practice, from the ethical, the proper roles of representa-tive and expert in a democratic decision-making process would be simple. For two reasons this is not possible. First, as has already been noted, most value judgments are made in terms of intermediate values, which themselves involve factual questions. Second, if factual decisions are entrusted to the experts, sanctions must be available to guarantee that the experts will conform, in good faith, to the value judgments that have been democratically formulated.

Critics of existing procedures for enforcing responsibility point to the high degree of ineffectiveness of these procedures in prac-tice.[24] But there is no reason to conclude that the procedures are inherently valueless. First, for the reasons already explained, self-responsibility of the administrator is no answer to the problem. Second, the fact that pressure of legislative work forbids the re-view of more than a few administrative decisions does not destroy the usefulness of sanctions that permit the legislative body to hold the administrator answerable for *any* of his decisions. The antici-pation of possible legislative investigation and review will have a powerful controlling effect on the administrator, even if this poten-tial review can be actualized only in a few cases. The *function* of deciding may be distributed very differently in the body politic from the *final authority* for resolving disputed decisions.

It would not be possible to lay down any final principles with re-gard to a subject so controversial, and so imperfectly explored.[25] Nevertheless, if the distinction of factual from ethical questions is a valid one, these conclusions would seem to follow:

1. Responsibility to democratic institutions for value determina-tion can be strengthened by the invention of procedural devices permitting a more effective separation of the factual and ethical ele-

---

[24] Cf. Friedrich, *op. cit.,* pp. 3–8. It should be pointed out again that Friedrich does not propose to dispense with democratic control, but to supplement it with other sanctions.

[25] I. G. Gibbon treats of this question in "The Official and His Authority," *Public Administration,* 4:81–94 (Apr., 1926), arriving at conclusions substantially in agreement with those set forth here.

ments in decisions. Some suggestions will be offered along these lines in later chapters.

2. The allocation of a question to legislature or administrator for decision should depend on the relative importance of the factual and ethical issues involved, and the degree to which the former are controversial. A proper allocation will become increasingly possible, without overburdening the legislature, to the extent that Point 1 above is successfully carried out.

3. Since the legislative body must of necessity make many factual judgments, it must have ready access to information and advice. However, this must take the form not merely of recommendations for action, but of factual information on the objective consequences of the alternatives that are before the legislative body.

4. Since the administrative agency must of necessity make many value judgments, it must be responsive to community values, far beyond those that are explicitly enacted into law. Likewise, though the function of making value judgments may often be delegated to the administrator, especially where controversial issues are not involved, his complete answerability, in case of disagreement, must be retained.

If it is desired to retain the terms "policy" and "administration," they can best be applied to a division of the decisional functions that follows these suggested lines. While not identical with the separation of "value" from "fact," such a division would clearly be dependent upon that fundamental distinction.

It would be naïve to suggest that the division of work between legislature and administrator in any actual public agency will ever follow very closely the lines just suggested. In the first place the legislative body will often wish, for political reasons, to avoid making clear-cut policy decisions, and to pass these on to an administrative agency.[26] In the second place the administrator may be very different from the neutral, compliant individual pictured here. He may (and usually will) have his own very definite set of personal values that he would like to see implemented by his administrative organization, and he may resist attempts by the legislature to as-

[26] This point is ably discussed by Leys, *op. cit.*, pp. 20–22.

sume completely the function of policy determination, or he may sabotage their decisions by his manner of executing them.

Nevertheless, it would probably be fair to say that the attainment of democratic responsibility in modern government will require an approximation to those lines of demarcation between legislature and administrator that were outlined above.

A Note on Terminology

Before concluding this chapter, it should be pointed out that the term "policy" is often used in a much broader and looser sense than the meaning given here. In private management literature, particularly, "policy" often means either (a) any general rule that has been laid down in an organization to limit the discretion of subordinates (e.g. it is "policy" in B department to file a carbon of all letters by subject), or (b) at least the more important of these rules, promulgated by top management (e.g. an employee is allowed two weeks' sick leave per year). In neither of these usages is it implied that policy has any ethical content. Serious ambiguity would be avoided if different terms were used for these three concepts— the one discussed in preceding paragraphs, and the two listed just above. Perhaps the ethical premises of management could be called "legislative policy"; the broad non-ethical rules laid down by top management, "management policy"; and other rules, "working policy."

In addition to these several kinds of policy, or authoritatively promulgated rules, there are to be found in almost every organization a large number of "practices" which have not been established as orders or regulations, and which are not enforced by sanctions, but which are nevertheless observed in the organization by force of custom or for other reasons. Often, the line between policy and practice is not sharp unless the organization follows the "practice" (or "policy") of putting all its policies in writing.

CONCLUSION

This chapter has been devoted to an explanation of the distinction between the value elements and the factual elements in decision-making. It has been shown, furthermore, that this distinction is the basis for the line that is commonly drawn between questions of policy and questions of administration.

In the next chapter, the anatomy of decision will be further examined, with special reference to the concept of "rationality" in decision-making. The emphasis will remain upon the logical rather than the psychological aspects of decision.

Chapter IV

RATIONALITY IN ADMINISTRATIVE BEHAVIOR

IN CHAPTER III it was concluded that the correctness of an administrative decision is a relative matter—it is correct if it selects appropriate means to reach designated ends. The rational administrator is concerned with the selection of these effective means. For the construction of an administrative theory it is necessary to examine further the notion of rationality and, in particular, to achieve perfect clarity as to what is meant by "the selection of effective means." The process of clarifying this idea will throw considerable light, in turn, upon the concepts of "efficiency" and "coordination" —both of central importance to administrative theory.

Little will be said in this chapter about what goes on in the mind of a person making decisions—treatment of the subject from a psychological standpoint will be reserved for Chapter V. The present chapter will be concerned with the objective environment of decision—with the actual consequences that follow on choice. Choice, in so far as it is rational and cognizant of its objective conditions, involves a selection of one alternative from among several. The alternatives differ with respect to the consequences that flow from them, and an analysis of decision-making in its objective aspects will refer primarily to these variable consequences of choice.

Although this emphasis upon consequences will give the present chapter a definitely "rationalistic" bias, concentration on the rational aspects of human behavior should not be construed as an assertion that human beings are always or generally rational. That misconception, which permeated utilitarian political theory and a large part of classical economic theory, has been decisively refuted by modern developments in psychology and sociology.[1]

Since "good" administration is behavior that is realistically adapted to its ends, just as "good" business is economic behavior accurately calculated to realize gain, a theory of administrative decisions will of necessity be somewhat preoccupied with the rational aspects of choice. Later chapters of this study will pay more attention to the actualities of administrative behavior. The present chapter bears the same relation to these realistic analyses that a discussion of business principles and theories bears to a description of economic institutions and actual market behaviors; that is, it is not a description of how administrators decide so much as a description of how *good* administrators decide.[2]

MEANS AND ENDS

Fact and value, as already noted in Chapter III, are related to means and ends. In the process of decision those alternatives are chosen which are considered to be appropriate means for reaching desired ends. Ends themselves, however, are often merely instrumental to more final objectives. We are thus led to the conception of a series, or hierarchy, of ends. Rationality has to do with the construction of means-ends chains of this kind.[3]

[1] The naïve utilitarian view is nowhere more strikingly set forth than by Jeremy Bentham, *op. cit.*, pp. 1–7, *passim*. On the other hand, rationalism is implicit rather than explicit in Adam Smith. See *An Inquiry into the Nature and Causes of the Wealth of Nations* (New York: E. P. Dutton & Co., 1914), pp. 12–15. The criticism of rationalism has perhaps been most strongly urged by the Freudians, but is a matter of general acceptance among almost all modern schools of sociology and psychology. See, for example, Harold D. Lasswell, *Psychopathology and Politics* (Chicago: University of Chicago Press, 1930), pp. 28–37; Sigmund Freud, "The Unconscious," *Collected Papers* (London: L. and V. Woolf, 1925), 4:98–136; Vilfredo Pareto, *The Mind and Society* (New York: Harcourt, Brace & Co., 1935), *passim*.

[2] The Appendix discusses at greater length the distinction between a practical science of administration (the study of what administrators "ought") and a sociology of administration (the study of what administrators "do").

[3] Talcott Parsons analyzes social action systems with the help of these same terms in *The Structure of Social Action* (New York: McGraw-Hill Book Co., 1937), pp. 44, 49, 228–241.

The Hierarchy of Ends

Even at the physiological level means-end relationships serve to integrate behavior. At this level muscular tensions are coordinated for (as a means of) the performance of simple physiological acts—walking, reaching and grasping an object, turning the eyes toward an object. In the adult, these simple movements are largely unconscious and automatic; but the child must with great difficulty learn them, and this learning, although not at a reflective level, is not at all unlike the learning of an adult in a means-end situation.

But the taking of a step, the grasping of an object, is usually itself a means to a broader end. The clearest way to determine which ends are sought for their own sake, and which for their usefulness as means to more distant ends, is to place the subject in situations where he must choose between conflicting ends.

The fact that goals may be dependent for their force on other more distant ends leads to the arrangement of these goals in a hierarchy—each level to be considered as an end relative to the levels below it and as a means relative to the levels above it. Through the hierarchical structure of ends, behavior attains integration and consistency, for each member of a set of behavior alternatives is then weighed in terms of a comprehensive scale of values—the "ultimate" ends. In actual behavior, a high degree of conscious integration is seldom attained. Instead of a single branching hierarchy, the structure of conscious motives is usually a tangled web or, more precisely, a disconnected collection of elements only weakly and incompletely tied together; and the integration of these elements becomes progressively weaker as the higher levels of the hierarchy—the more final ends—are reached.

The hierarchy of means and ends is as characteristic of the behavior of organization as it is of individuals. As a matter of fact, the mode of specialization which in Chapter II was called "organization by purpose" is nothing other than the arrangement of the organization structure to parallel the system of means and ends involved in the accomplishment of its purposes. Thus, the fire department has as its purpose the reduction of fire losses; but the means to the attainment of this end are the prevention of fires and the extinguishment of fires. These two principal means are often represented in the organization structure by a fire prevention bureau and the fire fighting forces, respectively. Since the latter must, in order to accomplish their purpose, be dispersed over the city, we find at the next level organization units specialized by area.

It is also as true of organizational as of individual behavior that the means-end hierarchy is seldom an integrated, completely connected chain. Often the connections between organization activities and ultimate objectives is obscure, or these ultimate objectives are incompletely formulated, or there are internal conflicts and contradictions among the ultimate objectives, or among the means selected to attain them. Thus, decision-making in the Work Projects Administration was complicated by the competing claims of "pump-priming" and immediate relief to the unemployed as agency objectives. In War Production Board decision-making, it was necessary to balance war needs against civilian requirements.

Sometimes the lack of integration in an organization's means-end hierarchy is due to refusal of the policy-making body to decide a "hot" issue of policy—Congress' refusal, for example, to determine for Selective Service the relative weight to be given to family status and occupation in deferments from military service. Sometimes the means-end connections themselves are obscure. For example, to say that it is the objective of an army to defeat the enemy leaves a great deal of room for dispute and inconsistency as to the proper strategies for achieving this end. (The controversy in this country between the "Germany first" and "Japan first" factions comes to mind in this connection.)

Both organizations and individuals, then, fail to attain a complete integration of their behavior through consideration of these means-end relationships. Nevertheless, what remains of rationality in their behavior is precisely the incomplete, and sometimes inconsistent, hierarchy that has just been described.

Limitations of the Means-End Schema

This analysis of rational behavior in terms of a means-end hierarchy may lead to inaccurate conclusions unless certain cautions are observed.

First, the ends to be attained by the choice of a particular behavior alternative are often incompletely or incorrectly stated through failure to consider the alternative ends that could be reached by selection of another behavior. It is not enough, in selecting a cantilever design for a bridge across a particular river, to know that this design will serve the purpose of bridging the river. The wisdom of the choice depends on whether the cantilever design will bridge the river more effectively and more economically than a suspension bridge, or a viaduct, or some other design. Rational decision-making always requires the comparison of alternative means in terms of the respective ends to which they will lead. As will be seen in Chapter VIII, below, this means that "efficiency"— the attainment of maximum values with limited means—must be a guiding criterion in administrative decision.

Second, in actual situations a complete separation of means from ends is usually impossible, for the alternative means are not usually valuationally neutral. It is from this difficulty that so many futile arguments arise as to whether "the ends justify the means." In the case of the Prohibition Amendment, for example, the means employed involved so many value questions—questions of personal liberty, proper police methods, etc.-—that these soon overshadowed in importance the "ultimate" objective of temperance. Hence it was fallacious to talk of prohibition as merely a means to the highly desirable end of temperance. The particular means used to attain this particular end had many consequences other than the specific end being sought, and these other unsought ends had to be given their proper weight in considering the desirability of the means.

Third, the means-end terminology tends to obscure the role of the time element in decision-making. If an end is some condition or state to be realized, then only one state may be realized at one time but many states over a period of time, and choice is influenced not only by particular ends but also by expectations of what ends may be realized at different times. Choice imposes two problems: (1) If a particular end is to be realized at a given time, what alternative ends must be relinquished for that time? (2) If a particular end is to be realized at a given time, how does this limit the ends that may be realized at other times? When Louis XV said, "Après nous le déluge," he was expressing the factual judgment that achievement of his particular short-run ends entailed some unfortunate long-run consequences; and he was also expressing a value-judgment—one of indifference for long-term consequences. Economists would say that he discounted time heavily.

The time element enters into decision-making in still another way. Some decisions are irrevocable in the sense that they create a new situation which, in turn, influences the decisions that follow them. In economic situations this is illustrated by the existence of fixed costs. If a manufacturer is deciding whether he will build a factory to make shoes, his problem is to determine whether the revenue he will get by selling the shoes will reimburse him for his expenditure. But, if he already *has* a shoe factory, the cost of this factory is a "sunk" cost that cannot be recovered; and he will continue to make shoes, even at an over-all loss, provided his revenues cover any new and additional costs that he must incur to make them. The decision to build the factory, therefore, influences his subsequent decisions. It is the existence of these long-term, irrevocable decisions that more than anything else accounts for the relative consistency of both personal and organizational behavior over periods of time. It also accounts for a certain "inertia" in the adjustment to new situations.

These objections do not mean that the language of ends and means is unusable; they simply mean that it must be employed with considerable care and sophistication. Under some circumstances another terminology may be clearer, and it is the purpose of the next section of this chapter to suggest such a terminology.

ALTERNATIVES AND CONSEQUENCES

The objections that have been raised to the means-end schema are (a) that it obscures the comparative element in decision-making, (b) that it does not achieve a successful separation of the factual elements in decision from the value elements, and (c) that it gives insufficient recognition to the time variable in purposive behavior. A theory of decisions in terms of alternative behavior possibilities and their consequences meets all these objections.

Behavior Alternatives[4]

At each moment the behaving subject, or the organization composed of numbers of such individuals, is confronted with a large number of alternative behaviors, some of which are present in consciousness and some of which are not. Decision, or choice, as the term is used here, is the process by which one of these alternatives for each moment's behavior is selected to be carried out. The series of such decisions which determines behavior over some stretch of time may be called a *strategy*.

If any one of the possible strategies is chosen and followed out, certain consequences will result. The task of rational decision is to select that one of the strategies which is followed by the preferred set of consequences. It should be emphasized that *all* the consequences that follow from the chosen strategy are relevant to the evaluation of its correctness, not simply those consequences that were anticipated.

The task of decision involves three steps: (1) the listing of all the alternative strategies; (2) the determination of all the consequences that follow upon each of these strategies; (3) the comparative evaluation of these sets of consequences. The word "all" is used advisedly. It is obviously impossible for the individual to know *all* his alternatives or *all* their consequences, and this impossibility is a very important departure of actual behavior from the model of objective rationality. As such, it will receive extended consideration in Chapter V.

Time and Behavior

There is nothing which prevents the subject, or the organization, having chosen one strategy on Monday, from selecting a different one on Tuesday. But the Monday decision, in so far as it has been partly acted out before its reconsideration, has already

[4] The theory presented here was worked out by the author in 1941. Its present reformulation has been greatly influenced by the remarkable work of John von Neumann and Oskar Morgenstern, *The Theory of Games and Economic Behavior* (Princeton: Princeton University Press, 1944), chap. 2. It is fair to point out that von Neumann first published that portion of his theory which is germane to the present discussion in 1928, "Zur Theorie der Gesellschaftsspiele," *Math. Annalen* 100:295-320 (1928).

narrowed down the strategies available on Tuesday. This has been pointed out above in the illustration of the shoe factory. Hence, the individual or organization can be committed to a particular line of action from the fact that, having once initiated it, it appears preferable to continue with it rather than to relinquish completely the portion which has already been carried out.

This time-binding character of strategies deserves the greatest emphasis, for it makes possible at least a modicum of rationality in behavior, where, without it, this would be inconceivable. For example, an individual who has spent seven years of his life preparing to be a physician and ten more practicing that profession does not ordinarily have to spend any more time deciding whether he should be a physician or not. Alternative occupations are practically closed to him by virtue of the investment he has already made in the strategy pursued thus far.

Similarly, an organization that is manufacturing shoes does not need to reconsider every day (although it may need to reconsider at intervals) whether it should be in the automobile business instead. This narrows appreciably the alternatives that must be considered by the individual at each moment, and is certainly a necessary, though not a sufficient, condition of rationality.

Knowledge and Behavior

The function of knowledge in the decision-making process is to determine which consequences follow upon which of the alternative strategies. It is the task of knowledge to select from the whole class of possible consequences a more limited subclass, or even (ideally) a single set of consequences correlated with each strategy. The behaving subject cannot, of course, know directly the consequences that will follow upon his behavior. If he could, a sort of reverse causality would be operating here—future consequences would be determinants of present behavior. What he does is to form *expectations* of future consequences, these expectations being based upon known empirical relationships, and upon information about the existing situation.

This may be illustrated in the case of a typical administrative decision process—the selection of personnel. Data are gathered about each of the candidates for a position, from examinations, service ratings, and other sources. These data are used as a basis for comparative prediction to determine which of the candidates will perform most satisfactorily on the job. If the predictions are accurate, then a correct decision can be made.

It has already been remarked that the subject, in order to perform with perfect rationality in this scheme, would have to have a complete description of the consequences following from each alternative strategy and would have to compare these consequences. He would have to know in every single respect how the world would be changed by his behaving one way instead of another, and he would have to follow the consequences of behavior through unlimited stretches of time, unlimited reaches of space, and unlimited sets of values. Under such conditions even an approach to rationality in real behavior would be inconceivable. Fortunately, the problem of choice is usually greatly simplified by the tendency of the empirical laws that describe the regularities of nature to arrange themselves in relatively isolated subsets. Two behavior alternatives, when compared, are often found to have consequences that differ in only a few respects and for the rest are identical. That is, the differential consequences of one behavior as against an alternative behavior may occur only within a brief span of time and within a limited area of description. If it were too often true that for want of a nail the kingdom was lost, the consequence chains encountered in practical life would be of such complexity that rational behavior would become virtually impossible.

In one respect the decision problem in private organizations is much simpler than in public agencies. The private organization is expected to take into consideration only those consequences of the decision which affect *it,* while the public agency must weigh the decision in terms of some comprehensive system of public or community values. For example, when the president of a private corporation decides to give his son a position in the firm, he has to take into consideration the effect the appointment will have upon the efficiency of the enterprise; but a man in the same relative position in the public service has to be concerned equally about the effect of this step upon "equality of opportunity in the public service." This distinction between private and public management is hardly one of black and white, for an increasing number of private businesses are becoming "affected with a public interest," and an increasing number of private executives are concerning themselves with their responsibilities of trusteeship toward the community, even beyond the limits that the law imposes on them.

The fact that consequences usually form "isolated" systems provides both scientist and practitioner with a powerful aid to rationality, for the scientist can isolate these closed systems in his experimental laboratory, and study their behavior, while the practitioner may use the laws discovered by the scientist to vary certain environmental conditions without significantly disturbing the remainder of the situation.

There still remain two important distinctions between a problem of scientific discovery and a problem of decision. First of all, it is a valid scientific problem to deduce the empirical laws that would hold under certain simplified hypothetical conditions, even though these conditions do not prevail in practice—the theoretical scientist can talk about "rigid bodies," "perfect vacuums," "frictionless fluids," etc. But the practitioner must allow for the effects of elasticity, air pressure, or friction, if they are present and substantial, no matter how much this complicates his problem of selecting the correct alternative. Second, the scientist can choose to study only those consequences of the system that he wishes to be concerned with, and ignore the others. It is a valid scientific problem to ask: "What effect upon the total weight of this airplane will specified changes in design have?" The problem of practical decision, however, is to balance a possible weight-saving against an increase in cost, or a loss of maneuverability, or other qualities. The practitioner can never choose to disregard conditioning facts or consequences simply because they fall outside the scope of his theory.

Group Behavior

Further complications are introduced into the picture if more than one individual is involved, for in this case the decisions of the other individuals will be included among the conditions which each individual must consider in reaching his decisions. That is, each individual, in order to determine uniquely the consequences of his actions, must know what will be the actions of the others. This is a factor of fundamental importance for the whole process of administrative decision-making.

There is really a serious circularity involved here. Before A can rationally choose his strategy, he must know which strategy B has chosen; and before B can choose his strategy, he must know A's. This may be illustrated by the game of matching pennies. There are two participants. The first, out of the sight of his opponent, places a coin with either head or tail uppermost upon a table, and covers it with his hand; the second tries to guess whether head or tail is up. The first participant must decide which choice he thinks the second will make, and then must place the coin in the opposite fashion; the second participant must decide which estimate the first has made of the situation. Both of them cannot be right for, if the first estimates correctly the second's choice, then the second will have incorrectly estimated the choice of the first, and vice versa. The resulting behavior system will be of a highly indeterminate nature, for the instability of each of the behavior choices leads to the instability of the other.

While the illustration may appear trivial, a little reflection will convince the reader that this game is a model for any purely competitive activity involving two participants—military strategy being perhaps the most important practical example.[5]

At the opposite extreme from a purely competitive situation is one where two or more participants share a common goal, and where each has sufficient information as to what the others are going to do to enable him to make correct decisions. This is precisely what is meant by "teamwork." The purpose of signals in football, or bidding in bridge, is to enable each player in a team to form accurate expectations as to what his teammates are going to do, so that he can determine the proper means for cooperating with them to reach the common aim. A major purpose of the planning and organizing that precedes any administrative activity is not

[5] Cf. Col. J. F. C. Fuller, *The Foundations of the Science of War* (London: Hutchinson & Co., 1925), p. 183.

merely to put each participant in the job he can best fill, but to permit each to form accurate expectations as to what the others are going to do. Perhaps it would clarify discussion of administrative theory to use the term "cooperation" for activity in which the participants share a common goal, and "coordination" for the process of informing each as to the planned behaviors of the others. Hence, cooperation will usually be ineffective—will not reach its goal, whatever the intentions of the participants—in the absence of coordination.

If the activity is competitive, then, it may exhibit a certain instability, for each individual will readjust his behavior if he "finds out" the intentions of his opponent, or even as a defensive tactic to prevent the opponent from finding out his own. But this same instability may result even if the activity is cooperative, provided the participants are insufficiently informed. In an organization, for example, where responsibilities have not been allocated with sufficient definiteness, two executives may write conflicting letters to the same person on the same matter, while in another case a letter may remain unwritten because each expects the other to do it.

To state the matter formally, in a cooperative pattern both participants prefer the same set of consequences; hence, if each anticipates the other correctly, they will both act so as to secure these consequences. In a competitive pattern, the optimum outcome for the first participant is not the optimum for the second. Hence the realization by the first participant of the consequence he prefers will frustrate the other participant—e.g., the rule of the market is to buy cheap and sell dear, but if the buyer buys cheap the seller will not have sold dear. Even a cooperative pattern may be unstable if each participant is unable to predict what the other is going to do. In these cases, coordination of the behaviors of the two participants is necessary in order that they may realize the possibility that they both prefer. Here conflict of aims is not in question, but imperfect knowledge.

Administrative organizations are systems of cooperative behavior.[6] The members of the organization are expected to orient

[6] Why and to what extent the participants in such organizations share a common goal will be discussed in chap. vi.

their behavior with respect to certain goals that are taken as "organization objectives." This leaves the problem of coordinating their behavior—of providing each one with knowledge of the behaviors of the others upon which he can base his own decisions. In cooperative systems, even though all participants are agreed on the objectives to be attained, they cannot ordinarily be left to themselves in selecting the strategies that will lead to these objectives; for the selection of a correct strategy involves a knowledge of each as to the strategies selected by the others.[7]

VALUE AND POSSIBILITY

There remains for discussion the third element in decision-making; namely, the process of determining preferences among consequences. This process may be termed *valuation*. To each strategy corresponds a unique set of consequences. Rational behavior involves a listing of the consequences in their order of preference, and the choice of that strategy which corresponds to the alternative highest on the list.

The System of Values—Utility Surfaces

Since the values that are present in the various alternatives are both numerous and diverse, the individual in exercising his preference must weigh them and choose among them. The economists have developed a conceptual scheme for describing this process which is very similar indeed to the scheme used here.

The individual's choices among competing values may be described by a set of indifference curves. These curves indicate which sets of possible consequences are equivalent to each other or mutually "indifferent" to choice. To illustrate with the economist's favorite goods—nuts and apples—the indifference curves tell whether a combination of ten nuts and five apples is preferred by an individual to a combination of five nuts and seven

---

[7] This is the fundamental criticism that the theory of anarchism has always failed to meet. That theory appears to posit that, given common goals, participants in a social scheme will automatically select for themselves their own most effective roles.

apples, or whether the first combination is less desirable, or whether the individual is indifferent as between the two.

Empirical limitations upon choice are introduced into the economist's scheme by the individual's stock of goods, and by the price structure. It is assumed that the individual starts with a specified number of nuts and apples, that he may exchange one for the other at a specified rate of exchange, and that he then attempts to select that amount of exchange for which his preference is greatest.[8]

Relation of Value, Experience, Behavior

The significance of the "means-end" relationship now becomes clearer. It is clear that the "means-end" distinction does not correspond to the distinction between fact and value. What then is the connection between the two sets of terms? Simply this: A means-end chain is a series of anticipations that connect a value with the situations realizing it, and these situations, in turn, with the behaviors that produce them. Any element in this chain may be either "means" or "end" depending on whether its connection with the value end of the chain, or its connection with the behavior end of the chain, is in question.

The means-character of an element in a means-end chain will predominate if the element is toward the behavior end of the chain; the end-character will predominate if the element is descriptive of the consequences of behavior. If this be so, terms that are descriptive of the consequences of a behavior may be taken as indicia of the values adhering to that behavior. While the economist talks of economic goods as the values that are the goals of economic activity, in actuality, of course, the economic goods are merely indicia of the existence of a state of affairs from which value can be obtained—the possibility of consuming the goods.[9]

[8] Henry Schultz, *The Theory and Measurement of Demand* (Chicago: University of Chicago Press, 1938), pp. 12–35.
[9] Frank Knight considers a major weakness of classical economics to be its failure to recognize economic gain as a purely intermediate link in a means-end chain, leading to "prestige" and "comfort"; and likewise its failure to recognize as an end valued for its own sake the very economic activity which leads to gain. See his *Risk, Uncertainty, and Profit* (Boston: Houghton Mifflin Company, 1921), pp. xii–xx.

The psychological act of evaluating alternatives usually consists in measuring these alternatives in terms of certain value-indices that have been found in fact to be generally associated with the realization of the values themselves—money, for example, may come to stand as an index of the values that money can purchase. These value-indices involve an important factual element, for they presuppose that an alternative characterized by a high value-index will possess a correspondingly high value. For example, if a federal loan agency spends only a small percentage of its funds in the administration of its loans, this may be an index of efficiency, for, *all other things being equal,* low administrative expenses are to be desired. But of course in this case the ratio of administrative to total expenses would *not* be a good value-index, because in the absence of definite evidence that the quality of investigation is not changed, it is highly unsafe to assume that all other factors remain the same when administrative costs are reduced.

If the means-end relationship is defined in this way, it does not permit a sharp separation of value from fact, for the same behavior may have as consequence more than one value—it may be a member of more than one means-end chain. A relief policy, for example, in which family budgets are set at a very low level in order to provide clients with an incentive to seek and accept private employment, may also have as its consequences a high incidence of malnutrition and disease among the families of relief clients. An acceptable policy cannot be determined merely by considering one of these means-end chains and ignoring the other.

DEFINITIONS OF RATIONALITY

A principal aim of this chapter has been to build the foundations upon which a clear understanding of the concept of "rationality" could be erected. Clarity does not necessarily imply simplicity, however. Roughly speaking, rationality is concerned with the selection of preferred behavior alternatives in terms of some system of values whereby the consequences of behavior can be evaluated. Does this mean that the process of adaptation must be conscious, or are unconscious processes included as well? It has been shown that many of the steps in mathematical invention—than which there can presumably be nothing more rational—are subconscious; and this is certainly true of the simpler processes of equation-solving.[10] Moreover, if consciousness is not stipulated as an element of rationality, are only deliberate processes of adaptation admitted, or non-deliberate ones as well? The typist trains herself to strike a particular key in response to the stimulus of a particular letter. Once learned, the act is unconscious, but deliberate. On the other hand, any person instinctively withdraws a finger that has been burned. This is "rational" in the sense that it serves a useful purpose, but is certainly neither a conscious nor a deliberate adaptation.

Shall we, moreover, call a behavior "rational" when it is in error, but only because the information on which it is based is faulty? When a subjective test is applied, it is rational for an individual to take medicine for a disease if he believes the medicine will cure the disease. When an objective test is applied, the behavior is rational only if the medicine is in fact efficacious.

Finally, in terms of what objectives, whose values, shall rationality be judged? Is behavior of an individual in an organization rational when it serves his personal objectives, or when it serves the organizational objectives? Two soldiers sit in a trench opposite a machine-gun nest. One of them stays under cover. The other, at the cost of his life, destroys the machine-gun nest with a grenade. Which is rational?

Perhaps the only way to avoid, or clarify, these complexities is to use the term "rational" in conjunction with appropriate adverbs. Then a decision may be called "objectively" rational if *in fact* it is the correct behavior for maximizing given values in a given situation. It is "subjectively" rational if it maximizes attainment relative to the actual knowledge of the subject. It is "consciously" rational to the degree that the adjustment of means to ends is a conscious process. It is "deliberately" rational to the degree that the adjustment of means to ends has been deliberately brought about (by the individual or by the organization). A decision is "organi-

[10] See Jacques Hadamard, *Essay on the Psychology of Invention in the Mathematical Field* (Princeton: Princeton University Press, 1945).

zationally" rational if it is oriented to the organization's goals; it is "personally" rational if it is oriented to the individual's goals. In the ensuing discussion, the term "rational" will always be qualified by one of these adverbs unless the meaning is clear from the context.

CONCLUSION

The object of this chapter has been to explore the anatomy of decision with a view to establishing a terminology and a framework of analysis that permit a realistic investigation of administrative decision. To this end, the objective environment surrounding choice was examined. This environment was described as a set of alternative behaviors, each leading to definite anticipated consequences.

Knowledge is the means of discovering which of all the possible consequences of a behavior will actually follow it. The ultimate aim of knowledge, in so far as it is part of the process of choice, is to discover a single unique possibility which is consequent on each behavior alternative, although in practice this aim is of course only imperfectly attained.

Knowledge about the consequences of behavior was thus identified as a primary influence on choice. The second influence was found to lie in the preferences of the behaving individual for one set of consequences as compared with another. The problem of choice is one of describing consequences, evaluating them, and connecting them with behavior alternatives.

It was found that means and ends do not completely correspond to facts and values, respectively, but that there is some connection between the two sets of terms. A means-end chain was defined as a series of causally related elements ranging from behaviors to the values consequent on them. Intermediate ends in such a chain serve as value-indices; and, using them, we can evaluate alternatives without a complete exploration of the final ends, or values, inhering in them.

The notion of alternatives casts considerable light on the patterns of interpersonal behavior. The relationship of the values of interacting individuals with the consequences of their joint behavior determines whether the behavior pattern will be competitive or cooperative. It was seen that instability in the behavior pattern may result when the pattern is competitive or when each of the participants in the pattern errs in predicting the behavior of the others.

Finally some definitions have been laid down to distinguish various meanings of rationality: objective, subjective, conscious, deliberate, organizational, and personal.

This chapter has barely touched on the psychological aspects of choice. In the next chapter an attempt will be made to contrast the psychological and the logical elements in the choice process. In later chapters of this study the analytic tools developed in this and the next chapter will be used to study some of the concepts that are central to administrative decision: authority, efficiency, identification, influence, and communication.

Chapter V

THE PSYCHOLOGY OF ADMINISTRATIVE
DECISIONS

THE ARGUMENT of the present chapter can be stated very simply. It is impossible for the behavior of a single, isolated individual to reach any high degree of rationality. The number of alternatives he must explore is so great, the information he would need to evaluate them so vast that even an approximation to objective rationality is hard to conceive. Individual choice takes place in an environment of "givens"—premises that are accepted by the subject as bases for his choice; and behavior is adaptive only within the limits set by these "givens."

If the psychological environment of choice, the "givens," were determined in some accidental fashion, then adult behavior would show little more pattern or integration than the behavior of children. A higher degree of integration and rationality can, however, be achieved, because the environment of choice itself can be chosen and deliberately modified. Partly this is an individual matter: the individual places himself in a situation where certain stimuli and certain items of information will impinge on him. To a very important extent, however, it is an organizational matter. One function that organization performs is to place the organization members in a psychological environment that will adapt their decisions to the organization objectives, and will provide them with the information needed to make these decisions correctly.

The material of the chapter will be presented in three parts. In the first part, the reasons will be set forth in detail why individual behavior must perforce fall far short of the standard of rationality.

The second part of the chapter will examine how the psychological environment of choice is, in fact, formed. It will be shown that this environment is the unifying element that fits a whole sequence of momentary choices into a consistent pattern.

In the final part, the role of the organization in establishing the psychological environment of choice will be studied. It will be seen how the organization selects the individual's ends, how it trains him in skills, and how it provides him with information. In the course of this discussion it will begin to appear that organization permits the individual to approach reasonably near to objective rationality.[1]

THE LIMITS OF RATIONALITY

Objective rationality, as that term was defined in the previous chapter, would imply that the behaving subject molds all his behavior into an integrated pattern by (a) viewing the behavior alternatives prior to decision in panoramic fashion, (b) considering the whole complex of consequences that would follow on each choice, and (c) with the system of values as criterion singling out one from the whole set of alternatives.

Real behavior, even that which is ordinarily thought of as "rational" possesses many elements of disconnectedness not present in this idealized picture. If behavior is viewed over a stretch of time, it exhibits a mosaic character. Each piece of the pattern is integrated with others by their orientation to a common purpose; but these purposes shift from time to time with shifts in knowledge and attention, and are held together in only slight measure by any con-

[1] The entire chapter draws heavily upon psychology for its premises. A fundamental difficulty that must be faced by any social scientist who wishes to use the products of psychological research in dealing with his subject is that the psychologists themselves are divided into warring schools. Fortunately, most of the psychological topics that are relevant to the present study are not subjects of controversy among these schools. Because it is one of the few psychological theories that are oriented around the concepts of choice and purpose, Tolman's analysis of *Purposive Behavior in Animals and Men* (New York: D. Appleton-Century Co., 1932), has perhaps contributed more than any other treatise to the terminology and viewpoint of this chapter. For traditional psychological topics such as "habit," "attention," and the like, an analysis sufficient for the purposes of this study may be found in any of the numerous textbooks. As a matter of fact, most of the references here are to William James, *The Principles of Psychology* (New York: Henry Holt & Co., 1925), and to John Dewey, *Human Nature and Conduct* (New York: Modern Library, 1930).

ception of an over-all criterion of choice. It might be said that behavior reveals "segments" of rationality—that behavior shows rational organization within each segment, but the segments themselves have no very strong interconnections.

Actual behavior falls short, in at least three ways, of objective rationality as defined in the last chapter:

(1) Rationality requires a complete knowledge and anticipation of the consequences that will follow on each choice. In fact, knowledge of consequences is always fragmentary.

(2) Since these consequences lie in the future, imagination must supply the lack of experienced feeling in attaching value to them. But values can be only imperfectly anticipated.

(3) Rationality requires a choice among all possible alternative behaviors. In actual behavior, only a very few of all these possible alternatives ever come to mind.

Incompleteness of Knowledge

The first limitation upon rationality in actual behavior has been mentioned in Chapter IV.[2] Rationality implies a complete, and unattainable, knowledge of the exact consequences of each choice. In actuality, the human being never has more than a fragmentary knowledge of the conditions surrounding his action, nor more than a slight insight into the regularities and laws that would permit him to induce future consequences from a knowledge of present circumstances.

For instance, to achieve a completely successful application of resources to a city's fire protection problem, the members of the fire department would need to know in comprehensive detail the probabilities of fire in each portion of the city—in fact, in each structure—and the exact effect upon fire losses of any change in administrative procedure or any redistribution of the fire-fighting forces.

Even to state the problem in this form is to recognize the extent to which complete rationality is limited by lack of knowledge. If each fire were reported to the department at the moment ignition occurred, fire losses would miraculously decline. Lacking such

[2] See pp. 68–70, *supra*.

omniscience, the fire department must devote considerable effort to securing as promptly as possible, through special alarm systems and otherwise, information regarding situations where its action is needed.[3]

This point has been developed in some detail in order to emphasize that it poses an extremely practical problem of administration —to secure an organization of the decision-making process such that relevant knowledge will be brought to bear at the point where the decision is made. The same point might have been illustrated with respect to a business organization—the dependence of its decisions, for example, on the correct prediction of market prices.

The human being striving for rationality and restricted within the limits of his knowledge has developed some working procedures that partially overcome this difficulty. These procedures consist in assuming that he can isolate from the rest of the world a closed system containing only a limited number of variables and a limited range of consequences.

There is a story to the effect that a statistician once found a very high correlation between the number of old maids and the size of the clover crop in different English counties. After puzzling over this relation for some time, he was able to trace what appeared to him to be the causal chain. Old maids, it appeared, kept cats; and cats ate mice. Field mice, however, were natural enemies of bumblebees, and these latter were, in turn, the chief agents in fertilizing the flowers of the clover plants. The implication, of course, is that the British Parliament should never legislate on the subject of marriage bonuses without first evaluating the effect upon the clover crop of reducing the spinster population.

In practical decision-making, devious consequences of this sort must of necessity be ignored.[4] Only those factors that are most closely connected with the decision in cause and time can be taken into consideration. The problem of discovering what factors are, and what are not, important in any given situation is quite as essen-

[3] With respect to similar considerations involved in military tactics, see *United States Army Field Service Regulations, 1923* (Washington: Government Printing Office, 1924), p. 4.
[4] Cf. Dewey, *The Public and Its Problems* (New York: Henry Holt & Co., 1927), pp. 106–107.

tial to correct choice as a knowledge of the empirical laws governing those factors that are finally selected as relevant.

Rational choice will be feasible to the extent that the limited set of factors upon which decision is based corresponds, in nature, to a closed system of variables—that is, to the extent that significant indirect effects are absent. Only in the cases of extremely important decisions is it possible to bring to bear sufficient resources to unravel a very involved chain of effects. For instance, a very large amount spent for research to determine the indirect effects of a governmental fiscal policy upon employment in the economy would, if it achieved its aim, be well spent. On the other hand, a physician treating a patient does not take time to determine what difference the life or death of his patient will make to the community.

Difficulties of Anticipation

It is a commonplace of experience that an anticipated pleasure may be a very different sort of thing from a realized pleasure. The actual experience may be considerably more or less desirable than anticipated.

This does not result merely from failure to anticipate consequences. Even when the consequences of a choice have been rather completely described, the anticipation of them can hardly act with the same force upon the emotions as the experiencing of them. One reason for this is that the mind cannot at a single moment grasp the consequences in their entirety. Instead, attention shifts from one value to another with consequent shifts in preference.

Valuation, therefore, is limited in its accuracy and consistency by the power of the individual to trace the varied value elements in the imagined consequence and to give them the same weight in anticipation as they will have for him in experience.

This is probably an important influence in "risky" behavior. The more vividly the consequences of losing in a risky venture are visualized—either through past experience of such consequences or for other reasons—the less desirable does the risk assumption appear. It is not so much that the experience of loss leads to attaching a higher probability to the occurrence of loss as that the desire to avoid the consequences of loss has been strengthened.

The Scope of Behavior Possibilities

Imagination falls down also in conceiving all the possible patterns of behavior that the individual might undertake. The number of things that a man, restricted only by physical and biological limitations, could do in even so short an interval as a minute is inconceivable. He has two legs, two arms, a head, two eyes, a neck, a trunk, ten fingers, ten toes, and many sets of voluntary muscles governing each. Each of these members is capable of complex movements individually or in coordination.

Of all these possible movements, only a very few come to mind at any moment as possible behavior alternatives. Since each alternative has distinct consequences, it follows that many sets of possible consequences never reach the stage of valuation, since it is not recognized that they are possible consequents of available behavior alternatives.

Relatively speaking, of course, human beings come much closer to exploiting in purposive action their physiological capacities of movement than other animals. The relatively simple "tool behaviors" of which the great apes are capable [5] are very elementary, judged by human standards.

In some fields, considerable ingenuity has been shown in devising methods for exploiting possibilities of behavior. Elaborate devices have been constructed in phonetics for observing and correcting lip and tongue movements. Time-and-motion studies are made to observe, in great detail, hand movements in industrial processes, to improve these movements, and to facilitate them through revision of the process. In the same category could be placed the whole field of tool-invention and skill-training. Both involve a close observation of behavior processes, and a consequent enlargement of the alternatives available for choice.

PURPOSIVE BEHAVIOR IN THE INDIVIDUAL

These remarks concerning the departure of actual behavior from the norm of rationality serve already to indicate some of the char-

[5] See Tolman, *op. cit.*, pp. 219–226, and the literature there cited.

acteristics of the psychological process of choice. It is time now to examine these characteristics more systematically.

Docility

As was pointed out in Chapter IV, the simplest movement—taking a step, focusing the eyes on an object—is purposive in nature, and only gradually develops in the infant from its earliest random undirected movements. In achieving the integration the human being exhibits *docility;* that is, he observes the consequences of his movements and adjusts them to achieve the desired purpose.[6]

Docility is characterized, then, by a stage of exploration and inquiry followed by a stage of adaptation. It can be observed in the behavior of individuals and in the behavior of organizations. A man learning to operate an overhead crane first obtains information from someone skilled in its operation as to how it is controlled and what the functions are of the various instruments and levers. He then supplements his information by experimenting with the crane, gradually learning from practice what reaction he can expect from the equipment when he manipulates it in a particular way. When he has reached this point, he is able to use the crane to accomplish his purposes—to adapt the manipulation to his ends.

Similarly, a new publishing firm must learn, from its own experience or from that of other firms, how many copies of a particular book are likely to be sold, and what kind of advertising is effective in selling it. Having learned what results a particular advertising technique will produce, the organization can intelligently adjust its techniques to the particular objectives it is trying to reach. This last example illustrates also the great part that judgment and estimate play in the adaptive process in most practical situations.

[6] The term "docility" is used here in its proper dictionary sense of "teachability." Since the word has no good synonym, it is unfortunate that in general speech it has taken on the connotations of tractability, submissiveness or pliancy. Tolman, whose treatment is closely followed in this discussion, defines docility as "that character of behavior . . . which consists in the fact that, if a given behavior-act in a given environment proves relatively unsuccessful, i.e., does not get the demanded type of goal-object at all or gets there only by a relatively long distance, it will, on subsequent occasions, tend to give way to an act or acts which will tend to get the organism to this demanded type of goal-object and will tend to get him to it by a relatively short route" (*op. cit.*, pp. 442–443).

Characteristics of Human Docility

Docility is of course, quite as characteristic of the behavior of higher animals as it is of human behavior. There are, however, a number of rather striking differences between animal and human docility. The animal's learning is primarily of a trial-and-error character. That is, learning does not show itself until he has had an opportunity, by actually experiencing them, to observe the consequences of his behaviors. The human being's power to observe regularities in nature of a very general sort, and to communicate with other human beings, helps him to shorten materially this learning process.

In the first place, a previous experience with other choices (of the same sort) may enable him to infer something about the character of the particular choice with which he is faced. Likewise, he may experiment ideationally rather than in actual behavior: he may trace in his mind the consequences of each behavior alternative and select one of them without actually trying any of them out. For example, an engineer may explore in his mind or on paper several plans for a sewer, and may be able to determine quite accurately their respective performance without putting any of them to an actual trial.[7]

In the second place, communication gives the human being a tremendous advantage over the animal in learning. The engineer designing a pavement does not base his attempts entirely upon experimentation, ideational or actual, but uses reference sources, descriptions of the conclusions that other persons have reached on the basis of long experimentation and research in this field—although he may select and modify this accumulated experience on the basis of his own success and failure. Under some circumstances, moreover, learning is dependent entirely on communication, and even the subsequent test of success or failure is not available to the individual. This is true of many professional disciplines. In the field of medicine, for instance, the individual practitioner is seldom able

---

[7] As a matter of fact, the difference between men and animals in this respect is probably one of degree rather than kind. Tolman, for instance, shows that the rat has a considerable capacity for generalization (*ibid.*, pp. 187–190).

to determine from what happens to his small group of patients the efficacy of particular modes of treatment, especially in the case of diseases he meets only infrequently. He must base his treatment on doctrine developed by medical scientists with special facilities for controlled research. The function of research, and especially experimental research, is to adapt behavior to purpose when the consequences of behavior are not easily evaluated outside the controlled conditions of the laboratory.

The possibility of purposive behavior derives, then, from recognition of the consequences that follow on particular behaviors. The human being's advantage is that he does not have to determine these consequences separately for each particular decision with which he is faced. By the use of the experimental method, by communication of knowledge, by theoretical prediction of consequences, a relatively little bit of experience can be made to serve as the basis for a wide range of decisions. As a result a remarkable economy of thought and observation is achieved.

Memory

The role of memory in rational behavior hardly requires comment. When similar problems recur, it is memory that stores up the information gathered, or even the conclusions reached, in solving the first problem, and makes these available, without new inquiry, when the next problem of the same kind is encountered.

It has often been remarked that memory may be either natural or artificial—information may be stored in the mind, or it may be recorded on paper in such a way as to be accessible. The artificial kind of memory that consists of libraries, files, and records is the kind of most importance in organization.

For any kind of memory, whether natural or artificial, to be useful, there must be mechanisms that permit the memory to be drawn upon when needed. The letter that is lost in the files and the figure that has slipped the mind are equally useless items of memory unless they can be located. Hence human rationality relies heavily upon the psychological and artificial associational and indexing devices that make the store of memory accessible when it is needed for the making of decisions.

Habit

An equally important mechanism that assists in the preservation of useful behavior patterns is habit.[8] Habit permits conservation of mental effort by withdrawing from the area of conscious thought those aspects of the situation that are repetitive.

In learning to typewrite, the student tries to pay close attention to each minute movement of his fingers, and to the relation of each mark on the copy to each key on the instrument. Only through a gradual and fumbling adjustment of his movements does he achieve the necessary coordination of eye with hand. When, by practice, a certain point in skill has been reached, it proves no longer necessary to give attention to integrations at this lowest level. The mere desire for the end of the action—the letter to be printed—brings about the act without further will. When this step has been reached, habit or skill takes over the integration which was first achieved by attention and desire to learn.

Habit performs an extremely important task in purposive behavior, for it permits similar stimuli or situations to be met with similar responses or reactions, without the need for a conscious rethinking of the decision to bring about the proper action. Habit permits attention to be devoted to the novel aspects of a situation requiring decision. A large part of the training that goes to make a championship football team, crew, army battalion, or fire company is devoted to developing habitual responses that will permit immediate reactions to rapidly changing situations.[9]

Habit, like memory, has an artificial organization counterpart, which has been termed by Stene "organization routine."[10] In so far as methods of handling recurring questions become matters of organization practice, perhaps embodied in manuals of practice and procedure, they cease to be objects of reconsideration when these questions arise. The close relation between habit and memory is evi-

[8] Dewey (*Human Nature and Conduct*, pp. 14–131, 172–181) early emphasized the important role of habit in social behavior. James, in his *Psychology*, contributed a classic chapter to the psychological literature on habit (chap. iv).

[9] John Dewey, *The Public and Its Problems*, pp. 159–161.

[10] Edwin O. Stene, "An Approach to a Science of Administration," *American Political Science Review*, 34:1129 (Dec., 1940).

dent here as it is in the case of the habits of individual persons. If a formal criterion were needed, it might be said that a matter has become part of the organization routine when it is settled by reference to accepted or approved practices rather than by consideration of the alternatives on their merits.

Habit must not be thought of as a purely passive element in behavior (either individual or organizational), for once a habit has been established the mere presence of the stimulus tends to release the habitual behavior without further conscious thought. Under such circumstances, it may actually require conscious attention to prevent the response from occurring even if changed circumstances have made it inappropriate. The automobile driver who is habituated to the application of his brakes on the approach of danger has difficulty restraining himself from this response when he skids on an icy pavement. This is a point that has far-reaching implications for organization, and must be considered at greater length.

Role of Positive Stimuli

If rationality is to be achieved, a period of hesitation must precede choice, during which the behavior alternatives, knowledge bearing on environmental conditions and consequences, and the anticipated values must be brought into the focus of attention. Psychologically speaking, such a hesitation marks a relatively sophisticated level of behavior. Simpler behavior patterns may be described as those responses to stimuli that occur upon presentation of the stimulus and with little or no hesitation.

The distinction between the stimulus-response pattern of behavior and the hesitation-choice pattern gives a clue to the respective roles of nonrational and rational in the complete behavior pattern. Considering the limitations, just described, in human capacity to meet the demands of rationality, the hesitation preceding choice could conceivably lengthen into inaction. The individual, realizing his inability to take into consideration all the factors relevant to his choice, and despairing of rationality, might vacillate among the available alternatives until the time for action was past. In fact, choice and action usually take place long before attention has been given even to those elements in the situation that are within grasp.

A stimulus, external or internal, directs attention to selected aspects of the situation to the exclusion of competing aspects that might turn choice in another direction. Within the central nervous system are built up channels that permit impulses to be translated into action while leaving large portions of the central system undisturbed.

Conscious attention is not a necessary element in this process. The consciousness that accompanies the "startle pattern" of behavior is not the cause of the response—it merely accompanies, or even succeeds, the response. However, since we are concerned primarily with decision points, and with responses to new situations, we may consider first the role of attention in the selective process—that is, in the channelizing of stimuli.

William James, who was not troubled by behavioristic scruples, described attention as follows:

Every one knows what attention is. It is the taking possession by the mind, in clear and vivid form, of one out of what seem several simultaneously possible objects or trains of thought. Focalization, concentration, of consciousness are of its essence. It implies withdrawal from some things in order to deal effectively with others, and is a condition which has a real opposite in the confused, dazed, scatterbrained state which in French is called *distraction,* and *Zerstreutheit* in German.[11]

Tolman, more cautiously, prefers to avoid the term and speaks instead of "selective responsiveness to stimuli." [12]

Attention, then, refers to the set of elements that enter into consciousness at any given time. It is clear that consciousness is not a necessary precondition to docility, and that even behaviors that are not in the focus of attention are capable of purposive adjustment. Certainly consciousness and attention are not involved in the simpler types of conditioned response—e.g., in the development of motor skills. In most cases, there seems to be a close relation, however, between the spheres of attention and of rationality. That is, docility is largely limited by (1) the span of attention, and (2) the area within which skills and other appropriate behaviors have become habitual. Hence to a considerable extent, the limits upon ra-

[11] *The Principles of Psychology,* 1:403–404.
[12] *Op. cit.,* pp. 35–36.

tionality described above are resultants of the limits of the area of attention.

Now it has already been noted that in so far as a part of behavior is governed by habit, it passes out of the area of conscious attention. For example, in a consideration of behavior alternatives, attention is not usually directed to possible movements of individual muscles. Instead, the behavior alternatives that actually come to attention are habitual integrations of such unitary movements—walking, writing, pronouncing, etc.; only under unusual circumstances is there a conscious attempt to analyze these integrations. Once the stimulus is received for the initiation of such movements, they go to completion without further consideration.

The same responsiveness in habitual manner to stimuli occurs at even higher levels of integration. A typist who receives some printed matter for copying converts it into typewritten form almost without the necessity of a single conscious or original decision. To the man on an assembly line, the presence on the belt in front of him of a partially finished product is the only stimulus necessary to initiate the whole series of skilled movements that represent his contribution to the manufacture of the product. The individual sitting down at the dinner table finds in the food before him the sufficient stimulus for the complex process of eating and can carry on this process without conscious attention—meanwhile devoting his attention to conversation.

It appears, then, that in actual behavior, as distinguished from objectively rational behavior, decision is initiated by stimuli which channel attention in definite directions, and that the response to the stimuli is partly reasoned, but in large part habitual. The habitual portion is not, of course, necessarily or even usually irrational, since it may represent a previously conditioned adjustment or adaptation of behavior to its ends.

In executive positions characterized by great busyness on the part of their occupants, a great many stimuli for decision come from outside the individual. A difficult case is referred upward for appellate review; a caller or a member of another organization insists on discussing a problem with the "top man." Innumerable other persons, problems, and things are constantly being forced on his attention.

In any such position the particular questions to be decided will depend largely on the accident of what stimuli are presented.

Not only do the stimuli determine what decisions the administrator is likely to make, but they also have a considerable influence on the conclusion he reaches. An important reason for this is that the very stimulus which initiates the decision also directs attention to selected aspects of the situation, with the exclusion of others. For example, a fire chief pictures a city in which fire losses are extremely low—which seems to him a good thing. His knowledge tells him that progress toward this desirable state of affairs could be made by purchase of a new piece of equipment. The demands of rationality would require, of course, that before deciding whether a new piece of equipment is needed he consider the other purposes for which the money could be spent: street repairs, an addition to the municipal hospital, and so on. That this description is not far from the actualities of administrative behavior will be amply demonstrated in later chapters.[13]

Almost all human beings have the feeling, at one time or another, that there are more things that they would like to do than there is time to do them. That is, there are more possible stimuli for behavior than could be acted out if they were all simultaneously present to the attention. Rationality demands that a conscious choice be made among competing "goods" instead of leaving the choice to the caprice of the attention-directing stimuli.

Determinants of the Psychological Environment

In so far, then, as choice is initiated by impingement upon the individual of accidental and arbitrary stimuli, it would seem that the

[13] The reader who is interested in further examples of this stimulus-response type of thinking will find fascinating materials in several fields. First, let him turn to autobiography and try to ascertain how each subject chose his particular profession. The autobiographies of Viscount Haldane and of William Alanson White both illustrate the point well: *Richard Burdon Haldane: An Autobiography* (London: Hodder & Stoughton, 1931), and *The Autobiography of a Purpose* (Garden City: Doubleday, Doran & Co., 1938). Next, let him turn to recent literature on propaganda technique and note the generous use of attention-directing devices by the propagandist. The supporting schedules of budget documents and the testimony taken at budget hearings are also filled with examples of attention channelized toward particular values.

integrated busyness of the adult is simply a more patterned busyness than the random movements and shifting attentions of the child. The organized wholes of which it is composed are larger and more complex but, as wholes, no more closely related to any over-all system of values than those of the child. The study of administrative behavior as a rational activity would hardly seem useful unless this difficulty can be removed by showing that the stimuli that initiate choice are not, or at least need not be, arbitrary, when viewed from the standpoint of the organization as a whole rather than from that of an individual member.[14]

The next question that must be considered, then, is how the stimuli themselves originate that are instrumental in initiating the decisional process.

A man in a room with a shelf full of books may glance over the titles and deliberately choose one of them to read for an hour. Once he has opened the book, if it is not too dull and he is not interrupted, the symbols which it places before his eyes will be the most important, perhaps the only, stimuli engaging his attention during the ensuing hour. Hence, his choice of a book determines these subsequent stimuli.

Now consider an illustration of a slightly more practical sort. A man has formed the habit of glancing at his calendar pad when he comes to the office each morning. On Thursday he receives a letter which will need to be answered the next Tuesday. He places a note

[14] The pragmatists would seem to take the position that human beings are concerned with rationality only in the first sense—in terms of adjustive responses to arbitrary stimuli. John Dewey, in *Human Nature and Conduct* (pp. 261–262), says: "The action of deliberation, as we have seen, consists in selecting some foreseen consequence to serve as a stimulus to present action. . . . But the selected consequence is set in an indefinite context of other consequences just as real as it is. . . . The 'ends' that are foreseen and utilized mark out a little island in an infinite sea. This limitation would be fatal were the proper function of ends anything else than to liberate and guide present action out of its perplexities and confusions. But this service constitutes the sole meaning of aims and purposes. Hence their slight extent in comparison with ignored and unforeseen consequences is of no import in itself." See also *The Public and Its Problems,* p. 200. Dewey's later views set forth in *Logic. The Theory of Inquiry,* chap. ix, pp. 159–180 (New York: Henry Holt & Co., 1938), are in closer accord with the point of view of the present study—that the behavior of the individual acquires a wider context of rationality through the environment of choice social organization provides for him.

on his pad, knowing that this note will provide the stimulus to act on the following Tuesday.

A third illustration involves the deliberate development of a skill. A person who uses the typewriter once in a while may fall into the "hunt and peck" system of typing because, at any given moment when he wishes to type, this is the fastest way of spelling out the words. If he anticipates, however, that he will make considerable use of the typewriter over a period of time, he may take the pains to develop the habits associated with the touch system. Then in the long run the stimuli that he wishes to translate into typewritten words will receive a more effective response than if he had not previously developed this skill.

A final illustration is provided by the lines of communication in an administrative organization. Each member of the organization requires certain information in order to make correctly those decisions for which he is responsible. To make certain that the necessary information is presented to each member, a regular system of records and reports is devised, which automatically directs these stimuli into the proper channels.

These illustrations give some notion of the mechanisms that bring about the integration of behavior in a broad pattern. Two principal sets of mechanisms may be distinguished: (1) those that cause behavior to persist in a particular direction once it has been turned in that direction, and (2) those that initiate behavior in a particular direction. The former are for the most part—though by no means entirely—internal. Their situs is the human mind, and to this extent their description and functioning is a problem for psychology, and can only be touched upon in the present study.

Behavior-initiating mechanisms, on the other hand, are largely external to the individual, although they usually imply his sensitivity to particular stimuli. Being external, they can be interpersonal— they can be invoked by someone other than the person they are intended to influence, and consequently, they play a central role in administrative organization.

The mechanisms of initiation have already been sufficiently illustrated for present purposes. The next few pages will dispose briefly of the mechanisms of behavior-persistence. That done, it will be possible to reconstruct a picture of rational behavior, giving a central place to the mechanisms of integration.

The Mechanisms of Behavior-Persistence

Attention and behavior, once initiated in a particular direction, tend to persist in that direction for a considerable interval of time. This is true even when the original choice of activity was a matter of relative indifference.

One important reason for behavior-persistence has already been discussed in Chapter IV. Activity very often results in "sunk costs" of one sort or another that make persistence in the same direction advantageous. An administrator may feel considerable doubt that a particular activity should be undertaken; but, once the responsibility has been assumed, it may be advantageous to continue rather than lose the time and effort that have already been expended. Another way of stating this is to say that activities are usually continued at least until a point of "consummation" has been reached— a point where the values produced by sunk costs have been harvested.

A second reason for persistence is that the activity itself creates stimuli that direct attention toward its continuance and completion. This has already been pointed out—a book, if it is well written, tends to hold attention to the limits of its covers until it has been read through. But the same thing can be equally well illustrated from almost any administrative situation. An engineer, arriving at his office, finds on his desk a set of plans for a street on which he was working the previous day. Immediately, his attention is directed to these plans and the problems involved in completing them, and no further external stimuli may be needed to keep him at work on the plans for the remainder of the day.

It may be seen that a large part of this stimulation is "internal," and proceeds along the associational paths that have been built up in the mind. If the pattern of associations is rich, the mind acts as a sort of closed circuit, repeatedly bringing thought back to the subject of concern whenever it strays. As is well known, any considerable degree of concentration (i.e., internal stimulation) will actually decrease the individual's sensitivity to external stimuli.[15]

A third factor making for persistence, and one closely related to "sunk costs," is one that might be labeled "make-ready" costs. In the case of many repetitive tasks, the time of preparing to perform the task, and the time required to turn from that task to another, make it advantageous to persist in the performance of the one task rather than to perform a variety.

THE INTEGRATION OF BEHAVIOR

It is time now to turn from the mechanisms that make integration possible to the pattern of behavior that results from the operation of these mechanisms. The process involves three principal steps:

(1) The individual (or organization) makes broad decisions regarding the values to which he is going to direct his activities, the general methods he is going to use to attain these values, and the knowledge, skills, and information he will need to make particular decisions within the limits of the policy laid down and to carry out the decisions. The decisional activity just described might be called *substantive planning*.

(2) He designs and establishes mechanisms that will direct his attention, channel information and knowledge, etc., in such a way as to cause the specific day-to-day decisions to conform with the substantive plan. This decisional activity might be called *procedural planning,* and corresponds to what was earlier described as "constructing the psychological environment of decision."

(3) He executes the plan through day-to-day decisions and activities that fit in the framework provided by steps (1) and (2).

In reality, the process involves not just three steps but a whole hierarchy of steps, the decisions at any given level of generality providing the environment for the more particular decisions at the next level below. The integration of behavior at the highest level is brought about by decisions that determine in very broad terms the

15 The subject cannot be pursued further at this point, but a wealth of illustrative material will be found in the psychological literature. See, for example, James' chapters in *The Principles of Psychology* on "The Stream of Thought," "Association," and "Will" (chaps. ix, xiv, and xxvi).

values, knowledge, and possibilities that will receive consideration. The next lower level of integration, which gives greater specificity to these very general determinants, results from those decisions that determine what activities shall be undertaken. Other levels follow, each one determining in greater detail a subarea lying within the area of the level above.

At the higher levels of integration only the very general aspects of the situation can be given consideration. Particularization can take place only when attention is directed to the more detailed possibilities and consequences. Hence, a fundamental problem of administrative theory is to determine how this plexus of decisions should be constructed—what the proper division of labor is between the broad "planning" decisions and the narrower "executory" decisions. A second fundamental problem is that of procedural planning—to devise mechanisms that will make effective the control of the executory decisions by the planning decisions.

Types of General Decisions

It should be made clear that actual events are determined by choice among on-the-spot alternatives for immediate behavior. In a strict sense, a decision can influence the future in only two ways: (1) present behavior, determined by this decision, may limit future possibilities,[16] and (2) future decisions may be guided to a greater or lesser degree by the present decision. It is from this possibility of influencing future choice by present decisions that the idea of an interconnected plexus of decisions derives. The first type of influence has already been discussed, but the second requires further consideration.

When a problem of a particular kind has several times arisen for decision, it may lead to a generalized query of the following kind: "What criteria can I discover which can be used as a basis for choice whenever a problem of this kind arises?" For example, the experienced fire fighter asks, "Are there any underlying principles of fire fighting which can be applied to the many fire situations with which I deal?"

When the problem has been posed and a solution reached, then a

[16] See chap. iv, pp. 67–68, *supra*.

decision has been made that will guide all further decisions on this subject. This it may do by selecting (1) particular values as criteria for the later decisions, (2) particular items of empirical knowledge as relevant to the later decisions, (3) particular behavior alternatives as the only ones needing consideration for later choice.

(1) The specialization of administrative functions, each with its own "objective," directs each portion of the organization toward the realization of a particular restricted set of values. To accept "reducing fire losses" as the objective of a fire department is to establish a criterion of value that will guide the fire department administrator in all his decisions.

(2) In many fields, general decisions are reached as to the facts that should be taken into consideration in making any subsidiary decision. The engineer, for instance, has routine procedures of calculation for determining whether a given bridge design allows the required factor of safety in bearing its stresses.

(3) Similarly, in many fields, general decisions determine the behavior alternatives that are to be considered when a specific choice is faced. A football team goes on the field with a definite repertoire of "plays" which it can call into use at appropriate moments. A policeman, seeing an infraction of the law, is trained to respond in terms of "arrest," "warning," or "report."

The psychological mechanisms by which these general criteria, previously decided upon, are brought to bear upon an immediate problem for choice have already been described.[17] By creating internal and external stimuli, these prior decisions determine the framework of attention with which the mind responds to the specific choice-situation. This narrow frame of attention is in distinct contrast with the broader area of reference that is involved when the prior, controlling decision is made. That is, the set of factors taken into consideration when it is determined that "a fire department will be established with the objective of minimizing fire losses" is quite different from the set that influences a fire-fighter to decide, "I had better connect a $2\frac{1}{2}$-inch line to this hydrant." This stratification of decisions makes it possible for each choice to be guided directly or indirectly by much broader considerations of ra-

[17] *Supra.*

tionality than would be possible if it had to be made "on the spot" without benefit of previous consideration. Hence, we are led to a concept of "planned" behavior as the proper means for maintaining rationality at a high level.

The Planning Process

The psychological processes involved in planning consist in selecting general criteria of choice, and then particularizing them by application to specific situations.[18] A designing engineer selects as his objective a railroad to extend between cities A and B through mountainous country. After a preliminary examination of the topography, he selects two or three general routes that seem feasible. He then takes each of these routes as his new "end"—an intermediate end—and particularizes it further, using more detailed topographical maps.

His thought processes might be described as a series of hypothetical implications: "If I am to go from A to B, routes (1), (2), and (3) seem more feasible than the others; if I am to follow route (1), plan (1a) seems preferable; if route (2), plan (2c); if route (3), plan (3a)"—and so on, until the most minute details of the design have been determined for two or three alternative plans. His final choice is among these detailed alternatives.

This process of thought may be contrasted with a single choice among *all* the possible routes. The latter method is the one dictated by logic, and is the only procedure that guarantees that the decision finally arrived at is the best. On the other hand, this method requires that all the possible plans be worked out in full detail before any decision is reached. The practical impossibility of such a procedure is evident. The planning procedure is a compromise, whereby only the most "plausible" alternatives are worked out in detail.

Let us present another illustration. Suppose the problem be to select a dam site for a storage reservoir. For simplicity, it will be assumed that the desideratum is to secure a specified volume of water storage at a minimum cost, and that water storage above the specified amount will be of no value. Usually the real problem is not so simple. The cost can be estimated, for each point along the river, of

[18] Cf. MacMahon, Millett, and Ogden, *op. cit.*, p. 17.

building a dam with the required storage capacity. However, to make an accurate estimate, detailed studies would need to be made of the foundation conditions at each point. Then, this huge array of cost estimates could be compiled and the dam site with least cost selected.

Actually, the engineer proceeds quite differently. By inspection of a topographic map, he immediately picks out a half-dozen "plausible" dam sites, and forgets the rest. He is sufficiently familiar with dam construction costs to know—with a fair degree of certainty—that any other site he might choose would have a higher construction cost. Next, he makes an approximate estimate of dam costs for each of the plausible sites, assuming "normal" foundation conditions. Finally, he selects the most promising sites and makes careful foundation studies as a basis for final estimates.

At each step in this process there is a chance that the dam site which really is most desirable will be eliminated without complete analysis. He must exercise great skill in determining the degree of approximation that is allowable at each point in the procedure.

The Function of Social Organization

It was mentioned several times in this chapter that the mechanisms leading to the integration of behavior might be interpersonal. If organizations and social institutions be conceived, in the broad sense, as patterns of group behavior, it is not hard to see that the individual's participation in such organizations and institutions may be the source of some of his most fundamental and far-reaching integrations. The organizational influences on the individual are of two principal kinds:

(1) Organizations and institutions permit stable expectations to be formed by each member of the group as to the behavior of the other members under specified conditions. Such stable expectations are an essential precondition to a rational consideration of the consequences of action in a social group.[19]

(2) Organizations and institutions provide the general stimuli and attention-directors that channelize the behaviors of the mem-

---

[19] Cf. Stene's discussion of "organization routine" *op. cit.*, p. 1129.

bers of the group, and that provide those members with the intermediate objectives that stimulate action.[20]

No pattern of social behavior could survive, of course, that did not anticipate and provide in some manner for the satiation of the stimuli of hunger, sexual desire, and fatigue. Beyond this, institutional arrangements are subject to infinite variation, and can hardly be said to follow from any innate characteristics of man. Since these institutions largely determine the mental sets of the participants, they set the conditions for the exercise of docility, and hence of rationality in human society.

The highest level of integration that man achieves consists in taking an existing set of institutions as one alternative and comparing it with other sets. That is, when man turns his attention to the institutional setting which, in turn, provides the framework within which his own mental processes operate, he is truly considering the consequences of behavior alternatives at the very highest level of integration. Thought at this comprehensive level has not been common to all cultures. In our Western civilization it has perhaps been confined to (1) the writings of utopian political theorists and (2) the thought and writings surrounding modern legislative processes.[21]

Human rationality, then, gets its higher goals and integrations from the institutional setting in which it operates and by which it is molded. In our democratic culture, legislation is the principal designer and arbiter of these institutions. Administrative organizations cannot perhaps claim the same importance as repositories of the fundamental human values as that possessed by older traditional institutions like the family. Nevertheless, with man's growing economic interdependence, and with his growing dependence upon the

[20] Cf. Dewey, *The Public and Its Problems*, p. 54.

[21] It has often been shown that the concept of "law-making" as distinct from "law-finding" is a relatively recent development. See, for example, C. J. Friedrich, *Constitutional Government and Politics* (New York: Harper & Bros., 1937), and Charles G. Haines, *The American Doctrine of Judicial Supremacy* (New York: Macmillan Co., 1914), pp. 12–13, 18–24. Hence, only in recent times has legislation involved a conscious consideration of the possibilities of alternative institutional patterns. Karl Mannheim has emphasized the importance of the deliberate fashioning of the institutional environment in his recent study, *Man and Society in an Age of Reconstruction* (London: Kegan Paul, 1940), pp. 149–155.

community for essential governmental services, formal organization is rapidly assuming a role of broader significance than it has ever before possessed. This is not without its advantages, for administrative organizations are usually constructed and modified with a deliberation and freedom from tradition which—though far from complete—gives them great adaptability to meet new needs with new arrangements.

The behavior patterns which we call organizations are fundamental, then, to the achievement of human rationality in any broad sense. The rational individual is, and must be, an organized and institutionalized individual. If the severe limits imposed by human psychology upon deliberation are to be relaxed, the individual must in his decisions be subject to the influence of the organized group in which he participates. His decisions must not only be the product of his own mental processes, but also reflect the broader considerations to which it is the function of the organized group to give effect.

Mechanisms of Organization Influence

The means that the organization employs to influence the decisions of individual members have already been outlined in the introductory chapter. They will be analyzed at length in later chapters and therefore require only brief discussion at this point.

(1) The organization divides work among its members. By giving each a particular task to accomplish, it directs and limits his attention to that task. The personnel officer concerns himself with recruitment, training, classification, and other personnel operations. He need not give particular concern to the accounting, purchasing, planning, or operative functions, which are equally vital to the accomplishment of the organization's task, because he knows they have been provided for elsewhere in the organization structure.

(2) The organization establishes standard practices. By deciding once for all (or at least for a period of time) that a particular task shall be done in a particular way, it relieves the individual who actually performs the task of the necessity of determining each time how it shall be done.

(3) The organization transmits decisions downward (and laterally or even upward) through its ranks by establishing systems of authority and influence. The most familiar form this takes is the hierarchy of formal authority; but of equal importance are the assignment to particular individuals of the formal function of advising, and the growth in any actual organization of an informal system of influence based partly upon formal status, and partly upon social relationships.

(4) The organization provides channels of communication running in all directions through which information for decision-making flows. Again these channels are both formal and informal. The formal channels are partly based on, and partly separate from, the lines of formal authority, and the informal channels are closely related to the informal social organization.

(5) The organization trains and indoctrinates its members. This might be called the "internalization" of influence, because it injects into the very nervous systems of the organization members the criteria of decision that the organization wishes to employ. The organization member acquires knowledge, skill, and identifications or loyalties that enable him to make decisions, by himself, as the organization would like him to decide.

The Process of Coordination

One of the principal functions of these organizational influences has already been alluded to in this and the previous chapter: to bring about coordination in the activities of the organization members. As has been explained, the effectiveness of an individual in achieving his aims in any social situation will depend not only upon his own activity, but also on how well that activity relates to what the other individuals concerned are doing. In any large organization—the Federal government is an excellent example—the task of relating the activities of one individual or unit to those of others becomes one of the greatest importance, complexity, and difficulty. War activities have illustrated this strikingly on numerous occasions. An administrator responsible for airplane gasoline production may wish to issue orders—quite logical for the execution of his task—that would interfere with the task of another administrator responsible for rubber production. The procurement of steel for merchant shipping may conflict with the procurement of steel for warships, or for tanks. The execution of a large military operation may require the coordination, in time, of a host of preparatory activities. These illustrations could be multiplied many times.

Viewed from the position of the individual in organization, coordination involves several elements: the relation of the individual's objectives and intermediate aims to those of other segments of the organization; the individual's assessment of the alternatives available to him and to the other members of the group; and his expectations as to the courses of action that will be followed by the others.

Self-Coordination. In the simplest situations, the individual participant can bring his activities into coordination with the activities of others through simple observation of what they are doing. In a group of three or four painters working together, each one may take a part of the job, and the entire group may work as a team with each one fitting in where he thinks his efforts will be most effective and will interfere least with the others. Occasionally a command may be given; but most of the adjustments take place silently and without discussion.

Anyone who has observed an unorganized group of persons act in an emergency has seen organized behavior of this variety. Of course, if the group has been organized previously to the emergency or if one or more members of the group are recognized as "leaders," the mechanism of coordination may be much more elaborate, involving vocal commands.

In most situations, the successful performance of a task by a group of persons requires a slightly higher degree of coordination. For instance, it may be necessary for effective performance that they all apply their efforts simultaneously. Even under such circumstances, the coordination may not be deliberate nor involve explicit commands. The various members of the group may merely accept one member as the "leader" and adjust their movements to his—a group of men moving a heavy load, for example.

All these situations where self-coordination is possible require that the individual be able to observe the behaviors of the organization members and adjust his to theirs. Where this direct observation is not possible—as in most situations of any complexity—the organization itself must provide for the coordination.

Group Versus Individual Alternatives. The individual views the attainment of his objectives as dependent upon the particular course of behavior he follows. For each of the courses of action open to him there is a distinct set of consequences or results. Rational choice, as has been explained, consists in selecting and bringing about the result that is preferred to the others.

When choice takes place in a group situation, the consequences of a course of action become dependent not only upon the individual's selection of a particular alternative, but upon the selections of the other members of the group as well. Only when the behaviors of the others are taken as "constants"—that is, when expectations are formed regarding their behaviors—does the problem of choice take on a determinate form. When such expectations have been formed, the only remaining independent variable is the individual's own choice, and the problem of decision reduces to the former case.

Hence, the set of alternatives available to the *group* must be carefully distinguished from the set of alternatives available to the *individual.* The latter is only a subset of the former, a different subset for each given set of behaviors of the other members of the group. The alternative that the individual actually selects for his own behavior may be quite distinct from the alternative that he would select if he could determine the behaviors of all the other group members.

If the individual's expectations of the behaviors of his colleagues are accurate they will usually be rather different from the way he wishes his colleagues would behave. Since his own decision, to be rational, must be related to his expectations rather than his wishes, he must aim not at that alternative *among all those possible for the group* which he prefers, but at that alternative *among all those possible for him* which he prefers.

That a distinction must be made between a plan of campaign that depends on the opponent's doing the wished-for thing, and a plan that depends upon the opponent's doing the "correct" thing is a cardinal principle of military tactics, and indeed of any competitive activity. A plan of the first kind never succeeds, for its success depends upon the false assumption that the opponent will do what you want him to do. In the practical world, plans are characterized as "utopian" whose success depends on wished-for behavior on the part of many individuals, but which fail to explain how this wished-for behavior will, or can, be brought about.

Now a very special situation arises when all the members of the group exhibit a preference for the same values and for the same outcomes out of all those possible of realization by the group. All the firemen fighting a fire are agreed on the aim of their joint behavior—to extinguish the fire as quickly as possible. In such a case there is one set of behaviors for the members of the group which, on entirely objective empirical grounds, is the most expeditious for the accomplishment of this aim. The members of the group may disagree as to what this best solution is, but any such disagreement is on a factual level—a question of judgment, not of values.

The attainment of the "best" result implies that each member of the group knows his place in the scheme and is prepared to carry out his job with the others. But, unless the intentions of each member of the group can be communicated to the others, such coordination is hardly possible. Each will base his behavior on his expectations of the behaviors of the others, but he will have no reason to expect that they will fit into any preconceived plan. Lacking formal coordination, the result will be highly fortuitous.

Under most practical conditions, self-coordination is infinitely less effective than a predetermined scheme of action that relieves each member of the group of the task of anticipating the behavior of the others as a basis for his own.

Communication, then, is essential to the more complex forms of cooperative behavior. The process of coordination in these more complicated situations consists of at least three steps: (1) the development of a plan of behavior for *all* the members of the group (not a set of individual plans for each member); (2) the communication of the relevant portions of this plan to each member;

and (3) a willingness on the part of the individual members to permit their behavior to be guided by the plan.

This process is not unlike that whereby the individual integrates his own behavior into a coordinated pattern. In the integration of the group, communication fills the gap—supplies the nerve tissue, so to speak—left by the absence of any organic connection among the individuals.

The Group Plan. The idea of a plan for the behavior of a group does not involve any metaphysical notions of a "group mind." It is a specification as to how a number of persons shall behave, rather than a specification as to how one person shall behave. The plan has its existence on paper, or in the respective minds of the individuals who create it. These individuals may be many, or few; they may belong to the group, or they may not. All that is required is that, before the plan is acted out, it shall be communicated to the group members who are to do the acting.

In the discussion thus far, it has been assumed that a plan will come into being only when there is perfect agreement among the group members as to which of all the possibilities available to the group they would like to see realized. As a matter of fact, this is not strictly necessary. Group coordination may be possible in many cases where different individuals have different notions of the "optimum." It is necessary only that they agree in finding one plan preferable to any alternative that would be open to them *as individuals* if there were no cooperation.[22]

Since the present discussion is concerned not so much with the reasons why individuals cooperate as with the mechanisms that make cooperation possible, the subject of the "group plan" may now be left, to be more fully discussed in the next chapter.

Communication. General organization decisions can control the behavior of the individual only through psychological mechanisms that bring values and knowledge to bear upon each individual de-

[22] An extreme form of this proposition was used by Hobbes in his demonstration that social organization can arise even from a state of *bellum omnium contra omnes*. Other contract theorists, notably Locke, felt impelled to postulate a natural identity of interests. For a penetrating discussion of the motivational bases of cooperation see R. M. MacIver, *Community: A Sociological Study* (London: Macmillan & Co., 3rd ed., 1924), particularly Bk. II, chaps. ii and iii.

cision at the time it is made. In group behavior, there is a similar necessity of communicating the group plan to the individuals who are to carry it out. This does not mean that the whole plan must be communicated, but that each individual must know what he is to do.

No step in the administrative process is more generally ignored, or more poorly performed, than the task of communicating decisions. All too often, plans are "ordered" into effect without any consideration of the manner in which they can be brought to influence the behavior of the individual members of the group. Procedural manuals are promulgated without follow-up to determine whether the contents of the manuals are used by the individuals to guide their decisions. Organization plans are drawn on paper, although the members of the organization are ignorant of the plan that purports to describe their relationships.

Failures in communication result whenever it is forgotten that the behavior of individuals is the tool with which organization achieves its purposes. The question to be asked of any administrative process is: How does it influence the decisions of these individuals? Without communication, the answer must always be: It does not influence them at all.

Acceptance of the Plan. The final step in coordination is acceptance by each of the organization members of his part in the group plan. The problem of securing this acceptance will furnish the principal topic of the next two chapters.

SUMMARY

In the course of this chapter both the limits and the possibilities of human rationality have been examined. The limits of rationality have been seen to derive from the inability of the human mind to bring to bear upon a single decision all the aspects of value, knowledge, and behavior that would be relevant. The pattern of human choice is often more nearly a stimulus-response pattern than a choice among alternatives. Human rationality operates, then, within the limits of a psychological environment. This environment imposes on the individual as "givens" a selection of factors upon which he must base his decisions. However, the stimuli of decision can themselves be controlled so as to serve broader ends, and a sequence of individual decisions can be integrated into a well conceived plan.

The deliberate control of the environment of decision permits not only the integration of choice, but its socialization as well. Social institutions may be viewed as regularizations of the behavior of individuals through subjection of their behavior to stimulus-patterns socially imposed on them. It is in these patterns that an understanding of the meaning and function of organization is to be found.

Chapter VI

THE EQUILIBRIUM OF THE ORGANIZATION

IN CHAPTER V some mechanisms were described that permit the behavior of the individual to be integrated with that of the rest of the organization of which he is a part. These mechanisms do not explain, however, why the individual is willing to participate in the organized group at all, and to submit his personal aims to the established organization objectives. An organization is, after all, a collection of people, and what the organization does is done by people. The activities of a group of people become organized only to the extent that they permit their decisions and their behavior to be influenced by their participation in the organization.

INDUCEMENTS

The clue to the participation of individuals in organization lies in the remarks made in Chapter I regarding the organized group as a system in equilibrium. Individuals are willing to accept organization membership when their activity in the organization contributes, directly or indirectly, to their own personal goals. The contribution is direct if the goals set for the organization have direct personal value for the individual—church membership is a typical example of this. The contribution is indirect if the organization offers personal rewards—monetary or other—to the individual in return for his willingness to contribute his activity to the organization. Employment in a business concern is a typical example of this. Sometimes these personal rewards are directly related to the size and growth of the organization—as in the case of the stockholders of a business; sometimes, not very directly—as in the case of most wage earners. The characteristics of these

three bases for participation are sufficiently distinct to make it
worth while to consider them separately : personal rewards deriving
directly from the accomplishment of the organization objective;
personal inducements offered by the organization and closely related
to its size and growth; and personal rewards derived from inducements offered by the organization but unrelated to the organization
size and growth. Organizations are ordinarily made up of three
groups of individuals, in each of which one of these types of motivation prevails; and it is the presence of these three groups that
gives administration its specific character.

The phrase "personal goals" which is used here should be understood in a broad sense. It is by no means restricted to egoistic goals,
much less to economic goals. "World peace" or "aid to the starving
Chinese" may be just as much a personal goal for a particular
individual as another dollar in his pay envelope. The fact that
economic incentives frequently predominate in business and governmental organizations should not obscure the importance of other
types of inducements. Nor should intangible egoistic values, such
as status, prestige, or enjoyment of organization associations, be
forgotten.

In Chapter I it was explained that in business organizations the
"customers" are a group that has, predominantly, the first type of
motivation—direct interest in organization objectives; employees,
the third type; and the entrepreneur the second type. This is true,
of course, only to a very rough approximation, and the necessary
qualifications will be set forth later in the chapter.

The members of an organization, then, contribute to the organization in return for inducements that the organization offers them.
The contributions of one group are the source of the inducements
that the organization offers others. If the sum of the contributions
is sufficient, in quantity and kind, to supply the necessary quantity
and kinds of inducements, the organization survives and grows;
otherwise it shrinks and ultimately disappears unless an equilibrium
is reached.[1]

[1]This idea of an equilibrium is due to C. I. Barnard. See his *The Functions of
the Executive* (Cambridge: Harvard University Press, 1938), pp. 56–59 and
chaps. xi and xvi.

TYPES OF ORGANIZATION PARTICIPANTS

Organization members may be classified in other ways than in terms of the inducements they receive for their participation. They may be classified in terms of the types of contributions they make to the organization: specific services (a supplier of material); money or other neutral services that may be employed as incentives (customers); and time and effort (employees).

Still a third method of classification would distinguish those who control the organization—that is, have a right to fix the terms on which the others will be permitted to participate in it—from the remaining participants. The various possible combinations of inducements, contributions, and control arrangements make for a considerable variety of organizational forms, and this variety must be taken into consideration in the succeeding discussion.

ORGANIZATION GOALS AS INDUCEMENTS

Most organizations are oriented around some goal or objective which provides the purpose toward which the organization decisions and activities are directed. If the goal is relatively tangible—e.g., making shoes—it is usually not too difficult to assess the contribution of specific activities toward it, and hence to evaluate their usefulness. If the goal is less tangible—like that of a religious organization—it becomes more debatable whether a particular activity contributes to the goal; and hence there may be considerable controversy, even among those who wish to work for the goal, as to how it is to be attained. Even where the goal is tangible there may be some activities whose relation to it is so indirect, though not necessarily any less substantial for that indirectness, that the problem of evaluation is difficult. It is much easier to budget, for example, for the production line than for the advertising department or for supervision.

It has been fashionable in the literature of business administration to debate whether "the" purpose of a business organization is service or profit. There really is no problem to debate about. Certain individuals, primarily the customers, contribute to the organization because of the service it provides; others, the entrepreneurs, because of the profits they may derive. When the system of organization behavior itself is examined, it is found that both service and profit aims influence decisions. It is for terminological convenience that the label of "organization objective" is here applied to the service aim.

Application to Specific Organization Types

In the case of the business organization the organization goal—the output of product—is a personal goal for individuals who are ordinarily not considered members of the organization, that is, the customers.[2] In return for this product the customers are willing to offer money, which provides a principal inducement for the employees and entrepreneurs to participate in the group. The relation of customers to the organization is distinguished not only by the type of inducement they receive, but also by the fact that it is based on a contract or bargain for a specific product without, ordinarily, any assumption of permanence or continuity in the relationship.

In the case of a government agency the organization goal is a personal goal for the ultimate controlling body of the organization —the legislature—and for the citizen. The relationship here is in part the same as in a business organization, in that the legislators, viewed as "customers," furnish the agency with its funds. It is decidedly different in that, first, they retain final legal control over the organization, and second, their "personal" motivation is based, in turn, on their peculiar status as elected representatives. To examine the way in which legislators make value judgments in determining the policy of governmental agencies would lead away from the present study into a study of the whole legislative process.

In volunteer organizations the organization objective is ordinarily the direct inducement that secures the services of the or-

[2] Barnard, in *The Functions of the Executive,* was perhaps the first writer to insist that the customers must be considered as a part of the system of organization activity in any theory of administration. His views on this point have still apparently not gained wide acceptance among writers on administration. As pointed out earlier, the important question here is not how "organization membership" is to be defined but whether or not the behavior of customers is to be included in the analysis of the organization.

ganization members. The peculiar problems of administration in volunteer organizations derive from the facts that the contributions are often on a part-time basis, that the various participants may have conflicting interpretations of the organization objective, and that the organization objective may play such a modest role in the participant's system of values that it offers only a mild inducement for cooperation. In this respect, the volunteer shares many of the characteristics of the customer of a business organization, although the former contributes services to the organization instead of money.

Adaptation of the Organization Objective

The organization objective is by no means a static thing. In order to survive, the organization must have an objective that appeals to its customers,[3] so that they will make the contributions necessary to sustain it. Hence, organization objectives are constantly adapted to conform to the changing values of customers, or to secure new groups of customers in place of customers who have dropped away. The organization may also undertake special activities to induce acceptance of its objectives by customers—advertising, missionary work, and propaganda of all sorts.

Hence, although it is correct to say that organization behavior is oriented toward the organization objective, this is not the whole story; for the organization objective itself changes in response to the influence of those for whom the accomplishment of that objective secures personal values.

The modification of the organization objective usually represents a compromise of the interests of several groups of potential participants, in order to secure their joint cooperation where each group individually is unable to attain its own objectives unaided. Hence the organization objective will seldom coincide exactly with the personal objectives of even those participants whose interest in the organization lies in its attainment of its goal. The crucial issue for any such individual is whether the organization objective is

[3] The word "customer" is used in a generic sense here to refer to any individual —customer, legislator, or volunteer—for whom the organization objective has personal value.

sufficiently close to his personal goal to make him choose to participate in the group rather than try to attain his goal by himself or in some other group. As will be seen, this process of compromise takes place, whether the controlling group of the organization is itself directly interested in the organization objective, or whether the inducement it receives from the organization is of some other type.

Loyalty of Employees to Organization Objective

Although the organization objective is of greatest importance in relation to the behavior of those participants who have been called "customers," almost all the members of an organization become imbued, to a greater or lesser degree, with the organization aim, and are influenced by it in their behavior. This has already been pointed out in the case of volunteer organizations; it is also true, although to a lesser extent, of governmental agencies and commercial organizations. It is one component, and a very important one, of organizational loyalty. If the objective has any appearance of usefulness, the organization members, whose attention is continually directed to it by their everyday work, will acquire an appreciation of its importance and value (often an exaggerated appreciation), and the attainment of the value will come, to that extent, to have personal value for them. It will be seen later that, in addition to this loyalty to the organization objective, there may also develop in employees a very different loyalty—a loyalty to the organization itself and an interest in its survival and growth.

INCENTIVES FOR EMPLOYEE PARTICIPATION

To an employee of a non-volunteer organization the most obvious personal incentive that the organization offers is a salary or wage. It is a peculiar and important characteristic of his relation with the organization that, in return for this inducement, he offers the organization not a specific service but his undifferentiated time and effort. He places this time and effort at the disposal of those directing the organization, to be used as they see fit. Thus, both the customer relation (in the commercial organization) and the employee relation originate in contract, but in contracts of very different sorts. The employment contract results in the creation of a continuing authority relation between the organization and the employee.

How can this be? Why does the employee sign a blank check, so to speak, in entering upon his employment? First, from the viewpoint of the organization, nothing would be gained by offering an inducement to the employee unless the latter's behavior could be brought into the system of organization behavior through his acceptance of its authority. Second, from the viewpoint of the employee, the precise activities with which his time of employment is occupied may, within certain limits, be a matter of relative indifference to him. If the orders transmitted to him by the organization remain within these limits of acceptance, he will permit his behavior to be guided by them.

What determines the breadth of the area of acceptance within which the employee will accept the authority of the organization? It certainly depends on the nature and magnitude of the incentives the organization offers. In addition to the salary he receives, he may value the status and prestige that his position in the organization gives him, and he may value his relations with the working group of which he is part. In setting his task, the organization must take into consideration the effect that its orders may have upon the employee's realization of these values. If the employee values white-collar status, for example, he may be completely unwilling to accept assignments that deprive him of that status even when the work he is asked to perform is not inherently unpleasant or difficult.

There is great variation among individuals in the extent to which opportunities for promotion act as incentives for participation. Promotion is, of course, both an economic and a prestige incentive. Burleigh Gardner has pointed out the importance for administrative theory of the presence in organizations of certain highly "mobile" individuals, i.e. individuals who have a strong desire for advancement. It would be a mistake (which Gardner carefully avoids) to assume that these desires provide a strong incentive in all individuals.[4]

We find, then, that those participants in organization who are called its employees are offered a variety of material and non-material incentives, generally not directly related to the attainment of the organization objective nor to the size and growth of the organization, in return for their willingness to accept organization decisions as the basis for their behavior during the time of their employment. The area within which organization authority will be accepted is not unlimited, and the boundaries will depend on the incentives that the organization is able to provide. In so far as these incentives are not directly dependent upon the organization objective, modification of that objective will not affect the willingness of employees to participate, and hence the latter group will exert little influence in the determination of the objectives.

VALUES DERIVED FROM ORGANIZATION SIZE AND GROWTH

The third type of incentive that induces individual participation in organization derives from the size and growth of the organization. These might be referred to as "conservation" values. Most prominent in the group for whom these values are important is the entrepreneur. It is true that the entrepreneur, to the extent that he is an "economic man," is interested in profits, and not in size and growth. In practice this objection is not serious: first because profits usually are, or are thought to be, closely related to size and growth; and secondly because most entrepreneurs are interested in nonmaterial values, such as prestige and power, as well as profit. This attachment to conservation objectives is even more characteristic of the professional managerial group who exercise the active control of most large business enterprises.

Conservation objectives may provide important values, also, for the other employees of the organization as well, particularly those who are mobile. An organization that is growing and prospering

---

[4] On this and other aspects of the problem of incentives see Burleigh B. Gardner, *Human Relations in Industry* (Chicago: Richard D. Irwin, 1945), particularly chaps. i and viii.

offers greater opportunities for prestige and advancement than one that is static or declining. Conservation values are not, therefore, completely independent in practice from values of the second type, though for purposes of analysis there is some advantage in considering them separately.

Interest in conservation of the organization provides the basis for an organizational loyalty distinct from that previously mentioned. The individual who is loyal to the *objectives* of the organization will resist modification of those objectives, and may even refuse to continue his participation if they are changed too radically. The individual who is loyal to the *organization* will support opportunistic changes in its objectives that are calculated to promote its survival and growth.

Loyalty to the organization itself is perhaps the type of loyalty most characteristic of commercial organizations, but both species prevail widely in both public and private administration, commercial and noncommercial. Some of the most striking manifestations of conflict between these two types of loyalty are to be found in religious and reform organizations, where there is often controversy as to the extent to which organization objectives shall be modified to insure survival. This was certainly one basis for the Stalinist-Trotskyist rivalry. As previously indicated, the motives of the opportunists in such a controversy may, of course, be tactical rather than egoistic. The opportunist, assessing unfavorably the chances of survival without adaptation, may prefer half a loaf to no bread, while the "idealist" may assess the chances of survival more optimistically, or may consider that the concession in objectives more than outweighs the improvement in survival chances. Both types of loyalty will be discussed more fully in a later chapter.

ORGANIZATION EQUILIBRIUM AND EFFICIENCY

The basic value criteria that will be employed in making decisions and choices among alternatives in an organization will be selected for the organization primarily by the controlling group—the group that has the power to set the terms of membership for all the participants. If the group that holds the legal control fails to exercise this power, then, of course, it will devolve on individuals further down the administrative hierarchy.

Whatever group exercises the power of determining the basic value criteria will attempt to secure through the organization its own personal values—whether these be identified with the organization objective, with the conservation objectives, with profits or what not. But their power of control does not in any sense imply that the control group exercises an unlimited option to direct the organization in any path it desires, for the power will continue to exist only so long as the controlling group is able to offer sufficient incentives to retain the contributions of the other participants to the organization. No matter what the personal objectives of the control group, their decisions will be heavily influenced by the fact that they can attain their objectives through the organization only if they can maintain a positive balance of contributions over inducements, or at least an equilibrium between the two.

For this reason the controlling group, regardless of its personal values, will be opportunistic—will appear to be motivated in large part at least by conservation objectives. It may be worth while to illustrate this more fully in the case of widely different organization types.

Equilibrium in Commercial Organizations

In business organizations, the control groups can ordinarily be expected to be oriented primarily toward profits and conservation.[5] They will attempt to maintain a favorable balance of incoming contributions over outgoing incentives in two ways: first by modifying the organization objective in response to customer demand; and second, by employing the resources, monetary contributions, and employees' time and effort in such a manner as to attain a maximum of inducement to employees, and a maximum of attainment of organization objectives with these resources. A detailed examination of the way in which this is accomplished leads to the

[5] This may be less true in recent years than formerly, and less true in businesses "affected with a public interest" than in others. In some areas of enterprise, particularly the public utility field, a "trusteeship" concept has grown up that leads the active control group to identify itself—to what degree the writer is not prepared to estimate—with the organization objective.

theory of what the economist calls "the economics of the firm." Such an examination cannot be undertaken here. One point does require notice, however: the second type of adjustment—that of using the given resources as effectively as possible in the light of the organization objective—makes efficiency a basic value criterion of administrative decision in such organizations.

It might be asked why most commercial organizations, if their basic adjustment is opportunistic, do tend usually to maintain fairly stable objectives. The answer to this is threefold. First, there are "sunk costs" which make immediate and rapid adjustment unprofitable even from the standpoint of conservation. Second, the organization acquires know-how in a particular field—really an intangible sunk cost, or more properly, "sunk asset." Third, the organization acquires goodwill, which is also a sunk asset that may not be readily transferable to another area of activity. Stated differently, a change in organization objectives ordinarily entails decreased efficiency in use of resources (sunk costs and know-how) and a loss of incentives otherwise available to maintain a favorable balance (goodwill).

Equilibrium in Governmental Agencies

In the governmental agency the "customer," i.e., the legislative body, is the ultimate controlling group. Since this group can contribute to the organization whatever funds are necessary to attain the organization objective, it is less obvious on casual examination that such an organization is a system in equilibrium. It may be expected, also, that opportunistic modification of the organization objective is less prominent in such organizations than in commercial organizations.

Closer examination tends to reduce the importance of these differences. First, the legislature and the electorate to which it is responsive have changing tastes and objectives. Second, the control of the legislative body over the public agency is usually of a relatively passive and general nature, and the real initiative for the formulation of objectives often—perhaps almost always—lies in the top administrative group. This group may be strongly imbued with the organization objectives, with conservation aims, or both, and, within the limits of its discretion, may play very much the same role as the management group in commercial organizations.

In any event, efficiency comes forth again as a basic criterion of decision in the public organization, since the controlling group will attempt to attain a maximum of organization objectives, however these be determined, with the resources at its disposal.

Equilibrium in Non-Profit Private Organizations

The non-profit organization (a professional association, or a private school, for example) is likely to differ from the ordinary business organization in several respects. For one thing, there is not a conflict—always possible in business organizations—between profit aims, and the other types of objectives discussed. Moreover, the control group is likely to be identified closely with the organization objective, and hence opportunism, though an important element in the equilibrium of such organizations, is likely to be of the type previously described as "tactical." On the other hand, the criterion of efficiency will play the same role in these organizations as in the others that have been described.

Elements in Common

These illustrations will perhaps serve to suggest the wide variety of possible organization forms. The reader undoubtedly can suggest other forms from his own experience and is aware of the numerous modifications these forms can undergo, particularly with respect to the motivation of the control group.

The same analysis can be applied to *segments* of organizations, the departments, divisions, and sections of which they are built. The administrators directing these segments, within the limits of discretion permitted them, behave in a fashion quite comparable to the groups that control autonomous organizations.

These illustrations indicate that there are at least two elements common to all organizational forms. They all have some equilibrating mechanism or mechanisms; and in all of them efficiency is a basic criterion of administrative choice.

The Criterion of Efficiency

The criterion of efficiency is such an important element in organization decision-making that an entire chapter will be devoted to it. Before leaving the present discussion, however, it may be well to give the term a more precise definition. The criterion of efficiency demands that, of two alternatives having the same cost, that one be chosen which will lead to the greater attainment of the organization objectives; and that, of two alternatives leading to the same degree of attainment, that one be chosen which entails the lesser cost.

Where resources, objectives, and costs are all variable, organization decisions cannot be reached purely on the basis of considerations of efficiency. Where the amount of resources and the organization objectives are givens, outside the control of the administrator, efficiency becomes the controlling determinant of administrative choice.

CONCLUSION

The organization has been described in this chapter as a system in equilibrium, which receives contributions in the form of money or effort, and offers inducements in return for these contributions. These inducements include the organization goal itself, conservation and growth of the organization, and incentives unrelated to these two.

The organization equilibrium is maintained by the control group, whose personal values may be of various kinds, but who assume the responsibility of maintaining the life of the organization in order that they may attain these values.

The remaining chapters of this volume will contain a development of the topics introduced thus far. The authority relationship will be examined more closely, the concept of efficiency will be analyzed, a study will be made of organizational loyalties, and the mechanisms of organization influence over the individual will be discussed in some detail. With this material at hand, it will be possible to draw a comprehensive picture of the anatomy of organization and the processes of decision in administration.

Chapter VII

THE ROLE OF AUTHORITY

HAVING discussed the processes whereby the individual becomes a member of an organization, we come to the next problem, which is how the organization fits the individual's behavior into an overall pattern—how it influences his decisions. Two aspects of influence may be distinguished: the stimuli with which the organization seeks to influence the individual; and the psychological "set" of the individual, which determines his response to the stimuli. These may be termed the "external" and "internal" aspects of influence, respectively.

For purposes of exposition, it is not convenient to separate completely the external and internal aspects of influence. Each plays a greater or lesser role in all the principal modes of influence: authority, communication, training, efficiency, and identification (organizational loyalty). Each of these topics will be considered, in turn, in the following chapters.

In this and the following chapters it is necessary to keep constantly in mind the idea of a decision as a conclusion drawn from a set of premises—value premises, and factual premises. Organizational influence upon the individual may then be interpreted not as determination by the organization of the decisions of the individual, but as determination for him of *some* of the premises upon which his decisions are based. Hence the several modes of influence by no means exclude one another. When the individual decides upon a particular course of action, some of the premises upon which this decision is based may have been imposed upon him by the exercise of the organization's authority over him, some may have been the result of his training, others of his desire for efficiency, still others of his organizational loyalty, and so forth.

Of all the modes of influence, authority is the one that chiefly distinguishes the behavior of individuals as participants of organizations from their behavior outside such organizations. It is authority that gives an organization its formal structure, and the other modes of influence may best be discussed after this structure has been specified.

In the behavior of organized human groups we often find a unity and coordination of behavior so striking that it has led many social thinkers to draw an analogy between the group and the individual, and even to postulate a "group mind." [1] The mechanism whereby this coordination is achieved is not easily perceived. In the case of the individual, there is a perfectly tangible structure of nerve fibers, capable of transmitting impulses from any part of the body to any other part, and capable of storing and transforming those impulses in a central nucleus. In the case of the social group, no physiological structure is present whose anatomy can be explored in the search for clues to the underlying mechanism.

The way in which such coordination is accomplished has already been partly described, in the last part of Chapter V. A plan of action is developed for the group, and this plan is then communicated to the members of the group. The final step in the process is the *acceptance* of this plan by the members. Authority plays a central role in this acceptance.

Coordination then results when the behavior of the individual is guided by his expectations of the behavior of the other members of the group. In the simplest cases, as we have seen, this adaptation may be self-induced. But for the coordination to reach any degree of complexity, it is necessary for the individual to make his specific decisions conform to some sort of group plan. Psychologically speaking, his realization that a particular behavior is a part of his role under the plan must be a sufficient stimulus to bring about the behavior in question.

The mental processes involved are seldom entirely deliberate or conscious. Most of the behaviors resulting in coordination are in

[1] For two decisive refutations of "group mind" theories see Floyd H. Allport, *Institutional Behavior* (Chapel Hill: University of North Carolina Press, 1933), chaps. i–iii, and R. M. MacIver, *Community,* Bk. II, chap. ii, and App. A.

large part habitual or reflexive. A soldier obeying a command does not reflect on the philosophy of obedience, but he *does* set himself a rule of behavior which makes his choices responsive to the command. Instead of being guided at each moment by a decision, "I will attack now," the soldier comprehends all such decisions under the general rule, "I will attack when ordered to do so."

An analysis of organized behavior of all sorts will demonstrate that such behavior results when each of the coordinated individuals sets for himself a criterion of choice that makes his own behavior dependent upon the behavior of others. In the simplest cases he makes his own decision at each point as to what those adjustments should be. In slightly more complex forms of organization, *he sets himself a general rule which permits the communicated decision of another to guide his own choices* (i.e. to serve as a premise of those choices) *without deliberation on his own part on the expediency of those premises.*

AUTHORITY

Even the very simple illustrations that have been presented of organized behavior exhibit, in embryo at least, the phenomenon of authority. "Authority" may be defined as the power to make decisions which guide the actions of another. It is a relationship between two individuals, one "superior," the other "subordinate." The superior frames and transmits decisions with the expectation that they will be accepted by the subordinate. The subordinate expects such decisions, and his conduct is determined by them.[2]

The relationship of authority can be defined, therefore, in purely objective and behavioristic terms. It involves behaviors on the part of both superior and subordinate. When, and only when, these behaviors occur does a relation of authority exist between the two persons involved. When the behaviors do not occur there is no authority, whatever may be the "paper" theory of organization.

The behavior pattern of the superior involves a command— an imperative statement concerning the choice of a behavior alter-

[2] For other descriptions of authority see L. D. White, *Introduction to the Study of Public Administration* (New York: Macmillan Company, 1939), pp. 44–46, and C. I. Barnard, *The Functions of the Executive*, p. 163.

native by the other—and an expectation that the command will be accepted by the other as a criterion of choice.[3]

The behavior pattern of the subordinate is governed by a single indeterminate decision, or criterion for decision, to "follow that behavior alternative which is selected for me by the superior." That is, he holds in abeyance his own critical faculties for choosing between alternatives and uses the formal criterion of the receipt of a command or signal as his basis for choice.[4]

Now since the relation of authority involves a particular criterion of choice as the basis for the subordinate's behavior, it is clear that two persons may stand in a relation of authority at one moment and not at the next. For the subordinate's behavior may be governed at the first moment by a command, and not at the next. Nor does it follow that when two persons recognize each other as "superior" and "subordinate" respectively, all the verbalizations of the first which affect the behaviors of the second are "commands." The willingness of the subordinate to accept a command, *if given,* does not imply that all, or even most, of his behavior choices are governed by commands.

It is necessary to distinguish, therefore, between specific behaviors which are momentary instances of the exercise of authority, and the roles played by two persons over a period of time which involve an *expectation of obedience* by the one and a *willingness to obey* by the other.

Distinction Between Influence and Authority

The relation of authority by no means comprehends all situations where the verbalizations of one person influence the behavior of another. The verbs "persuade," "suggest," etc., describe several kinds of influence which do not necessarily involve any relationship of authority. The characteristic which distinguishes authority from other kinds of influence is one already mentioned above, namely, that a subordinate holds in abeyance his own critical faculties for choosing between alternatives and uses the formal

[3] This idea was central to the utilitarian concept of the state. See, for example, Jeremy Bentham, *A Fragment on Government* (Oxford: Clarendon Press).
[4] Cf. Ordway Tead, *Human Nature and Management* (New York: McGraw-Hill, 1929), p. 149, and Stene, *op. cit.,* p. 1131.

criterion of the receipt of a command or signal as his basis for choice. On the other hand, a person who receives a suggestion accepts it as only one of the evidential bases for making his choice —but the choice he will make depends upon conviction. Persuasion, too, centers around the reasons for or against a course of action. Persuasion and suggestion result in a change in the evidential environment of choice which may, but need not, lead to conviction. Obedience, on the other hand, is an abdication of choice.

Confusion among these terms results from the fact that all three phenomena—persuasion, suggestion, and command—are frequently present in a single situation. Even where a behavior can be secured by the exercise of authority, a superior often and perhaps usually prefers to employ suggestion or persuasion. Some reasons for this will be discussed presently. But confusion will be avoided if it is remembered—as has been pointed out already—that the mere fact that two persons accept the roles of superior and subordinate does not imply that all, or even most, of their behaviors will be instances of the exercise of authority.

The line of demarcation between suggestion and command is perhaps not so clear as would be suggested by this discussion, however. Certain subtleties are concealed in the term "conviction," which was used as the distinguishing criterion.

A conviction, as used in this connection, is a belief in a factual or value premise which is relevant to a particular decision. Belief in a factual proposition may be induced in a number of ways, one of which is *proof*.

But we are convinced of a great number of things which never have been proved to us logically or empirically. Most persons in this country would agree that the atom bomb has been invented, though they would be hard put to demonstrate this either by pure logic or by the evidence of the senses. Likewise, few persons before taking prescribed medicines ask their physicians for a demonstration of the curative properties of the prescription.

In other words, conviction often results from the social transmission of factual statements, even in the absence of proof. So, a secretary who has been instructed by her employer to investigate a particular question of office procedure may report: "I have looked into the problem, and suggest that you act in this manner." This suggestion may be accepted without any review of its evidential basis by the employer, merely on the strength of his confidence in the secretary. Here is evident the same relaxation of critical faculties that we have said was characteristic of the relation of authority.

Statements, then, may convince without proving by virtue of the status or position of the person making the statement. An individual who does not have a recognized status, or who is not recognized by his associates as expert with respect to a certain kind of knowledge will have a more difficult time convincing his listeners that a recommendation is sound than one who possesses the credentials of "expertness." Recommendations are judged partly on their merits, but partly on the merits of the persons making the recommendations. This is true both because the individuals acting upon the recommendations often do not have the expertise needed to judge them, and because pressure of time requires them to accept the recommendations of those whom they trust. This is an important reason for the resistance that is usually experienced in any organization to suggestions that are made outside the line of duty, or that are volunteered through other than the usual lines of communication.

It should not be implied that this resistance to "irregular" suggestions is entirely a weakness of organization. The specialization of decision-making functions, and the fixing of responsibility for particular kinds of expertness upon particular individuals is an important source of organizational efficiency that must be balanced against the potential loss of independent ideas which results.

At the expense of a possible abuse of the term, we shall use "authority" broadly, and comprehend under it all situations where suggestions are accepted without any critical review or consideration. If this definition is accepted, it follows that when A is superior to B at one moment, B may act as superior to A at the next moment. What is meant, then, when A is described as *the* superior of B?

Authority and the "Last Word"

In the situations that have been discussed, a subordinate accepts commands in the absence of a determinate choice of his own. But a subordinate may also accept commands in opposition to a determinate choice of his own. In such a case, the element of authority in the behavior pattern is unequivocal. When there is a disagreement between two persons, and when the disagreement is not resolved by discussion, persuasion, or other means of conviction, then it must be decided by the authority of one or the other participant. It is this "right to the last word" which is usually meant in speaking of "lines of authority" in an administrative organization. Too often, however, the element of disagreement in obedience is overemphasized at the expense of the other elements of the situation. The term "authority" would be too narrowly employed if it were restricted to such instances of disagreement.

A final complication must be added to the notion of authority. If authority were evidenced entirely in the acceptance of explicit commands, or in the resolution of disagreements, its presence or absence in any relationship could be sought in the presence or absence of these tangible concomitants. But it is equally possible for obedience to anticipate commands. The subordinate may, and is expected to, ask himself "How would my superior wish me to behave under these circumstances?" Under such circumstances, authority is implemented by a subsequent review of completed actions, rather than a prior command. Further, the more obedient the subordinate, the less tangible will be the evidences of authority. For authority will need to be exercised only to reverse an incorrect decision.

This phenomenon has been pointed out by Friedrich,[5] who calls it a "rule of anticipated reactions." It affords a striking example of the manner in which expectations and anticipations govern hu-

[5] C. J. Friedrich, *op. cit.*, p. 16. Cf. Bentham's very interesting definition: "A tacit *expression of will* is that which is conveyed by any other signs than words whatsoever; among which none are so efficacious as acts of punishment annexed in times past, to the non-performance of acts of the same sort with those that are the objects of the will that is in question" (*A Fragment on Government*, p. 138).

man behavior, and the difficulties which result from this for the analysis of human institutions. The difficulty in determining authority relations because of the operation of the rule of anticipated reactions is common to all "power" situations. Any study, for instance, of a governor's veto power must take into consideration what bills failed of passage in the legislature because of the anticipation of veto, and what bills were passed for the very same reason.[6]

Any study of power relations which confines itself to instances where the sanctions of power were invoked misses the essential fact of the situation. To avoid this fallacy, authority has been defined in this study not in terms of the sanctions of the superior, but in terms of the behaviors of the subordinate.

The Sanctions of Authority

Having decided, tentatively at least, what authority is, we must examine the circumstances surrounding its exercise. Why and to what extent will a subordinate accept the decisions of another as governing his own conduct?

The superior-subordinate relationship is one of many possible examples of the role-taking which characterizes broad areas of human conduct. Perhaps the most important basis for such role-taking is custom. That is, a great deal of conduct requires no further explanation than that, under the circumstances, it is the socially "expected" conduct. For the reasons why particular conduct is dictated by custom it would be necessary to study the social history of the society in question.[7]

The "institutions" of a society may be regarded as rules specifying the roles that particular persons will assume in relation to one another under certain circumstances. The range of possible roles and possible behaviors is as broad as the ingenuity of man for dramatic invention.[8]

One of the socially determined roles in many societies is that

[6] Leslie Lipson, *The American Governor: From Figurehead to Executive* (Chicago: University of Chicago Press, 1939), pp. 210–212.
[7] This is, of course, a central problem of sociology and social psychology.
[8] For a further discussion of this problem, see Charner M. Perry, "The Relation Between Ethics and Political Science," *International Journal of Ethics,* 47:169–170, 172–174 (Jan., 1937).

of "employee." The particular content of the role—the degree of obedience expected—will vary with the social situation. The American workingman today, for example, probably has a somewhat narrower zone of acceptance, so far as the employer's instructions are concerned, than his father had. In part this may be due to his stronger bargaining position, or conversely, the weaker sanctions of the employer; but there is probably also present here a more fundamental change in social attitudes as to what it is "proper" for an employer to ask an employee to do. This changed attitude is reflected also in social legislation limiting the terms of the employment contract.

There are wide differences, too, among different types of employees in their expectations of the authority relations in their positions. Professional men and skilled workmen are apt to have relatively narrow zones of acceptance, particularly in the areas of their own professional competences or skills.

No attempt will be made here to explain the genesis of these social attitudes that establish an expectation of obedience in certain situations, nor their dependence upon and relation to other attitude clusters in the society. There has been much speculation that the central attitudes of a society must be reflected in administrative organization, so that administration in a democracy will be in some sense "democratic" while administration in a totalitarian system will be "authoritarian." Thus far, the thesis has been expounded, but by no means demonstrated.

There are a number of other, more specific, factors which induce acceptance of authority in organization. In a broad sense they might be called "sanctions," although that word is usually confined to the stimuli which act through punishment, while some of the factors listed below are more properly classified as rewards.

(1) The social sanctions are the first to be noted, and perhaps the most important. Not only does society set up in the individual expectations of obedience in certain social situations, but the individual who fails to accept his role will feel, in one way or another, the social disapprobation of his fellows. Insubordination can be as embarrassing, under these circumstances, as failure to wear a necktie to church.

On the other hand, in so far as fellow employees may receive vicarious satisfaction when an individual "tells off" the boss, social sanctions may operate to decrease the effectiveness of authority. The extent to which group attitudes of acceptance or resistance will condition the individual's reactions to authority has been much emphasized in the Hawthorne studies.[9]

(2) Psychological differences between individuals may play an important part in enforcing such relations. Though the study of leadership is in a very primitive stage, there are some indications that there may be certain personality types that lead, and others that follow.[10]

(3) Purpose has been stressed by students of administration as a sanction of prime importance. As already pointed out in Chapter VI, in voluntary organizations efforts are contributed largely because the contributor is sympathetic to the purpose of the organization. He is willing to obey commands because he realizes that the coordination secured thereby is useful to the attainment of the joint purpose.[11]

Several conditions must be satisfied if purpose is to be an effective sanction of authority. The subordinate must have confidence that the command is issued in furtherance of a purpose with which he is in sympathy. Second, he must have confidence that the command will be effective in achieving this purpose. This confidence may be based less on his own knowledge of the correctness of the command (as a matter of fact, such acceptance would fall outside our definition of authority) than on his faith in the ability of those who issued the command, his recognition that they have information he does not have, and his realization that his efforts and those of fellow workers will be ineffective in reaching the desired objective without some coordination from above. Within limits, he will even accept commands he knows to be incorrect because he

[9] See, for example, F. J. Roethlisberger and W. J. Dickson, *Management and the Worker* (Cambridge: Harvard University Press, 1939).
[10] Charles E. Merriam, *Political Power* (New York: McGraw-Hill Book Co., 1934), pp. 24–46, and Harold D. Lasswell, *Psychopathology and Politics*, pp. 38–64, 78–152.
[11] C. I. Barnard, *op. cit.*, pp. 165–166, and Luther Gulick, "Notes on the Theory of Organization," in Gulick and Urwick, eds., *op. cit.*, pp. 37–38.

does not wish to challenge or unsettle a system of authority that he believes to be beneficial to his aims in the long run.

(4) More formal sanctions in our society are based on the relation between the "job" and economic security and status. Thus, obedience may be the price of retaining the position, securing a higher salary or other advantages. The facts that most organizations will tolerate large quantities of insubordination—particularly if it is not verbalized—without dismissal, and that many organization members are not desirous of promotion, diminish the importance of these sanctions as means for securing acceptance of authority in the day-by-day work of an organization.

(5) Particularly in the case of individuals not much affected by influences in the third and fourth categories, simple unwillingness or disinclination to accept responsibility may be a major reason for the acceptance of decisions made by others. If the assigned task is not unduly unpleasant, many individuals would prefer being told what to do to being forced to make the decisions themselves. As a matter of fact, this is probably characteristic of most individuals when the decision in question lies outside the area of their experience and competence. The psychological roots of this lie deeper than a mere fear of the consequences which may be forthcoming in case of an incorrect decision, and there is great variability among individuals in this characteristic.

The Limits of Authority

The most striking characteristic of the "subordinate" role is that it establishes an area of acceptance [12] in behavior within which the subordinate is willing to accept the decisions made for him by his superior. His choice is then determined, always within the area of acceptance, by his superior, and the relation of superior-subordinate holds only within this area. Acceptance may be due to any of the influences discussed in the previous section, and may take place when the subordinate does not care which alternative is selected, or

[12] This concept is adopted from Barnard (*op. cit.*, pp. 168–169), who, however, does not develop to any great extent the positive significance of what he calls the "zone of indifference."

when the sanctions are sufficiently strong to induce him to carry out an undesired alternative.

The magnitude of the area is influenced by a large number of circumstances. A voluntary organization with poorly defined objectives has perhaps the narrowest range of acceptance.[13] An army, where the sanctions as well as the customs are of extreme severity, has the broadest area of acceptance.[14]

Restraint of the superior is as important as obedience of the subordinate in maintaining the relationship. Modern writers on administration have emphasized the need for restraint by recommending the use when possible of other means of influence, leading to conviction, rather than authority, leading often to nothing more than acquiescence.

The corresponding limitations of political authority have been discussed by Professor Charles E. Merriam.[15] Theoreticians of history have often questioned the extent to which "leaders" really lead. How broad is the area of indifference within which a group will continue to follow its leadership? In a very real sense, the leader, or the superior, is merely a bus driver whose passengers will leave him unless he takes them in the direction they wish to go. They leave him only minor discretion as to the road to be followed.

THE USES OF AUTHORITY

Authority has been described as a relation that secures coordinated behavior in a group by subordinating the decisions of the individual to the communicated decisions of others. Thus, the exercise of authority in a group makes possible a large degree of separation of the decision-making processes from actual performance, or what might be called vertical "specialization" in decision-making.

Just as a steersman may permit his moment-to-moment decisions to be controlled by a course laid out beforehand on the map, so a member of an organization submits his behavior to the control of

[13] *Ibid.,* p. 155.
[14] Military literature shows a clear recognition of the importance of the area of acceptance as a fundamental element in tactics. Cf. Col. J. F. C. Fuller's graphic description of the psychology of battle (*op. cit.,* pp. 140–141).
[15] See the chapter "The Poverty of Power" in his *Political Power* (pp. 156–183).

the decision-making portion of the organization. In the first case, the coordination takes place in the behavior of a single individual over a period of time. In the second case, the coordination takes place in the behavior of a number of individuals, over a short or long period of time. The principle involved in both cases is the same: the subordination of specific to general decisions.

Vertical specialization, or specialization in decision-making, is possible, of course, without the use of authority. A unit may be given a purely advisory or "staff" status in an organization, and yet, through its recommendations, actually make decisions that are accepted elsewhere in the organization. However, in so far as the recommendations of a staff agency are accepted without reexamination on their merits, the agency is really exercising authority, as we have defined that term; and it would be difficult to cite examples from organization where an effective specialization of the decision-making process exists without the exercise of at least some authority to maintain it.

The wide employment of authority as a tool for coordination of group activity reflects the important uses to which this tool may be put. Three functions of authority deserve special notice:

(1) It enforces responsibility of the individual to those who wield the authority;
(2) It secures expertise in the making of decisions;
(3) It permits coordination of activity.

Responsibility

Writers on the political and legal aspects of authority have emphasized that its function is to enforce the conformity of the individual to norms laid down by the group, or by its authority-wielding members.[16] The enactments of a legislature, for instance, are accepted as authoritative not only by the administrative hierarchy employed by the state, but by all the persons subject to its jurisdiction. When disobedience occurs, an elaborate set of sanctions may be invoked and applied against the recalcitrant member. The central

[16] Charles E. Merriam, *Political Power*, p. 16, and *History of the Theory of Sovereignty Since Rousseau* (New York: Columbia University Press, 1900); C. J. Friedrich, *Responsible Bureaucracy* (Cambridge: Harvard University Press, 1932), pp. 20–24.

core of many of the most important social institutions consists of a system of authority, and a set of sanctions for enforcing it. The state itself is the primary example, but the law of property, the church, and even the family also fall in this category.[17]

This aspect of authority is of considerable importance for our own discussion. The notion of an administrative hierarchy in a democratic state would be unthinkable without the corresponding notion of a mechanism whereby that hierarchy is held to account.[18] The question of responsibility must be a central issue in any discussion of the relation between administrative and legislative bodies, or in any analysis of administrative law.

When authority is employed to enforce responsibility, sanctions will probably play an important part in the process; and this accounts for the attention which is usually given to the subject of sanctions in discussions of authority. Even in this connection, the importance of sanctions should not be overemphasized, however. The person who accepts the authority of a legislature, a property holder, or a father within a particular institutional setting, is probably motivated much more by socially indoctrinated ethical notions than by the fear of sanctions. That is, the individual in a particular society believes that he *ought* to obey the laws adopted by the constituted authorities and that he *ought* to recognize property rights. To explain away the whole system of authority and responsibility in terms of sanctions is to oversimplify the situation.

Expertise

An extremely important function of authority is to secure decisions of a high quality of rationality and effectiveness. It has long

[17] For an interpretation of "property" in terms of power and decision, see John R. Commons, *Institutional Economics* (New York: Macmillan Co., 1934), pp. 397–401; Morris R. Cohen, *Law and the Social Order* (New York: Harcourt, Brace & Co., 1933), pp. 44–45; and Albert Kocourek, *Jural Relations* (Indianapolis: Bobbs-Merrill Co., 1927), pp. 305–334.

[18] For variant notions as to the form this responsibility should take, see John M. Gaus, "The Responsibility of Public Administration," in *The Frontiers of Public Administration*, ed. Gaus, White, and Dimock (Chicago: University of Chicago Press, 1936), pp. 26–44; C. J. Friedrich, *Responsible Bureaucracy;* C. J. Friedrich, "Public Policy and the Nature of Administrative Responsibility," in *Public Policy, 1940* (Cambridge: Harvard University Press, 1940), pp. 3–24; Herman Finer, "Administrative Responsibility in Democratic Government," *Public Administration Review*, 1:335–350 (Summer, 1941).

been recognized that specialization is of fundamental importance to administrative efficiency, and it is hardly necessary to repeat here the stock examples which show how specialization may increase productivity.[19] These advantages of specialization are quite as important when the specialization concerns the process of "deciding" as when it concerns the processes of "doing."

The city manager of a small community is a jack-of-all-trades: he must have the skills of an engineer, accountant, executive, foreman, bill collector, and mechanic. He is also an intellectual jack-of-all-trades: he must, by himself, make almost all the decisions that guide his activities and those of his few subordinates during the working day; he must decide when to repair a street, or build a sewer; he must anticipate his equipment and personnel needs, purchase the equipment, and hire employees; he must decide what policing is needed, and what health services.

The administrator of a large city's governmental organization is in a very different situation. If his staff is large enough, he may hire an engineer to direct public-works activities, and to make the technical decisions in that area. He may have one or more personnel specialists and a purchasing agent. Foremen will exercise actual supervision over working crews. Every decision for the city's operation will receive relatively specialized and expert consideration.

To gain the advantages of specialized skill in a large organization, the work of the organization is subdivided, so far as possible, in such a way that all processes requiring a particular skill can be performed by persons possessing that skill. Likewise, to gain the advantages of expertise in decision-making, the responsibility for decisions is allocated, so far as possible, in such a way that decisions requiring particular knowledge or skill will rest with individuals possessing that knowledge or skill. This involves a subdivision of the decisions governing the organization into numerous component decisions, and a restriction of the activities of each member of the organization to a very few of these components.

A fundamental device for securing expertise in organization de-

[19] L. Gulick, "Notes on the Theory of Organization," in Gulick and Urwick, *op. cit.*, pp. 3–4.

cisions is to locate the expert in a strategic position in the formal hierarchy of authority—that is, in a position where his decisions will be accepted as decisional premises by the other organizational members. This is a major advantage of organization by "process." When all activities to which engineering decisions are relevant are organized in a single department, then it is easy to allocate the function of decision in such a way as to secure the necessary technical competence.[20]

So long as the communication of decisions is restricted to the formal hierarchy of authority, however, it is not possible to secure the several kinds of technical assistance that are often needed for a single decision. A small school department, for instance, may lack the technical medical facilities for making decisions with regard to its school health services, or the engineering advice needed in the maintenance of the school plant.

To secure all the advantages, therefore, of expertise in decision-making, it is necessary to go beyond the formal structure of authority. The "authority of ideas" must gain an importance in the organization coordinate with the "authority of sanctions."

The emphasis in this discussion has thus far been on the *technical* knowledge needed for decisions. Expertise may apply to other types of information as well. Modern police departments in large cities have central dispatching rooms which receive information, by telephone or otherwise, of incidents requiring police attention, and which assign policemen by radio, to investigate these incidents. The importance which the dispatching rooms have for the process of decision (in this case the assignment of policemen) lies in their strategic location with respect to relevant incoming information. Again, the formal structure of authority may play only a small part in this process, and may actually, except in cases of disagreement, be disregarded by the lines of communication.

In the organizational hierarchy, the superior ordinarily enjoys, by virtue of his position, the same advantage of information over his subordinate. The extent to which this advantage is real, and the extent to which it is mythical, may depend in large part upon

[20] Cf. Frederick W. Taylor, *The Principles of Scientific Management* (New York: Harper & Bros., 1911), pp. 99–113.

the design of the lines of communication in the organization. The superior who possesses such advantages of information will have much less occasion to invoke the formal sanctions of authority than the superior whose subordinates are in a better situation than he, from the standpoint of information, to make the decision.

Coordination

The third function of authority, to secure coordination, was discussed at some length in the earlier sections of this chapter. Coordination should be clearly distinguished from expertise. Expertise involves the adoption of a *good* decision. Coordination is aimed at the adoption by all the members of the group of the *same* decision, or more precisely of mutually consistent decisions in combination attaining the established goal.

Suppose ten persons decide to cooperate in building a boat. If each has his own plan, and they don't bother to communicate their plans, it is doubtful that the resulting craft will be very seaworthy. They would probably have better success if they adopted even a very mediocre design, and then all followed this same design.

In the first portion of the Waterloo campaign, Napoleon's army was divided in two parts. The right wing, commanded by the Emperor himself, faced Blücher at Ligny; the left wing, under Marshal Ney, faced Wellington at Quatre Bras. Both Ney and the Emperor prepared to attack, and both had prepared excellent plans for their respective operations. Unfortunately, both plans contemplated the use of Erlon's corps to deliver the final blow on the flank of the enemy. Because they failed to communicate these plans, and because orders were unclear on the day of the battle, Erlon's corps spent the day marching back and forth between the two fields without engaging in the action on either. Somewhat less brilliant tactical plans, coordinated, would have had greater success.

By the exercise of authority, it is possible to centralize the function of deciding, so that a general plan of operations will govern the activities of all members of the organization. Again, this procedure is analogous to the process whereby an individual plans his own activities over an extended period of time.

Coordination may be exercised in both a procedural and a substantive sense. By procedural coordination is meant the specification of the organization itself—that is, the generalized description of the behaviors and relationships of the members of the organization. Procedural coordination establishes the lines of authority, and outlines the sphere of activity and authority of each member of the organization.

Substantive coordination is concerned with the *content* of the organization's activities. In an automobile factory, an organization chart is an aspect of procedural coordination, while blueprints for the engine block of the car being manufactured are an aspect of substantive coordination.

UNITY OF COMMAND

In Chapter II some remarks were made on the inadequacy of the doctrine of unity of command, as that doctrine is usually stated. It was pointed out there that, in a trivial sense, unity of command is always achieved, for if a subordinate is instructed to base a decision on two conflicting premises he will obviously be able to accept only one of them, and has to disregard the other. Hence, when unity of command is urged, this cannot be all that is meant.

As was also explained in Chapter II, unity of command is usually taken to mean that any one individual in an administrative organization will accept the authority of only one other person in the organization. The validity of this principle as a part of sound organization procedure was criticized on the ground that it does not give any reason why an individual cannot accept certain decisional premises from one superior and other non-conflicting premises from another. He may, for example, accept the authority of a "line" superior in determining the program of his unit, while he accepts the authority of the accounting department as to what financial records he shall keep. Or, to use the example of Taylor's "functional foremanship," he may accept the instructions of one foreman as to the speed of his lathe, and those of another foreman as to its proper maintenance.

Perhaps the purpose that is to be served by establishing unity of command will be better understood if the results which such unity is supposed to bring about are examined. It is certainly undesirable for the organization that the subordinate who receives conflicting commands relating to the *same* decisional premise should be either punished for not carrying out both commands, or placed in a position where he may carry out either command that he prefers. In the first case the subordinate will be demoralized by the impossible situation in which he is placed; in the second case he will retain his original discretion, hence will not be subject to any real authority. Moreover the superior, unless he can hold the subordinate responsible for carrying out instructions, cannot himself be held responsible for results. There is no question that these difficulties are real and fundamental; the only issue is whether unity of command is the sole or best solution.

On the contrary, there would seem to be at least four methods in common use for preventing or resolving conflicts in authority:

1. Unity of command in the traditional sense—each individual receives orders from one and only one superior.

2. Unity of command in the narrower sense defined in Chapter II —an individual may receive orders from several superiors, but in case of a conflict there is one and only one whom he is supposed to obey.

3. Division of authority—each unit in the organization is assigned some specific area over which it has exclusive authority, and the decisional premises of any individual that fall within this area are subject to that authority.

4. A system of rank—an individual is subject to the authority of all other individuals of a certain rank. If he receives conflicting orders, he follows the last one received, but is bound to bring the conflict to the attention of the person issuing the order. Authority relations between commissioned officers and men in the Army and Navy follow this general procedure.

These procedures, particularly the second, third, and fourth, are not necessarily mutually exclusive, and may be used in combination in a single organization.

The Hierarchy of Authority

The arrangement of the organization members in a hierarchy or pyramid of command affords the basis for either the first or the second method of avoiding conflicts in authority. Consistent adherence to such an arrangement either prevents the issuance of conflicting commands to a subordinate by different supervisors, or, if two individuals on the same level of the pyramid happen to work at cross purposes, automatically terminates the conflict between them by submitting it to the decision of a common superior in the hierarchy. The administrative hierarchy, therefore, provides a determinate procedure that decides who is to decide.

In actual practice, the hierarchy of authority usually represents a compromise between the two theories of unity of command listed above; that is, the lines of authority in the hierarchy provide the normal (but almost never the exclusive) channels for the transmission of commands and orders, and when overlapping of orders does occur the hierarchy is referred to in resolving the conflict.

Division of Authority

The hierarchy of authority might be described as a division of authority according to persons—each individual is assigned authority (exclusive authority, if the first theory is followed) over a specified group of subordinates. It is equally possible to divide authority according to subject matter—each individual is assigned authority over some specified aspect of the organization's work. In the literature this is often termed a "functional" allocation of authority.

Authority over subject matter is allocated by the issuance of authoritative communications—instructions, duties manuals, and the like—delineating the area within which each member of the group is to confine his activities, and within which the decisions of each member are to have an authoritative character in the group. Instead of deciding, in each particular case of conflict, what decisions are to be obeyed and what decisions are not, a general rule is laid down beforehand, granting each member of the group a certain sphere of decision within which he is to have authority.

If the work of members of the group were carried on in mutual isolation, there would be no need of a division of authority, beyond the establishment of the hierarchy. Normally, however, the manner in which each member of the group performs his work closely affects the work of each other member. The slowdown of one man on the assembly line may disrupt the entire line. The delay of a purchasing agent may affect a construction gang. A backlog on a reviewing officer's desk may hold up correspondence.

Even where there is a hierarchy of authority, then, it is usually necessary to divide the organization also along functional, or subject-matter, lines. There are two criteria for measuring the success of an allocation of authority: (1) the extent to which it aids or hinders the work of the group, and (2) the extent to which it minimizes jurisdictional disputes. The two criteria do not necessarily coincide. For instance, a division of authority in an automobile plant on the basis of the place of residence of the buyer of each car would probably be univocal, but would hardly facilitate the process of manufacture. To be successful, the division of authority must be adapted to the division of work—that is, to the technology of the work process.

Even under the best conditions, cases will occur where jurisdiction is doubtful. This is especially probable where two portions of the organization are organized on diverse principles: line and auxiliary, functional and geographical. In such cases, the need reappears for an appellate process to settle the dispute. The hierarchy of authority may be used for this purpose, or special appellate agencies may be used.

Where a formal division of authority on a subject-matter basis exists, however, a dispute is settled on a somewhat different basis from that in a simple hierarchy, where it is referred to a common superior—even though the process may be the same. When there is no division of authority, each separate dispute is submitted to the superior and is decided by him on its merits. Where there is a division of authority, the issue to be decided is not the specific question in dispute so much as the question of jurisdiction.

In the latter process, which we may call "adjudication," the superior must concern himself not so much with the content of the decision or its expediency, as with its "legality"—that is, the competence of the decider, in terms of the formal organizational structure. Without this division of authority, the superior would be concerned principally with the merits of the specific case.

For example, there may be a disagreement between a purchasing agent and a line officer as to the specifications for stationery. The line officer may wish one brand and quality, the purchasing agent may insist on delivering another to him. If this were merely a question of a hierarchy of authority, the common superior to these two men would be faced with the question of which type of paper was more desirable for the contemplated use.

In an organization with formal allocations of authority, the question would not be submitted to the superior in this form. Instead, each subordinate would claim that decisions specifying the quality of paper lay within *his* sphere of authority. Instead of deciding which paper was best, the superior would be forced to decide *which officer should decide which paper was best*. Instead of a question of technology, he would be faced with a *question of administration*.

In practice, of course, the issue is seldom decided on such a clearcut basis. The administrative superior will generally inquire both into questions of authority and into the merits of the case. Considerations of expediency influence him more when jurisdictional lines are vague than when the allocation of authority is clear. On the other hand, in order to maintain the lines of authority and the division of work in his organization, he must often support a particular decision because it lay within the sphere of authority of the decider rather than because it was the correct decision.

Even with these qualifications the illustration just given is a grave oversimplification of the actual problem, for it gives consideration only to the maintenance of the authority relation. In practice, when a conflict of authority is appealed to an administrator he must take into consideration (1) the effect his decision will have on the lines of authority, (2) the effect it will have upon organization policy, and (3) the information the conflict gives him with respect to the soundness and competence of his subordinates. The first point has already been discussed.

With respect to the second point, it is probably true that the administrator will be inclined to look into the merits of the dispute rather than to decide it on jurisdictional grounds, if it is an important question of organizational policy. As a matter of fact, jurisdictional disputes are an important means of bringing to the top administrator significant issues of policy, and of preventing these from being decided at lower levels without his knowledge. Similarly (this bears on the third point), they are a means of informing him about the characteristics and viewpoints of his subordinates. Particularly when policy in the organization is in its formative stages, there may be important advantages, therefore, to the top administrator in a somewhat indefinite allocation of authority that would permit such disputes to arise. Certainly the technique of "playing one against the other" is used by top administrators so often that it cannot be casually dismissed as poor administration.

If the administrator uses this technique of maintaining control over the decisions of his subordinates, he is faced with the very delicate tasks of preventing organizational and jurisdictional lines from dissolving completely, and of preventing the differences among subordinates which he adjudicates from degenerating into personal quarrels or feuds among subunits of the organization for power and influence. Regardless of these dangers, to avoid the use of such methods may lead to virtual abdication.

Rank

Rank, as a basis for authority relations, is always employed in connection with a hierarchy of authority. In military organizations, and some others, it is absolutely necessary to provide a continuity of authority, and a certainty in authority relations at all times. This is accomplished by the system of rank. When emergency, death, or absence of an officer temporarily disrupts the normal organizational pattern, rank is used to reestablish a system of authority.

This device, too, creates administrative complexities. An enlisted man, on a mission for one office, may be given conflicting instructions by another officer. The only safeguard here is the restraint of each officer, and his knowledge that he will be held to an accounting for a disruption of the administrative organization through the abuse of his authority.

The Application of Sanctions

It may be well to repeat at this point that authority, as the term is used in this volume, refers to the *acceptance* by the subordinate of the decisions of the superior and not the power of the superior to apply sanctions in case of noncompliance. In most present-day organizations an employee's immediate superior does not possess the unregulated power of hiring and firing, although, regardless of whether there is a formal service rating scheme, that superior's estimate of him will probably be a major factor in determining his chances of promotions, pay increases, and the like.

As the power of the immediate superior to impose sanctions is circumscribed, he must rely more and more on other more positive incentives to enforce his authority. On the other hand those who have the power to apply sanctions will, by their use of this power, either reinforce or weaken the lines of authority that have been established. Inability to discipline, either directly or by appeal to his superiors, a subordinate who is disloyal will rapidly destroy the authority of any individual in the administrative hierarchy.

Hence, when the power to discipline rests with the immediate superior, the system of authority in the organization will generally take on and retain rather definite hierarchical structure. Each individual will know who the "boss" is. It may be conjectured that under these conditions those individuals who, according to the plan of organization, exercise zoned "functional" authority without disciplinary powers will take on more nearly an advisory than an authoritative role.

It will be noticed that, regardless of whether the power to apply sanctions is distributed throughout the administrative hierarchy or is concentrated in the higher levels of that hierarchy, "unity of command" will generally be observed to the extent that a given individual will not be subjected to sanctions from two independent sources. This is a distinct, and narrower, concept of unity of command than the two stated previously, for it refers not to the right to issue orders, but to the power to impose sanctions for noncompliance with orders.

Concluding Comments

This volume is primarily a work of description rather than prescription. No attempt will be made to state definite principles as to the proper use of these several devices for the allocation of authority, but some tentative comments may be offered. Virtually no organization attempts to get along without some sort of hierarchy of authority. Some organizations operate on the theory that this hierarchy defines the sole channels of authority, others on the theory that the hierarchy is to be reverted to only in case of conflicts of authority. Whatever the theory, the practice almost always represents some compromise between these two.

In almost all organizations, authority is also zoned by subject matter; and the subject-matter allocation will sometimes conflict with the hierarchical allocation. In these cases the hierarchy is used as a mechanism for resolving jurisdictional disputes. These disputes afford the top administrator an important source of information as to what is going on at lower levels, and he will not be inclined to try to eliminate them entirely, even if he could, by a watertight allocation of authority. The distribution of the power to apply sanctions, and the use of this power, will have a considerable influence on the sharpness of the lines of authority and on the relative importance of hierarchical and subject-matter authority.

In some organizations the hierarchy and the zoning of authority will need to be supplemented by a system of rank to prevent breaks in the continuity of command.

FORMAL AND INFORMAL ORGANIZATION

The manner in which authority is used to maintain coordination in organization has already been discussed. Procedural coordination—the specification of the lines of authority, and the spheres of activity and authority of each organization member—creates a *formal organization,* a set of abstract, more or less permanent relations that govern the behavior of each participant. It will be noticed that authority enters into the formal organization in two ways: first, the authority of those individuals who exercise control over the group is employed to establish and enforce the scheme of formal organization; second, the scheme of formal organization itself prescribes the lines of authority and division of work that shall be followed in carrying out the work of the organization.

To illustrate, Acts of Congress may set up a Department of Agriculture, specify the general departmental organization, and the responsibilities of the agency. The Secretary of Agriculture, deriving authority from this formal organization plan, may then himself create a formal structure *within* the department, dividing work, and further delegating his authority.

In addition to allocating zones of activity and establishing authority relationships, the scheme of formal organization may also establish procedures, and lines of communication. The body of regulations will establish who may employ or fire whom; who will give orders to whom; who is responsible for particular jobs; whose signature a particular type of decision must have; and so forth. For the most part, these relationships can be described rather abstractly, without reference to the particular content of the organization's work.

This formal scheme of organization will always differ from the organization as it actually operates in several important respects. First, there will be many omissions in it—the actual organization will exhibit many interpersonal relationships that are nowhere specified in the formal scheme. The vice president in charge of sales frequently plays golf with the comptroller, and on these occasions they discuss business problems. Second, the interpersonal relations in the organization as it operates may be in actual contradiction to the specifications. The operator of a lathe may refuse to accept his foreman's instructions as to the speed at which he should operate his machine on a particular job. The organization scheme may provide that Department A will be informed of certain decisions made in Department B, but this is not done.

The term "informal organization" refers to interpersonal relations in the organization that affect decisions within it but either are omitted from the formal scheme or are not consistent with that scheme. It would probably be fair to say that no formal organization will operate effectively without an accompanying informal organization. Every new organization must have its initial "shake-down cruise" before it will run smoothly; and each new organization member must establish informal relations with his colleagues before he becomes a significant part of the working organization.

Even if it were desirable, the formal structure could not be specified in such detail as to obviate the need for an informal supplement. On the other hand, the formal structure performs no function unless it actually sets limits to the informal relations that are permitted to develop within it. In particular, it is an important function of the formal organization to prevent the development of organization politics—struggle for influence and authority—to a point that would be deleterious to the functioning of the organization; and a further function to detect and eliminate unnecessary duplication and overlapping in the work of the parts of the organization. Perhaps a more positive function of the formal, in relation to the informal, structure is to encourage the development of the latter along constructive lines. That is, a proper allocation of duties and the maintenance of adequate channels of communication may both relieve the need for the growth of informal channels, and encourage cross-fertilization and attitudes of cooperation within the informal structure.

PSYCHOLOGY AND THE THEORY OF AUTHORITY

It is important to note that propositions about human behavior, *in so far as it is rational,* do not ordinarily involve propositions about the psychology of the person who is behaving. Let us explain this rather paradoxical statement. In a given situation, and with a given system of values, there is only one course of action which an individual can rationally pursue. It is that course which under the given circumstances maximizes the attainment of value. Hence, psychological propositions, other than descriptions of an individual's value system, are needed only to explain why his behavior, in any given instance, *departs* from the norm of rationality.

Likewise, propositions about the behavior of members of an organization, *in so far as that behavior is governed by the system of authority in the organization,* do not ordinarily involve propositions about the psychology of the person who is behaving. That is, in so far as a person is obedient to the decisions of another, his psychology has nothing to do with his behavior. Hence, psychological propositions are important for determining the area within which authority will be respected, but have no significance for determining what behavior will be *within this area.*

It should be added, of course, that in many cases it is very difficult for the superior to control the interpretation and application that is given his orders by the subordinate, and in so far as this is true the attitudes of the latter are of very considerable importance. Apart from actual insubordination, an order may be carried out intelligently or unintelligently, promptly or slowly, enthusiastically or grudgingly. The statement of the previous paragraph might be more cautiously restated : Psychological propositions are important for determining the area within which authority will be respected, and the degree to which the intent of the order-giver will actually be carried out; but in so far as the authority is actually accepted they have no significance for determining what the subordinate's behaviors will be.

For illustration let us consider the literature on military psychology. This literature is concerned with one central problem— how to enlarge the area within which the soldier, when faced with the dangers of battle and the hardships of campaign life, will obey his superiors.[21]

If the obedience of soldiers were perfect, then military operations would be limited only by the soldiers' physiological endurance —their marching endurance, and their vulnerability to the effects of bullets. A unit could fail in an attack only through the physical extermination of its members by the enemy, and the only data needed in planning operations would be statistical information on the effects of fire under different conditions.[22]

Actually, however, before a unit is exterminated, it will usually reach a point where its members will refuse obedience. They will

[21] Col. J. F. C. Fuller, *op. cit.,* pp. 140–141 ; Ardant du Picq, *Etudes sur le combat* (Paris : Hachette et Cie., 1880), pp. 7–8, and *passim.*
[22] In the recent war this was evidently nearly true of Japanese soldiers. If so, the limits of authority here were physiological rather than psychological.

refuse to advance when ordered to do so, or they will surrender to the enemy. The real limiting factors, then, in an attack, are the psychological factors which determine when the soldiers will refuse further obedience to commands. To be sure, behind disobedience or surrender will lie the fear of extermination, but the actual amount of destruction necessary before morale fails varies within wide limits under different circumstances.[23]

Psychology, then, enters into administration as a *condition*, just as physiological, physical, or other environmental factors may enter in. It is part of the technology of administration, rather than a part of the administrative theory itself.

SUMMARY

In this chapter the behavior of the organized group was explored with a view to isolating some of its salient characteristics. An individual acts as a member of a group when he applies the same general scale of values to his choices as do other members of the group, and when his expectations of the behavior of other members influence his own decisions.

In all but the simplest varieties of group behavior, definite procedures are adopted for securing coordination. A procedure is coordinative when it adapts the behavior of each individual to a plan for the group. In all cases, coordination requires communication of at least certain critical elements in the group situation to the members of the group.

When coordination goes farther than mere communication, when it deliberately influences the behavior of group members in desired directions, it ordinarily involves some measure of authority. Authority is exercised over an individual whenever that individual, relaxing his own critical faculties, permits the communicated decision of another person to guide his own choice.

Authority is only one of a number of forms of influence. Its distinguishing characteristic is that it does not seek to convince the subordinate, but only to obtain his acquiescence. In actual exercise,

[23] Col. Gen. von Balck, *Tactics,* trans. Walter Krueger (Fort Leavenworth, Kans.: U.S. Cavalry Association, 1911), pp. 185–200.

of course, authority is usually liberally admixed with suggestion and persuasion. An important function of authority is to permit a decision to be made and carried out, even when agreement cannot be reached. Perhaps this arbitrary aspect of authority has been overemphasized, however, in discussions of the concept. In any case, the arbitrary element in authority is limited to the "area of acceptance" of the subordinate.

The magnitude of the area of acceptance depends upon the sanctions which authority has available to enforce its commands. At least as important as the negative sanctions—physical and economic force—are community of purpose, social acceptance, and personality.

In administration the avoidance of contradictory authority-relations is sometimes an important problem. The problem is met by establishing a determinate hierarchy of authority, and by zoning authority along functional or other lines. It is seldom possible, however, to eliminate twilight zones within which conflicts of authority may occur. It is an important administrative task to maintain the organization structure by adjudicating "boundary disputes" with respect to authority.

Coordination is only one of the three functions which authority performs in administrative organization. Authority is also an important factor in the enforcement of responsibility, and in the specialization of decision-making.

The problem of responsibility, which has already been discussed at length in Chapter III, arises whenever it is desirable or necessary to enforce the adherence of the individual to the group plan. Sanctions play a more important part in the responsibility-enforcing function of authority than in its other uses.

The advantages which are obtained from the division and specialization of work may also be claimed for the division and specialization of the decision-making function. Authority, by permitting the decision reached by one member in an organization to influence the behavior of other members, makes possible the specialization of decision-making.

A formal organization is a plan for the division of work and the allocation of authority. The organization plan gives to each member of the group his status and role in relation to the other members, but it specifies the *content* of his work and his decisional function only in very general terms. It is to the substantive aspects of decision—the criteria of choice rather than the procedure of choice—that we must turn next.

Chapter VIII

COMMUNICATION

THE ROLE of communication in the influencing of decisions has been mentioned many times in the preceding pages and particularly in the last chapter. It is time now to examine more systematically this important aspect of the decisional process.

The first topic to be taken up will be the nature and functions of communication systems. This will be followed by a discussion of formal and informal channels of communication. A third section of the chapter will be devoted to those elements in an administrative organization which are specialized for the function of communication; while the final section will discuss the role of training in communication.

NATURE AND FUNCTIONS OF COMMUNICATION

Communication may be formally defined as any process whereby decisional premises are transmitted from one member of an organization to another. It is obvious that without communication there can be no organization, for there is no possibility then of the group influencing the behavior of the individual. Not only is communication absolutely essential to organization, but the availability of particular techniques of communication will in large part determine the way in which decision-making functions can and should be distributed throughout the organization. The possibility of permitting a particular individual to make a particular decision will often hinge on whether there can be transmitted to him the information he will need to make a wise decision, and whether he, in turn, will be able to transmit his decision to other members of the organization whose behavior it is supposed to influence.

Communication in organizations is a two-way process: it comprehends both the transmittal *to* a decisional center (i.e. an individual vested with the responsibility for making particular decisions) of orders, information, and advice; and the transmittal of the decisions reached *from* this center to other parts of the organization. Moreover, it is a process that takes place upward, downward, and laterally throughout the organization. The information and orders that flow downward through the formal channels of authority and the information that flows upward through these same channels are only a small part of the total network of communications in any actual organization.[1]

The information and knowledge that has a bearing on decisions arises at various points in the organization. Sometimes the organization has its own "sensory organs"—the intelligence unit of a military organization, or the market analysis section of a business firm. Sometimes individuals are recruited and installed in positions for the knowledge they are presumed already to possess—a legal division. Sometimes the knowledge develops on the job itself—the lathe operator is the first one to know when his machine breaks down. Sometimes the knowledge is knowledge of other decisions that have been made—the executive turns down one request for expenditure of funds because he knows that he has already committed these funds to another use.

In all these cases particular individuals in the organization are possessed of information that is relevant to particular decisions that have to be made. An apparently simple way to allocate the function of decision-making would be to assign to each member of the organization those decisions for which he possesses the relevant information. The basic difficulty in this is that not all the information relevant to a particular decision is possessed by a single individual. If the decision is then dismembered into its component premises and these allocated to separate individuals, a communication process must be set up for transmitting these components from the separate centers to some point where they can be combined and transmitted, in turn, to those members in the organization who will have to carry them out.

---

[1] Barnard's discussion of communications (*op. cit.* pp. 175–181) suffers somewhat from his identification of communication channels with channels of authority.

Only in the case where the man who is to carry out a decision is also the man best fitted to make that decision is there no problem of communication—and in this exceptional case there is of course no reason for organization. In all other cases means must be devised for transmitting information from its organizational sources to decisional centers, from centers where component decisions are made to centers where these are combined, and from the latter to the points in the organization where the decisions are to be carried out.

Military organization has developed especially elaborate procedures for accomplishing the gathering and transmittal of information. An important reason for this is that the information on which military decisions—particularly tactical decisions—depend is of a rapidly changing nature, ascertainable only at the moment of decision.

Military information is essential to the efficient preparation and execution of strategical and tactical plans. It constitutes a vital element in the commander's estimate of the situation and decision. Continuous research of information by all available means throughout the course of operations is necessary to the successful operations of all units . . .

Information collected by combat units in the field relates chiefly to the enemy forces with which they are in contact . . .

The necessary orientation is given to the research of information by the issuance of instructions to subordinate units indicating the points of greatest importance to the execution of the commander's plan of operations and to the security of the command. . . .

Each unit commander, in his own zone of operation, directs the research of information in accordance with instructions received, and in addition independently carries out such researches as are dictated by his special situation or required for the execution of the operation in which he is engaged.

The evaluation, collation, and analysis of military information is the duty of the intelligence division of the general staff of large units and of the intelligence agencies of brigades, regiments, and battalions . . .

Analysis of the information received leads to a more or less complete reconstruction of the enemy's situation and activities and frequently furnishes the best indication of his intentions.[2]

[2] *U.S. Army Field Service Regulations, 1923*, pp. 25–26.

The difficulties of transmission from sources of information to decision centers tend to draw the latter toward the former, while the difficulties of transmission from decision centers to points of action create a pull in the opposite direction. The task of properly locating decision centers is one of balancing these opposing pulls.

The pulls that tend to bring about a centralization of the decision-making functions and a consequent separation of decision from action have already been discussed from a slightly different viewpoint in the previous chapter. These pulls are the need for responsibility, expertise, and coordination. The two principal pulls in the opposite direction—that of decentralization—are, first, the fact that a very large portion of the information that is relevant to decisions originates at the operating level, and second, that the separation of decision from action increases the time and man-power costs of making and transmitting decisions.

FORMAL AND INFORMAL COMMUNICATION

The formal system of communications in any organization—those channels and media of communication which have been consciously and deliberately established—is soon supplemented by an equally important informal network of communications based on social relations within the organization. The relationship between the formal and the informal system is best understood through an examination of the media of communication.

Media of Formal Communication

The most obvious media of communication are the spoken word and memoranda and letters addressed from one member of an organization to another. A number of specialized written media need to be distinguished from the ordinary memorandum or letter. First, there is "paper flow"—the movement of a document from one point to another of an organization where it is successively processed. Next there are records and formal reports. Finally, there are manuals of organization practice and procedure.

Oral Communications. Only to a limited extent is any formal system of oral communications ordinarily established in the scheme of organization. To a certain degree the system of formal authority creates a presumption that oral communication will take place primarily between individuals and their immediate superiors or subordinates; but these are certainly never the exclusive channels of communication.

To a certain degree, also, the formal organization may place limits upon the ease with which upward communication takes place. Individuals at higher levels of the organization may be relatively inaccessible to all except their immediate subordinates. In military organizations, formal rules are developed to govern this matter of "accessibility"—the private speaks to the captain by permission of the sergeant—but in other organizations, even when the executive maintains an official "open door" policy, accessibility is regulated by informal social controls plus the device of a private secretary. In this case accessibility is really governed by the informal rather than the formal organization.

Physical propinquity may be a very real factor in determining the frequency of oral communication, and hence, the layout of offices is one of the important formal determinants of the communication system. Even the advent of the telephone has not very much diminished the importance of this factor, since a telephone conversation is by no means equivalent to a face-to-face contact.

Memoranda and Letters. The flow of memoranda and letters is more often subjected to formal control, particularly in large organizations, than is oral communication. In some organizations it is actually required that all written communications follow the lines of authority; but this is not common. Slightly more common is the requirement that communications skip not more than one link in the chain of authority. That is, if two individuals in different divisions of the same department wish to communicate, the communication must go to the first division head, from him to the second division head, and thence to the second individual, by-passing the head of the department.

In most organizations, however, no such strict requirements are imposed, except in the transmission of orders—a topic that has been covered in the previous chapter. "Clearance" rules are quite frequently established, however, that require copies of communications to be sent up the regular channels when the communication itself has cut across lines.

Paper-Flow. In certain cases—this is typical of organizations handling financial matters, like insurance companies, accounting departments, and Federal lending agencies—the organization's work, or some part of it, centers around the processing of a piece of paper. In a life insurance company, for example, applications are received, examined, accepted or rejected, policies issued, policyholders billed for premiums, premiums processed, and benefits paid. The file representing the individual policy is the focal center of the organization's work. This file is moved from one point in the organization to another for various types of action—reviewing the application, recording a change of beneficiary, approving payment of benefits, and so on. As it moves it carries with it all the information regarding that policy which is needed in taking the required administrative action. The individual at that point *to which* it is moved for a particular action presumably possesses the knowledge of company regulations that must be applied to the policy information in order to reach a decision as to its disposition. The file permits the combining of the information relating to the indivdual policyholder, which originates in the field, with the information relating to the company's practices and obligations, which originates in the central office. In this case the combining is accomplished by moving the information obtained in the field into the central office for decision through the flow of paper. In other situations this might be done by transmitting the central office information to the field through instructions, manuals, and the like.

Records and Reports. A vital part of the formal communications system of almost every organization is the system of records and reports. In the case of letters and memoranda, the individual initiating the communication must reach the decision that there is a need for transmission of certain information, and will decide what is to be transmitted. The distinguishing characteristic of records and reports is that they specify for the person who makes them out on what occasions he is expected to make reports (periodically or on the occurrence of a particular event or circumstance), and what information he is to include in them. This is highly important, for it largely relieves each organization member of the important but difficult task of continually deciding what part of the information he possesses should be passed on to other organization members, and in what form.

Manuals. The function of manuals is to communicate those organization practices which are intended to have relatively permanent application. In their absence, permanent policies will reside only in the minds of permanent organization members, and will soon cease to have any great influence upon practice. The preparation and revision of manuals serves to determine whether the organization members have a common understanding of the organization structure and policies. An important use of manuals, either in connection with or apart from a period of vestibule training, is to acquaint new organization members with these policies.

An almost inevitable consequence of the preparation and use of manuals is to increase the degree of centralization in decision-making. In the interest of "completeness" and "uniformity" the individuals preparing a manual almost always include in it matters that have previously been left to individuals to decide, and embody these matters in organization policy. This is by no means all sheer gain, for "completeness" and "uniformity" unless required in the interest of coordination, do not have any particular value for an organization.

Informal Communications

No matter how elaborate a system of formal communications is set up in the organization, this system will always be supplemented by informal channels. Through these informal channels will flow information, advice, and even orders (the reader will recall that, in terms of our definitions, an authority relation can exist even though the superior is not vested with any sanctions). In time, the actual system of relationships may come to differ widely from those specified in the formal organization scheme.

The informal communications system is built around the social relationships of the members of the organization. Friendship between two individuals creates frequent occasions for contact and "shop talk." It may also create an authority relationship if one of the individuals comes to accept the leadership of the other. In this way "natural leaders" secure a role in the organization that is not always reflected in the organization chart.

The informal communication system takes on additional importance when it is remembered that the behavior of individuals in organizations is oriented not only toward the organization's goals but also to a certain extent toward their personal goals, and that these two sets of goals are not always mutually consistent. Hence, when organization members deal with one another, each must attempt to assess the extent to which the other's attitudes and actions are conditioned by personal rather than organizational motives. When a primary relationship has been established between them, it becomes easier for each to make this assessment, and easier for them to be frank in regard to their motives. Requests for cooperation will less often meet with the reaction: "You run your department, and I will run mine." (This problem of identification with, or loyalty to, a particular segment of the organization will be discussed more fully in Chapter X below.)

Primary relationships can be unfriendly, of course, just as easily as they can be friendly, although there is what might be called a "presumption of friendliness" in most social relationships in our society. It becomes a major task of the executives, then, to maintain attitudes of friendliness and cooperation in these direct personal relationships so that the informal communication system will contribute to the efficient operation of the organization rather than hinder it.

The informal communications system is sometimes used by organization members to advance their personal aims. From this arises the phenomenon of cliques—groups that build up an informal network of communications and use this as a means of securing power in the organization. Rivalry among cliques, in turn, may lead to general unfriendliness in social relationships and defeat the purpose of the informal communications system.

There has been little systematic analysis of the way in which the formal organization structure encourages or hinders the formation of cliques, or of the techniques that can be used by executives to deal with cliques and minimize their harmfulness. On the first score, it may be conjectured that weakness of the formal system of communications and failure to secure an adequate measure of coordination through that system probably encourage the development of cliques. The coordinating function that cliques perform under such circumstances is closely analogous to the coordinating function performed by political machines in a highly decentralized governmental structure like the American system.

A great deal of the informal communication in any organization is far less deliberate than the activities of cliques or even the conversations of executives who lunch together. In addition to these there is the great mass of communication that goes under the head of "gossip." In most organizations the "grapevine" probably plays, on the whole, a constructive role. Its chief disadvantages are, first, that it discourages frankness, since confidential remarks may be spread about, second, that the information transmitted by the grapevine is very often inaccurate. On the other hand, in addition to transmitting information that no one has thought to transmit formally, the grapevine is valuable as a barometer of "public opinion" in the organization. If the administrator listens to it, it apprises him of the topics that are subjects of interest to organization members, and their attitudes toward these topics. Even for this latter purpose, of course, the grapevine needs to be supplemented by other channels of information.

Personal Motivation and Communication

We have just seen that personal motivation may have considerable influence upon the growth of the informal communication system. In particular, individuals may develop this system as a means of increasing their own power and influence in the organization. There is another way in which personal motivation affects communication—both formal and informal. Information does not *automatically* transmit itself from its point of origin to the rest of the organization; the individual who first obtains it must transmit it. In transmitting it, he will naturally be aware of the consequences its transmission will have for him. When he knows that the boss is going to be "burned up" by the news, the news is very likely to be suppressed.[3]

Hence, information tends to be transmitted upward in the organization only if (1) its transmission will not have unpleasant consequences for the transmitter, or (2) the superior will hear of it anyway from other channels, and it is better to tell him first, or (3) it is information that the superior needs in his dealings with his own superiors, and he will be displeased if he is caught without it. In addition, there is often failure to transmit information upward simply because the subordinate cannot visualize accurately what information his superior needs in order to make his decisions.

A major communications problem, then, of the higher levels of the administrative hierarchy is that much of the information relevant to the decisions at this level originates at lower levels, and may not ever reach the higher levels unless the executive is extraordinarily alert. As has already been pointed out, an important function of a system of formal records and reports is to transfer from the subordinate to the superior the responsibility for deciding what information will be transmitted upward.

There is a converse problem that arises when a superior withholds information from a subordinate. This, again, may be accidental—the superior does not realize that his subordinate needs the information. On the other hand, the superior may use his exclusive possession of information as a means of maintaining his authority over the subordinate. It is hard to see that the latter, which is usually a symptom of an incompetent and insecure executive, has any constructive function in organization. The former, equally unfortunate, is of frequent occurrence in most organizations, largely because of lack of sufficient consideration to the needs of downward transmission of information other than orders.

Receptivity to Communications

Consideration has been given thus far principally to the source of communications. Attention must be given also to their destina-

[3] This point has been very well discussed by Burleigh Gardner in *Human Relations in Industry*, chap. ii, and the present exposition follows closely Gardner's analysis.

tion. It has been pointed out that the attention that will be given a communication by its recipient is not simply a matter of logic. The source of the communication, and the way in which it is presented, will determine for its recipient how much consideration he will give it. If formal channels are maintained, communications flowing through these channels will have their effect enhanced by the authority which their "official" character gives them. Unsolicited information or advice, on the other hand, may be given little or no attention.

This dependence of the weight of a communication upon its source applies in upward as well as downward transmittal—suggestions transmitted upward may receive scanty consideration unless the person offering the suggestion is in a formal advisory position and transmits it "through channels." Much frustration results therefrom, particularly in the lower levels of the organization, but it is hard to see how this can be completely eliminated without destroying the organization structure.

The attention a communication will receive will also depend upon its form. In the discussion of the authority relation in the previous chapter, emphasis was placed on the acceptance of authority by the subordinate. The crucial point is whether the recipient of an order, or of any other kind of communication, is influenced by the communication in his actions or decisions, or whether he is not. The problem of securing employees' compliance with a safety rule is not very different from the problem of securing a customer's acceptance of a particular brand of soap. In some cases formal authority may be a sufficient inducement for the subordinate to comply; but usually the communication must reason, plead, and persuade, as well as order, if it is to be effective.

In the same connection, consideration must be given to whether the communication should be oral or written; and whether it should be in formal or informal language. In every case the state of mind of the recipient, his attitudes and motivations, must be the basic factors in determining the design of the communication. The function of the communication, after all, is not to get something off the mind of the person transmitting it, but to get something into the mind and actions of the person receiving it.

Because of the great importance of communication to their functioning, most organizations, even of moderate size, develop certain specialized communications tasks. Decision-centers themselves—that is, executive positions—must often be staffed with persons who can assist the executive in his communications functions. The organization develops specialized repositories of its official "memory"—files, records, libraries, follow-up systems. Organization units may be established to handle specific information-gathering functions: accounting, inspection, administrative analysis, intelligence, and the like. The larger the organization, the farther it becomes possible to carry this specialization.

Organization of Decision-Centers

A number of the communications tasks of the administrator need not be performed personally, but may be delegated to staff assistants in his office. Included among these are the drafting of outgoing communications, the screening of incoming communications, and liaison.

The drafting of outgoing communications hardly requires comment. It is one of the common functions of secretaries, and important executives often have assistants with such functions. Perhaps the most elaborate specialization of this sort is the Bureau of the Budget in the Executive Office of the President, which has, as one of its important functions, the drafting of presidential orders, as well as the drafting of bills for submission to Congress.

The possibility of this type of division of work does have one important consequence. It means that, by the attachment of specialists to the executive's office, outgoing communications can receive a review from the standpoint of their respective specialties without complicating the scheme of authority. This system is perhaps best developed in military organization, where an artillery officer, for example, on the divisional commander's staff will work out the artillery phases of an operational plan, and so forth. The executive himself—and in the military example, his chief of staff—

exercises the function of coordinating and balancing these specialties.

The review of incoming communications to determine which should receive the personal attention of the executive is also a delegable function that is specialized for important executive positions. In some cases this extends to the preparation of analyses and recommendations for the executive which are transmitted to him with the communication. In other cases, the executive's staff may be able to take action on the communication, by-passing him completely.

The delegation by the executive to his staff of the function of liaison with subordinates or with other organization units creates somewhat more delicate problems than the other two types of delegation. Unless the relationships are carefully defined, the subordinates of the executive may fail to recognize that the liaison officer is exercising authority not on his own initiative, but as representative of his chief. As a result of this ambiguity, considerable resentment may develop against the liaison officer and he may lose his usefulness. In many civilian organizations the distinction between an assistant department head and an assistant *to* the department head is not clearly understood, and such organizations would do well to observe the care with which this distinction is made in military organization.

Repositories of Organization "Memory"

Since an organization is not an organism the only memory it possesses, in the proper sense of the term, is the collective memory of its participants. This is insufficient for organization purposes, first, because what is in one man's mind is not necessarily available to other members of the organization, and, second, because when an individual leaves an organization the organization loses that part of its "memory."

Hence organizations, to a far greater extent than individuals, need artificial "memories." Practices which would become simply habitual in the case of the individual must be recorded in manuals for the instruction of new organization members. Among the repositories which organizations may use for their information are records systems, correspondence and other files, libraries, and follow-up systems.

All these devices are familiar. They in themselves create difficult problems of organization—what types of information are to be recorded, in what manner they are to be classified and filed, the physical location of the files, and so forth; but it is hardly profitable to discuss these problems in the abstract.

Investigatory Facilities

Most organizations, or particular decision-centers in organization, require information in addition to that which comes to them normally in the course of their work. This necessary information is of two kinds: external—that which is to be obtained from sources outside the organization; and internal—that which is to be obtained within the organization. In any large organization units can be identified whose function it is to secure one or the other of these types of information. The patent department in industrial concerns is such a unit, one of whose primary functions is to keep continual watch on patent and product development in the company's field by checking the *Patent Office Gazette,* manufacturers' catalogues, periodicals, and trade literature. The accounting department is the outstanding example of a unit whose function it is to obtain internal information.

The external investigatory unit does not require much discussion. The chief problem in fitting it into the organization is to locate it in such a manner that the information it receives will be transmitted promptly and in usable form to the appropriate points in the organization. This inevitably leads to questions, like those asked of any service unit, as to how far the function should be specialized and how far it should be decentralized among the operating units. Other such units are the intelligence units in military organization, market research units in business concerns, a fire alarm bureau, and a police communications system.

There are several varieties of internal investigatory units in addition to accounting. Perhaps the most significant are independent inspectional units (like the Inspector General's Office of the Army) and analysis units (the Department of Investigation of New York

City, or the Division of Administrative Management of the United States Bureau of the Budget).

In the case of accounting for money, the need for a flow of information independent of the regular channels of authority is universally accepted as almost self-evident. The functions of the typical accounting unit have been very much broadened, however, beyond the simple audit for honesty. It is quite frequently used nowadays as a source of information for determining whether expenditures are conforming to the plan laid down in the budget. Accounts are used also as a basis for cost analysis which, in turn, contributes to future executive decisions. In these capacities, accounting information has become one of the most important tools in the executive review of operations.

Accounting controls have probably never been carried further than they have by the Comptroller General of the United States. That office has for a number of years maintained a continual pre-audit of Federal expenditures and has disallowed those which it considered to be not in conformity with Congressional authorizations. This has created a system of dual authority over expenditures in the Federal government that has generally received adverse comment from persons who have studied it. It should be recognized, however, that this is merely an extreme form of the problem that arises whenever control functions of *any* sort are vested in an accounting unit. To the extent that the accountant has authority to set limits to the actions of executives in the line organization, his authority cuts across the regular lines of authority, and unity of command in the broad sense of that term is violated.

Independent inspectional organizations create problems of dual command similar to those created by accounting controls. Even where, as is usually the case, the inspectional unit has no power but that of reporting its findings to the top executive, the line organization will become responsive to its viewpoints. The seriousness of this problem is mitigated somewhat—with a weakening in the effectiveness of the inspectional unit—by the fact that its intervention is usually intermittent rather than continuous. At any rate, whatever the problems it creates, the top administrator often finds the inspectional unit an invaluable aid because it gives him information that simply would not be transmitted up through the line organization.

Another way in which the top levels of the hierarchy gain knowledge about the operation of the organization is by undertaking, at intervals, a comprehensive analysis and survey of the organization or some part of it. In this they may be assisted by an administrative analysis unit which specializes in such work. Such a survey may be confined to questions of organization structure, or it may include an analysis of the program of activity. In most cases these two are so inextricably interwoven that both are involved.

TRAINING AND COMMUNICATION

The whole subject of training involves other questions than those of communication. Nevertheless the role of training in administration is perhaps best understood by viewing it as one of several alternative means for communicating decisional premises to organization members. If, for example, a particular job in an organization requires certain legal knowledge, (a) a lawyer may be appointed to the position; (b) instructions and manuals may be provided to the person selected, with careful supervision of his work; or (c) he may be trained after selection. All these are, in a sense, training procedures, but in (a) the organization depends upon pre-service training, in (b) upon day-to-day supervision as a training device, in (c) upon formal training.

Military organizations have long provided striking demonstrations of the use that can be made of formal training in indoctrinating large numbers of new members in highly complicated and unfamiliar tasks in a short time. In civilian organizations, where new members are seldom employed in such large numbers, and where the new employees are usually at least partly trained at the time of their recruitment, the possibilities of formal training have been much less fully realized. In military organizations instruction in "how to do it" is carried on almost entirely through the formal training process, while operational orders are generally restricted to "what to do." In many civilian organizations instruction in "how to do it" is left pretty much to the supervisory staff. Undoubtedly the poorest method of communicating operational procedures is to rely solely on written instructions and manuals.

Perhaps the greatest difficulty in the use of formal training methods is to secure in the group being trained an attitude of receptivity. Every teacher recognizes—often with a great feeling of helplessness—that motivation is the key to the learning process. The trainee must have an interest in learning, and, moreover, he must be convinced that he does not already know the things in which he is to be trained. The problem of motivation is at a minimum in the vestibule training of new employees. It may be very serious indeed in the training of employees who have already been performing their jobs for a considerable period of time.

Training requires of the trainee a certain attitude of deference toward the teacher, and an admission of incomplete knowledge that many individuals who have reached a mature age and a responsible position find quite galling. When in-service training deals with such individuals—skilled workmen, supervisors, executives—considerable attention must be given to the prestige and acceptability of the instructor and the practicality of the training materials. One of the reasons for the success of the conference method in training such groups is that it minimizes the "teaching" role of the instructor, and creates the illusion that the new ideas are originating in the group itself. Of course this is not entirely an illusion; but it is more of an illusion than the theorists of conference-method training like to admit.

Training is applicable to the process of decision wherever the same elements are involved in a large number of decisions. Training may supply the trainee with the facts necessary in dealing with these decisions; it may provide him a frame of reference for his thinking; it may teach him "approved" solutions, or it may indoctrinate him with the values in terms of which his decisions are to be made.

Training, as a mode of influence upon decisions, has its greatest value in those situations where the exercise of formal authority through commands proves difficult. The difficulty may lie in the need for prompt action, in spatial dispersion of the organization, or in the complexity of the subject matter of decision which defies summarization in rules and regulations. Training permits a higher degree of decentralization of the decision-making process by bringing the necessary competence into the very lowest levels of the organizational hierarchy.

CONCLUSION

This chapter has been concerned with the organization communications system—particularly those aspects of it which supplement the system of authority. It has been shown that the specialization of decision-making functions is largely dependent upon the possibility of developing adequate channels of communication to and from decision centers. Generally the organization structure will include the specification of a formal system of communication —including channels for oral and written communications, paper-flow, records and reports, and manuals—but this will be supplemented by a rich network of informal communications based upon the social relationships that develop in the organization.

Personal motives may lead organization members to try to divert the communications system to their own uses, and may lead them also to withhold information from superiors and colleagues. Personal motives and attitudes also influence the reception given to those communications that are transmitted, and the ability of an individual to influence others by his communications will depend upon his formal and informal position of authority, and upon the intelligibility and persuasiveness of the communication itself.

Organizations usually develop units that are specialized for particular communications functions. These include staff aids, repositories of organization "memory," and investigatory units, both internal and external.

Training is one of several alternative methods of communication that proves particularly useful in transmitting job "know-how." Its successful use, however, hinges on the possibility of obtaining favorable attitudes in the trainees toward the training program.

Chapter IX

THE CRITERION OF EFFICIENCY

In the preceding two chapters attention has been concentrated on the way in which the organization brings its influence to bear on its individual members. Through the system of authority and the other types of communication that have been discussed, the organization provides the individual with some of his principal premises of decision: it specifies his fundamental value-premises—the organization objectives—and it supplies him with relevant information of all sorts that is necessary if he is to implement these values. It is time now to turn to the "internal" aspects of decision, and to see how the organizationally supplied premises are synthesized by the individual into a completed decision. Crucial to the synthesis are the decisional premises that the individual himself supplies, and the most important of these, aside from the information that originates with him, are the criterion of efficiency [1] and the individual's organizational identifications or loyalties. These will provide the subject matter of this and the following chapter, respectively.

Because the criterion of efficiency is rather more complicated in its application to noncommercial than to commercial organizations, a large part of this chapter will be taken up with the problem of extending the concept of efficiency so that it becomes applicable to the former as well as to the latter.

THE NATURE OF EFFICIENCY

The criterion of efficiency is most easily understood in its application to commercial organizations that are largely guided by the

---

[1] The theory of efficiency, along the lines developed here, has been proposed in C. E. Ridley and H. A. Simon, *Measuring Municipal Activities* (Chicago: International City Managers' Association, 1938).

profit objective. In such organizations the criterion of efficiency dictates the selection of that alternative, of all those available to the individual, which will yield the greatest net (money) return to the organization. This "balance sheet" efficiency involves, on the one hand, the maximization of income, if costs are considered as fixed; and on the other hand, the minimization of cost, if income is considered as fixed. In practice, of course, the maximization of income and the minimization of cost must be considered simultaneously— that is, what is really to be maximized is the difference between these two.

It will be seen that the criterion of efficiency is closely related to both organization and conservation objectives, as those terms have been defined in Chapter VI. It is related to the organization objective in so far as it is concerned with the maximization of "output." It is related to conservation objectives in so far as it is concerned with the maintenance of a positive balance of output over input.

The simplicity of the efficiency criterion in commercial organizations is due in large part to the fact that money provides a common denominator for the measurement of both output and income, and permits them to be directly compared. The concept must be broadened, therefore, if it is to be applicable to the process of decision where factors are involved that are not directly measurable in monetary terms. Such factors will certainly be present in noncommercial organizations where monetary measurement of output is usually meaningless or impossible. They will also be present in commercial organizations to the extent that those controlling the organization are not solely directed toward the profit motive—i.e. where they are concerned with questions of the public interest or employee welfare even when those factors are not directly related to the profit and loss statement. Moreover, nonmonetary factors will also be involved in the internal operation even of purely commercial organizations where specific activities are concerned whose relation to the profit-and-loss statement cannot be assessed directly. For example, decisions in a personnel department cannot always be evaluated in monetary terms, because the monetary effect of a particular personnel policy cannot be directly determined.

The Cost Element in Decision

In both commercial and noncommercial organizations (except for volunteer organizations) the "input" factor can be largely measured in money terms. This is true even when the organization objectives are broader than either profit or conservation of the organization. That is, even if the organization is concerned with the cost *for the community,* this cost can be fairly valued in terms of the goods and services that the organization buys.[2]

This point may not be entirely evident in the case of the evaluation of the services of employees. The tasks to which employees are assigned are not all equal with respect to agreeableness, hazard, and the like; and, to the extent that they are not, the money wage (unless this accurately reflects these elements—which it usually does not) is not an accurate measure of input in an organization where employee welfare takes its place among the organization objectives. In such cases, organization decisions must balance not only money input against output, but money input against output *and* employee welfare.

There are other cases, too, where input is not accurately measured by money cost to the organization. An industrial concern, for example, which is not penalized for the smoke and soot it distributes over the community has a cost factor, provided the organization objectives include concern for community welfare, that does not appear in the accounts.

When the decision is being made for a public agency that embraces among its objectives the general stability and prosperity of the economy—the Federal government, for example—still other considerations must enter in. In the case of a private business, interest on invested capital, at the market rate, must be included in calculations as a cost. In the case of government, if the effect of spending is to employ investment capital that would otherwise be idle, the interest on this capital is not really a cost from the standpoint of the economy as a whole. Moreover, the "output" of govern-

---

[2] For an elaboration of this point, and statements of the qualifications that must be appended to it to make it strictly accurate, the reader is referred to the literature on welfare economics. See, for example, A. C. Pigou, *The Economics of Welfare* (London: Macmillan & Co., 1924).

ment investment may include effects of this investment on the level of income and employment in the economy, and these effects must be included in the measurement of product.

Likewise, when a private business employs an unemployed person his wage is an ordinary cost; while when the government employs such a person it makes use of a resource that would otherwise not be utilized, and hence the wages of those employed do not involve any real cost from the standpoint of the community.

These comments are not intended to defend any particular concept of the role of government spending in a modern economy—a subject that evokes sufficient controversy among the various competing schools of modern economists—but merely to point out that the criterion of efficiency cannot be applied to decisions in governmental agencies without consideration of the economic effects that the activities of these agencies may have. In the language of the economist, the problem of efficiency in the public agency must be approached from the standpoint of the general, rather than the partial, equilibrium.

Positive Values in Decision

While the negative values involved in decision can usually be summarized in terms of time or money costs, the positive values present a somewhat more complex picture. As we have seen, in a commercial enterprise, money value of output plays somewhat the same role as cost of production (input) in summarizing the value element involved. From a positive standpoint the kind of product manufactured is a valuationally neutral element. Not so in the case of public services. Hence, some substitute must be found in public administration for money value of output as a measure of value.

This substitute is provided by a statement of the objectives of the activity, and by the construction of indices that measure the degree of attainment of these objectives. Any measurement that indicates the effect of an administrative activity in accomplishing its final objective is termed a measurement of the *result* of that activity.[3]

Definition of Objectives. The definition of objectives for public

[3] Ridley and Simon, *op. cit.,* p. 1.

services is far from a simple task. In the first place, it is desirable to state the objectives so far as possible in terms of values. That is, only if they are expressions of relatively final ends are they suitable value-indices. When objectives are stated in terms of intermediate goals, there is a serious danger that decisions governed by the intermediate end will continue to persist even when that end is no longer appropriate to the realization of value. The proliferation of forms and records in an administrative agency, for instance, frequently evidences a failure to reconsider activities which are aimed at some concrete end in terms of the broader values which that end is supposed to further.

On the other hand, however, the values which public services seek to realize are seldom expressible in concrete terms. Aims, such as those of a recreation department—to "improve health," "provide recreation," "develop good citizens"—must be stated in tangible and objective terms before results can be observed and measured. A serious dilemma is posed here. The values toward which these services should be directed do not provide sufficiently concrete criteria to be applied to specific decisional problems. However, if value-indices are employed as criteria in lieu of the values themselves, the "ends" are likely to be sacrificed for the more tangible means—the substance for the form.

Further difficulty arises in the lack of a common denominator of value. An activity may realize two or more values, as in the case of the recreation department mentioned above. What is the relative importance of the various values in guiding the department's activities? The health department provides an illustration of the same problem. Shall the department next year redistribute its funds to decrease infant mortality or to increase the facilities of the venereal disease clinic? Observations of results, measured in terms of value-indices, can merely tell the extent to which the several objectives are realized if one or the other course of action is taken. Unless both activities are directed toward exactly the same value, measurement of results cannot tell which course of action is preferable. Rationality can be applied in administrative decisions only after the relative weights of conflicting values have been fixed.

The question of who should construct the system of values or preferences which underlie the administrator's decisions has already been discussed in Chapter III. We wish here only to emphasize that somewhere, sometime in the administrative process weights actually are assigned to values. If this is not done consciously and deliberately, then it is achieved by implication in the decisions which are actually reached. It is not possible to avoid the problem by hiding it among the unexpressed premises of choice.

Accomplishment a Matter of Degree. Defining objectives does not exhaust the value element in an administrative decision. It is necessary to determine, in addition, the degree to which the objective is to be attained. A city charter or ordinance may define the function of the fire department as "protecting the city from damage due to fire"; but this does not imply that the city will wish to expand the fire-fighting facilities to the point where fire damage is entirely eliminated—an obviously impossible task. Moreover, it begs the question to say that the fire department should reduce losses "as far as possible," for how far it is possible to reduce losses depends on the amount of money available for fire protection and fire prevention services.

Value questions are not eliminated from the fire protection problem of that city until it has been determined that (1) the fire department should aim to limit fire losses to x dollars per capita, and (2) the city council will appropriate y dollars which, it is anticipated on the basis of available information, will permit (1) to be carried out. Values are involved, then, not only in the definition of objectives, but in the determination as well of the level of adequacy of services which is to be aimed at. Attainment of objectives is *always* a matter of degree.

The processes of "policy determination," as they take place in our governmental institutions, seldom cope with these questions of degree in determining the objectives of governmental services. It will be urged in later sections of this chapter that extension of policy determination to such questions is of fundamental importance for the maintenance of democratic control over the value elements in decision. It will be shown that a large measure of this procedural reform can be attained by a modification and extension of budgetary techniques.

Distributive Values. Thus far, the discussion has centered on values which are "aggregates." That is, the community measures its fire loss in terms of total dollars of destruction during the year. It does not distinguish the loss of $1,000 in Smith's store from a loss of $1,000 in Jones' store. The police department, in attempting to reduce the number of robberies, does not give a robbery on Third Street a different weight from a similar robbery on Fourth Street.

Nevertheless, questions of "distributive" value enter into almost every administrative decision—if in no other way than in an assumption of "equal weight" like those cited above. A playground built on the West Side will not serve children on the East Side. If chess classes are offered at the social center, there may be no facilities available for persons interested in social dancing.

Many distributive questions are geographical, but they may involve social, economic, or innumerable other "class" distinctions. The importance of such considerations in administration can be appreciated when it is recognized that agencies for assessment administration, administrative tribunals, and even welfare agencies are concerned primarily with questions of distributive rather than aggregate value.

As will be shown later, distributive questions are also of great importance when the work of an organization is specialized by "area" or by "clientele." In these cases, the objective of the organizational unit is immediately restricted to a particular set of persons, and interjurisdictional problems of the greatest consequence may arise.

A Common Denominator for Value—the Criterion of Efficiency

A fundamental problem involved in reaching a decision is the discovery of a common denominator between the two values which have been mentioned: low cost and large results. How is the choice made when the two conflict? Four relations are conceivable between choices A and B. If I_A is the input for A, and I_B for B, and O_A and O_B are the respective outputs, then these four possible relations may be expressed as follows:

1. I_A is less than I_B, and O_A is greater than O_B.
2. I_B is less than I_A, and O_B is greater than O_A.
3. I_A is less than I_B, and O_A is less than O_B.
4. I_B is less than I_A, and O_B is less than O_A.

In cases 1 and 2 the choice is unequivocal; but not so in cases 3 and 4. That is, when possibility A involves a larger cost than possibility B, but produces a smaller result, B obviously is preferable. But when possibility A involves a lower cost as well as a smaller result than B, cost must be weighed against result before a choice can be made.

The path to the solution of this difficulty has already been indicated. Underlying all administrative decisions is a limitation—a "scarcity"—of available resources. This is the fundamental reason why time and money are costs. Because they are limited in quantity, their application to one administrative purpose prevents the realization of alternative possibilities. Hence, the administrative choice among possibilities can always be framed as a choice among alternatives involving the same cost, but different positive values.

An administrative choice is incorrectly posed, then, when it is posed as a choice between possibility A, with low costs and small results, and possibility B, with high costs and large results. For A should be substituted a third possibility C, which would include A *plus* the alternative activities made possible by the cost difference between A and B. If this is done, the choice resolves itself into a comparison of the results obtainable by the application of fixed resources to the alternative activities B and C. The efficiency of a behavior is the ratio of the results obtainable from that behavior to the maximum of results obtainable from the behaviors which are alternative to the given behavior.

The criterion of efficiency dictates that choice of alternatives which produces the largest result for the given application of resources.

It should be noted that this criterion, while it supplies a common denominator for the comparison of administrative alternatives, does not supply a common numerator. Even though all decisions be made in terms of alternative applications of the same resources, the problem still remains of comparing the values which are attained by the different courses of action. The efficiency criterion neither solves nor avoids this problem of comparability.

Note on the Term "Efficiency"

The term "efficiency" has acquired during the past generation a number of unfortunate connotations which associate it with a mechanistic, profit-directed, stop-watch theory of administration. This is the result of the somewhat careless use of the term by over-enthusiastic proponents of the "scientific management" movement. Nevertheless, no other term in the language comes so close as "efficiency" to representing the concept described in this chapter. The term has therefore been employed, with the hope that the reader will understand the criterion in the sense in which it has just been defined, and will be able to dissociate from it any unfortunate connotations it may have had in his mind.

Until practically the end of the nineteenth century, the terms "efficiency" and "effectiveness" were considered almost as synonymous. The Oxford Dictionary defines "efficiency": "Fitness or power to accomplish, or success in accomplishing, the purpose intended; adequate power, effectiveness, efficacy."

In recent years, however, "efficiency" has acquired a second meaning: the ratio between input and output.[4] In the words of the *Encyclopaedia of the Social Sciences:*

> Efficiency in the sense of a ratio between input and output, effort and results, expenditure and income, cost and the resulting pleasure, is a relatively recent term. In this specific sense it became current in engineering only during the latter half of the nineteenth century and in business and in economics only since the beginning of the twentieth.[5]

The use of the term by leaders of the scientific management movement added still a third meaning. Again quoting from the *Encyclopaedia of the Social Sciences:*

[4] An early application of the engineering concept to the social field is that of F. Y. Edgeworth, who on p. 2 of his *Mathematical Psychics* (London: Kegan Paul & Co., 1881) defined efficiency essentially as it is defined in this study: ". . . efficiency being thus defined: one engine is more efficient than another if, whenever the total quantity of fuel consumed by the former is equal to that consumed by the latter, the total quantity of energy yielded by the former is greater than that yielded by the latter."

[5] "Efficiency," *Encyclopaedia of the Social Sciences,* 5:437.

The foundation of modern scientific management may be dated from F. W. Taylor's paper, *A Piece Rate System,* in which he described his pioneer method of establishing standards of job performance at the Midvale steel plant. When such standards were set, it became customary to refer to the ratio of actual performance to the standard performance as the efficiency of labor, a use somewhat different from that of the mechanical engineers, who apply the term to the ratio of actual output to an actual input.[6]

Harrington Emerson, another pioneer in the scientific management movement, and one who preferred the term "efficiency engineering," is reported to have defined efficiency as "the relation between what is accomplished and what might be accomplished." In this connection, he speaks of the "efficiency percent of the employee."[7]

It must be noted that there is a difference in computing an output-input ratio in the physical and in the social sciences. For the engineer, both output and input are measured in terms of energy. The law of conservation of energy tells him that the output of useful energy cannot exceed the energy input. Hence arises the concept of "perfect" efficiency—that is, a situation in which output equals input. In the social sciences, output and input are seldom measured in comparable units; and even when they are, as in a comparison of cost of fire protection with dollar losses from fire, there is no "law of conservation of energy" which prevents the output from exceeding the input. Hence, the concept of perfect efficiency, if it is used at all, must be redefined. As a matter of fact, the concept of perfect efficiency will not be required in the present study. Actual problems, as they present themselves to the administrator, are always concerned with *relative* efficiencies, and no measure of *absolute* efficiency is ever needed. Moreover, the theory does not require a numerical measure of efficiency, but merely a comparison of *greater* or *less* between the efficiencies of two alternative possibilities. Under these circumstances, the definitions of efficiency as ratio of output to input and as ratio of the actual to the maximum possible amount to the same thing.

[6] *Loc. cit.*
[7] Horace Bookwalter Drury, *Scientific Management* (New York: Columbia University Press, 1915), pp. 114, 115.

An Economic Analogy

It can be seen that the criterion of efficiency as applied to administrative decisions is strictly analogous to the concept of maximization of utility in economic theory. It is not asserted here that the criterion of efficiency always does dominate administrators, decisions, but rather that if they were rational it would. There is no assertion that such rationality is a common characteristic of actual behavior. On the other hand, the doctrine of maximization of utility has been commonly set forth in the economic literature as an explanatory doctrine as well, that is, as descriptive of actual behavior in the market. This difference between the two propositions should be kept carefully in mind.

The analogy between the two propositions extends also to the assumptions which underlie them. The first of these is that there is a scarcity of applicable resources. A second assumption is that the activities concerned are "instrumental" activities—that is, activities that are carried on for the positive values they produce, in the form of some kind of "result." Third, both propositions involve the comparability, at least subjectively, of the values in terms of which results are measured. (This assumption has already been discussed in the previous section.)

The broad scope of the analogy will become increasingly clear as the discussion proceeds. It will be seen that the problem of administrative decisions can be translated into a problem in the theory of production, and that concepts and theorems developed in economic theory have wide applicability to administrative decisions.

CRITICISMS OF THE EFFICIENCY CRITERION

Criticisms of "efficiency" as a guide to administration have been frequent and vociferous.[8] One group of criticisms need not concern us here, for they refer to definitions of the term different from the one proposed here. In this category must be placed attacks on efficiency which equate the term with "economy" or "expenditure re-

[8] See instances cited by Marshall E. Dimock, "The Criteria and Objectives of Public Administration," in *The Frontiers of Public Administration,* ed. Gaus, White, and Dimock, pp. 116-133.

duction." As we have used "efficiency," there is no implication whatsoever that a small expenditure—or, for that matter, a large expenditure—is *per se* desirable. It has been asserted only that if two results can be obtained with the same expenditure the greater result is to be preferred. Two expenditures of different magnitude can, in general, be compared only if they are translated into opportunity costs, that is, if they are expressed in terms of alternative results.

"Mechanical" Efficiency

Others have objected to "efficiency" on the ground that it leads to a "mechanical" conception of admiration. This objection, too, must result from the use of the term in quite a different sense from that proposed here. For a mere criterion of preference among possibilities does not in any manner limit the administrative techniques which may be employed in attaining the possibilities, nor, as we shall see in the next section, does it in any way reduce the role of the administrator's judgment in reaching decisions. Furthermore, the efficiency criterion is in the most complete accord with a viewpoint that places the social consequences of administration in the forefront of its determining influences.

"The Ends Justify the Means"

Two other lines of criticism assert that the criterion of efficiency leads to an incorrect relationship between "means" and "ends." On the one hand it is alleged that, in the interests of efficiency, ends are taken to justify any appropriate means. As we have noted in Chapter IV, the terms "means" and "ends" must be employed carefully in order to avoid contradictions; and for this reason we have preferred to talk of the value and factual aspects of alternatives. Suffice it to say that if the evaluation of the results of administrative activity takes into account *all* the significant value elements of the administrative alternatives, no undue subordination of "means" to "ends" can result.

"Ruthless" Efficiency

On the other hand, it is charged that efficiency directs all attention to the means, and neglects the ends. This charge has already been answered in pointing out the integral role which valuation plays in the employment of a criterion of efficiency. It may be freely admitted that efficiency, as a scientific problem, is concerned chiefly with "means," and that "efficient" service may be efficient with respect to any of a wide variety of ends. But merely to recognize that the process of valuation lies outside the scope of science, and that the adaptation of means to ends is the only element of the decisional problem that has a factual solution, is not to admit any indifference to the ends which efficiency serves. Efficiency, whether it be in the democratic state or in the totalitarian, is the proper criterion to be applied to the factual element in the decisional problem. Other, ethical, criteria must be applied to the problem of valuation.

Common to all these criticisms is an implication that an "efficiency" approach involves a complete separation of "means" and "ends." We have already seen that, strictly speaking, this is not the case—that the only valid distinction is one between ethical and factual elements in decision. Yet, in the actual application of the efficiency criterion to administrative situations, there is often a tendency to substitute the former distinction for the latter, and such a substitution inevitably results in the narrower, "mechanical" efficiency which has been the subject of criticism.

How this substitution comes about may be briefly explained. The ethical element in decision consists in a recognition and appraisal of all the value elements inhering in the alternative possibilities. The principal values involved are usually expressed as "results" of the administrative activity, and, as we have seen, the activity itself is usually considered as valuationally neutral. This leads to the isolation of two values: (1) the positive values expressed as "results," and (2) the negative values, or opportunity costs, expressed in terms of time or money cost.

In fact, to consider the administrative activity itself as valuationally neutral is an abstraction from reality which is permissible within broad limits but which, if carried to extremes, ignores very important human values. These values may comprehend the remuneration and working conditions (using these terms broadly) of the members of the group which carries out the activity.

We may enumerate some of these value elements more explicitly:

1. If cost is measured in money terms, then the wages of employees cannot be considered as a valuationally neutral element, but must be included among the values to be appraised in the decision.

2. The work pace of workers cannot be considered as a valuationally neutral element—else we would be led to the conclusion that a "speed-up" would always be eminently desirable.

3. The social aspects of the work situation cannot be considered as a valuationally neutral element. The decision must weigh the social and psychological consequences of substituting one type of work-situation for another.

4. Wage policies, promotional policies, and the like need to be considered not only from the viewpoint of incentives and result-efficiency, but also from that of distributive justice to the members of the group.

It must be emphasized, then, that when a choice between alternatives involves any valuationally significant difference in the work activity this difference must be included among the values to be weighed in reaching a decision.

Valuational Bias

A closely related fallacy in the application of the efficiency criterion is to include in the evaluation of alternatives only those values which have been previously selected as the *objective* of the particular administrative activity under consideration. The effects of some administrative activities are confined to a rather limited area, and indirect results do not then cause much difficulty. The activities of the fire department usually have an effect on fire losses, but very little relation to the recreation problem in the community (unless ardent fire fans form a large part of the community). Hence the fire chief does not have to take recreation values into consideration in reaching his decisions. It is very fortunate that the consequences of human activities are so strictly segregated; if they were not, the problem of reaching rational decisions would be impossible.[9] But the mere fact that activities do not *usually* have valuationally significant indirect effects does not justify us in ignoring such effects if they are, *in fact*, present. That is, the fire chief cannot, merely because he is a fire chief, ignore the possibility of

[9] See pp. 81–83, *supra*.

accidents in determining the speed at which his equipment should respond to alarms.

This all seems commonplace, yet we shall devote a large portion of the next chapter to showing that, in actuality, administrators in reaching decisions commonly disclaim responsibility for the indirect results of administrative activities.[10] To this point of view we oppose the contrary opinion that the administrator, serving a public agency in a democratic state, must give a proper weight to *all* community values that are relevant to his activity, and that are reasonably ascertainable in relation thereto, and cannot restrict himself to values that happen to be his particular responsibility. Only under these conditions can a criterion of efficiency be validly postulated as a determinant of action.[11]

Of course, the extent to which administrators can, in practice, give consideration to "indirect" effects is severely limited by the psychological considerations analyzed at length in Chapter V. Many effects not directly related to the objective of the organization will perforce be ignored because the administrator's span of attention is limited, and because there are often severe limits on the time available for making decisions.

FACTUAL ELEMENTS IN DECISION [12]

We have seen that the criterion which the administrator applies to factual problems is one of efficiency. The resources, the input, at the disposal of the administrator are strictly limited. It is not his function to establish a utopia. It is his function to maximize

[10] For a superlative illustration of the difficulty of securing administrative responsibility for indirect effects see Karl E. Stromsen, "The Usefulness of Central Review of Bureau Communications," *Case Reports in Public Administration*, No. 16, compiled by a Special Committee on Research Materials, Committee on Public Administration, Social Science Research Council (Chicago: Public Administration Service, 1940). The entire analysis assumes that organizational relevance is the ruling criterion of whether an indirect effect should be given administrative consideration.

[11] Dewey finds in these indirect effects the basic characteristic which distinguishes a "public" from a "private" transaction. See *The Public and Its Problems*, pp. 12–13.

[12] This section is based on Herbert A. Simon, "Comparative Statistics and the Measurement of Efficiency," *National Municipal Review*, 26:524–527 (Nov., 1937).

the attainment of the governmental objectives (assuming they have been agreed upon), by the efficient employment of the limited resources that are available to him. A "good" public library, from the administrative standpoint, is not one that owns all the books that have ever been published, but one that has used the limited funds which are allowed it to build up as good a collection as possible under the circumstances.

When a decision is made in terms of the criterion of efficiency, it is necessary to have empirical knowledge of the results that will be associated with each alternative possibility. Let us consider a specific municipal function, the fire department. Its objective is the reduction of the total fire loss, and results will be measured in terms of this loss.

The extent of the fire loss will be determined by a large number of factors. Among these are natural factors (frequency of high winds, heavy snowfall, severe cold weather, hot dry weather, tornadoes, hurricanes and cyclones, earthquakes, and floods), structural and occupancy factors (exposure hazards, physical barriers, density of structures, type of building construction, roof construction, contents, and risk of occupancy), the moral hazard (carelessness and incendiarism), and finally the effectiveness of the fire department itself. The loss, then, will be a function of all these variables, including the performance of the fire department itself. The fire chief must know how the activities of his department affect the loss if he is to make intelligent decisions.

How does the fire department perform its task? It inspects buildings to eliminate fire hazards, it carries on campaigns of education against carelessness, it fights fires, it trains firemen, it investigates and prosecutes incendiaries.

But we can carry the analysis a step farther. Of what does firefighting consist? A piece of apparatus must be brought to the scene of action, hose laid, water pumped and directed upon the flames, ladders raised, and covers spread over goods to reduce water damage. Again, each of these activities can be analyzed into its component parts. What does laying a hose involve? The hose must be acquired and maintained. Equipment for carrying it must be acquired and maintained. Firemen must be recruited and trained.

The firemen must spend a certain amount of time and energy in laying the hose.

A final level of analysis is reached by determining the cost of each of these elements of the task. Thus, the whole process of fire-fighting can be translated into a set of entries in the city's books of accounts.

The problem of efficiency is to determine, at any one of these levels of analysis, the cost of any particular element of performance, and the contribution which that element of performance makes to the accomplishment of the department's objectives. When these costs and contributions are known, the elements of performance can be combined in such a way as to achieve a maximum reduction in fire loss.

There are at least four rather distinct levels at which the analysis of the administrative situation may be carried out. At the highest level is the measurement of results, of the accomplishment of agency objectives. Contributing to these results are the elements of administrative performance. Subordinate to these, in turn, is input measured in terms of effort. Effort, finally, may be analyzed in terms of money cost.

The mathematically minded will see in this structure a set of equations—strictly identical with the economist's "production functions." The first equation expresses the results of government as a function of the performance of certain activities. Further equations express these performance units as functions of less immediate performance units, the latter in terms of units of effort; and finally effort is expressed as a function of expenditures. The problem of efficiency is to find the maximum of a production function, with the constraint that total expenditure is fixed.

The Determination of Social Production Functions

It follows from the considerations which have been advanced that that portion of the decision-making process which is factual, which is amenable to scientific treatment, resolves itself into the determination of the production functions of administrative activities. This is a research task of the first magnitude, and one which as yet has hardly been touched.

Progress toward an understanding of these functions involves a series of well defined steps:

(1) The values, or objectives, affected by each activity must be defined in terms that permit their observation and measurement.

(2) The variables, extra-administrative as well as administrative, that determine the degree of attainment of these functions must be enumerated.

(3) Concrete, empirical investigations must be made of the way in which results change when the extra-administrative and administrative variables are altered.

The necessary scope and difficulty of a research program which would make a substantial contribution to our knowledge of these functions can hardly be exaggerated. The principal progress to date has been in the first step,[13] and, as yet, empirical studies involving steps 2 and 3 are almost nonexistent.[14]

But if such research is difficult it is also indispensable. It is hard to see how rationality can play any significant role in the formulation of administrative decisions unless these production functions are at least approximately known. Nor can the problem be avoided by falling back on the "common sense" of administrators—their "intuition" and "practical insight" in dealing with situations for which "long experience" has qualified them. Anyone who has had close contact with administrative situations can testify that there is no correlation between the ability of administrators and their confidence in the decisions they make—if anything the correlation is an inverse one. The ablest administrators are the first to admit that their decisions are, in general, the sheerest guesswork; that any confidence they evidence is the protective shield with which the practical man armors himself and his subordinates from his doubts.

The fact of the matter is that momentous decisions are made every day as to the allocation of resources to one or another competing purpose, and that, particularly in noncommercial organizations, the decisions are made in an almost complete absence of the

[13] For a bibliography of writings on this subject see Ridley and Simon, *op. cit.,* pp. 68–74.
[14] Herbert A. Simon et al., *Determining Work Loads for Professional Staff in a Public Welfare Agency* (Berkeley: Bureau of Public Administration, University of California, 1941).

evidence which would be necessary to validate them. The principal reason for this, of course, is the difficulty, except in enterprises that have a relatively tangible product, of determining the actual production functions.

To recognize how far actual decisions fall short of rationality is no criticism of the administrator, who must act whether or not he possesses the information that would be necessary for the complete rationality of his decisions. It is, however, a criticism of apologies that would make his ignorance a virtue, and would question the need for extensive programs of research in this direction.[15]

FUNCTIONALIZATION IN RELATION TO EFFICIENCY

A few words need to be said now about the bearing of this efficiency criterion upon organizational problems. In an earlier chapter it was noted that specialization in organization often follows functional lines. This functionalization involves the analysis of the organization objective into subsidiary objectives. One or more of the subsidiary objectives may be assigned to each of the organizational units.

Thus, a fire department may be divided into a fire prevention bureau, and a number of fire-fighting divisions. The function, or objective, of the former will be defined in terms of prevention, that of the latter in terms of extinguishment. A health department may include a communicable diseases division, a division for prenatal care, a vital statistics division, and so forth. Similar illustrations can be found in every field of governmental service.

Under these circumstances, there will be a hierarchy of functions and objectives corresponding to the hierarchy of divisions and bureaus in the agency. In general, the hierarchical arrangement of functions will correspond to a means-end relationship. Fire losses, for instance, can be conceived as a product of number of fires by average loss per fire. Hence, a fire department might take reduction

---

[15] Even Barnard, whose critical insight usually saves him from the "practical man" fallacy, credits the intuitional faculties with considerably more validity than seems to be due them. See his "Mind in Everyday Affairs," reprinted as an appendix in *The Functions of the Executive*, pp. 301–322.

in number of fires and reduction in average loss per fire as subsidiary objectives, and assign these objectives to subsidiary units in the organization.

There are several prerequisites to effective functionalization. First, as indicated above, the general objective must be analyzed into subsidiary objectives, standing in a means-end relation with it. But further, the technology of the activity must be such that the work of the agency can be broken into distinct portions, each contributing primarily toward one, and only one, of the subsidiary objectives. Thus, it would be useless to divide a recreation department into "good citizenship," "health," "enjoyment," and "education" divisions. Although these might be defended as subsidiary objectives of recreation work, it would be impossible to devise a scheme of organization which would break activities into component parts, each contributing to only one of these objectives.

Value and Limits of Functionalization

The so-called "functional principle" of organization is thus seen to be a of a rather complex nature. It assumes the possibility of a parallel functionalization of objectives and of activities. Where such parallelism is absent, the mere analysis of an objective into its components does not afford any basis for organization.

If the limitations of functionalization are apparent, so also are some of its values. For, if the activities of an organizational unit are directed toward a particular well defined objective, then the problem of decision-making in that unit is correspondingly simplified. The value elements to be considered in weighing alternatives can all be related to the organizational objective. A fire prevention division need consider only the impact of its activities upon the number of fires that will occur.

On the other hand, if the functionalization is unrealistic—if it does not fit the technological picture—then functionalization may lead to deterioration in the quality of decisions. For in this case the values which are affected by the unit's activities, but which are not comprehended in the statement of the organizational objective, will be neglected in the decision-making process.

Specialization by "Area" and "Clientele"

It has not generally been recognized in the literature of administration that specialization by "area" and "clientele" are, in fact, merely a particular kind of functionalization. This follows from the fact, already noted, that the complete definition of an objective involves the specification of the group of persons to whom the value in question refers.

The fire department of Podunk, for instance, has as its objective not "minimization of fire losses," but "minimization of fire losses *in Podunk*."

If specialization by area and specialization by clientele are merely forms of functionalization, then, to be successful they must satisfy the conditions of effective functionalization: (1) it must be technologically feasible to split the work activity, as well as the objective, along functional lines; (2) these segregated work activities must not affect, to a substantial degree, values extraneous to the specified functions.

The first point may again be illustrated by a health department. It would not be technologically feasible to divide a contagious disease program into two portions, one aiming to reduce contagious diseases among men the other among women.

The second point will be developed at length in Chapter X. By way of illustration we need only to recall the frequent newspaper accounts of buildings which burn to the ground when a fire department refuses, or is unable, to cross a jurisdictional line.

EFFICIENCY AND THE BUDGET [16]

As a practical application of the approach set forth in this chapter, we may consider the public budget-making process, and the form which this process will have to take if it is to conform to the requirements of rationality.

It has been asserted that the concept of efficiency involves an

[16] This section is adapted from Herbert A. Simon, "Measurement Techniques in Administrative Research," *Civic Affairs*, 8:1 ff. (May, 1941).

analysis of the administrative situation into a positive value element (the results to be attained) and a negative value element (the cost). For the practical execution of this analysis, a technique is needed that will enable the administrator to compare various expenditure alternatives in terms of results and costs. The budget document will provide the basis for such a comparison.

The essence of the public budget process is that it requires a comprehensive plan to be adopted for *all* the expenditures that are to be made in a limited period. But if the budget is to be used as an instrument for the control of efficiency, substantial improvements must be made in present techniques.

Inadequacy of Customary Budget Methods

What does the typical governmental budget include? It tells how much each department will be allowed to spend during the subsequent year, and how it may spend it. How are the particular figures to be found in budgets arrived at? How is it determined that 14 per cent of the budget shall be devoted to fire protection and 11.6 per cent to highways?

A different answer to this question would be given in every community in which it was asked. Some budgets are made by copying off the figures of the previous year's expenditures. Some are constructed by increasing or decreasing appropriations by a fixed percentage. Some are determined by allotting to each department a certain percentage of its request—he who shouts loudest gets most. Some have even less systematic plans.

If this seems exaggerated, the following justifications for increased appropriations in the supporting schedules of one city budget should serve to convince even the most skeptical:

"Salaries should be commensurate with duties and responsibilities of office."

"Naturally with increased work more supplies will be necessary and the cost will be greater. My postage bills alone amount to $2,500 a year."

"Time and skill required for this work before and after election."

"A larger increase was asked last year and refused." [17]

There are, of course, a few exceptional cities and other agencies which attempt to substitute a more rational budget review for this hit-or-miss process. A number of federal departments, including the Department of Agriculture, may be cited in this connection.[18]

The Long-Term Budget

If budgeting is to serve as a basis for the rational allocation of expenditures, two comprehensive budgets must be substituted for the present inadequate documents: an annual budget and a long-term budget. However, since the annual budget is merely a segment of the long-term budget, only the latter need be discussed.

The long-term budget will be made up of several parts: (1) long-term estimates of trends in problem-magnitude for the various departments—distribution and concentration of burnable values which must be protected against fire, mileage of streets which must be kept clean, population which must be served by libraries, etc.; (2) long-term estimates of service adequacy—that is, the level of services which the city intends to provide its citizens, so many acres of park per 1,000 population, a specified fire loss, etc.; (3) a long-term work program, showing in work units the services which will have to be provided and facilities to be constructed to achieve the program outlined in items (1) and (2); and (4) a financial program which will relate the work program to the fiscal resources of the community.

Item (1) involves primarily factual considerations. The determination of item (2) is primarily a matter of value judgments. Items (3) and (4), after the first two items have been determined, become largely factual questions. Hence, it would seem to be a legislative task to weigh (2) against (4), and to determine the budget program. On the other hand, the legislature would need as-

---

[17] I will permit the city from whose budget these examples are drawn to remain anonymous.

[18] Verne B. Lewis, "Budgetary Administration in the Department of Agriculture," in John M. Gaus and Leon O. Wolcott, *Public Administration and the U.S. Department of Agriculture* (Chicago: Public Administration Service, 1941), pp. 403–462; MacMahon, Millett, and Ogden, *op. cit.*, pp. 171–185.

sistance in developing the factual information for (1), (2), and (3).

Under present budgetary procedure, items (1) and (2) are seldom even a part of the budget document, and the entire discussion is carried on in terms of items (3) and (4). Furthermore, usually a single budget plan is presented to the legislature, for its approval or amendment. It would seem much preferable, if the necessary information were available, to present directly to the legislature the policy issues involved in (2), and to present the legislature with alternative budget plans, indicating the implications for policy of increases and curtailments of expenditure. Modifications along these lines would seem to be absolutely essential if the legislature is to be returned to a place of influence in the determination of public policy.

Too often, under current practice, the basic decisions of policy are reached by technicians in the agency entrusted with budget review, without any opportunity for review of that policy by the legislature. That this condition is tolerated results partly from general failure to recognize the relative element in governmental objectives.[19] Since most legislative declarations of policy state objectives of governmental activity without stating the level of adequacy which the service is to reach, it is impossible for an "expert" to reach on factual grounds a conclusion as to the adequacy of a departmental appropriation. Hence, present procedures would not seem to safeguard sufficiently democratic control over the determination of policy.[20]

Progress Toward a Long-Term Budget

Public agencies have made considerable progress within the past few years toward long-term plans that include a work program and a financial plan. Little progress has as yet been made toward a program that will tell the legislator and the citizen what this program means to him in terms of specific governmental services. Further-

[19] See pp. 47–55, 177, *supra*. Cf. Gaston Jeze, *Théorie Générale du Budget* (Paris: M. Giard, 1922), pp. i–iii.
[20] John Dewey has done much to develop a democratic philosophy of the relation of expert to public. In *The Public and Its Problems* (p. 208) he states the essential thesis of the present study.

more, little progress has as yet been made toward estimating the cost of maintaining governmental services at a particular level of adequacy, or determining when expenditures should, in the interests of efficiency, be turned from present channels into other, more useful directions.

Illustration of a Rational Budget

As an illustration of the line of development which needs to be pursued, the budget procedure of the California State Relief Administration will be described briefly. The agency for several years employed a well designed procedure of budget estimating. One reason for its successful performance of this difficult task was the nature of its objectives.

The major task of an unemployment relief agency is to provide a minimum level of economic security to needy families. The family budget which the agency employs to effect its policies provides an immediate translation of "cost" into "result." That is, it is immediately possible to visualize what a specific expenditure means in terms of the level of economic assistance which the agency provides. The policy-forming body can decide how large a family budget it is willing to authorize, and this decision can be immediately translated into cost terms. In this way "service adequacy" is determined.

Similarly, the State Relief Administration had worked out a detailed procedure for estimating over a period of time how many cases would be eligible for assistance; that is, what the problem-magnitude would be. With these two steps completed—the level of service determined and the problem magnitude estimated—it was a simple matter to develop the work budget and estimate financial needs.

This illustration has been oversimplified to emphasize its salient features. An unemployment relief agency must provide certain types of service as well as cash relief. The operating expenses of the agency have been left out of consideration also.[21] But, except for this oversimplification and these omissions, the budget procedure which has been described closely approximates the ideal of a rational budget process.

[21] Simon et al., *op. cit.*

SUMMARY

In this chapter we have seen that, in the factual aspects of decision-making, the administrator must be guided by the criterion of efficiency. This criterion requires that results be maximized with limited resources.

On the other hand, criteria of "correctness" have no meaning in relation to the purely valuational elements in decision. A democratic state is committed to popular control over these value elements, and the distinction of value from fact is of basic importance in securing a proper relation between policy-making and administration.

Improvement in the quality of decision awaits empirical research into the production functions that relate activities to results. Our knowledge of these functions is fragmentary at present, yet they are indispensable as a tool of reason, without which it operates in a factual vacuum.

The value of organization along functional lines lies in its facilitation of decisional processes. Functionalization is possible, however, only when the technology permits activities to be segregated along parallel lines.

A potent device for the improvement in governmental decision-making processes, both legislative and administrative, is the budget document. The improvement of budgetary methods will (1) permit a more effective division of labor between the policy-forming and administrative agencies, and (2) focus attention upon the social production functions and their critical role in decision-making.

Chapter X

LOYALTIES AND ORGANIZATIONAL IDENTIFICATION

THE VALUES and objectives that guide individual decisions in organization are largely the organizational objectives—the service and conservation goals of the organization itself. Initially, these are usually imposed on the individual by the exercise of authority over him; but to a large extent the values gradually become "internalized" and are incorporated into the psychology and attitudes of the individual participant. He acquires an attachment or loyalty to the organization that automatically—i.e. without the necessity for external stimuli—guarantees that his decisions will be consistent with the organization objectives. This loyalty may itself have two aspects: it may involve an attachment to the service goals of the organization (what was called in Chapter VI the "organization objective"), and it may involve also an attachment to the conservation and growth of the organization itself.

In this way, through his subjection to organizationally determined goals, and through the gradual absorption of these goals into his own attitudes, the participant in organization acquires an "organization personality" rather distinct from his personality as an individual. The organization assigns to him a role: it specifies the particular values, facts, and alternatives upon which his decisions in the organization are to be based. For a park foreman the alternatives take the form of grass-cuttings, planting, road maintenance work, clean-up work, and so forth; the values are legislatively and socially determined standards of appearance, cleanliness, recreation use-value; the facts are budgets, work methods, unit costs. The foreman is not ordinarily expected to give serious thought to the alternative possibility of eliminating the park entirely, and making a subdivision of it. Yet this possibility may merit quite as serious attention as the proper location of a flower-bed. It is not considered because it is not his "business." [1]

The broader decisions in the organization determine what each man's "business" is—what his frame of reference in decision-making is to be. It has already been explained, in Chapter V, why the creation of this organizational role and personality is essential to rationality in administrative decision. By limiting the range within which an individual's decisions and activities are to lie, the organization reduces his decisional problems to manageable proportions.

SOCIAL VERSUS ORGANIZATIONAL VALUES

When it is recognized that actual decisions must take place in some such institutional setting, it can be seen that the "correctness" of any particular decision may be judged from two different standpoints. In the broader sense it is "correct" if it is consistent with the general social value scale [2]—if its consequences are socially desirable. In the narrower sense, it is "correct" if it is consistent with the frame of reference that has been organizationally assigned to the decider.

This distinction is well illustrated in the literature of what is called "welfare economics." [3] In a private economy, the institution of private property permits a considerable degree of decentralization in decision-making. It is assumed that each individual will make his decisions in terms of the maximization of his "profit" or "utility." A decision is "correct" if it achieves this maximization. But the welfare economist evaluates decisions from another standpoint. He wants to know the extent to which the maximization of personal utility is compatible with the maximization of social value. When

[1] Cf. Dewey, *The Public and Its Problems*, p. 22.
[2] The phrase "social value" is not entirely a happy one, particularly in view of the insistence upon ethical relativism in chap. iii. It is used here for lack of a more descriptive and accurate term, and an attempt will be made below to explain exactly what is meant.
[3] A. C. Pigou, *The Economics of Welfare* (London: Macmillan & Co., 1924).

choice is viewed from within the individual's environment, advertising is explainable as a technique for increasing profit. Viewing choice from the social viewpoint, the welfare economist questions the social value of energies expended on advertising.[4]

This distinction between general social value and organizational value leads, in turn, to a third notion of correctness—the "correctness" of the organizational environment itself. That is, the social value of the organizational structure may be determined by noting the degree of coincidence between the organizationally correct and the socially correct decisions.

A private economy, for instance, is commonly justified on the ground that a high degree of coincidence exists between the two kinds of correctness. When it is recognized that under certain circumstances—conditions of monopoly, for instance—a considerable discrepancy arises, changes are demanded in the environment of decision (trust-busting, rate regulation, or the like) that will eliminate or reduce the discrepancies.

Meaning of the Phrase "Social Value"

The term "social value," as used here, is best understood in terms of a hierarchy of organizations, or social institutions. A society establishes certain very general values through its basic institutional structure, and attempts to bring about some conformity between these general values and the organizational values of the various groups that exist within it. This has already been illustrated in the previous paragraph. In the same way, any large organization—a business firm or a government—seeks to bring the organizational goals of its parts—departments, bureaus, and so forth—into conformity with the objectives of the organization as a whole.

What is meant by "social value" here is the objectives of some larger organization or social structure in relation to the "organizational values" of its components. Viewed from the standpoint of the legislative body or the citizenry, in so far as these have any

---

[4] See, for example, Elizabeth Ellis Hoyt, *Consumption in Our Society* (New York: McGraw-Hill Book Co., 1938), pp. 104–105. There is no intent to assert here that advertising is always socially valueless, but merely to point out that the value of advertising to the firm does not necessarily measure its value to society.

formulated objectives, the objectives of the Department of the Interior or the United States Steel Corporation are organizational objectives. Viewed from the standpoint of the Secretary of the Interior or the president of the steel company, the objectives of his agency are the "social objectives" to which the organizational objectives of the component divisions and bureaus must conform.

Since it is difficult to establish subsidiary objectives that will always be consistent with the general objective, the individual who is a member of the subsidiary organization will sometimes make decisions that are consistent with the partial objective of his particular organizational component, but inconsistent with the broader goal of the organization as a whole. It is this problem—of reconciling the "role-taking" that the organization imposes on individuals with the achievement of goals transcending these particular roles—that provides the principal subject-matter of this chapter.

An Example of the Conflict

By way of illustration, let us consider the decision-making process in a specific organizational setting. In California, prior to July, 1941, responsibility for the care of unemployed persons was divided between two agencies: the State Relief Administration cared for *employable* unemployed persons and their families; the county welfare departments cared for *unemployable* unemployed persons. The division of function was largely historical in origin and was not supported by any very cogent reasons; but that is beside the point.

From the standpoint of the state as a whole, the objective of welfare administration was to care for the unemployed and to guarantee them a certain minimum standard of living. It was desirable, moreover, to accomplish this objective as efficiently as possible. That is, once the rules of eligibility had been established and standards for the size of family budgets determined, the administrative task was to see that eligible persons, and only eligible persons, qualified for relief; that their budgets conformed to the standards authorized; and that these ends were attained with the least possible expenditure of funds. The State Relief Administration was presumably trying to accomplish this objective with its area of activity limited to employable persons, while the county welfare departments were aiming at the same objective with their areas of activity limited to unemployable persons.

But if these objectives are viewed organizationally, a competitive element immediately enters into the decisions of the state and county administrative officials, respectively. One way in which the state agency could increase its efficiency (measured in terms of its own limited objective, and not in terms of the objective of the state as a whole) was to make certain that any unemployable persons on its rolls were discovered and transferred to the county. One way in which the county agency could increase its efficiency (measured, again, in terms of the limited organizational objective) was to make certain that any employable persons on its rolls were discovered and transferred to the state.

As a result, each organization sought the relative maximization of its own objective, and a great deal of time, effort, and money was spent by these agencies in attempting to shift clients from one to the other in border-line cases. This competitive activity is entirely understandable from the point of view of the organizational objectives of each organization, but it contributed nothing toward the maximization of the broader social value.

It should be noted, however, that there is nothing inevitable about this development. Decisions are not made by "organizations" but by human beings behaving as members of organizations. There is no logical necessity that a member of an organization shall make his decisions in terms of values which are organizationally limited. Nevertheless, in example after example, we can find individuals behaving as though the institutions to which they belong were "economic men," always calculating the "institutional utility," in terms both of service and conservation goals, in each decision. How can this phenomenon be explained? To understand it, we must make clear first the distinction between men's personal and organizational decisions.

Impersonality of Organization Decisions

Barnard has very clearly pointed out that the decisions which a person makes as a member of an organization are quite distinct from his personal decisions:

The system, then, to which we give the name "organization" is a system composed of the activities of human beings. What makes these activities a system is that the efforts of different persons are here coordinated. For this reason their significant aspects are not personal. They are determined by the system either as to manner, or degree, or time. Most of the efforts in cooperative systems are easily seen to be impersonal. For example, a clerk writing on a report form for a corporation is obviously doing something at a place, on a form, and about a subject that clearly never could engage his strictly personal interest. Hence, when we say that we are concerned with a system of coordinated human efforts, we mean that although persons are agents of the action, the action is not personal in the aspect important for the study of cooperative systems.[5]

At a later point, Barnard shows clearly why this is so. Personal considerations determine whether a person will participate in an organization; but, if he decides to participate, they will not determine the content of his organizational behavior:

Every effort that is a constituent of organization, that is, every coordinated cooperative effort, may involve two acts of decision. The first is the decision of the person affected as to whether or not he will contribute this effort as a matter of personal choice. It is a detail of the process of repeated personal decisions that determine whether or not the individual will be or will continue to be a contributor to the organization. . . . This act of decision is *outside* the system of efforts constituting the organization . . . although it is, as we have seen, a subject for organized attention.

The second type of decisions has no direct or specific relation to personal results, but views the effort concerning which decision is to be made non-personally from the viewpoint of its organization effect and of its relation to organization purpose. This second act of decision is often made in a direct sense by individuals, but it is impersonal and organizational in its intent and effect. Very often it is also organizational in its process, as for example in legislatures, or when boards or committees determine action. The act of decision is a part of the organization itself.

This distinction between the two types of decision is frequently recognized in ordinary affairs. We very often say or hear sentences similar

[5] C. I. Barnard, *op. cit.*, p. 77.

to this: "If this were my business, I think I would decide the question this way—but it is not my personal affair"; or, "I think the *situation* requires such and such an answer—but I am not in a position to determine what ought to be done"; or "The decision should be made by someone else." This is in effect a restatement, with a different emphasis, of the suggestions in Chapter VII that a sort of dual personality is required of individuals contributing to organization action—the private personality, and the organization personality.[6]

Once the system of values which is to govern an administrative choice has been specified, there is one and only one "best" decision, and this decision is determined by the organizational values and situation, and not by the personal motives of the member of the organization who makes the decision. Within the area of discretion, once an individual has decided, on the basis of his personal motives, to recognize the organizational objectives, his further behavior is determined not by personal motives, but by the demands of efficiency.

There is a limit, however, to this proposition. There is an area of acceptance within which the individual will behave "organizationally." When the organizational demands fall outside this area, personal motives reassert themselves, and the organization, to that extent, ceases to exist.

When a person is behaving impersonally, then, an organizational value scale is substituted for his personal value scale as the criterion of "correctness" in his decisions. Hence, his decision may be considered as a variable, depending for its specific character upon the particular organizational value scale which governs it.

We still do not have an answer to the question of why an individual employs one particular organizational value scale as his criterion of choice, rather than one or more of all the innumerable other scales he might use. We can now turn our attention to this question.

ORGANIZATIONAL IDENTIFICATION

To designate the phenomenon we are discussing, we may introduce the term "identification" which has already had some currency

[6] *Ibid.*, pp. 187–188.

in political theory. "Identification" is used in psychoanalytic literature to denote a particular kind of emotional tie. Freud describes the nature of the tie thus:

It is easy to state in a formula the distinction between an identification with the father and the choice of the father as an object. In the first case one's father is what one would like to *be,* and in the second he is what one would like to *have.* The distinction, that is, depends upon whether the tie attaches to the subject or to the object of the ego.[7]

Freud hypothesized, further, that identification is a fundamental mechanism in group cohesion:

We already begin to divine that the mutual tie between members of a group is in the nature of an identification of this kind, based upon an important emotional common quality; and we may suspect that this common quality lies in the nature of the tie with the leader.[8]

Lasswell, presumably adopting the term from Freud, devotes an entire chapter [9] to "Nations and Classes: The Symbols of Identification." Nowhere, however, does he define the term, other than to speak of "identifying symbols like 'nation,' 'state,' 'class,' 'race,' 'church,' " and to define a "sentiment area" as "the locus of those who are mutually identified." Further, he nowhere asserts that the underlying psychological mechanism is identical with the Freudian concept of identification.

Meaning of Identification

To make explicit the definition of the concept which Lasswell names, we will say that *a person identifies himself with a group when, in making a decision, he evaluates the several alternatives of choice in terms of their consequences for the specified group.* We shall not assume that the mechanism underlying this phenomenon is the Freudian one. In fact, in this case as in many others, the Freudian hypothesis appears to be a greatly oversimplified one.

When a person prefers a particular course of action because it is "good for America," he identifies himself with Americans; when

[7] Sigmund Freud, *Group Psychology and the Analysis of the Ego* (New York: Boni and Liveright, 1922), p. 62.
[8] *Ibid.,* p. 66.
[9] H. D. Lasswell, *World Politics and Personal Insecurity* (New York: Whittlesey House, 1935), pp. 29–51. The quotations are from p. 7.

he prefers it because it will "boost business in Berkeley," he identifies himself with Berkeleyans. A person is said to act from "personal" motives when his evaluation is based upon an identification with himself or with his family.

The group with which a person identifies himself can be characterized by the geographical area which it inhabits, its economic or social status in the society, and any number of other criteria. The "nation" is an example of geographical identification; the "proletariat" and "women" are examples of economic and social identification symbols. Examples of identifications which are important to our political institutions may be found in the literature on legislative processes and pressure groups.[10]

The identification of the individual may be either with the organization objective or with the conservation of the organization. For example, a person making a decision can identify himself with the function or objective of education—he can evaluate all alternatives in terms of their effect upon education. On the other hand, he may identify himself with a particular educational organization—he may resist the transfer of certain recreational functions from a school department to a park department—and seek the conservation and growth of that organization. As pointed out in Chapter VI, two types of organizational loyalty must be distinguished, corresponding to these two kinds of identification.

These identifications with group or with function are such an all-pervasive phenomenon that one cannot participate for fifteen minutes in political or administrative affairs, or read five pages in an administrative report, without meeting examples of them.

Newspapers carry frequent illustrations of such identifications. Following is a brief news item about the California highway system:

California can hardly think of spending $150,000,000 to bring its highways up to military standards when the network of rural roads is seriously in need of reconstruction, State Highway Engineer Charles H. Purcell said today.

---

[10] Cf. E. Pendleton Herring, *Group Representation Before Congress* (Baltimore: Johns Hopkins Press, 1929), pp. 1–12. and *passim,* and H. D. Lasswell, *Politics: Who Gets What, When, How* (New York: McGraw-Hill Book Co., 1936), pp. 1–28, 29–51, 129–232.

Purcell told a legislative interim committee the chief concern of the State Division of Highways was how to obtain the $442,500,000 required to make the rural roads adequate to carry normal civilian traffic in the next ten years.

If the War Department wants some 5,887 miles of California's strategic highways improved to its standards, the State engineer declared, it was the "primary responsibility" of the Federal Government to advance the money. The same highways system, he added, is considered adequate for civil use.[11]

The Highway Engineer apparently conceives it to be his function to choose between competing possibilities for highway construction in terms of the value of "civilian need" rather than the value of "military need" or some composite of both values. He further implies in his statement that, when funds are spent through a *state* agency, values to the state are to be given a weight in the decisions for allocating these funds, while values which may diffuse across state boundaries are not to be considered. Neither criticism of, nor agreement with, this position is intended here. The points to be noted are that the Engineer's judgments are consequences of his organizational identifications, and that his conclusions can be reached only if these identifications be assumed.

The hearings before the House Committee on Appropriations of the United States Congress are a fertile source of illustrations of the phenomenon of identification. The following example will suffice:

Mr. Oliver: That, of course, is all worth-while service, but how do you feel you are accomplishing practical, concrete results from the studies and surveys you are making in the different directions referred to?

Miss Anderson: Well, that is very difficult to say, because it is intangible in a way.

Mr. Oliver: In other words, it is information which, of course, either the States or some organizations in the States should take up, and acting on the suggestions you make, provide some remedy or relief?

Miss Anderson: Yes. For instance, take the State of Connecticut. There has been a great deal of information given to the State of Con-

[11] Oakland (Calif.) *Tribune,* Oct. 13, 1941.

necticut, and I have no doubt that the information that we gave them on these conditions, and what they have followed up themselves since, will manifest itself in certain legislation in the next session of their legislature.

Mr. Oliver: Now, why should not the States undertake to collect that information? Why should they be expected to send to Washington, many, many miles away, and call on the Federal Government to collect information which is much more readily available to them and to their own officials?

Miss Anderson: The Labor Department in only one or two States in the country are able to collect that material themselves. They have not set up that kind of investigational organization.

Mr. Oliver: Is not this true: So long as the Federal Government willingly responds to requests of that character—and it appears from your statement that each year you are being called on to become active in a new field—just so long as ready response is made to requests, the States will decline to do that which primarily should devolve upon them?

A little later in the dialogue the Congressman adds:

Mr. Oliver: How long, in times like these, should we continue to render a service of that character for the States which all seem to concede is primarily a duty devolving on the State? [12]

It is clear that although the Congressman states his first argument in terms of efficiency, the real issue in his mind is an organizational one. An activity which might be of legitimate value if pursued by a State is to be valued less highly if pursued by a Federal agency because it "is primarily a duty devolving on the State." We will forgive the Congressman the supreme illogic of his qualifying phrase "in times like these." It is significant, however, that his illogic, quite as much as his logic, stems from an organizational identification.

The Psychology of Identification

No single or simple mechanism is likely to explain realistically the phenomenon of identification. Some of the contributory factors may be enumerated:

[12] U.S. Congress, Subcommittee of House Committee on Appropriations, *Hearing on Department of Labor Appropriation Bill for 1934* (Washington: Government Printing Office, 1933), pp. 74–76.

1. *Personal Interest in Organizational Success.* The decision which is made in terms of organizational values is, to that extent, impersonal; but attachment to the organization derives from personal motives. The individual is willing to make impersonal organizational decisions because a variety of factors, or incentives, tie him to the organization—his salary, prestige, friendship, and many others.

Many of these personal values are dependent not only on his connection with the organization, but also on the growth, the prestige, or the success of the organization itself. His salary and his power are both related to the size of the unit that he administers. Growth of the organization offers to him and to his employees salary increases, advancement, and opportunity to exercise responsibility. A large budget will enable him to undertake activities and services which will excite the interest and admiration of his professional peers in other organizations. Consequently, these motives lead to an identification with conservation goals.

Conversely, failure of the organization, or curtailment of its budget, may mean salary reduction, loss of power, or even unemployment to the administrator. At the very least it forces on him the unpleasant duty of dismissing personnel and seriously impairs the incentive of possible advancement for his subordinates.

2. *Transfer of Private-Management Psychology.* The private segment of our economy operates on the assumption that management will make its decisions in terms of profit to the individual business establishment. This institutional psychology of choice may easily be carried over to the public segment of the economy through lack of recognition of the fundamental differences in the assumptions that underlie these two segments. The executive who is accustomed to thinking in terms of "my" business, is apt to think in terms of "my" county, or "my" department. Again, this motive would lead primarily to identification with conservation rather than with particular organization objectives. These same attitudes may be present in persons who, while they never have had administrative responsibility in the private segment of the economy, have absorbed

these notions from a predominantly private-economy cultural environment.[13]

It would be an interesting subject of research to determine the extent to which private-management attitudes persist in a communistic economy like that of Soviet Russia. It would be extremely difficult, however, to separate this factor from the elements of personal motivation which would continue to bind the individual to the organization even in a nationalized economy.

The illustration drawn from the administration of public welfare in the state of California [14] is a good example of the consequences which flow from a "private" conception of organizational efficiency. So zealous were the state and county agencies, respectively, in rejecting clients who were the "responsibility" of the other that it proved politically impossible in most counties of the state to set up an impartial medical board to pass on the employability of doubtful cases.

3. *Focus of Attention.* A third element in the process of identification is the focusing of the administrator's attention upon those values and those groups which are most immediately affected by the administrative program. When an administrator is entrusted with the task of *educating* Berkeley's children, he is likely to be more clearly aware of the effect of any particular proposal upon their learning, than of its possible indirect effects upon their health—and vice versa. He identifies himself, then, with the organization objective.

It is clear that attention may narrow the range of vision by selecting particular values, particular items of empirical knowledge, and particular behavior alternatives for consideration, to the exclusion of other values, other knowledge, and other possibilities. Identification, then, has a firm basis in the limitations of human psychology in coping with the problem of rational choice.

[13] Several individuals who read an earlier draft of this study questioned the existence of this transfer of private-management psychology. The writer knows of no available empirical evidence that would definitely prove or disprove the existence of such a transfer. He can only say that the hypothesis that such exists seems plausible to him, and that both the existence of the transfer and its importance if it does exist would be very fruitful objects of empirical investigation.
[14] See pp. 201–202, *supra.*

From this point of view, identification is an important mechanism for constructing the environment of decision. When identification is faulty, the resulting discrepancies between social and organizational values result in a loss of social efficiency. When the organizational structure is well conceived, on the other hand, the process of identification permits the broad organizational arrangements to govern the decisions of the persons who participate in the structure. Thereby, it permits human rationality to transcend the limitations imposed upon it by the narrow span of attention.[15]

An example of the manner in which the focus of attention of participants in an administrative structure is determined by their position in the structure came to the author's attention while he was making a study of the administration of recreation activities in Milwaukee. The playgrounds in that city had been constructed by the Playground Division of the Department of Public Works, but activities on the grounds were supervised by the Extension Department of the School Board. Maintenance of the grounds had also been turned over to the latter agency, and there was some belief that maintenance was inadequate.

It is understandable that the Extension Department, suddenly confronted with vast new financial obligations by the expansion of physical facilities, should attempt to minimize cost of maintenance so as not to divert funds from supervisory activities. The fact that the early construction work was highly experimental has resulted in maintenance costs beyond original expectations. It is likewise understandable that the Playground Division, whose work has been the construction of physical facilities, should consider it a false economy to inadequately provide for the maintenance of those facilities.

There has been a difference in emphasis, for example, as to the place of landscaping in the playground design. The Playground Division has stressed the importance of proper landscaping in affecting public attitudes toward playgrounds. It has insisted that the playground should be an asset to the appearance of the neighborhood.

The Extension Department spent the first ten years of its existence working with the meagerest physical facilities. The playgrounds were

[15] See chap. v, pp. 100–102. Karl Mannheim (*op. cit.*, pp. 52–57, 290) has emphasized this same point.

for the most part hot and dusty with no thought of landscaping. From those ten years of experience the Department learned that the success of a playground depends primarily upon leadership rather than upon physical plant.

Each department understands fully that both objectives are desirable, and to a certain extent necessary, in the administration of a successful program. The question is not "which" but "how much," and since it is the Extension Department which has charge of the funds maintenance activities have suffered to a certain degree.[16]

Identification and Adequacy

One of the most common consequences of functional identification is a failure to balance costs against values in making administrative decisions. The accomplishment by an administrative program of its organizational goals can be measured in terms of *adequacy* (the degree to which its goals have been reached) or of *efficiency* (the degree to which the goals have been reached relative to the available resources). To use a very crude example, the adequacy of the recent war production program would be measured in terms of the size and equipment of the armed force put into the field; its efficiency in terms of a comparison of the production actually attained with what could have been attained with a best use of national resources. American war production turned out to be of a high degree of adequacy; whether it was efficient is quite another question.

The tendency of an administrator who identifies himself with a particular goal is to measure his organization in terms of adequacy rather than efficiency.[17] It is not always recognized by these specialists that there is absolutely no scientific basis for the construction of so-called "standards of desirable service" or "standards of minimum adequate service" for a particular function, until it is known what this service will cost, what resources are available for financing

[16] Herbert A. Simon, "Administration of Public Recreational Facilities in Milwaukee," unpublished manuscript, 1935, p. 38.

[17] Since, as pointed out in chap. vi, such identifications are more frequent in public administration than in the administration of commercial enterprises, the problem discussed in this section is primarily (but not entirely) a problem of public administration.

it, and what curtailment in other services or in private expenditures would be required by an increase in that particular service.

What annual report is ever published which does not include some such recommendation as the following:

The chief and very urgent recommendation at the close of this fiscal year is for an increase in staff. This is especially necessary in the Minimum Wage Division, the work of which has increased enormously since the Supreme Court decision validated minimum-wage legislation. Many States still in the early stages of wage-law administration are looking to the Women's Bureau for help in organization, in securing the necessary wage and hour data, and in the all-important work of bringing uniformity into the setting of rates and the practice of enforcement. Frequent visits to the States, and meetings in Washington of State officials, are necessary. The staff of this Division must be increased, as it is not able to meet all the demands upon it.[18]

That is the universal administrative plaint. "The budget is *inadequate*." Now, between the white of adequacy and the black of inadequacy lie all the shades of gray which represent degrees of adequacy. Further, human wants are insatiable in relation to human resources. From these two facts we may conclude that the fundamental criterion of administrative decision must be a criterion of *efficiency* rather than a criterion of *adequacy*. The task of the administrator is to maximize social values *relative* to limited resources.[19]

If, then, the process of identification leads the administrator to give undue weight to the particular social values with which he is

[18] U.S. Department of Labor, 25th Annual Report of the Secretary, Fiscal Year Ended June 30, 1937 (Washington: Government Printing Office, 1937), p. 136.
[19] We must not commit the opposite error of making budget decisions in terms of *economy*—that is, reduction of expenditures without regard to service. This seems to be the fundamental objection to entrusting undue influence in budget matters to a controllership or treasury agency as recommended, for instance, by the British Machinery of Government Committee: "On the whole, experience seems to show that the interests of the taxpayer cannot be left to the spending Departments; that those interests require the careful consideration of each item of public expenditure in its relation to other items and to the available resources of the State, as well as the vigilant supervision of some authority not directly concerned in the expenditure itself; and that such supervision can be most naturally and effectively exercised by the Department which is responsible for raising the revenue required." (Great Britain, Ministry of Reconstruction, *Report of the Machinery of Government Committee*, Cd. 9230 [London: H.M. Stationery Office, 1918, reprinted 1925], pp. 18–19.)

concerned, he is in no position, psychologically speaking, to make a satisfactory decision as to the amount of money which should be allocated to his function, or as to the relative merits of his claims upon public funds, as compared with the claims of competing units.[20]

Budgetary procedures are the most important means of translating questions of adequacy into questions of efficiency. The budget, first of all, forces a simultaneous consideration of all the competing claims for support. Second, the budget transports upward in the administrative hierarchy the decisions as to fund allocation to a point where competing values must be weighed, and where functional identifications will not lead to a faulty weighting of values.

MODIFYING IDENTIFICATIONS THROUGH ORGANIZATION

It would seem that a major problem in effective organization is to specialize and subdivide activities in such a manner that the psychological forces of identification will contribute to, rather than hinder, correct decision-making.

[20] The importance of "location" to the psychology of the administrator is accepted, even in lay circles, as a natural attribute of institutional thought. This is humorously, but convincingly, illustrated by an incident reported in the gossip column of the *San Francisco News,* Feb. 12, 1942. The item refers to the San Francisco Utilities Department, which controls the city's Water Department and the Hetch Hetchy Power development as well as other local utilities:

"While Utilities Manager Cahill was in Washington for 10 days that lasted a month, Nelson Eckart, head of the Water Department, filled his own job, the top Hetch Hetchy post of the late A. T. McAfee, and Cahill's overall job, too. Forrest Gibbon, executive secretary, had to tell who he was by the hat he was wearing.

"On Cahill's return, Eckart's first words were, 'Here's the key to the powder house, here's the aspirin bottle, I quit.' But it was some days before Cahill discovered all the triple-personality kinks which had brought Eckart to the brink of madness. He discovered, in fact, a letter Waterman Eckart had written asking money for more water-works, another letter Hetch Hetchy Eckart had written asking for more HH dough, and a final letter Acting Utilities Manager Eckart had written denying both of his own requests. Naturally, Cahill asked what the devil.

"'From up here,' Eckart explained, 'things don't look the same as they do from down there.'"

Thomas Becket seems to have been a highly institutionalized personality—his loyalties shifting with his office. See his biography in the *Encyclopædia Britannica,* 11th Ed. (Vol. III, p. 609), where his relations to Henry II are explained in institutional terms.

Modes of Specialization

The way in which activities are subdivided in the organization will have a major influence on identification. The administrative segregation of a function will be satisfactory to the extent that (1) the activities involved in the performance of the function are independent of the other activities in the organization, (2) indirect effects of the activity, not measurable in terms of the functional objective, are absent, and (3) it is possible to set up lines of communication which will bring to the unit responsible for the performance of the function the knowledge necessary for its successful execution.

All three of these are technical and factual questions. This means that any attempt to devise an administrative organization for carrying on a service by means of an armchair analysis of the agency's function into its component parts is inherently sterile. Yet a large part of the administrative research, so called, which has been carried on in the last generation is exactly of this nature.

Allocation of the Decision-Making Function

To the extent that identifications modify decisions, the effective allocation of decision-making functions must take these identifications into consideration.

If any basic principle governs this allocation, it is that each decision should be located at a point where it will be of necessity approached as a question of efficiency rather than a question of adequacy. That is, it is unsound to entrust to the administrator responsible for a function the responsibility for weighing the importance of that function against the importance of other functions. The only person who can approach competently the task of weighing their relative importance is one who is responsible for both or neither.

This presupposes, however, that persons *will* identify themselves with their organizational units. While we have indicated that there are a number of factors making for such identification, it should not be supposed that it is ever complete or consistent. The administrator who is faced with a choice between social and organizational values usually feels a twinge of conscience, stronger or weaker, when he puts organizational objectives before broader social ones. There is no inevitability in any particular identification.

It might be hoped, then, that it would be feasible to broaden, to some degree, the area of identification which governs the administrator's decisions. Steps might be taken to transfer allegiance from the smaller to the larger organizational units, and from the narrower to the broader objectives. To the extent that this is achieved, the precise location of decision-making functions is of less importance.

Lord Haldane's Committee deplored what they called the traditional attitude of antagonism between the Treasury and the other departments. I do not know myself that I have been particularly conscious of it, but there is no doubt that in many departments there are individuals who seem to believe in the Russian proverb, "Whose bread I eat his songs I sing," and who think it is incumbent upon them as members of a particular department to show what they conceive to be their loyalty to that department by supporting it, right or wrong. Such a view I believe to be a thoroughly mistaken one. The loyalty of every citizen in the State is to the country at large. It is the country's bread that he eats, not the bread of the Ministry of Health or the Department of Agriculture, or the Exchequer and Audit Department. If he finds something which he thinks it is in the interest of the country to point out, he ought not to be deterred from doing his plain duty by the feeling that he might be disliked in his own department or might prejudice his personal advancement. That, of course, is still more true when you take departments collectively, and when you get one department very jealous of another department, very angry if there is any poaching on its preserves, upon which follow barren interminable interdepartmental correspondence.[21]

Here clearly, is the end to be aimed at; but it will take more than hope and preaching to reach it. If personal motives, private-business attitudes, and limitations of the span of attention are the factors making for narrow organizational identifications, then any attempt to weaken such identifications, or to transfer them, must modify

[21] Henry Higgs, "Treasury Control," *Journal of Public Administration*, 2:129 (Apr., 1924).

these same factors. Loyalty to the larger group will result when loyalty to that group is rewarded even in conflict with loyalty to the smaller group. Loyalty to the larger group will result when the distinction is clearly understood between the private-economy and public-economy modes of thought. Loyalty to the larger group will result when administrative situations are understood in terms of efficiency rather than adequacy.

Psychological Types in Decision

These considerations suggest that a very fundamental classification of administrative types might be developed in terms of the variant thought-processes underlying decision. The development of this theme would carry us too far afield from our main topic, but a few remarks may serve by way of illustration.

Observation indicates that, as the higher levels are approached in administrative organizations, the administrator's "internal" task (his relations with the organization subordinate to him) decreases in importance relative to his "external" task (his relations with persons outside the organization). An ever larger part of his work may be subsumed under the heads of "public relations" and "promotion." The habits of mind characteristic of the administrative roles at the lower and higher levels of an organization undoubtedly show differences corresponding to these differences in function.

At the lower levels of the hierarchy, the frame of reference within which decision is to take place is largely given. The factors to be evaluated have already been enumerated, and all that remains is to determine their values under the given circumstances. At the higher levels of the hierarchy, the task is an artistic and an inventive one. New values must be sought out and weighed; the possibilities of new administrative structures evaluated. The very framework of reference within which decision is to take place must be constructed.

It is at these higher levels that organizational identifications may have their most serious consequences. At the lower level, the identification is instrumental in bringing broad considerations to bear on individual situations. It assures that decisions will be made responsibly and impersonally. At the higher levels, identifications serve to predetermine the decision, and to introduce among its assumptions unrecognized and unverified valuations.

SUMMARY

In this chapter we have examined a specialized but fundamentally important element in the psychological environment of decision—namely, the element of identification. Identification is the process whereby the individual substitutes organizational objectives (service objectives or conservation objectives) for his own aims as the value-indices which determine his organizational decisions.

Through identification, organized society imposes upon the individual the scheme of social values in place of his personal motives. An organizational structure is socially useful to the extent that the pattern of identifications which it creates brings about a correspondence between social value and organizational value.

The psychological bases of identification are obscure, but seem to involve at least three elements: personal interest in institutional success, a transfer to public agencies of a private-management philosophy, and limitations upon the area of attention which prevent more than a restricted sphere of values from coming within its purview.

The principal undesirable effect of identification is that it prevents the organized individual from making correct decisions in cases where the restricted area of values with which he identifies himself must be weighed against other values outside that area. The organization structure must be designed, and decisions allocated within it, so as to minimize the decisional bias arising from this cause. Two important applications may be mentioned. To avoid biases of identification, budget decisions must be made at a point in the organization where they will be viewed from a standpoint of efficiency rather than adequacy—that is, where the real alternatives of cost as well as value are posed. Likewise, the success of functional specialization will depend, in part, on the absence of value-consequences that lie outside the area of functional identification, for the presence of such consequences will introduce serious biases into decision.

If identification is highly useful in depersonalizing choice within an organization and enforcing social responsibility, it may be equally harmful if it colors and distorts the decisions that precede the establishment of the organizational structure itself. The construction of socially useful organizations requires an unprejudiced assessment of all the values involved. Prejudice is bound to enter if the assessor's judgment is warped by his identifications. Hence, the personal loyalty to organizational values which is generally so useful an aspect of behavior in an organization may be correspondingly harmful when encountered in the fields of invention and promotion, that is, in the tastes of the administrator at the higher levels of the hierarchy.

Chapter XI

THE ANATOMY OF ORGANIZATION

IT IS time now to draw the threads of discussion together, and to see whether they weave any pattern for administrative organization. The reader may wish, first of all, to review Chapter I, which gives something of an overview of the topics that have been taken up thus far.

In the present chapter, as in previous ones, no attempt will be made to offer advice as to how organizations *should* be constructed and operated. The reader has been warned before that this volume deals with the anatomy and physiology of organization and does not attempt to prescribe for the ills of organization. Its field is organizational biology, rather than medicine; and its only claim of contribution to the practical problems of administration is that sound medical practice can only be founded on thorough knowledge of the biology of the organism. Any prescriptions for administrative practice will be only incidental to the main purpose of description and analysis.

The central theme around which the analysis has been developed is that organization behavior is a complex network of decisional processes, all pointed toward their influence upon the behaviors of the operatives—those who do the actual "physical" work of the organization. The anatomy of the organization is to be found in the distribution and allocation of decision-making functions. The physiology of the organization is to be found in the processes whereby the organization influences the decisions of each of its members—supplying these decisions with their premises.

THE PROCESS OF COMPOSITE DECISION

It should be perfectly apparent that almost no decision made in an organization is the task of a single individual. Even though the final responsibility for taking a particular action rests with some definite person, we shall always find, in studying the manner in which this decision was reached, that its various components can be traced through the formal and informal channels of communication to many individuals who have participated in forming its premises. When all of these components have been identified, it may appear that the contribution of the individual who made the formal decision was a minor one, indeed.[1]

We may see the treasurer of a corporation affix his signature to a contract whereby the corporation borrows a sum of money to finance a particular project. The treasurer evidently has authority to make this decision for the organization and to commit the organization to it; but what steps preceded his decision? Perhaps the chief engineer (acting, no doubt, on information and analyses communicated to him by his subordinates) decides that for the adequate operation of a technological system there should be a particular structure that his department has designed at an anticipated cost of five hundred thousand dollars. The general manager to whom he reports does not object to the proposal from the technological standpoint, but doubts that its value is sufficient to justify so large an expenditure; but before making a decision he consults the president or some members of the board as to their willingness to approve the risk of additional investment, as to the feasibility of financing, and as to the time of financing. This results in a decision to ask for a revision and curtailment of the proposal, and plans are redrafted in the engineering department to reduce the cost to four hundred thousand dollars. The proposal is then formally drawn up, approved by the chief engineer and the officers, and presented to the board. The questions then are: should the project be approved, and how should it be financed? It is approved, but it is suggested that in view of the danger of error of estimate, financing to the amount of four hundred fifty thousand dollars should be sought because otherwise the

---

[1] I am indebted to Mr. Barnard, through correspondence, both for the term "composite decision" and for the particular example of composite decision that is given here. The reader can undoubtedly supply many comparable examples from his own organizational experience.

financial position of the company would be embarrassed if the cost should exceed four hundred thousand. Then, after much discussion, it is decided to finance by means of a mortgage loan at an interest rate not exceeding a certain amount, preferably placed with Company X, and the officers are authorized by the board of directors to proceed. Company X, however, when consulted is not interested in the proposal at the interest rate suggested and on examination of the plans thinks the engineering aspects call for revision. The matter goes through the same process again, and so on.

In the end, the officer making the final negotiation or signing the contract, though appearing to decide at least the major questions, is reduced almost to performing a ministerial function. The major decisions were made neither by the board nor by any officer, nor formally by any group; they evolved through the interaction of many decisions both of individuals and by committees and boards. No one man is likely to be aware of all the decisions entering into the process or of who made them, or of the interaction through a period of time that modified decisions at one point and another. That decision is almost always a composite process of this sort will be illustrated further in a later section of this chapter that deals with the planning process.

From the standpoint of process, it is useful to view composite decision from the standpoint of the individual who makes a decision, in order to see (a) how much discretion is actually left him, and (b) what methods the organization uses to influence the decisional premises he selects.

The Degrees of Influence

Influence is exercised in its most complete form when a decision promulgated by one person governs every aspect of the behavior of another. On the parade ground, the marching soldier is permitted no discretion whatsoever. His every step, his bearing, the length of his pace are all governed by authority. Frederick the Great is reported to have found the parade-ground deportment of his Guards perfect—with one flaw. "They breathe," he complained. Few other examples could be cited, however, of the exercise of influence in unlimited form.

Most often, influence places only partial limits upon the exercise of discretion. A subordinate may be told *what* to do, but given considerable leeway as to *how* he will carry out the task. The "what" is, of course, a matter of degree, and may be specified within narrower or broader limits. A charter which states in general terms the function of a city fire department places much less severe limits upon the discretion of the fire chief than the commands of a captain at the scene of a conflagration place on the discretion of the firemen.

A realistic analysis of influence in general and authority in particular must recognize that influence can be exercised with all degrees of specificity. To determine the scope of influence or authority which is exercised in any concrete case, it is necessary to dissect the decisions of the subordinate into their component parts, and then determine which of these parts are determined by the superior and which are left to the subordinate's discretion.

In Chapter III it was shown that a rational decision can be viewed as a conclusion reached from premises of two different kinds: value premises and factual premises. Given a complete set of value and factual premises, there is only one decision which is consistent with rationality. That is, with a given system of values, and a specified set of alternatives, there is one alternative that is preferable to the others.

The behavior of a rational person can be controlled, therefore, if the value and factual premises upon which he bases his decisions are specified for him. This control can be complete or partial—all the premises can be specified, or some can be left to his discretion. Influence, then, is exercised through control over the premises of decision. It is required that the decisions of the subordinate shall be consistent with premises selected for him by his superior. The scope of authority, and conversely the scope of discretion, are determined by the number and importance of the premises which are specified, and the number and importance of those which are left unspecified.

As pointed out previously, discretion over value premises has a different logical status from discretion over factual premises. The latter can always be evaluated as "right" or "wrong" in an objective, empirical sense. To the former, the terms "right" and "wrong" do not apply. Hence, if only factual premises are left to the subordinate's discretion, there is, under the given circumstances, only one decision which he can "correctly" reach. On the other hand, if value premises are left to the subordinate's discretion, the "correctness" of a decision will depend upon the value premises he has selected, and there is no criterion of right or wrong which can be applied to his selection.

When it is admitted that authority need extend to only a few of the premises of decision, it follows that more than one order can govern a given decision, provided that no two orders extend to the same premise. An analysis of almost any decision of a member of a formal organization would reveal that the decision is responsive to a very complex structure of influence.

Military organization affords an excellent illustration of this. In ancient warfare, the battlefield was not unlike the parade ground. An entire army was often commanded by a single man, and his authority extended in a very complete form to the lowest man in the ranks. This was possible because the entire battlefield was within range of a man's voice and vision, and because tactics were for the most part executed by the entire army in unison.

The modern battlefield presents a very different picture. Authority is exercised through a complex hierarchy of command. Each level of the hierarchy leaves an extensive area of discretion to the level below, and even the private soldier, under combat conditions, exercises a considerable measure of discretion.

Under these circumstances, how does the authority of the commander extend to the soldiers in the ranks? How does he limit and guide their behavior? He does this by specifying the general mission and objective of each unit on the next level below, and by determining such elements of time and place as will assure a proper coordination among units. The colonel assigns to each battalion in his regiment its task; the major, to each company in his battalion; the captain, to each platoon in his company. Beyond this, the officer does not ordinarily go. The internal arrangements of Army Field Service Regulations specify that "an order should not trespass upon the province of a subordinate. It should contain everything beyond the independent authority of the subordinate, but nothing more." [2]

[2] U.S. Army Field Service Regulations, 1923, p. 7.

So far as field orders go, then, the discretion of an officer is limited only by the specification of the objective of his unit, and its general schedule. He proceeds to narrow further the discretion of his subordinates so far as is necessary to specify what part each subunit is to play in accomplishing the task of the unit.

Does this mean that the discretion of the officer is limited only by his objective or mission? Not at all. To be sure, the field order does not go beyond this point. It specifies the *what* of his action. But the officer is also governed by the tactical doctrine and general orders of the army which specify in some detail the *how*. When the captain receives field orders to deploy his company for an attack, he is expected to carry out the deployment in accordance with the accepted tactical principles in the army. In leading his unit, he will be held accountable for the *how* as well as the *what*.

When we turn our attention, finally, to the man who carries out the army's task—the private soldier—we see that a great mass of influences bear upon the decisions which he makes. The decision that he will participate in an attack may have been made by a divisional, or even a corps, commander. His precise geographical location and place in the attack will be determined with ever increasing degrees of specificity by general, colonel, major, captain, lieutenant, sergeant in turn. But that is not all. The plan of attack which the captain determines upon will be a result not only of the field orders he receives, but also of the tactical training he has received, and his intelligence of the disposition of the enemy. So also the private, as he moves forward to the attack in the skirmish line, must thenceforth rely more and more upon the influences of his training and indoctrination.

To understand the process of decision in an organization, it is necessary to go far beyond the on-the-spot orders that are given by superior to subordinate. It is necessary to discover how the subordinate is influenced by standing orders, by training, and by review of his actions. It is necessary to study the channels of communication in the organization in order to determine what information reaches him which may be relevant to his decisions. The broader the sphere of discretion left to the subordinate, the more important become those types of influence which do not depend upon the exercise of formal authority.

The Modes of Influence

The ways in which the organization brings its influence to bear on the decisions of the individual have been enumerated in Chapter I. The "external" influences include authority, advice and information, and training. The "internal" influences include the criterion of efficiency and organizational identifications. Each of these has been discussed at length in preceding chapters, and that discussion does not need repetition here.

It is a fundamental problem of organization to determine the extent to which, and the manner in which, each of these forms of influence is to be employed. To a very great extent, these various forms of influence are interchangeable, a fact that is far more often appreciated in small than in large organizations.

The simplest example of this is the gradual increase in discretion that can be permitted to an employee as he becomes familiar with his job. A secretary learns to draft routine correspondence; a statistical clerk learns to lay out his own calculations. In each case training has taken the place of authority in guiding the employee's decisions.

"Functional supervision" often takes the form of advice rather than authority. This substitution of advice for authority may prove necessary in many situations in order to prevent conflicts of authority between line officers, organized on a geographical basis, and experts organized on a functional basis.

To the extent to which these forms of influence supplement, or are substituted for, authority, the problem of influence becomes one of internal education and public relations. Following is an example of this kind of influence:

To the administration of a big department, the staff of the department themselves constitute a kind of inner "public," the right orientation of whose attitudes to each other in their mutual office contacts, in the inevitable absence of the direct personal touch which secures it in a small organization, would seem *prima facie* to call for just the same kind of attention, the same "practical psychology" or "salesmanship," as their attitude to members of the outside public. . . .

Consider, for example, the machinery for preparing official instructions to the staff. . . . Do not official instructions tend to be drafted too rationalistically? Is not the draftsman's attention often concentrated too exclusively on framing a logical statement setting accurately and comprehensively what *ought* to be done? . . . But after all, the primary object of an instruction is not to be admired by critical specialists in the same office; an instruction is intended to be acted on, and that by people who are as a rule neither critical, nor specialists, nor in the same office—in other words, to produce such an impression on the *ultimate* recipient that on receiving it, he *will* forthwith proceed to do what is required of him.[3]

Administrators have increasingly recognized in recent years that authority, unless buttressed by other forms of influence, is relatively impotent to control decision in any but a negative way. The elements entering into all but the most routine decisions are so numerous and so complex that it is impossible to control positively more than a few. Unless the subordinate is himself able to supply most of the premises of decision, and to synthesize them adequately, the task of supervision becomes hopelessly burdensome.

When viewed from this standpoint, the problem of organization becomes inextricably interwoven with the problem of recruitment. For the system of influence which can effectively be used in the organization will depend directly upon the training and competence of the employees at the various levels of the hierarchy. If a welfare agency can secure trained social workers as interviewers and case workers, broad discretion can be permitted them in determining eligibility, subject only to a sampling review, and a review of particularly difficult cases.

If trained workers can be obtained only for supervisory positions, then the supervisors will need to exercise a much more complete supervision over their subordinates, perhaps reviewing each decision, and issuing frequent instructions. The supervisory problem will be correspondingly more burdensome than in the first example, and the effective span of control of supervisors correspondingly narrower.

[3] H. Townshend, " 'Practical Psychology' in Departmental Organization," *Journal of Public Administration*, 12:66.

Likewise, when an organization unit is large enough to retain within its own boundaries the specialized expertise that is required for some of its decisions, the need for functional supervision from other portions of the organization becomes correspondingly less. When a department can secure its own legal, medical, or other expert assistance, the problems of functional organization become correspondingly simpler, and the lines of direct authority over the department need less supplementation by advisory and informational services.

Hence, problems of organizaton cannot be considered apart from the specifications of the employees who are to fill the positions established by the organization. The whole subject of job classification needs to be brought into much closer coordination with the theory of organization. The optimum organizational structure is a variable, depending for its form upon the staffing of the agency. Conversely, the classification of a position is a variable, depending upon the degree of centralization or decentralization which is desired or anticipated in the operation of the organizational form.

PLANNING AND REVIEW IN THE PROCESS OF COMPOSITE DECISION

There are two administrative techniques that are of key importance in the process of composite decision and in bringing to bear on a single decision a multiplicity of influences. Reference has already been made to them from time to time, but they deserve more systematic discussion as a part of the over-all decisional structure of the organization. The first of these is planning—a technique whereby the skills of a variety of specialists can be brought to bear on a problem before the formal stage of decision-making is reached. The second is review—a technique whereby the individual can be held accountable for the "internal" as well as the "external" premises that determine his decision.

The Planning Process

Plans and schedules are perhaps not strictly distinguishable from commands, since they usually derive their authority from an order. None the less, they are of special interest as devices for influencing decisions because of the immense amount of detail which it is possible to include in them, and because of the broad participation that can be secured, when desirable, in their formulation. Let us consider the last point first. An example is given by Sir Oswyn Murray:

There is very little that is haphazard or disconnected about the array of Admiralty Departments. The noteworthy thing about them is not their number or variety, so much as their close inter-connection and the manner in which they combine to serve those administrative ends which I mentioned at the beginning of my paper. Perhaps I can best illustrate this by describing briefly the procedure followed in the design and production of a new battleship, which always seems to me to be the very romance of cooperation.

We start with the First Sea Lord and his Assistant Chief of Naval Staff laying down in general terms the features that they desire to see embodied in the new design—the speed, the radius of action, the offensive qualities, the armour protection. Thereupon the Director of Naval Construction, acting under and in consultation with the Controller, formulates provisional schemes outlining the kind of ship desired, together with forecasts of the size and cost involved by the different arrangements. To do this he and his officers must have a good general knowledge—in itself only attainable by close relations with those in charge of these matters—of the latest developments and ideas in regard to a great range of subjects—gunnery, torpedo, engineering, armour, fire-control, navigation, signalling, accommodation, and so on—in order to be reasonably sure that the provision included in his schemes is such as is likely to satisfy the experts in all these subjects when the time for active cooperation arrives.

With these alternative schemes before them, the Sea Lords agree on the general lines of the new ship, which done, the actual preparation of the actual designs begins. The dimensions and shape of the ship are drawn out approximately by the naval constructors. Then the Engineer-in-Chief and his Department are called in to agree upon the arrangement of the propelling machinery, the positions of shafts, propellers, bunkers, funnels, etc., and at the same time the cooperation of the Director of Naval Ordnance is required to settle the positions of the guns with their barbettes, and magazines and shell rooms and the means of supplying ammunition to the guns in action.

An understanding between these three main departments enables further progress to be made. The cooperation of the Director of

Torpedoes and the Director of Electrical Engineering is now called for to settle the arrangements for torpedo armament, electric generating machinery, electric lighting, etc. So the design progresses and is elaborated from the lower portions upwards, and presently the Director of Naval Construction is able to consult the Director of Naval Equipment as to the proposed arrangements in regard to the sizes and stowage of the motor boats, steamboats, rowing and sailing boats to be carried, as well as of the anchors and cables; the Director of the Signal Department as to the wireless telegraphy arrangements; the Director of Navigation as to the arrangements for navigating the ship, and so on. In this way the scheme goes on growing in a tentative manner, its progress always being dependent on the efficiency of different parts, until ultimately a more or less complete whole is arrived at in the shape of drawings and specifications provisionally embodying all the agreements. This really is the most difficult and interesting stage, for generally it becomes apparent at this point that requirements overlap, and that the best possible cannot be achieved in regard to numbers of points within the limit set to the contractors. These difficulties are cleared up by discussion at round-table conferences, where the compromises which will least impair the value of the ship are agreed upon, and the completed design is then finally submitted for the Board's approval. Some fourteen departments are concerned in the settiement of the final detailed arrangements.[4]

The point which is so clearly illustrated here is that the planning procedure permits expertise of every kind to be drawn into the decision without any difficulties being imposed by the lines of authority in the organization. The final design undoubtedly received authoritative approval; but, during the entire process of formulation, suggestions and recommendations flowed freely from all parts of the organization without raising the problem of "unity of command." It follows from this that to the extent to which planning procedures are used in reaching decisions, the formal organization has relevance only in the final stages of the whole process. So long as the appropriate experts are consulted, their exact location in the hierarchy of authority need not much affect the decision.

This statement must be qualified by one important reservation.

[4] Sir Oswyn A. R. Murray, "The Administration of a Fighting Service," *Journal of Public Administration*, 1:216–217 (July, 1923).

Organizational factors are apt to take on considerable importance if the decision requires a compromise among a number of competing values which are somewhat incompatible with one another. In such a case, the focus of attention and the identification of the person who actually makes the decision are apt to affect the degree to which advice offered him by persons elsewhere in the organization actually influences him. This factor is present in the example of the warship just cited.

This same illustration throws in relief the other aspect of the planning procedure which was mentioned above—that the plan may control, down to minute details, a whole complex pattern of behavior. The completed plan of the battleship will specify the design of the ship down to the last rivet. The task of the construction crew is minutely specified by this design.

The Process of Review

Review enables those who are in a position of authority in the administrative hierarchy to determine what actually is being done by their subordinates.

Methods of Review. Review may extend to the *results* of the subordinates' activities, measured in terms of their objectives; the tangible *products,* if there are such, of their activities; or the method of their *performance.*

When authority is exercised through the specification of the objective of the organizational unit, then a primary method of review is to ascertain the degree to which the organizational objective is attained—its results. A city manager, for instance, may use measurements of results as a principal means of reviewing city departments. He may evaluate the fire department in terms of fire losses, the police department in terms of crime and accident rates, the public works department in terms of the condition of streets and the frequency of refuse collection.

A second very important method of review is one which examines the piece of completed work to see whether it meets the requirements of quantity and quality. This method assumes that the reviewing officer is able to judge the quality and quantity of the completed work with a certain degree of competence. Thus, a superior may review all outgoing letters written by his subordinates, or the work of typists may be checked by a chief clerk, or the work of a street repair crew may be examined by a superintendent.

It has not often enough been recognized that in many cases the review of work can just as well be confined to a randomly selected sample of the work as extended to all that is produced. A highly developed example of such a sampling procedure is found in the personnel administration of the Farm Credit Administration. This organization carries out its personnel functions on an almost completely decentralized basis, except for a small central staff which lays down standards and procedures. As a means of assuring that local practices follow these standards, field supervisors inspect the work of the local agencies, and in the case of certain personnel procedures, such as classification, the setting of compensation scales, and the development of testing materials, assure themselves of the quality of the work by an actual inspection of a sample. The same type of procedure is usually followed by state boards of equalization which review local assessments. Finally, welfare agencies in California, New York, and perhaps other states have developed an auditing procedure on a sampling basis, in order to review the work of local welfare agencies.

The third, and perhaps simplest, method of review is to watch the employee at work, either to see that he puts in the required number of hours, or to see that he is engaging in certain movements which if continued will result in the completion of the work. In this case, the review extends to procedures and techniques, rather than product or results. It is the prevalent form of review at the foremanship level.

Functions of Review. To determine what method of review should be employed in any concrete administrative situation, it is necessary to be quite clear as to what this particular review process is to accomplish. There are at least four different functions that a review process may perform: diagnosis of the quality of decisions being made by subordinates, modification through influence on subsequent decisions, the correction of incorrect decisions that have already been made, and enforcement of sanctions against subordinates so that they will accept authority in making their decisions.[5]

In the first place, review is the means whereby the administrative hierarchy learns whether decisions are being made correctly or incorrectly, whether work is being done well or badly at the lower levels of the hierarchy. It is a fundamental source of information, then, upon which the higher levels of the hierarchy must rely heavily for their decisions. With the help of this information, improvements can be introduced into the decision-making process.

This leads to the second function of review—to influence subsequent decisions. This is achieved in a variety of ways. Orders may be issued covering particular points on which incorrect decisions have been made, or laying down new policies to govern decisions. Employees may be given training or retraining with regard to those aspects of their work which review has proved faulty. Information may be supplied to them, the lack of which has led to incorrect decisions. In brief, change may be brought about in any of the several ways in which decisions can be influenced.

Third, review may perform an appellate function. If the individual decision has grave consequences, it may be reviewed by a higher authority, to make certain that it is correct. This review may be a matter of course, or it may occur only on appeal by a party at interest. The justifications of such a process of review are that (1) it permits the decision to be weighed twice, and (2) the appellate review requires less time per decision than the original decision, and hence conserves the time of better trained personnel for the more difficult decisions. The appellate review may, to use the language of administrative law, consist in a consideration *de novo,* or may merely review the original decision for substantial conformity to important rules of policy.

Fourth, review is often essential to the effective exercise of authority. As we have seen in Chapter VII, authority depends, to a certain extent, upon the availability of sanctions to give it force. Sanctions can be applied only if there is some means of ascertaining

[5] A somewhat similar, but not identical, analysis of the function of review can be found in Sir H. N. Bunbury's paper, "Efficiency as an Alternative to Control," *Journal of Public Administration,* 6:97–98 (Apr., 1928).

when authority has been respected, and when it has been disobeyed. Review supplies the person in authority with this information.

When we recall the "rule of anticipated reactions," we see that the anticipation of review and the invocation of sanctions secures conformity to authority of the decision made prior to review. It is for this reason that review can influence a prior decision.

CENTRALIZATION AND DECENTRALIZATION

Our examination of the process of composite decision, and particularly of the methods and functions of review in an organization, casts considerable light on the way in which decisional processes can best be distributed through the organization, and on the relative advantages and disadvantages in centralizing the processes of decision.

What has already been said with respect to this issue? In Chapter VII it was pointed out that the specialization and centralization of decision-making serves three purposes: it secures coordination, expertise, and responsibility. In Chapter III some pragmatic tests were suggested for arriving at a division of function between legislator and administrator. In Chapter VIII, the relation between centralization of decisions and the problems of communication was explored. In Chapter X, it was seen that a need for centralization sometimes arises from the faulty institutional identifications of the members of an organization. In the present chapter, it was urged that the capabilities of the members of an organization would be one determinant of the possible degree of decentralization. Are there additional considerations, beyond those already mentioned, that should carry weight in the allocation of decisions?

At the outset, one important distinction must be clearly understood. There are two very different aspects to centralization. On the one hand, decision-making powers may be centralized by using general rules to limit the discretion of the subordinate. On the other hand, decision-making powers may be centralized by taking out of the hands of the subordinate the actual decision-making function. Both processes may be designated as "centralization" because their result is to take out of the hands of the subordinate the actual weighing of competing considerations and to require that he accept the conclusions reached by other members of the organization.

The very close relationship between the manner in which the function of review is exercised, and the degree of centralization or decentralization should also be pointed out. Review influences decisions by evaluating them, and thereby subjecting the subordinate to discipline and control. Review is sometimes conceived as a means of detecting wrong decisions and correcting them. This concept may be very useful as applied to those very important decisions where an appellate procedure is necessary to conserve individual rights or democratic responsibility. Under ordinary circumstances, however, the function of correcting the *decisional processes* of the subordinate which lead to wrong decisions is more important than the function of correcting *wrong decisions*. As the resources of the subordinate for making correct decisions are strengthened, decentralization becomes increasingly possible. Hence, review can have three consequences: (1) if it is used to correct individual decisions, it leads to centralization, and an actual transfer of the decision-making function; (2) if it is used to discover where the subordinate needs additional guidance, it leads to centralization through the promulgation of more and more complete rules and regulations limiting the subordinate's discretion; (3) if it is used to discover where the subordinate's own resources need to be strengthened, it leads to decentralization. All three elements can be, and usually are, combined, in varying proportions.

But why should administration aim at decentralization? All of our analysis to this point has emphasized the important functions which the centralization of decision-making performs. Nevertheless, we are warned against a naïve acceptance of the advantages of centralization by the distrust which careful students of administration express for it. Sir Charles Harris, for example, has this to say:

If I appear before you as a thoroughgoing advocate of decentralization, it is as a convert to the faith in middle age. . . . At the beginning of my service I was greatly impressed by the lack of general knowledge and grasp of central principle displayed in the local decisions and actions that came under my notice. For years the conviction grew upon me that a larger measure of active control from the centre would conduce to both efficiency and economy of administration; and today, if I were to confine my view to particular details and to immediate results. I should still feel on that point no possible doubt whatever. It is when one falls back to Capability Brown's view-point, and tries to see the wood as well as the trees, that the certainty disappears.

. . . Simple centralization drives up the functions of decision and authorization to the top centre, it leaves action, when decided upon, to be carried out by the subordinate authority.

Don't cut down the discretion of the man below, or his class, by requiring submission to higher authority in the future, because he has made a mistake. Teach him and try him again; but if he is unteachable, shunt him.[6]

Almost any person, unless he recognizes the long-term consequences, feels "safer" if he makes decisions himself instead of delegating them to a subordinate. The superior rationalizes this centralization on a variety of grounds: he is more highly skilled or trained than the subordinate; if he makes the decision, he can be certain that it is decided as he would want it. What he does not always realize is that by concentrating the entire function of decision in himself, he is multiplying his work, and making the subordinate superfluous.

There are two principal reasons for decentralizing decisions even in cases where the superior is more highly trained than the subordinate. The first harks back to the distinction in Chapter IX between efficiency and adequacy. It is not enough to take into consideration the accuracy of the decision; its cost must be weighed as well. The superior is presumably a higher paid individual than the subordinate. His time must be conserved for the more important aspects of the work of the organization. If it is necessary, in order that he may make a particular decision, that he sacrifice time which should be devoted to more important decisions, the greater accuracy secured for the former may be bought at too high a price.

The second reason why decentralization is often preferable to centralization is that the referral of a decision upward in the hierarchy introduces new money and time costs into the decision-making

[6] Sir Charles Harris, "Decentralization," *Journal of Public Administration,* 3:117–133 (Apr., 1925).

process. Against any advantages of accuracy when the decision is made at the center must be balanced the cost of duplicating the decisional process, together with the cost of communicating the decisions.

To emphasize the costs of uneconomic standards of review, we cannot do better than quote an example cited by Ian Hamilton from his personal experience:

In 1896 I was Deputy Quartermaster-General at Simla; then, perhaps still, one of the hardest worked billets in Asia. After a long office day I used to get back home to dinner pursued by a pile of files three to four feet high. The Quartermaster-General, my boss, was a clever, delightful work-glutton. So we sweated and ran together for a while a neck and neck race with our piles of files, but I was the younger and he was the first to be ordered off by the doctors to Europe. Then I, at the age of forty-three, stepped into the shoes and became officiating Quartermaster-General in India. Unluckily, the Government at that moment was in a very stingy mood. They refused to provide pay to fill the post I was vacating and Sir George White, the Commander-in-Chief, asked me to duplicate myself and do the double work. My heart sank, but there was nothing for it but to have a try. The day came; the Quartermaster-General went home and with him went the whole of his share of the work. As for my own share, the hard twelve hours' task melted by some magic into the Socialist's dream of a six hours' day. How was that? Because, when a question came up from one of the Departments I had formerly been forced to compose a long minute upon it, explaining the case, putting my own views, and endeavoring to persuade the Quartermaster-General to accept them. He was a highly conscientious man and if he differed from me he liked to put on record his reasons—several pages of reasons. Or, if he agreed with me, still he liked to agree in his own words and to "put them on record." Now, when I became Quartermaster-General and Deputy-Quartermaster General rolled into one I studied the case as formerly, but there my work ended: I had not to persuade my own subordinates: I had no superior except the Commander-in-Chief, who was delighted to be left alone: I just gave an order—quite a simple matter unless a man's afraid: "Yes," I said, or "No!" [7]

[7] Sir Ian Hamilton, *The Soul and Body of an Army* (London: E. Arnold & Co., 1921), pp. 235-236.

There is an additional objection to centralization that goes beyond those already considered. It has been assumed thus far that, given ample time, the superior could make more accurate decisions than the subordinate. This will be true, however, only if the information upon which the decision is to be based is equally accessible to both. When decisions must be made against a dead line, or when the organization is characterized by geographical dispersion, this may be far from the case. The "facts of the case" may be directly present to the subordinate, but highly difficult to communicate to the superior. The insulation of the higher levels of the administrative hierarchy from the world of fact known at first hand by the lower levels is a familiar administrative phenomenon.

Centralization is sometimes urged as a necessary concomitant of the specialization of work. If work is specialized, then procedures must be introduced to secure coordination among the members of the group; and among the most powerful of coordinative procedures is the centralization of decisions. This is true; but in accepting this conclusion we must not blind ourselves to the very real disadvantages and costs that accompany specialization.

Interpersonal coordination involves communication of a plan. Complex and powerful as are the devices which can be used for such coordination, their effectiveness is in no way comparable to the coordinating power of the individual human nervous system. When the elements of the plan can be reduced to diagrams and maps, as in the case of a design for a ship or a bridge, interpersonal coordination can reach even minute detail. But the coordinative mechanisms of a skilled pianist, or of an engineer bringing all his skill and knowledge to bear on a problem of design, are far more intricate.

Successful use of the device of specialization to increase efficiency implies either that no coordination is required among the specialized segments of the complete task, or that this coordination can be achieved with the available techniques of interpersonal coordination. If neither of these conditions is fulfilled, then specialization must be sacrificed in order to retain the use of the individual brain as the coordinating mechanism. It is not very easy to thread a needle if one person holds the thread and another the needle. Here the task is to get thread and needle to the *same* place, and interpersonal coordination accomplishes this much less successfully than the coordination of the movements of the two hands by the human nervous system.

The quotation in which the procedure for designing a battleship was described [8] is another case in point. A careful analysis of the procedure reveals that there were involved in it not only the experts on various aspects of battleship design, but also a group of functionaries who might be described as "expert jacks-of-all-trades in battleship design." The Director of Naval Construction, and not the functional experts, lays down the general lines of the ship. To repeat:

Thereupon the Director of Naval Construction, acting under and in consultation with the Controller, formulates provisional schemes outlining the kind of ship desired, together with forecasts of the size and cost involved by the different arrangements. To do this he and his officers must have a good general knowledge—in itself only attainable by close relations with those in charge of these matters—of the latest developments and ideas in regard to a great range of subjects—gunnery, torpedo, engineering, armour, fire-control, navigation, signalling, accommodation, and so on—in order to be reasonably sure that the provision included in his schemes is such as is likely to satisfy the experts in all these subjects, when the time for active cooperation arrives.[9]

Only after the "jack-of-all-trades" has done his job are the experts called in for their suggestions. Next, a technique of interpersonal coordination, the conference, is used to reconcile the competing claims of experts. Finally, the plan is turned over again to the non-specialist for authorization.

We may conclude, then, that some measure of centralization is indispensable to secure the advantages of organization: coordination, expertise, and responsibility. On the other hand, the costs of centralization must not be forgotten. It may place in the hands of highly paid personnel decisions which do not deserve their attention. It may lead to a duplication of function which makes the subordinate superfluous. Facilities for communication must be available,

---

[8] See pp. 229–230, *supra.*
[9] Sir Oswyn A. R. Murray, *loc. cit.*

sometimes at considerable cost. The information needed for a correct decision may be available only to the subordinate. Finally, centralization leaves idle and unused the powerful coordinative capacity of the human nervous system, and substitutes for it an interpersonal coordinative mechanism. These are the considerations which must be weighed in determining the degree to which decisions should be centralized or decentralized.

LESSONS FOR ADMINISTRATIVE THEORY

In Chapter II the position was taken that the currently accepted "principles of administration" are little more than ambiguous and mutually contradictory proverbs, and that a new approach was needed to establish a consistent and useful administrative theory. This is a fact that is beginning to be recognized in the literature of administration. If we study the chain of publications extending from Mooney and Reiley through Gulick, the President's Committee controversy, to Schuyler Wallace and Benson, we see a steady shift of emphasis from the "principles of administration" themselves to a study of the *conditions* under which competing principles are respectively applicable. We no longer say that organization should be by purpose, but rather that under such and such conditions purpose organization is desirable, but under such and such other conditions, process organization is desirable. It is the central thesis of this study that an understanding of these underlying conditions for the applicability of administrative principles is to be obtained from an analysis of the administrative process in terms of decisions.

If this approach be taken, the rationality of decisions—that is, their appropriateness for the accomplishment of specified goals—becomes the central concern of administrative theory. As was pointed out, however, in Chapter II, if there were no limits to human rationality administrative theory would be barren. It would consist of the single precept: Always select that alternative, among those available, which will lead to the most complete achievement of your goals. The need for an administrative theory resides in the fact that there *are* practical limits to human rationality, and that these limits are not static, but depend upon the organizational environment in which the individual's decision takes place. The task of administration is so to design this environment that the individual will approach as close as practicable to rationality (judged in terms of the organization's goals) in his decisions.

The Area of Rationality

As has also been explained in Chapter II, when the limits to rationality are viewed from the individual's standpoint, they fall into three categories: he is limited by his unconscious skills, habits, and reflexes; he is limited by his values and conceptions of purpose, which may diverge from the organization goals; he is limited by the extent of his knowledge and information. The individual can be rational in terms of the organization's goals only to the extent that he *is able* to pursue a particular course of action, he has a correct conception of the *goal* of the action, and he is correctly *informed* about the conditions surrounding his action. Within the boundaries laid down by these factors his choices are rational—goal-oriented.

Rationality, then, does not determine behavior. Within the area of rationality behavior is perfectly flexible and adaptable to abilities, goals, and knowledge. Instead, behavior is determined by the irrational and nonrational elements that bound the area of rationality. The area of rationality is the area of adaptability to these nonrational elements. Two persons, given the same possible alternatives, the same values, the same knowledge, can rationally reach only the same decision. Hence, administrative theory must be concerned with the limits of rationality, and the manner in which organization affects these limits for the person making a decision. The theory must determine—as suggested in Chapter X—how institutionalized decision can be made to conform to values developed within a broader organizational structure. The theory must be a critique of the effect (judged from the point of view of the whole organization) of the organizational structure upon the decisions of its component parts and its individual members.

Perhaps an example of the way in which the organization can alter each of the three types of limits enumerated above will make the problem more concrete:

Limited Alternatives. Suppose a bricklayer is unable to work at an acceptable speed. There may be no lack of rationality in his behavior. The fact may be that his skills are not sufficiently developed to enable him to lay bricks rapidly. However, if attention were to be given to the skills themselves, if he were given instruction and training in proper methods, the impossible might readily become possible. Skills are examples of behavior patterns that in the short run limit the sphere of adaptability or rationality, but in the long run may, by training, open up entirely new behavior possibilities.

Reorientation of Values. Sometimes rationality is limited by the individual's failure to identify himself correctly with the goals of the whole organization. In certain situations, at least, it is possible to reorient an individual from identification with a subgoal of the organization to identification with a broader and more inclusive goal. The writer has had occasion in another context to point to this method for reorienting the behavior of a "rational person" by altering his framework of values. The problem dealt with in that situation was to control and modify the motivation of a group of social workers who were participating in an administrative experiment:

To the worker, the experiment might seem inconsistent with the objectives he was trying to attain in his daily job. The cooperation of such a worker could be obtained only by interpreting the study in terms of his more fundamental values and by showing him that these broader values would be benefited by a temporary sacrifice of some of his immediate objectives and attitudes. In this way his attention might be detached from the narrower frame of reference—the conditioned reflexes, so to speak—forced on him by his regular daily schedule of work. [10]

Limits of Knowledge. Where a particular item of knowledge is needed repeatedly in decision, the organization can anticipate this need and, by providing the individual with this knowledge prior to decision, can extend his area of rationality. This is particularly important when there are time limits on decision. Thus, a policeman is trained in methods of making arrests, handling unruly prisoners and the like, so that he will not have to figure these things out on the spot when occasion requires.

[10] Simon and Divine, *op. cit.*, p. 487.

Individual and Group Rationality

A decision is rational from the standpoint of the individual (subjectively rational) if it is consistent with the values, the alternatives, and the information which he weighed in reaching it. A decision is rational from the standpoint of the group (objectively rational) if it is consistent with the values governing the group, and the information that the group possesses relevant to the decision. Hence, the organization must be so constructed that a decision which is (subjectively) rational from the standpoint of the deciding individual, will remain rational when reassessed from the standpoint of the group.

Suppose that an officer orders a soldier under his command to capture a particular hill. Rationality (subjective) demands of him that he combine this objective, or value, with the skills he possesses for approaching hostile positions, and with the information his senses provide him regarding his situation.

On the other hand, rationality requires of the officer that the objective he assigns the soldier shall contribute to the broader objective of his unit (which usually implies that the soldier's objective must have a reasonable possibility of successful attainment), and that he provide the soldier with all available information that may assist him in his task. To say that the officer is rational means that the soldier's behavior continues to appear rational when evaluated from the broader viewpoint which the officer's position affords him.

This is the basic task of administration—to provide each "operative" employee with an environment of decision of such a kind that behavior which is rational from the standpoint of this environment is also rational from the standpoint of the group values and the group situation. Moreover, it must be taken into consideration that the establishment of an environment of decision for the individual involves problems of communication for the organization. These then are the basic elements from which a theory of organization can be constructed: (1) a decision made above the operative level must be communicated; (2) wherever a decision is made, its quality will depend on the environment that bounds the area of rationality of the person making the decision. With respect to the first element, the technology of communication (in the very broadest sense) is the limiting factor; with respect to the second, the limiting factors are the very factors that limit the area of individual rationality.

Importance of Organizational Location

Since administrative theory is concerned with control of the nonrational, it follows that, the larger the area of rationality, the less important is the administrative organization. For example, the function of plan preparation, or design, if it results in a written plan that can be communicated interpersonally without difficulty, can be located almost anywhere in the organization without affecting results. All that is needed is a procedure whereby the plan can be given authoritative status; and that can be provided in a number of ways. A discussion, then, of the proper location for a planning or designing unit is apt to be highly inconclusive, and may hinge on the personalities in the organization and their relative enthusiasm, or lack of it, toward the planning function.[11]

On the other hand, when factors of communication or identification are crucial to the making of a decision, the location of the decision in the organization is of great importance. The method of allocating decisions in the army, for instance, automatically (and "theoretically," I hasten to add) provides, at least in the period prior to the actual battle, that each decision will be made where the knowledge is available for coordinating it with other decisions. Similarly, we may note that final decisions regarding budget allowances are always entrusted to administrators who are not identified with the particular items to be allowed, but must weigh these items against alternative items.

---

[11] See, for instance, Robert A. Walker, *The Planning Function in Urban Government* (Chicago: University of Chicago Press, 1941), pp. 166–175. Walker makes out a case for attaching the planning agency to the chief executive. But he rests his entire case on the rather slender reed that "as long as the planning agency is outside the governmental structure, however, planning will tend to encounter resistance from public officials as an invasion of their responsibility and jurisdiction." The verb "will" seems entirely too strong for the facts of the case.

THE ROLE OF THE ADMINISTRATOR

It may be appropriate to conclude this volume with a brief statement about the role and training of administrators. It has been suggested earlier that the decisions which might be uniquely designated as "administrative" decisions are those which are concerned with the decision-making process itself. That is, such decisions do not determine the content of the organization's work, but rather how the decision-making function is to be allocated and influenced in that particular organization.

But to say that in any organization certain "administrative" decisions have to be made, is not to say that the person who happens to be designated an "administrator" in that organization makes, or should make, only administrative decisions. Whether or not it is desirable that there *should* be functionaries whose tasks are confined within these limits, it is certainly not an accurate description of administrative organizations as they exist today to define the administrator's task in those terms.

In almost all organizations he has a responsibility not only to establish and maintain the organizational structure, but also to make some of the broader and more important decisions regarding the content of the organization's work. To mention only one of these decisions, the higher administrator ordinarily has a considerable responsibility for budget decisions—that is, decisions as to the directions in which the organization's efforts should be applied. Further, to him falls the responsibility, within the limits of his discretion, of formulating organizational objectives—that is, the values that will guide decisions at all lower levels of the organization.

The statement, then, that as we proceed upward in the hierarchy "administrative" duties come to occupy more and more of the administrator's time, and "technical" duties less, must be interpreted with considerable caution. It is not true if the term "administrative duties" is taken to refer only to the organization-determining functions. It is true, if the broader decisional functions which fall to the administrator are considered as "administrative duties."

What is the difference between these latter functions and the "technical" functions at the lower levels of the hierarchy? Simply that the content decisions of the higher administrator deal with more ultimate purposes and more general processes than the decisions of the lower administrator. We might say that the lower administrator's purposes are the upper administrator's processes.

The stenographer's rationality is exercised in translating a piece of copy, whatever its content, into a typewritten manuscript. Her employer's rationality is exercised in determining the content of the copy, taking for granted the very element with which the stenographer is concerned—its translation into typewritten form.

If the Chief Engineer's decisions are less concerned with engineering technology than those of his designing engineers, with what are they concerned? If the Health Officer's decisions do not involve the minutiae of medical knowledge, what do they involve? They involve the application of the criterion of efficiency to the broader purposes of the organization. Since the broader purposes of governmental organizations (and, to a lesser extent, commercial organizations) are predominantly social, and the larger problems of means are principally economic and fiscal this means that the decisions of the higher administrators involve social science principles and economic calculations.

One further point should be noted that applies even to those decisions which deal with the organization structure itself. If, as has been suggested, administrative theory cannot be entirely freed from concern with the content of the organization's work, it follows that sound organizational decisions require also a knowledge of that content.

We see, then, that the work of the administrator, as organizations are now constituted, involves (1) decisions about the organization structure, and (2) the broader decisions as to the content of the organization's work. Decisions of neither type can rest entirely, or even primarily, upon a knowledge of or facility with administrative theory. The former must be firmly grounded in the organization's technology. The latter must be grounded in the organization's technology and requires in addition (a) a thorough appreciation of the theory of efficiency, and (b) a knowledge of those aspects of the social sciences which are relevant to the broader purposes of the organization.

If this analysis is correct, it has direct implications for the training of an "administrative class," that is, for the training of persons who are skilled in higher administration. In the first place, it casts grave doubts on the possibility of developing administrative ability apart from subject-matter competence except at the very highest levels of the hierarchy. In the second place, it indicates that the proper training of "administrators" lies not in the narrow field of administrative theory, but in the broader field of the social sciences generally.

CONCLUSION

Our study has not led us to any definitive administrative principles. It has, however, provided us with a framework for the analysis and description of administrative situations, and with a set of factors that must be weighed in arriving at any valid proposal for administrative organization. It has shown us, further, that currently accepted "principles" of administration suffer from internal ambiguity and mutual contradiction.

What are the next steps that research must take? First, it must develop adequate case studies of existing administrative situations. It will do well to initiate these on a small scale—dealing in minute detail with organizational units of moderate size. Only in this way can superficiality be avoided.

Second, techniques must be developed and improved for measuring the success of particular administrative arrangements. Specifically, the assumption so often made in administrative studies, that an arrangement is effective because it exists, is a circular argument of the worst sort. Students of administration are possessed of no occult vision which permits them, by simply observing an administrative organization, to determine whether it is "working" or not. The only procedure of evaluation that can possibly be valid is the comparison of alternative administrative schemes in terms of their objective results.

Finally, the valuable investigations already initiated of the "conditions" under which different administrative principles are validly applicable might well be extended with the use of the "decisional" framework described in this study.

WHAT IS AN ADMINISTRATIVE SCIENCE?

THE DISTINCTION made in Chapter III between the ethical and the factual helps to explain the nature of administrative science. Scientific propositions, it was said in that chapter, are statements about the observable world and the way in which it operates. Ethical propositions, on the other hand, are expressions of preferences. Do principles of administration qualify, under this definition, as scientific propositions, or do they contain an ethical element?

THEORETICAL AND PRACTICAL SCIENCES

Sciences may be of two kinds: theoretical and practical. Thus, scientific propositions may be considered practical if they are stated in some such form as: "In order to produce such and such a state of affairs, such and such must be done." But for any such sentence, an exactly equivalent theoretical proposition with the same conditions of verification can be stated in a purely descriptive form: "Such and such a state of affairs is invariably accompanied by such and such conditions." Since the two propositions have the same factual meaning, their difference must lie in the ethical realm. More precisely, the difference lies in the fact that the first sentence possesses an imperative quality which the second lacks. The first sentence can be said to be "true" or "false" only if this imperative aspect is ignored.

This situation is strictly analogous to that which we found to hold with respect to decisions. In so far as decisions can be said to be "correct," they can be translated into factual propositions. Their ethical element must be eliminated before the terms "true" and "false" can be applied to them. Similarly, the propositions of a practical science must be put in hypothetical form in order to eliminate the ethical element.

When factual propositions are selected primarily for their usefulness in deriving one imperative from another, they may be considered practical. In other cases, they are *theoretical*. It is clear that they differ from each other only with respect to the motives of the persons who employ them.

From the foregoing discussion, two definite conclusions may be drawn:

First, science is interested in sentences only with regard to their verification. Hence, science is concerned with the factual aspects of meaning, but not with the ethical.

Second, practical sciences differ from theoretical sciences, as those terms have been used here, only in their ethical aspects.

Propositions of an Administrative Science [1]

Propositions about administrative processes will be scientific in so far as truth and falsehood, in the factual sense, can be predicated of them. Conversely, if truth or falsehood can be predicated or a proposition concerning administrative processes, then that proposition is scientific.

It is sometimes thought that, since the words "good" and "bad" often occur in sentences written by students of administration, the science of administration contains an essential ethical element. If this were true, a science of administration would be impossible, for it is impossible to choose, on an empirical basis, between ethical alternatives. Fortunately, it is not true. The terms "good" and "bad" when they occur in a study on administration are seldom employed in a purely ethical sense. Procedures are termed "good" when they are conducive to the attainment of specified objectives, "bad" when they are not conducive to such attainment. That they are, or are not, so conducive is purely a matter of fact, and it is this factual element which makes up the real substance of an administrative science. To illustrate: In the realm of economics, the proposition "Alternative

[1] Luther Gulick has set forth substantially this same view with respect to the nature of administrative science. See "Science, Values, and Public Administration," in Gulick and Urwick, eds., *op. cit.*, pp. 191–193.

A is *good*" may be translated into two propositions, one of them ethical, the other factual:

"Alternative A will lead to maximum profit."

"To maximize profit is good."

The first of these two sentences has no ethical content, and is a sentence of the practical science of business. The second sentence is an ethical imperative, and has no place in any science.

Science cannot tell whether we *ought* to maximize profit. It can merely tell us under what conditions this maximization will occur, and what the consequences of maximization will be.

If this analysis be correct, then there are no *logical* differences which distinguish the sentences of one science from those of another. Whatever differences exist must arise from the subject matter of the several sciences, rather than from the intrinsic nature of their sentences.

THE NATURAL AND THE SOCIAL SCIENCES

The discussion thus far leads to the solution of one issue which has been debated by methodologists of the social sciences. It has often been argued that the social sciences involve ethical norms, and therefore lack the objectivity of the natural sciences. A recent statement of this view may be found in Robert S. Lynd's *Knowledge for What?* [2] Since it is clear that truth or falsehood cannot be predicated of ought-sentences, this distinction cannot be valid. If there are fundamental differences between the natural and the social sciences, they must lie in some other direction.

Another group of distinctions, although valid, must be dismissed as superficial. First, social phenomena are probably far more complex than the data with which the natural sciences are concerned. Consequently the task of discovering regularities underlying social phenomena might be expected to be more difficult. Second, experiments cannot be carried on in the social sciences without regard to the consequences for the objects of experimentation. The doctor in

[2] Robert S. Lynd, *Knowledge for What? The Place of Social Science in American Culture* (Princeton: Princeton University Press, 1939). A somewhat more sophisticated variant of this viewpoint runs through the writings of Frank H. Knight. See especially his review of "Bertrand Russell on Power," *International Journal of Ethics*, 49:253–285 (Apr., 1939), and the Preface to the reissue of his *Risk, Uncertainty and Profit*, pp. xv–xvi.

Arrowsmith had an unequaled opportunity to experiment with vaccine under controlled conditions; but his human values got the best of him, and he found himself unable to deprive his control subjects of the benefits of treatment. The validity of both of these distinctions may be granted, but they can hardly be considered fundamental. Complexity is a matter of degree, and it may well be questioned whether some of the more involved phenomena which have been dealt with in the physical sciences are not as complex as some of the simpler social phenomena. Experimentation, too, can hardly be the real distinction, for astronomy, the first developed of the natural sciences, has never had the advantages of the laboratory in discovering its laws.

Expectations as Factors in Social Behavior

If there is a fundamental difference between the social and the natural sciences, it derives from the fact that the social sciences deal with conscious human beings whose behavior is influenced by knowledge, memory, and expectation. Consequently, knowledge by the human beings themselves of the forces which mold their behavior may (but need not) alter that behavior. It is apparent today, for example, that public awareness of the uses to which propaganda was put in an earlier world war affected to some degree public reaction to propaganda in the Second World War.

This does not mean that it is impossible to state valid laws of human behavior. It simply means that one of the variables to be included in the statement of social laws is the state of knowledge and experience of the persons whose behavior the law purports to describe.[3] The more deliberate the behavior which forms the subject

[3] A careful search for discussions of this point in the literature of social science methodology revealed a brief but clear statement of the proposition in a paper by W. Edwin Van de Walle, "A Fundamental Difference Between the Natural and Social Sciences," *Journal of Philosophy*, 29:542–550 (Sept. 29, 1932). The distinction is closely allied to the differentiation between the artificial and the natural which was introduced into the field of sociology by Lester F. Ward, *Dynamic Sociology* (New York: D. Appleton & Co., 2nd ed., 1926). Cf. Joseph Mayer, "Scientific Method and Social Science," *Philosophy of Science*, 1:338–350 (July, 1934). But both in the writings of Ward and in Frank Knight's discussion of the same issue (*Risk, Uncertainty and Profit*, pp. xv–xxxii) the view is apparently taken that the "artificiality" of society implies that a science of sociology inevitably involves ethical assumptions. In the present study, the contrary view is taken.

matter of a science, the more important the role played by knowledge and experience.

This characteristic of purposive behavior, that is, its dependence on belief or expectation, has further consequences in the social field when group behavior is involved. The decision of each member of the group may depend on his expectation of the behavior of the other members of the group; that is, A's decision may depend on his expectation of B's behavior, while B's decision may depend on his expectation of A's behavior. In this way a certain indeterminacy may arise, as indeed it does in such social institutions as the stock market, where successful behavior involves outguessing other participants in the market with regard to these expectations.[4]

It is a fundamental characteristic of social institutions that their stability and even their existence depend on expectations of this sort. In so far as behavior of another person can be accurately predicted, it forms a portion of the objective environment, identical in its nature with the nonhuman portions of that environment.

Applying these considerations to the field of administration, we see first of all that the administrative organization implies purposive behavior on the part of its participants. Hence the expectations of these participants will be a factor in determining their behavior. Further, part of their expectations will involve expectations as to the behavior of other members of the administrative organization.

In this sense administration is not unlike play-acting. The task of the good actor is to know and play his role, although different roles may differ greatly in content. The effectiveness of the performance will depend on the effectiveness of the play and the effectiveness with which it is played. The effectiveness of the administrative process will vary with the effectiveness of the organization and the effectiveness with which its members play their parts.

---

[4] Frank Knight's fundamental thesis is that this "outguessing" is the explanatory mechanism for profit in a competitive economic system (*Risk, Uncertainty and Profit*, pp. 35–37, 333–335). See also analyses of the economic problem of duopoly, where the phenomenon of outguessing shows up to an extreme degree, in R. G. D. Allen, *Mathematical Analysis for Economists* (London: Macmillan & Co., 1938), pp. 200–204, 345–347, and references cited therein.

THE NATURE OF ADMINISTRATIVE PRINCIPLES

We may summarize the conclusions we have reached with respect to a science of administration. In the first place, an administrative science, like any science, is concerned purely with factual statements. There is no place for ethical assertions in the body of a science. Whenever ethical statements do occur, they can be separated into two parts, one factual and one ethical; and only the former has any relevance to science.

Using the terms "theoretical" and "practical" as they have been defined in this section, an administrative science may take either of these two modes. On the one hand, propositions about administration may be descriptions—with reference either to a particular organization or to organizations in general—of the way in which human beings behave in organized groups. This might be called a sociology of administration.

On the other hand, a practical science of administration consists of propositions as to how men would behave if they wished their activity to result in the greatest attainment of administrative objectives with scarce means.[5]

These two alternative forms of administrative science are exactly analogous to the two forms which economic science takes. First economic theory and institutional economics are generalized descriptions of the behavior of men in the market. Second, business theory states those conditions of business behavior which will result in the maximization of profit.

This treatise has included discussions of both the sociology of administration and the practical science of administration. Chapters IV, VI, VIII, and X have been concerned primarily with the former, and Chapters III, IX, and XI primarily with the latter.

[5] For a fuller discussion of the distinction between a sociology and a practical science of administration, see Richard A. Musgrave, "The Planning Approach in Public Economy: A Reply," *Quarterly Journal of Economics*, Feb., 1941, p. 324, and Herbert A. Simon, "The Planning Approach in Public Economy: Further Comment," *ibid.*, p. 329. For an example of the misconceptions which result from a failure to make this distinction, see the recommendations for research in administration set forth in V. O. Key, "The Lack of a Budgetary Theory," *American Political Science Review*, 34:1143 f. (Dec., 1940).

Part II

Chapter XII

ON THE CONCEPT OF ORGANIZATIONAL

GOAL[1]

FEW DISCUSSIONS of organization theory manage to get along without introducing some concept of "organization goal." In the classical economic theory of the firm, where no distinction is made between an organization and a single entrepreneur, the organization's goal—the goal of the firm—is simply identical with the goal of the real or hypothetical entrepreneur. In general, it is thought not to be problematical to postulate that individuals have goals. If it is not, this solution raises no difficulties.

When we are interested in the internal structure of an organization, however, the problem cannot be avoided in this way. Either we must explain organizational behavior in terms of the goals of the individual members of the organization or we must postulate the existence of one or more organization goals, over and above the goals of the individuals.[2]

The first alternative is an attractive one. It protects us from the danger of reifying the organization, of treating it as a superindividual entity having an existence and behavior independent of the behavior of its members. The difficulty with this alternative is that it is hard to carry off. The usual way it is attempted is by identifying the phrase "organization goals" with "goals of the

[1] Taken with minor revisions from the *Administrative Science Quarterly*, 9:1–22 (1964), reprinted with permission. I am grateful to Herbert Kaufman for helpful comments on the manuscript.
[2] The present discussion is generally compatible with, but not identical to, that of my colleagues, R. M. Cyert and J. G. March, who discuss organizational goals in chap. iii of *A Behavioral Theory of the Firm* (Englewood Cliffs, N.J.: Prentice-Hall, 1963). Their analysis is most germane to the paragraphs of this paper that treat of motivation for goals and organizational survival.

firm's owners" or, alternatively, "goals of the firm's top management," or "goals of those who hold legitimate authority to direct the organization."

But this solution raises new difficulties, for we often have occasion to observe that the goals that actually underlie the decisions made in an organization do not coincide with the goals of the owners or of top management but have been modified by managers and employees at all echelons. Must we conclude, then, that it is the goals of the latter—of subordinate managers and employees—that are governing organizational behavior? Presumably not, because the kinds of behavior taking place are not those we would expect if the managers and employees were consulting only their personal goals. The whole concept of an informal organization modified by, but not identical with, the goals either of management or of individual employees, becomes hazy and ambiguous if we follow this path.

Let us see if we can find a way between this Scylla and the Charybdis of reification. The first step toward clarification is to maintain a distinction between goals, on the one hand, and motives, on the other. By *goals* we shall mean value premises that can serve as inputs to decisions. By *motives* we mean the causes, whatever they are, that lead individuals to select some goals rather than others as premises for their decisions. In the next section we shall develop the concept of goal, defined as above. In subsequent sections we shall undertake to explicate the notion of *organization goal* and to clarify the relations between organization goals and personal motives.

Before we can define *organization goals* we shall have to be clear on what we mean by *goals of an individual*. We shall begin by considering the latter question.

GOALS AND DECISIONS: MULTIPLE CRITERIA

Our discussion of goals will be much simplified if we have a definite model before us of the situation we are considering. In recent years in the field of management science or operations research, we have learned to build formal models to characterize even quite elaborate and complex decision situations, and to use these models to reach "optimal" decisions. Since many of these models make use of the tool of linear programming, we will employ a linear programming framework to describe the decision situation. No mathematical knowledge will be assumed beyond the ability to read algebraic notation.[3]

The optimal diet problem is a typical simple linear programming problem. We are given a list of foods, and for each item on the list its price, its calorie content, and its proportions of each of the minerals and vitamins relevant to nutrition. Then we are given a set of nutritional requirements, which may include statements about minimum daily intake of minerals, vitamins, and calories, and may also put limits on maximum intake of some or all of these components.

The diet problem is to find that sublist of foods and their quantities that will meet the nutritional requirements at least cost. The problem can be formalized as follows:

Let the various foods be numbered from 1 through N, and the various nutritional components from 1 through M. Let x_i be the quantity of the ith food in the diet, y_j be the total quantity of the jth nutritional component in the diet, and p_i the price of the ith food. Let a_{ij} be the amount of the jth nutritional component in a unit quantity of the ith food; let b_j be the minimum requirement of the jth nutritional component, and c_j the maximum allowance. (Some of the b_j's may be zero, and some of the c_j's infinite.) Then:

$$\sum_i a_{ij}x_i = y_j, \qquad \text{for } j = 1, \ldots, M; \qquad (1)$$

i.e., the total consumption of the jth nutritional element is the sum of the quantities of that element for each of the foods consumed. The nutritional requirements can be stated:

$$c_j \geqq y_j \geqq b_j, \qquad \text{for } j = 1, \ldots, M; \qquad (2)$$

[3] There are now a substantial number of elementary discussions of linear programming in the management science literature. For a treatment that develops the point of view proposed here, see A. Charnes and W. W. Cooper, *Management Models and Industrial Applications of Linear Programming* (New York: Wiley, 1961), chap. i. See also Charnes and Cooper, Deterministic Equivalents for Optimizing and Satisfying under Chance Constraints, *Operations Research*, 11:18–39 (1963).

i.e., the total quantity of the jth element must lie between b_j and c_j. The quantity of each food consumed must be nonnegative, although it may be zero:

$$x_i \geq 0, \qquad i = 1, \ldots, N. \qquad (3)$$

Finally, the total cost of the diet is to be minimized; we are to find:

$$\underset{x}{Min} \underset{i}{\Sigma} \, x_i p_i. \qquad (4)$$

A diet (the solution is not necessarily unique) that satisfies all the relations (2), (3), (4) is called an *optimal* diet. A diet that satisfies the inequalities (2) and (3) (called *constraints*), but which is not necessarily a minimum cost diet, is called a *feasible* diet.

What is the goal of the diet decision? It would be an appropriate use of ordinary language to say that the goal is to minimize the cost of obtaining an adequate diet, for the condition (4) is the criterion we are minimizing. This criterion puts the emphasis on economy as the goal.

Alternatively, we might direct our attention primarily to the constraints, and in particular to the nutritional requirements (2). Then we might say that the goal is to find a nutritionally satisfactory diet that is economical. Although we still mention costs in this statement, we have clearly shifted the emphasis to the adequacy of the diet from a nutritional standpoint. The primary goal has now become good nutrition.

The relation between the criterion function (4) and the constraints (2) can be made even more symmetrical. Let us replace the criterion (4) with a new constraint:

$$\underset{i}{\Sigma} \, x_i p_i \leq k, \qquad (5)$$

that is to say, with the requirement that the total cost of the diet not exceed some constant, k. Now the set of feasible diets has been restricted to those that satisfy (5) as well as (2) and (3). But since the minimization condition has been removed, there is apparently no basis for choosing one of these diets over another.

Under some circumstances, we can, however, restrict the set of diets that deserve consideration to a subset of the feasible set. Suppose that all the nutritional constraints (2) are minimal constraints, and that we would always prefer, *ceteris paribus,* a greater amount of any nutritional factor to a smaller amount. We will say that diet A is dominated by diet B if the cost of diet B is no greater than the cost of diet A, and if diet B contains at least as much of each nutritional factor as does diet A, and more of at least one factor. We will call the set of diets in the feasible set that is undominated by other diets in that set the Pareto optimal set.

Our preference for one or the other of the diets in the Pareto optimal set will depend on the relative importance we assign to cost in comparison with amounts of nutritional factors, and to the amounts of these factors in relation with each other. If cost is the most important factor, then we will again choose the diet that is selected by criterion (4). On the other hand, if we attach great importance to nutritional factor *j,* we will generally choose a quite different feasible diet—one in which the quantity of factor *j* is as great as possible. Within the limits set by the constraints, it would be quite reasonable to call whatever criterion led us to select a particular member of the Pareto optimal set our goal. But if the constraints are strong enough, so that the feasible set and, *a fortiori,* the Pareto optimal set is very small, then the constraints will have as much or more influence on what diet we finally select than will the goal, so defined. For example, if we set one or more of the nutritional requirements very high, so that only a narrow range of diets also satisfy the budget constraint (5), then introducing the cost minimization criterion as the final selection rule will have relatively little effect on what diet we choose.

Under such circumstances it might be well to give up the idea that the decision situation can be described in terms of a simple goal. Instead, it would be more reasonable to speak of a whole set of goals—the whole set, in fact, of nutritional and budgetary constraints—that the decision-maker is trying to attain. To paraphrase a familiar epigram: "If you allow me to determine the constraints, I don't care who selects the optimization criterion."

MULTIPLE CRITERIA IN ORGANIZATIONS

To show the organizational relevance of our example it is necessary only to suppose that the decision we are discussing has arisen within a business firm that manufactures commercial stock feeds, that the nutritional requirements are requirements for hogs and the prices those of available feed ingredients, and that the finished feed prices facing the firm are fixed. Then minimizing the cost of feed meeting certain nutritional standards is identical with maximizing the profit from selling feed meeting those standards. Cost minimization represents the profit-maximizing goal of the company.

We can equally well say that the goal of the feed company is to provide its customers with the best feed possible, in terms of nutritional standards, at a given price, i.e., to produce feeds that are in the Pareto optimal set. Presumably this is what industry spokesmen mean when they say that the goal of business is not profit but efficient production of goods and services. If we had enlarged our model to give some of the prices that appear in it the status of constraints, instead of fixing them as constants, we could have introduced other goals, for example, the goal of suppliers' profits, or, if there were a labor input, the goal of high wages.[4]

We may summarize the discussion to this point as follows. In the decision-making situations of real life, a course of action, to be acceptable, must satisfy a whole set of requirements, or constraints. Sometimes one of these requirements is singled out and referred to as the goal of the action. But the choice of one of the constraints, from many, is to a large extent arbitrary. For many purposes it is more meaningful to refer to the whole set of requirements as the (complex) goal of the action. This conclusion applies both to individual and organizational decision-making.

[4] See "A Comparison of Organization Theories," in my *Models of Man* (New York: Wiley, 1957), pp. 170–182.

SEARCH FOR A COURSE OF ACTION

Thus far, we have assumed that the set of possible actions is known in advance to the decision-maker. In many, if not most, real-life situations, possible courses of action must be discovered, designed, or synthesized. In the process of searching for a satisfactory solution, the goals of the action—that is, the constraints that must be satisfied by the solution—may play a guiding role in two ways. First, the constraints may be used directly to synthesize proposed solutions (*alternative generation*). Second, the constraints may be used to test the satisfactoriness of a proposed solution (*alternative testing*). The former set of constraints will generally appear to us the more goal-like.[5]

We may illustrate these possibilities by considering what goes on in the mind of a chess player when he is trying to choose a move in a game. One requirement of a good move is that it put pressure on the opponent by attacking him in some way or by preparing an attack. This requirement suggests possible moves to an experienced player (alternative generation). For example, if the opponent's king is not well protected, the player will search for moves that attack the king, but after a possible move has been generated in this way (and thus automatically satisfies the requirement that it put pressure on the opponent), it must be tested against other requirements (alternative testing). For example, it will not be satisfactory if it permits a counterattack that is more potent than the attack or that can be carried out more quickly.

The decisions of everyday organizational life are similar to these decisions in chess. A bank officer who is investing trust funds in stocks and bonds may, because of the terms of the trust document, take as his goal increasing the capital value of the fund. This will lead him to consider buying common stock in firms in growth industries (alternative generation). But he will check

[5] For further discussion of the role of generators and tests in decision-making and problem-solving, see A. Newell and H. A. Simon, "The Processes of Creative Thinking," in H. E. Gruber, G. Terrell, and M. Wertheimer, eds., *Contemporary Approaches to Creative Thinking* (New York: Atherton, 1962), particularly pp. 77–91.

each possible purchase against other requirements: that the firm's financial structure be sound, its past earnings record satisfactory, and so on (alternative testing). All these considerations can be counted among his goals in constructing the portfolio, but some of the goals serve as generators of possible portfolios, others as checks.[6]

The process of designing courses of action provides us, then, with another source of asymmetry between the "goal-like" constraints that guide the actual synthesis and the constraints that determine whether possible courses of action are in fact feasible. In general, the search will continue until one decision in the feasible set is found, or, at most, a very few alternatives. Which member of the feasible set is discovered and selected may depend considerably on the search process, that is, on which requirements serve as generators, in the sense just defined, and which as tests.

In a multiperson situation, one man's goals may be another man's constraints. The feed manufacturer may seek to produce feed as cheaply as possible, searching, for example, for possible new ingredients. The feed, however, has to meet certain nutritional specifications. The hog farmer may seek the best quality of feed, searching, for example, for new manufacturers. The feed, however, cannot cost more than his funds allow; if it is too expensive, he must cut quality or quantity. A sale will be made when a lot of feed is feasible in terms of the requirements of both manufacturer and farmer. Do manufacturer and farmer have the same goals? In one sense, clearly not, for there is a definite conflict of interest between them: The farmer wishes to buy cheap, the manufacturer to sell dear. On the other hand, if a bargain can be struck that meets the requirements of both—if the feasible set that satisfies both sets of constraints is not empty —then there is another sense in which they do have a common goal. In the limiting case of perfect competition, the constraints imposed by the market and the technology actually narrow down the feasible set to a single point, determining uniquely the quantity of goods they will exchange and the price.

[6] G. P. E. Clarkson, "A Model of Trust Investment Behavior," in Cyert and March, *op. cit.*

The neatness and definiteness of the limiting case of perfect competition should not blind us to the fact that most real-life situations do not fit this case exactly. Typically, the generation of alternatives (e.g., product invention, development, and design) is a laborious, costly process. Typically, also, there is a practically unlimited sea of potential alternatives. A river valley development plan that aims at the generation of electric power, subject to appropriate provision for irrigation, flood control, and recreation will generally look quite different from a plan that aims at flood control, subject to appropriate provision for the other goals mentioned. Even though the plans generated in both cases will be examined for their suitability along all the dimensions mentioned, it is almost certain that quite different plans will be devised and proposed for consideration in the two cases, and that the plans finally selected will represent quite distinct points in the feasible set.

In later paragraphs we shall state some reasons for supposing that the total sets of constraints considered by decision-makers in different parts of an organization are likely to be quite similar, but that different decision-makers are likely to divide the constraints between generators and tests in quite different ways. Under these circumstances, if we use the phrase "organization goals" broadly to denote the constraint sets, we will conclude that organizations do, indeed, have goals (widely shared constraint sets). If we use the phrase "organization goals" narrowly to denote the generators, we will conclude that there is little communality of goals among the several parts of large organizations and that subgoal formation and goal conflict are prominent and significant features of organizational life. The distinction we have made between generators and tests helps resolve this ambiguity but also underlines the importance of always making explicit which sense of goal is intended.

MOTIVATION FOR GOALS

If by motivation we mean whatever it is that causes someone to follow a particular course of action, then every action is motivated—by definition. But in most human behavior the relation between motives and action is not simple; it is mediated by a whole chain of events and surrounding conditions.

We observe a man scratching his arm. His motive (or goal)? To relieve an itch.

We observe a man reaching into a medicine cabinet. His motive (or goal)? To get a bottle of lotion that, his wife has assured him, is very effective in relieving the itch of mosquito bites. Or have we misstated his motive? Is it to apply the lotion to his arm? Or, as before, to relieve the itch? But the connection between action and goal is much more complex in this case than in the previous one. There intervenes between them a means-end chain (get bottle, apply lotion, relieve itch), an expectation (that the lotion will relieve the itch), and a social belief supporting the expectation (that the wife's assurance is a reliable predictor of the lotion's efficacy). The relation between the action and the ultimate goal has become highly indirect and contingent, even in this simple case. Notice that these new complications of indirectness are superimposed on the complications we have discussed earlier—that the goal is pursued only within limits imposed by numerous side constraints (don't knock over the other bottles in the medicine cabinet, don't brush against the fresh paint, and so on).

Our point is identical with the point of the venerable story of the three bricklayers who were asked what they were doing. "Laying bricks," "Building a wall," "Helping to erect a great cathedral," were their respective answers. The investment trust officer whose behavior we considered earlier could answer in any of these modes, or others. "I am trying to select a stock for this investment portfolio." "I am assembling a portfolio that will provide retirement income for my client." "I am employed as an investment trust officer." Now it is the step of indirectness between the second and third answers that has principal interest for organization theory. The investment trust officer presumably has no "personal" interest in the retirement income of his client, only a "professional" interest in his role as trust officer and bank employee. He does have, on the other hand, a personal interest in maintaining that role and that employment status.

ROLE BEHAVIOR

Of course, in real life the line of demarcation between personal and professional interests is not a sharp one, for personal satisfactions may arise from the competent performance of a professional role, and both personal satisfactions and dissatisfactions may result from innumerable conditions that surround the employment. Nevertheless, it is exceedingly important, as a first approximation, to distinguish between the answers to two questions of motive: "Why do you keep (or take) this job?" and "Why do you make this particular investment decision?" The first question is properly answered in terms of the personal motives or goals of the occupant of the role, the second question in terms of goals that define behavior appropriate to the role itself.

Corresponding to this subdivision of goals into personal and role-defined goals, organization theory is sometimes divided into two subparts: (1) a theory of motivation explaining the decisions of people to participate in and remain in organizations; and (2) a theory of decision-making within organizations comprised of such people.[7]

In the motivational theory formulated by Barnard and me, it is postulated that the motives of each group of participants can be divided into *inducements* (aspects of participation that are desired by the participants) and *contributions* (aspects of participation that are inputs to the organization's production function but that generally have negative utility to participants). Each participant is motivated to maximize, or at least increase, his inducements while decreasing his contributions, and this motivation is a crucial consideration in explaining the decision to join (or remain). But "joining" means accepting an organizational role, and hence we do not need any additional motivational assumptions beyond those of inducements-contributions theory to explain the ensuing role-enacting behavior.

I hasten to repeat the caveat, introduced a few paragraphs

[7] For further discussion and references, see J. G. March and H. A. Simon, *Organizations* (New York: Wiley, 1958), chap. iv; also, Chapter VI of this book.

above, that in thus separating our consideration of organizational role-enacting behavior from our consideration of personal motivation—allowing the decision to join as the only bridge between them—we are proposing an abstraction from the complexities of real life. A good deal of the significant research on human relations and informal organization, which has contributed heavily in the last generation to our understanding of organizational behavior, has been concerned specifically with the phenomena that this abstraction excludes. Thus, desire for power and concern for personal advancement represent an intrusion of personal goals upon organizational role, as do the social and craft satisfactions and dissatisfactions associated with work.

To say that the abstraction is sometimes untenable is not to deny that there may be many situations in which it is highly useful. There are, first of all, many organizational decisions that simply do not affect personal motives at all—where organizational goals and personal goals are orthogonal, so to speak. As a trivial example, the secretary's inducement-contribution balance is generally in no whit affected by the choice between typing a letter to A or a letter to B or by the content of the letter. Second, personal motives may enter the decision process as fixed constraints (only courses of action that satisfy the constraints are considered, but the constraints have no influence on the choice of action within the set). Thus, the terms of the employment contract may limit work to a forty-hour week but may have little to say about what goes on during the forty hours.[8]

The abstraction of organizational role from personal goals turns out to be particularly useful in studying the cognitive aspects of organizational decision-making, for the abstraction is consonant with some known facts about human cognitive processes. Of all the knowledge, attitudes, and values stored in a human memory, only a very small fraction are evoked in a given concrete situation. Thus, an individual can assume a wide variety of roles when these are evoked by appropriate circumstances, each of which may interact only weakly with the others. At one time he

[8] See "A Formal Theory of the Employment Relation," in *Models of Man, op. cit.*

may be a father, at another a machinist, at another a chess player. Current information processing theories of human cognition postulate that there is only modest overlap of the subsets of memory contents—information and programs—that are evoked by these several roles. Thus, we might postulate that the day-to-day organizational environment evokes quite different associations out of the memory of the participant from those evoked when he is considering a change of jobs. To the extent this is so, it provides a further explanation of why his "personal" system of inducements and contributions, i.e., the utilities that enter into the latter decisions, will have no effect on his "organizational" decisions, i.e., those that are made while the first set is evoked.

The ability of a single individual to shift from one role to another as a function of the environment in which he finds himself thus helps to explain the extent to which organizational goals become internalized, i.e., are automatically evoked and applied during performance of the role. By whatever means the individual was originally motivated to adopt the role in the first place, the goals and constraints appropriate to the role become a part of the decision-making program, stored in his memory, that defines his role behavior.

INTERPERSONAL DIFFERENCES

Although the considerations introduced in the last section show that the uncoupling of organizational role from personal goals need not be complete, it may be useful to indicate a little more specifically how differences among individuals can affect their behavior in roles that are identical from an organizational standpoint.

A role must be understood not as a specific, stereotyped set of behaviors but as a *program* (as that word is understood in computer technology) for determining the courses of action to be taken over the range of circumstances that arise. In previous sections we have given examples of such programs and have shown that they can be highly complex; for instance, a single decision may be a function of a large number of program instructions or premises.

Thus, while we may conceive of an ideal type of role that incorporates only organizational goals among its premises, the roles that members of organizations actually enact invariably incorporate both organizational and personal goals. We have already seen how both can be part of the total system of constraints.

But interpersonal differences in the enactment of roles go far beyond the incorporation of personal goals in the role. Role behavior depends on means-end premises as well as goal premises. Thus, particular professional training may provide an individual with specific techniques and knowledge for solving problems (accounting techniques, legal techniques, and so on), which are then drawn upon as part of the program evoked by his role. In this way, a chief executive with an accounting background may find different problem solutions from a chief executive, in the same position, with a legal background.

An individual may incorporate in his role not only a professional style but also a personal style. He may bring to the role, for example, habits and beliefs that provide him with crucial premises for his handling of interpersonal relations. Thus, an authoritarian personality will behave quite differently from a more permissive person when both are in the same organizational role and pursuing the same organizational goals.

The leeway for the expression of individual differences in role behavior is commonly narrowest in the handling of those matters that come to the role occupant at the initiative of others and is commonly broadest in his exercise of initiative and in selecting those discretionary matters to which he will attend and give priority. In terms used in earlier paragraphs, premises supplied by the organizational environment generally control alternative selection more closely than alternative generation.

THE ORGANIZATIONAL DECISION-MAKING SYSTEM

Let us limit ourselves for the present to situations where occupational roles are almost completely divorced from personal goals and pursue the implications of this factoring of the behavior of organizational participants into its personal and organizational components. If we now consider the organizational decision-making programs of all the participants, together with the connecting flow of communication, we can assemble them into a composite description of the organizational decision-making system—a system that has been largely abstracted from the individual motives that determine participation.

In the simplest case, of a small, relatively unspecialized organization, we are back to a decision-making situation not unlike that of the optimal diet problem. The language of "goals," "requirements," "constraints" that we applied there is equally applicable to similarly uncomplicated organizational situations.

In more complicated cases, abstracting out the organizational decision-making system from personal motives does not remove all aspects of interpersonal (more accurately, interrole) difference from the decision-making process. For when many persons in specialized roles participate in making an organization's decisions, the total system is not likely to be monolithic in structure. Individual roles will differ with respect to the number and kinds of communications they receive and the parts of the environment from which they receive them. They will differ with repect to the evaluative communications they receive from other roles. They will differ in their search programs. Hence, even within our abstraction, which neglects personal motives, we can accommodate the phenomena of differential perception and subgoal formation. (See Chapter X, above.)

To make our discussion more specific, let us again consider a specific example of an organizational decision-making system—in this case a system for controlling inventory and production. We suppose a factory in which decisions have to be made about (1) the aggregate rate of production, that is, the work force that will be employed and the hours employees will work each week, (2) the allocation of aggregate production facilities among the several products the factory makes, and (3) the scheduling of the sequence in which the individual products will be handled on the production facilities. Let us call these the aggregate production decision, item allocation decision, and scheduling decision, respectively. The three sets of decisions may be made by different roles in the organization; in general, we would expect the aggregate decision to be handled at more central levels than the others. The real-world situation will always include complications beyond those we have described, for it will involve decisions with respect to shipments to warehouses, decisions as to which products to hold in warehouse inventories, and many others.

Now we could conceive of an omniscient Planner (the entrepreneur of classical economic theory) who, by solving a set of simultaneous equations, would make each and all of these interrelated decisions. Decision problems of this kind have been widely studied during the past decade by management scientists, with the result that we now know a great deal about the mathematical structures of the problems and the magnitude of the computations that would be required to solve them. We know, in particular, that discovery of the optimal solution of a complete problem of this kind is well beyond the powers of existing or prospective computational equipment.

In actual organizational practice, no one attempts to find an optimal solution for the whole problem. Instead, various particular decisions, or groups of decisions, within the whole complex are made by specialized members or units of the organization. In making these particular decisions, the specialized units do not solve the whole problem but find a "satisfactory" solution for one or more subproblems, where some of the effects of the solution on other parts of the system are incorporated in the definition of "satisfactory."

For example, standard costs may be set as constraints for a manufacturing executive. If he finds that his operations are not meeting those constraints, he will search for ways of lowering his costs. Longer production runs may occur to him as a means for accomplishing this end. He can achieve longer production runs if the number of style variations in product is reduced, so he proposes product standardization as a solution to his cost problem. Presumably he will not implement the solution until he has tested it against constraints introduced by the sales department—objections that refusal to meet special requirements of customers will lose sales.

Anyone familiar with organizational life can multiply examples of this sort, where different problems will come to attention in different parts of the organization, or where different solutions will be generated for a problem, depending on where it arises in the organization. The important point to be noted here is that we do not have to postulate conflict in personal goals or motivations in order to explain such conflicts or discrepancies. They could, and would, equally well arise if each of the organizational decision-making roles were being enacted by digital computers, where the usual sorts of personal limits on the acceptance of organizational roles would be entirely absent. The discrepancies arise out of the cognitive inability of the decision-makers to deal with the entire problem as a set of simultaneous relations, each to be treated symmetrically with the others.[9]

An aspect of the division of decision-making labor that is common to virtually all organizations is the distinction between the kinds of general, aggregative decisions that are made at high levels of the organization and the kinds of specific, item-by-item decisions that are made at low levels. We have already alluded to this distinction in the preceding example of a system for controlling inventory and production. When executives at high levels in such a system make decisions about "aggregate inventory," this mode of factoring the decision-making problem already involves radical simplification and approximation. For example, there is no single, well-defined total cost associated with a given total value of aggregate inventories. There will generally be different costs associated with each of the different kinds of items that make up the inventory (for example, different items may have different spoilage rates or obsolescence rates), and different probabilities and costs will be associated with stock-outs of each kind of item. Thus, a given aggregate inventory will have different costs depending on its composition in terms of individual items.

To design a system for making decisions about the aggregate work force, production rate, and inventories requires an assumption that the aggregate inventory will never depart very far from a typical composition in terms of individual item types. The

[9] For some empirical evidence, see Chapter XV, below.

assumption is likely to be tolerable because subsidiary decisions are continually being made at other points in the organization about the inventories of individual items. These subsidiary decisions prevent the aggregate inventory from becoming severely unbalanced, hence make averages meaningful for the aggregate.

The assumption required for aggregation is not unlike that made by an engineer when he controls the temperature of a tank of water, with a single thermometer as indicator, knowing that sufficient mixing of the liquid in the tank is going on to maintain a stable pattern of temperature relations among its parts. Without such a stable pattern it would be infeasible to control the process by means of a measurement of the average temperature.

If one set of decisions is made, on this approximate basis, about aggregate work force, production rate, and inventories, then these decisions can be used as constraints in making detailed decisions at subsidiary levels about the inventory or production of particular items. If the aggregate decision has been reached to make one million gallons of paint next month, then other decisions can be reached as to how much paint of each kind to make, subject to the constraint that the production quotas for the individual items should, when added together, total one million gallons.[10]

This simple example serves to elucidate how the whole mass of decisions that are continually being made in a complex organization can be viewed as an organized system. They constitute a system in which (1) particular decision-making processes are aimed at finding courses of action that are feasible or satisfactory in the light of multiple goals and constraints, and (2) decisions reached in any one part of the organization enter as goals or constraints into the decisions being made in other parts of the organization.

There is no guarantee that the decisions reached will be optimal with respect to any over-all organizational goal. The system is a loosely coupled one. Nevertheless, the results of the

[10] A system of this kind is developed in detail in "Determining Production Quantities under Aggregate Constraints," in C. Holt, F. Modigliani, J. Muth, and H. A. Simon, *Planning Production, Inventories, and Work Force* (Englewood Cliffs, N.J.: Prentice-Hall, 1960). Compare the discussion of composite decision in Chapter XI, above.

over-all system can be measured against one or more organizational goals, and changes can be made in the decision-making structure when these results are adjudged unsatisfactory.

Furthermore, if we look at the decision-making structure in an actual organization, we see that it is usually put together in such a way as to insure that the decisions made by specialized units will be made in cognizance of the more general goals. Individual units are linked to the total system by production schedules, systems of rewards and penalties based on cost and profit goals, inventory limits, and so on. The loose coupling among the parts has the positive consequence of permitting specific constraints in great variety to be imposed on subsystems without rendering their decision-making mechanisms inoperative.

THE DECISION-MAKING SYSTEM AND ORGANIZATIONAL BEHAVIOR

In the previous sections great pains were taken to distinguish the goals and constraints (inducements and contributions) that motivate people to accept organizational roles from the goals and constraints that enter into their decision-making when they are enacting those organizational roles. On the one hand, the system of personal inducements and contributions imposes constraints that the organization must satisfy if it is to survive. On the other hand, the constraints incorporated in the organizational roles, hence in what I have called here the organizational decision-making system, are the constraints that a course of action must satisfy in order for the organization to adopt it.

There is no necessary *logical* connection between these two sets of constraints. After all, organizations sometimes fail to survive, and their demise can often be attributed to failure to incorporate all the important motivational concerns of participants among the constraints in the organizational decision-making system. For example, a major cause of small business failure is working capital shortage, a result of failure to constrain actions to those that are consistent with creditors' demands for prompt payment. Similarly, new products often fail because incorrect assumptions about the inducements important to consumers are reflected in the constraints that guide product design. (It is widely believed that the troubles of the Chrysler Corporation stemmed from the design premise that car purchasers were primarily interested in buying a good piece of machinery.)

In general, however, there is a strong empirical connection between the two sets of constraints, for the organizations we will usually observe in the real world—those that have succeeded in surviving for some time—will be precisely those that have developed organizational decision-making systems whose constraints guarantee that their actions maintain a favorable balance of inducements to contributions for their participants. The argument, an evolutionary one, is the same one we can apply to biological organisms. There is no logical requirement that the temperatures, oxygen concentrations, and so on that are maintained in the tissues of a bird by its physiological processes should lie within the ranges required for its survival. It is simply that we will not often have opportunities for observing birds whose physiological regulators do not reflect these external constraints. Such birds are soon extinct.[11]

Thus, what the sociologist calls the functional requisites for survival can usually give us good clues for predicting organizational goals; however, if the functional requisites resemble the goals, the similarity is empirical, not definitional. What the goals are must be inferred from observation of the organization's decision-making processes, whether these processes be directed toward survival or suicide.

CONCLUSIONS

We can now summarize our answers to the question that introduced this paper: What it the meaning of the phrase "organizational goal"? First, we discovered that it is doubtful whether decisions are generally directed toward achieving *a* goal. It is

11 The relation between the functional requisites for survival and the actual constraints of the operating system is a central concept in W. R. Ashby's notion of a multistable system. See his *Design for a Brain* (2d ed.) (New York: Wiley, 1960).

easier and clearer to view decisions as being concerned with discovering courses of action that satisfy a whole set of constraints. It is this set, and not any one of its members, that is most accurately viewed as the goal of the action.

If we select any of the constraints for special attention, it is (1) because of its relation to the motivations of the decision-maker, or (2) because of its relation to the search process that is generating or designing particular courses of action. Those constraints that motivate the decision-maker and those that guide his search for actions are sometimes regarded as more "goal-like" than those that limit the actions he may consider or those that are used to test whether a potential course of action he has designed is satisfactory. Whether we treat all the constraints symmetrically or refer to some asymmetrically as goals is largely a matter of linguistic or analytic convenience.

When we come to organizational decisions, we observe that many, if not most, of the constraints that define a satisfactory course of action are associated with an organizational role and hence only indirectly with the personal motives of the individual who assumes that role. In this situation it is convenient to use the phrase organization goal to refer to constraints, or sets of constraints, imposed by the organizational role, which has only this indirect relation to the motives of the decision-makers.

If we examine the constraint set of an organizational decision-making system, we will generally find that it contains constraints that reflect virtually all the inducements and contributions important to various classes of participants. These constraints tend to remove from consideration possible courses of action that are inimical to survival. They do not, of course, by themselves, often fully determine the course of action.

In view of the hierarchical structure that is typical of most formal organizations, it is a reasonable use of language to employ "organizational goal" to refer particularly to the constraint sets and criteria of search that define roles at the upper levels. Thus it is reasonable to speak of conservation of forest resources as a principal goal of the U.S. Forest Service, or reducing fire losses as a principal goal of a city fire department. For high-level executives in these organizations will seek out and support actions that advance these goals, and subordinate employees will do the same or will at least tailor their choices to constraints established by the higher echelons with this end in view.

Finally, since there are large elements of decentralization in the decision-making in any large organization, different constraints may define the decision problems of different positions or specialized units. For example, "profit" may not enter directly into the decision-making of most members of a business organization. Again, this does not mean that it is improper or meaningless to regard profit as a principal goal of the business. It simply means that the decision-making mechanism is a loosely coupled system in which the profit constraint is only one among a number of constraints and enters into most subsystems only in indirect ways. It would be both legitimate and realistic to describe most business firms as directed toward profit making—subject to a number of side constraints—operating through a network of decision-making processes that introduces many gross approximations into the search for profitable courses of action. Furthermore, the goal ascription does not imply that any employee is motivated by the firm's profit goal, although some may be.

This view of the nature of organization goals leaves us with a picture of organizational decision-making that is not simple. But it provides us with an entirely operational way of showing, by describing the structure of the organizational decision-making mechanism, how and to what extent over-all goals, like "profit" or "conserving forest resources" help to determine the actual courses of action that are chosen.

Chapter XIII

THE FUTURE OF INFORMATION-PROCESSING TECHNOLOGY[1]

THE DAY before yesterday, in the beautiful and historic city of Guanajuato, I saw the impressive monuments located there that celebrate Mexico's political revolution—*La Alhóndiga* and the statue of *El Pípila*. But while exploring the city, I also saw a monument that celebrates today's technological revolution—an electronic computer, in the offices of the government of the State of Guanajuato. Indeed, in the present age, the presence of electronic computers has become a prime symbol of the explosion of technology.

But I must be careful in my use of terms. We use the words "revolution," "explosion," and "breakthrough" very freely nowadays. Hardly a day passes without a new "breakthrough" in toothpaste manufacture or the design of raincoats. If we are to avoid a Madison Avenue dilution of meanings, we must employ these terms accurately and sparingly. We must ask whether we are really justified in applying "revolution" to contemporary trends in technology generally, "explosion" to information specifically.

PLUS ÇA CHANGE, PLUS C'EST LA MEME CHOSE

Is there in fact, as is so often claimed, an "information explosion"? Why do we think so? If there is one, what does it signify?

Certainly the daily press has no doubts that information is ex-

[1] This chapter is based on a talk presented at the Institute of Management Science (TIMS) International Meeting in Mexico City, August 24, 1967. It is reprinted with permission from *Management Science*, 14:619–624 (1968).

ploding. A single issue of the Sunday *New York Times* yields the following two items:

In the financial section:

Will a full week of shorter trading hours bring happiness to brokerage firms whose back offices are jammed with paper work?

In the news columns:

George A. Miller, a professor of psychology at Harvard, warned that by 2000, the limit of man's mind to absorb information may be reached. "We may already be nearing some kind of limit for many of the less gifted among us, and those still able to handle the present level of complexity are in ever increasing demand."

These two items are simply a more or less random sample from the very much larger number I could quote—the first two that came to hand. The first conjures up a fascinating picture of the Stock Exchange slowly submerging under a tide of paper; the second promises prosperity to "those still able to handle the present level of complexity"—and I assume that means all of us present here.

How can we assess these developments and the others like them? How valid are the predictions of the impending Flood? To answer those questions, we must sort out the elements of stability and the elements of change in human affairs.

Change—extremely rapid change—there certainly is along technological and economic dimensions. We know that technology is advancing with great speed. We know that it is *beginning* to make possible for the first time in human history the elimination of acute poverty. We know that it is even providing means for combating the over-rapid growth of population—the most serious threat to that prospect of banishing poverty.

But (there is always a "but" at this point in the argument), if we measure the world by Man, by his values and his goals, we have good reason to doubt whether it is changing very much at all. Lesson 21 in the Spanish grammar I brought along to this meeting provides me with a splendid commentary on the stability of human affairs. In translation, the lesson reads:

News! I finish reading the paper. I have learned that prices have gone up. The weather continues to be bad and there may be a storm tonight. No solution has been reached in the dispute between the union and the factory management; it is probable that there will be another strike. It appears doubtful that the political parties will reach an agreement. The international situation is not improving. The other news is the same: accidents, crimes, deaths, births, and weddings.

I am sure the author of that passage intended it as no more than a lesson in Spanish vocabulary. It turns out to be a good description of the human condition—a condition that has not changed much since Greek times. Or at least since the time of Cervantes— for the adventures of Don Quixote are highly suggestive of events in the world today—even including tilting at windmills.

We must not suppose that with the progress of technology, or even with the progress of our economies, mankind will become deliriously happy. For Man's aspirations have a way of adjusting to his opportunities. We must not expect that technological progress will produce Utopia; it is reasonable to hope that it will bring relief to acute hardship and acute pain.

AN ESSAY INTO PREDICTION

With these cautions and reservations, let us turn back to the technology itself and examine the changes that are taking place in information production and processing. Ten years ago, at an Operations Research Society of America meeting in Pittsburgh, Allen Newell and I made some very specific ten-year predictions. I wish I could tell you now—since the deadline for the predictions is almost here—that each one had been exactly fulfilled. Unfortunately, that isn't the case. But rather than take much time here either to defend or to explain away our past predictions, I will simply make a few general comments about them, and then exercise proper caution by eschewing predictions for the future.

If I were to defend our predictions, my defense would take these lines: All the predictions were wrong in detail, but they were correct in their general import: the trend they foresaw and the rate of change. We did not guess correctly how research efforts would be allocated to specific areas, and we did not guess correctly the rank order by difficulty of specific problem areas. Hence, although musical composition, chess playing, and theorem proving by computer have made important progress, they have not yet reached our ten-year targets. On the other side of the account, fundamental understanding of natural language and progress in construction of high-level computer languages have advanced more rapidly than we would have dared predict a decade ago, as have automatic design by computers, visual displays for man-computer on-line interaction, and automatic character recognition.

Hence, in the light of the decade's progress, we remain unrepentant. We see no reason to revise our basic thesis: that electronic computers are general-purpose information-processing devices; that we will step-by-step learn to do with them any kind of thinking that Man can do; that with the help of computer simulation techniques, we will learn (and are learning) how Man thinks, and we will learn how to help him to think better.

ATTENDING TO THE INFORMATION THAT IS THERE

Grant me the premise for the moment that the technology of information processing is progressing as rapidly as these claims would imply—and the TIMS program at this meeting provides much additional evidence for that premise. If this is in fact occuring, why *won't* there be an information explosion? Let me propose a metaphor to explain why there won't—or needn't—be.

The mountain climber, Mallory, when asked why he wanted to climb Everest, gave his famous reply: "Because it is there." Not all of us accept that reply, at least for ourselves. Not all of us aspire to climb Everest or would look forward to the prospect with any relish or sense of purpose.

Now it is possible to be just as skeptical about processing information as about climbing mountains. Specifically, *information doesn't have to be processed just because it is there*. The telephone doesn't have to be answered just because it is ringing; the newspaper doesn't have to be read just because it has been tossed on our doorstep.

I hasten to acknowledge that information is sometimes ignored at our own peril. The inexhaustible Sunday *New York Times* again provides an example:

Tag Petersen, a traffic controller at a railway signal station told a court Friday that he permitted a train to go on Thursday although signals indicated the track was not clear. Since he had not heard from another train on the same tracks, he assumed it was in Nyborg, 20 miles to the East, according to schedule, and that the signals on his control board were in error.

In spite of this example and others of the same genre that could be produced, we are more often guilty of the opposite error—of supposing that all would be well "if we just had more information." I turn once more to the *Times* for an apt illustration:

A Nobel Prize winner at Stanford University thinks it is time for the polls to go to the people instead of the people going to the polls. "I believe that our engineers are in an advanced enough stage to put a simple electronic voting device in all homes," said Professor Robert Hofstadter, a 1961 prize winner in physics.

A qualified citizen could vote, say, in his own living room. Professor Hofstadter said "modern computers can assemble the data almost instantaneously and flawlessly to give a definite result on the issue."

We recognize this as an example of a pathetically naïve belief in the "technological fix." The following is a more frightening example (for, after all, we do not take physicists too seriously when they sound off on politics):

The U.S. State Department, drowning in a river of words estimated at 15 million a month to and from 278 diplomatic outposts around the world, has turned to the computer for help. Final testing is under way on a $3.5 million combination of computers, high-speed printers and other electronic devices. Officials say these will eliminate bottlenecks in the system, especially during crises when torrents of cabled messages flow in from world trouble spots.

When the new system goes into full operation this Fall, computers will be able to absorb cable messages electronically at a rate of 1,200 lines a minute. The old teletypes can receive messages at a rate of only 100 words a minute."

A touching faith in more water as an antidote to drowning! Let us hope that foreign ministers will not feel themselves obliged to process those 1,200 lines per minute just because they are there.

ATTENDING SELECTIVELY

It is ridiculous to suppose that we can save ourselves from drowning in information by installing faster printing devices. *Lack* of information is not the typical problem in our decision processes. The world is constantly drenching us with information through eyes and ears—millions of bits per second, of which, according to the best evidence, we can handle only about 50.

Saturation with information is no new thing. The movements of the stars, visible to Man throughout the tens of thousands of years of his history, contain all the information that is needed for Newton's laws of motions or the law of gravitation. The information was there all along. What was lacking, until a few hundred years ago, was the basis for selecting the tiny fraction of it that could be used to establish powerful generalizations.

We cannot avoid living in a world that drenches us with information—whether made by Man or nature—but we *can* select for our processing the information that is likely to be useful to us and ignore the rest. Gertrude Stein, in the opening pages of *The Autobiography of Alice B. Toklas,* said: "I like a view, but I like to sit with my back turned to it." We can follow Miss Stein's example for independence from the environment of information. Our scientific and technological knowledge, our decision-making and information-processing systems are means for permitting us to turn our back to the view—or to gaze on it very selectively, extracting from it just the parts we want.

In the same vein, most of the contemporary concern about the information explosion in science is misconceived, because it is based on a invalid model of the nature of scientific progress. Science does not advance by piling up information—it organizes information and compresses it. A generation ago, for example, organic chemistry was a mass of particulars only weakly organized by known theoretical generalizations. Today, although knowledge of organic chemistry has grown vastly, the principles of quantum mechanics provide powerful organizing means for that knowledge. As a result, it is undoubtedly easier today to gain a mastery of organic chemistry adequate for doing significant original work than it was in an earlier era when there was very much less known.

The example I have chosen is a spectacular but not an isolated one. In the scientific endeavor, "knowing" has always meant "knowing parsimoniously." The information that nature presents to us is unimaginably redundant. When we find the right way to summarize and characterize that information—when we find the pattern hidden in it—its vast bulk compresses into succinct equations, each one enormously informative.

A SCIENCE OF INFORMATION PROCESSING

Herein lies the real significance of today's information revolution. Information and the processing of information are themselves for the first time becoming the objects of systematic scientific investigation. We are laying the foundations for a science of information processing that we can expect will greatly increase our effectiveness in handling the information around us.

Thus, at a time when we are acquiring devices that will both transmit and process symbols at unprecedented rates, the most important change that is occurring is not the growth of these devices but the growth of an information science or computer science that will help us understand them. It is the growth in our understanding of how information can be transmitted, how it can be organized for storage and retrieval, how it can be used (and how it is used) in thinking, in problem-solving, in decision-making.

This growing understanding of information processing returns to us the decision of whether information must overflow and we must drown in it. It returns to us that decision, just as advances in medicine return to mankind the decision whether population must overflow and we must drown in our own numbers.

A major task ahead for science and technology is to design effective information-processing systems for making decisions in business and in government. It is important that we talk about designing "information-processing systems" and not just designing "computers." This choice of terms is not meant simply to emphasize that the computer programming system—"software" —is at least as important as hardware. That is true, but it is only part of the story. The design of such systems must encompass far more than the computer hardware and software; it must handle with equal care the information-processing characteristics and capabilities of the human members of organizations who constitute the other half of the system.

For generations to come, although the systems we call organizations will have some mechanized components, their most numerous and most crucial elements will continue to be men. The effectiveness of these systems in handling problems will depend more heavily on the effectiveness of the thinking, problem-solving, and decision-making that men do than upon the operation of the computers and their programs. Hence, in the period ahead of us, more important than advances in computer design will be the advances we can make in our understanding of human information processing—of thinking, problem-solving, and decision-making.

A TASK FOR MANAGEMENT SCIENCE

Management scientists will play a major role in these developments. They will carry a heavy responsibility for raising the level of rationality in the organizational decisions that will affect the fate of millions, sometimes even billions, of men.

Perhaps, if they are effective and fortunate, they will be able to raise the quality of decision-making in executive offices and chanceries to the point where the disasters that inept problem-solving all too frequently bring on us will become rare events.

Don Quixote symbolizes forcefully Man's frequent and pathetic incapacity to understand the world in which he lives. But Don Quixote, in the end, recognized his own madness and gained his freedom from it.

And so, in a world that sorely needs balance and clarity of thought, in a world where Man sometimes appears dangerously mad, we may be able, with our growing understanding of the technology of information processing, to restore a measure of reason.

Chapter XIV

APPLYING INFORMATION TECHNOLOGY
TO ORGANIZATION DESIGN[1]

IN THE PAST, organization theory has been mainly concerned with what might be called "organization for production"—that is, with systems that use the services of substantial numbers of employees to generate, more or less continuously, some kind of output or "product." The normative theory of organization, aimed at enhancing organizational efficiency and effectiveness, traditionally paid special attention to two problems: how to divide up the work for its efficient performance and in such a way as to keep the needs for coordination of the parts within manageable bounds; and how to construct and maintain mechanisms for coordinating the several organizational parts—especially authority mechanisms.

Research on "human relations" in organizations, beginning on a substantial scale in the 1930s, turned attention in organizational design to the linkage between the individual as organization member and the pattern of organizational activity. The principal normative concern here was to create organizational environments in which employees would be motivated to join the organization, to remain in it, and to contribute vigorously and effectively to its goals. As a result of theory and empirical research in human relations, the factory and office came to be viewed as relatively impoverished human environments—starving both the human mind and the human emotions. Proposals were advanced for the redesign of organizations in ways that would make work intellectually more stimulating (or less boring) and give the worker a

---

[1] Taken, with minor revisions, from *Public Administration Review*, 33:268–78 (1973), reprinted with permission.

greater feeling of participation in the decisions governing his activity. "Job enrichment" and "democratic management" are labels commonly applied to these emphases in organizational design.[2]

The human relations movement did not limit itself to redesigning organizations to achieve the traditional goals of organizational effectiveness and efficiency. It also raised fundamental value questions of whether organizations *should* be designed in these terms; or whether, on the other hand, there should be a deliberate sacrifice of effectiveness and efficiency in order to make work itself a rewarding and enjoyable part of human life. This value issue is sometimes obscured in the literature when the assumption is made, implicitly or explicitly, that "the happy employee is the productive employee." That assumption tends to prevail through the early writings on human relations but has been frequently questioned or attacked in recent years by the social critics of the New Left.

I do not intend to enter into that controversy here. I raise the issue because I think the debate has been carried out on premises that are less and less valid in today's organizations and will be still less valid in the organizations of the future. The attack on work in organizations as dehumanizing generally takes as its model of the organization a system engaged in mass repetitive processing of materials or symbols—the assembly line or a room full of clerks or draftsmen. Chaplin's movie, "Modern Times," exaggerates only slightly the portrait of the factory given in the human relations literature.

But with the introduction of highly automated machinery, and particularly with the introduction of mechanized information processing equipment, the assembly line becomes a rather rare form of organization of production, as does the repetitive unautomated clerical process. The human operative or clerk is less often a cog in the ongoing production process, or even the first-level controller of that process. He is more and more an observer, moderator, maintenance man, and repairman for a nearly auton-

---

[2] The names of Lewin, Roethlisberger, Likert, MacGregor, and Argyris will identify the general range of approaches and emphases within the human relations movement. Many other names could, of course, be added to the list, which is only illustrative.

omous process that can carry on for significant intervals of time without direct human intervention.

The question of whether "the happy employee is the productive employee" still needs asking under these new conditions of employment. But it is not obvious that the question will have the same answer it had in the past. The problems of cognitive impoverishment and alienation may be replaced by quite new problems—or may disappear altogether. My own assessment—based on direct observation and the studies of others of highly automated work situations—is that the new environment will be, for most workers, a more pleasant and humane environment than the old. We will need a great deal more experience with this new environment, however, to provide solid evidential foundations for that optimism.

But I am getting a bit ahead of my story, for I have not yet said why I think organizations are changing in the directions I have mentioned.

THE POST-INDUSTRIAL SOCIETY

Peter Drucker has used the phrase "post-industrial society" to describe the emerging world in which manufacturing production, and the activities associated with it, plays a much less central role than it did in the world of the past century. Organizations in the post-industrial society provide services, many of them intangible, more than they manufacture things. Already, a large part of the economic activity of our society consists in providing services for education, health, and leisure-time activities.

Providing services tends to pose different organizational problems from producing tangible goods. It is usually more difficult to define appropriate output measures for service organizations than for organizations that produce tangible commodities. Whatever problems are present in measuring the quality of goods are magnified greatly in measuring the quality of services. The point can be illustrated by comparing two versions of the same economic activity, first viewed as a goods-producing activity, then as a service-producing activity: that is, producing *houses* and *housing* respectively.

A house is a tangible commodity that can be manufactured and distributed through the usual market mechanisms; housing is a bundle of services provided by a dwelling in the context of a neighborhood, with schools, streets, shopping facilities, and a pattern of social interaction among the inhabitants. However complex it may be to define the qualities of a house, narrowly conceived as a structure, it is far more complex to define the qualities of housing, in the sense of a situation that creates and supports a pattern of social activity.

Related to the tendency of organizations in our society to broaden the definition of their goals from the production of tangible commodities to the production of bundles of services that may or may not be associated with tangible commodities, is a tendency to broaden their concern for the externalities associated with their activities. Externalities are simply those consequences of action that are not charged, through the existing market mechanisms, to the actors. The classical example is the factory smoke whose social costs have not generally been paid by the consumers of the factory's product.

It may be that organizations producing services usually have more and larger externalities associated with their activities than organizations producing goods; it may be that we are simply becoming more sensitive in our society to the indirect consequences of organizational activity directed toward specialized goals; it may be that, with the growth of population and technology, the actual interdependencies of organizations, and hence the externalities they cause, are becoming more extensive and significant. Whatever the reasons—and all three of those mentioned probably contribute to the trend—organizational decision-making in the organizations of the post-industrial world shows every sign of becoming a great deal more complex than the decision-making of the past. As a consequence of this fact, the decision-making process, rather than the processes contributing immediately and directly to the production of the organization's final output, will bulk larger and larger as *the* central activity in which the organization is engaged.

In the post-industrial society, the central probem is not how to organize to produce efficiently (although this will always remain an important consideration), but how to organize to make decisions—that is, to process information. Until recent years, decision-making was exclusively a human activity; it involved processes going on inside the human head and symbolic communication among humans. In our present world, decision-making is shared between the human and mechanized components of man-machine systems, the machines being those devices we call computers. The division of labor between the human and computer components in these systems has changed steadily over the past twenty years, and we can expect it to continue to change as the sophistication of computer technology—and particularly computer programming or software technology—grows.

The anatomy of an organization viewed as a decision-making and information-processing system may look very different from the anatomy of the same organization viewed as a collection of people. The latter viewpoint, which is the traditional one, focuses attention on the groupings of human beings—that is, the departmentalization. The former viewpoint, on the other hand, focuses on the decision-making process itself—that is, upon the flows and transformations of symbols. If we carve an organization, conceptually, into subsystems on the basis of the principal components into which the decision-making process divides, we may, and probably will, arrive at a very different dissection than if we carve it into its departmental and subdepartmental components. Moreover, the greater the interdependencies among the departmental components, the greater will be the difference in these two ways of conceptualizing the organization.

Both of these viewpoints are useful and even essential in arriving at sound designs for organizations. In this analysis, I shall emphasize the less conventional point of view and shall discuss the decision-making process disembodied, so to speak, from the flesh-and-blood (or glass and metal, as the case may be) decision-makers who actually carry out this process. Instead of watching a man or computer as information reaches him and he processes it and transmits new information in his turn, we will watch information as it flows from one man or computer to another and is transformed in the course of flow. This approach, if it has no other advantages (though I believe it does), will give us a fresh look at the design of organizations.

TWO REQUIREMENTS OF ORGANIZATIONAL DESIGN

The division of labor is quite as important in organizing decision-making as in organizing production, but what is being divided is different in the two cases. From the information-processing point of view, division of labor means factoring the total system of decisions that need to be made into relatively independent subsystems, each one of which can be designed with only minimal concern for its interactions with the others. The division is necessary because the processors that are available to organizations, whether humans or computers, are very limited in their processing capacity in comparison with the magnitude of the decision problems that organizations face. The number of alternatives that can be considered, the intricacy of the chains of consequences that can be traced—all these are severely restricted by the limited capacities of the available processors.

Any division of labor among decisional subsystems creates externalities, which arise out of the interdependencies among the subsystems that are ignored. What is wanted is a factorization that minimizes these externalities and consequently permits a maximum degree of decentralization of final decision to the subsystems, and a maximum use of relatively simple and cheap coordinating devices like the market mechanism to relate each of the decisional subsystems with the others.

Not only must the size of decision problems handled by organizations be reduced to manageable proportions by factorization, but the number of decisions to be processed must be limited by applying good principles of attention management. Attention management for an organization means exactly what it means for an individual human being: Processing capacity must be allocated to specific decision tasks, and if the total capacity is not adequate to the totality of tasks, then priorities must be set so that the most important or critical tasks are attended to.

The information-processing systems of our contemporary world swim in an exceedingly rich soup of information, of symbols. In a world of this kind, the scarce resource is not information; it is processing capacity to attend to information. Attention is the chief bottleneck in organizational activity, and the bottleneck becomes narrower and narrower as we move to the tops of organizations, where parallel processing capacity becomes less easy to provide without damaging the coordinating function that is a prime responsibility of these levels.

The richness of the informational environment and the scarcity of attention have many consequences for organizational design, some of which will be developed presently. At this point, only two further comments need to be made. First, the difficulty of coping with the information-rich environment is compounded by the fact that most information relevant to top-level and long-run organizational decisions typically originates outside the organization, and hence in forms and quantities that are beyond its control. This means that the organization must have an "interface" for ingesting such information selectively and for translating it into formats that are compatible with its internal information flows and systems.

Second, if attention is the scarce resource, then it becomes particularly important to distinguish between problems for decision that come with deadlines attached (real-time decisions), and problems that have relatively flexible deadlines. Rather different system designs are called for to handle these different kinds of decisions.

In summary, the inherent capacity limits of information-processing systems impose two requirements on organizational design: that the totality of decision problems be factored in such a way as to minimize the interdependence of the components; and that the entire system be so structured as to conserve the scarce resource, attention. The organizational design must provide for interfaces to handle information that originates outside the organization, and special provision must be made for decisions that have particular time limits associated with them.

Applying these basic design requirements make it easy to see the fallacy in some recent and more or less abortive approaches to the improvement of information systems: municipal data banks and management information systems. There was a great enthusiasm, only a couple of years ago, for developing comprehensive data banks for metropolitan areas—these data banks to incorporate in a single system all the myriad pieces of information about land and its uses, and about people and their activities, that are generated by the operations of urban government. As the result of several attempts to construct such systems, the enthusiasm has been much moderated, and several incipient undertakings of this kind have been abandoned. There were several reasons for the disenchantment that followed the initial attempts at constructing such systems. First, the data processing and data storage tasks proved much larger and more complex than had been imagined. Perhaps more crucial, it became less and less clear just how the data were to enter into the decision-making process, or indeed to just what decisions they were relevant.

The lesson is clear. There is no magic in comprehensiveness. It may be sufficient motive to climb a mountain "because it is there," but the mere existence of a mass of data is not a sufficient reason for collecting it into a single, comprehensive information system. Indeed, the problem is quite the opposite: of finding a way of factoring decision problems in order to relate the several components to their respective relevant data sources. Analysis of the decision-making system and its data requirements must come first; only then can a reasonable approach be made to defining the data systems that will support the decision-making process.

The history of management information systems has been nearly the same as the history of municipal data banks. In the enthusiasm to make use of the enormous power of computers, there was a tendency, in designing such systems, to take the existing source records as a starting point and to try to give top management access to all this information. The question was not asked, or not asked with sufficient seriousness, whether top management either wanted or needed such information, nor whether the information that top management needed and should want could in fact be derived from these particular source records. The systems were not designed to conserve the critical scarce resource—the attention of managers—and they tended to ignore the fact that the information most important to top managers comes mainly from external sources and not from the internal records that were immediately accessible for mechanized processing.

Thus many of the efforts to design information systems for municipalities and corporations fell into the fallacy of thinking that "more information is better." They took over, implicitly, the assumptions of a past society where information rather than attention was the scarce resource.

CHARACTERISTICS OF THE TECHNOLOGY

Good design requires bringing the desired ends into effective relation with the available means. To design effective decision-making organizations, we must understand the structure of the decisions to be made; and we must understand the decision-making tools at our disposal, both human and mechanical—men and computers.

The Human Components

In our fascination with the new capabilities that computers offer us, we must be careful not to forget that our human decision-makers have some pretty remarkable qualities too. Each human decision-maker is provided with a sizeable memory that is stocked cumulatively over a long period of years with various kinds of relevant and irrelevant information and skills. Each is able to communicate in natural language with his fellows, either in direct face-to-face settings or by remote devices like the telephone.

Suppose, for example, that we were interested in designing an organization that would lead us to the most expert source of information in the United States about any particular question that happened to arise. Now this expert information is stored both in human heads and in books. Moreover, the information in books is also indexed in human heads, so that usually the most expeditious way to find the right book is to ask a human who is an expert on the subject the book deals with. Not only are books indexed in human heads, but people are also. Taking these resources into account, the most powerful information-processing system for carrying out this search task is the aggregate of memory that is distributed among 200 million human heads, together with the telephone system that links these distributed memories. On receipt of the inquiry, I pick up the phone and call the person, among my acquaintances, whose field of expertness is as close as possible (it need not be very close at all). I ask him, not for the answer to the question, but for the name of the person in his circle of acquaintance who is closest to being an expert on the topic. I repeat the process until I have the information I want. It will be a rare instance when more than three or four calls are required.

Suppose that the question is whether whales have spleens. (I can't imagine why we want to know, but this example is as good as any other.) I call a biologist, who refers me to an ichthyologist, who refers me to a specialist on whales, who either knows the answer or can refer me to the book where I will find it.

I do not mean to propose that we junk all our other information systems and place sole reliance on the telephone and the vast distributed memory with which it connects us. However, this is a useful illustration of how we must think about information-processing systems—including human systems—their components and interconnections, if we are to design them well. We must learn to characterize them in terms of the sizes of their memories, the ways in which those memories are indexed, their processing rates, and the rapidity with which they can respond. The human components of information systems are just as describable as the machine components, and since World War II we have learned a great deal through psychological research about the parameters of the human system.

Our new and growing understanding of information processing enables us to look at familiar processing systems—man and telephone—in new ways. It also introduces us to new kinds of systems, which we put under the general label of "computers," that have capabilities of the most varied kinds.

The Computer as Memory

The computer is, first of all, a memory. I have already expressed my qualms about confusing the design of an information-*collecting* system with the design of an information-*processing* system. The fault, of course, is not in collecting information (although that may be costly in itself); it is in demanding the scarce attention of decision-makers to the information that has been collected. Memories, as components of information-processing systems, need to be viewed as stores of *potential* information, which, if indexed effectively, can become available at a reasonable cost whenever it is needed as input to a decision-making process.

Consider a man who has collected a library of 30,000 books. Even if he reads one book a day—a pretty good clip—it will take him 100 years to read through all the shelves. We may even consider it a bit ostentatious of him to have collected more books than he can possibly read—as though he were trying to impress us with his learning. However, we must not be too hasty in judging him. If his library is properly indexed, then our collector has potential access to *any* of the information in the 30,000 volumes. He is quite justified in collecting more volumes than he can read if he cannot predict in advance what particular information he will need in the future.

The computer memories that are employed today are not, in general, large compared with the paper-and-ink memories we call libraries. They are, in general, better indexed for rapid retrieval of information, and one of the important directions of technological progress since the computer has appeared on the scene has been our understanding of the indexing and information retrieval processes, and in our ability to carry these out mechanically.

The Computer as Processor

In addition to being a memory, the computer is also a processor that possesses quite general capabilities for handling symbols of all kinds, numerical and nonnumerical. This is the computer's most novel feature. Nonhuman memories have been familiar to man since the invention of writing. Nonhuman symbol manipulation is something quite new, and even after twenty years, we are just beginning to glimpse its potential.[3]

Up to the present time, perhaps the most important use of the computer in decision-making (though not the use that accounts for the bulk of computer time that is consumed by organizations) is to model complex situations and to infer the consequences of alternative decisions. Some of this modeling makes use of mathematical techniques, like linear programming, that permit the calculation of optimal courses of action, hence serve as direct decision-making tools. In other forms of modeling, the computer serves as a simulator, calculating out the alternative histories of a system that would follow on different decision strategies.

The term "management information system" has generally been construed narrowly and has been applied to large information storage and retrieval systems, like those mentioned earlier, in which the computer does only very simple processing of the information. The term would be better applied to the optimizing and simulation models that are increasingly used to illuminate various areas of management decision—models that are usually referred to as "operations research" and "strategic planning." Such models, however they are labeled, probably give us a better preview of the future uses of computers in organizational decision systems than do the explicitly named management information systems.

Let me cite one example of an area of application for a strategic planning model. In the next decades, our society faces some important and difficult policy decisions with respect to the production and use of energy. In the past, the national energy problem was perceived mostly as a resource problem, and it was left in considerable part to private management through market mechanisms.

[3] One evidence of the degree of novelty of the computer's capabilities is the resistance it evokes from those who refuse to see in it anything more than an enlarged desk calculator. Not since the Darwinian controversy of the past century have we seen such a passionate defense of the uniqueness of man against claims of kinship by systems that do not belong to his species.

Today, we see that the use of energy has important indirect consequences for the environment, and we see also that the adequacy of fuel resources for producing energy will depend on such broader trends as the rates of development of industrializing countries and the decisions we make with respect to R & D for energy technology.

The number of important variables involved in the energy picture is so large, and the interconnections among variables so intricate, that common sense and everyday reasoning no longer provide adequate guides to energy policies—if, indeed, they ever did. Nor is there a simple organizational solution of a traditional kind: establishing a federal agency with comprehensive jurisdiction over energy problems, or, alternatively, tinkering with the market mechanism. Agency reorganization is no solution for at least two reasons. First, energy problems cannot be separated neatly from other problems. What would be the relation of a comprehensive energy agency to environmental problems? The fragmentation of responsibility for energy policy in the federal government today is a consequence of the intertwining of those problems with others. Second, even if there were such an agency, it too would need a systematic framework within which to take up its decision problems. Tinkering with market mechanisms raises the same difficulty—without a decision framework, we do not know how to tinker.

Hence, the most important organizational requirement for handling energy policy in an intelligent way is the creation of one or more models—either of an optimizing or simulation type—to provide coherence to the decision-making process. No doubt, it is of some importance to locate the responsibility for developing and exploiting such models in appropriate places in the governmental and industrial structure. But the mere existence of the models, wherever located, cannot but have a major impact on energy policy decisions. Surprisingly, the first comprehensive models of the energy system are just now under construction, although the need for them has been fairly obvious for some years. The tardiness of response to the need is evidence both of the novelty of the modeling technology and the novelty of looking at organization as a collection of decision systems rather than a collection of agencies and departments.[4]

Computer Access to External Information

A third point must be made about the characteristics of the computer as a component of the organization's information processing system. I have mentioned as one limitation of the management information systems of recent years their great reliance on information that is generated internally, within the organization itself—for example, production and accounting information. A major reason for the emphasis on internal information is that, since the organization controls the production of this information, it is not hard to produce it in machine-readable form. Then no costly step is involved in getting it inside the computer.

If we examine the kinds of external information that executives use, we find that a large proportion of it is simply natural language text—the pages of newspapers, trade magazines, technical journals, and so on. Natural language text can, of course, be stored in computer memory after it is translated into some machine-readable form—punched cards, magnetic tape, or the like. Once stored in memory, computer programs can be written to index it automatically and to retrieve information from it in response to inquiries of a variety of kinds.

[4] We have now had a generation's experience with decision models for economic policy. The construction and testing of such models in the United States has been carried out in considerable part by nongovernmental agencies—the Cowles Foundation for Research in Economics and the Brookings Institution, for example. Since the day when President Nixon declared himself to be a Keynesian, the impact of decision models on government decisions could no longer be in doubt, although the impact certainly preceded that declaration by a decade or more. The econometric models have generally used classical analytic mathematical techniques, but the computer has been essential to carrying out the calculations. A somewhat different example is provided by several linear programming models that have been constructed, mainly under university auspices, to guide water policy decisions. In both these cases we see decision-making systems being designed in relative independence from reorganizations of a traditional kind. It is interesting to speculate whether all of the agency-shuffling reorganizations of federal agencies since 1937 have had as great an effect on public policy as these new decision-making systems.

The only barrier, therefore, to making available to the mechanized components of organizational information systems the same kind of external information that executives now rely upon is the cost of putting the information into machine-readable form. Technologically, the obstacle is not insuperable; it is possible to produce devices that will translate printed text into magnetic tape. The costs of doing this, however, are rather high, and the prospects do not appear bright for reducing them rapidly.

This particular Gordian knot should be cut, not untied. Every word that is now printed in a newspaper, journal, or book passes at some time during its prior history through a machine—typewriter or typesetting machine—that could produce a machine-readable version of the text at the same time that it produces the man-readable version, and at an insignificant incremental cost. Hence, we may look forward to a time in the near future when the written word will be almost universally available in both machine-readable and man-readable editions. Once the switchover begins, so that there is a market for the machine-readable versions, we can expect the conversion process to go very rapidly. It is a little like the telephone—the more people who have them, the more worthwhile it is to get one.

This development will open up a whole new range of application of computers to organization information systems. It will enable computers to serve as initial filters for most of the information that enters the organization from outside, and will thereby help reduce the attentional demands on executives.

Matching Techniques to Requirements

These comments will serve to indicate what is involved in fitting together the requirements of organization information systems with the characteristics of the information technology that is now available or emerging. The key to the successful design of information systems lies in matching the technology to the limits of the attentional resources. From this general principle, we can derive several rules of thumb to guide us when we are considering adding a component to an existing information-processing system.

In general, an additional component (man or machine) for an information-processing system will improve the system's performance only if:

1. Its output is small in comparison with its input, so that it conserves attention instead of making additional demands on attention;

2. It incorporates effective indexes of both passive and active kinds (active indexes are processes that automatically select and filter information for subsequent transmission);

3. It incorporates analytic and synthetic models that are capable not merely of storing and retrieving information, but of solving problems, evaluating solutions, and making decisions.

These heuristics are applicable to all components of information systems, not only to computers. It is a useful exercise, for example, to look at television in their light, as a component of a political information system. Television can be used to deliver lectures or to exhibit concrete scenes and events. As a source of lectures, its relatively undifferentiated mass audience is a severe handicap—for almost any individual member of the audience, we could devise a lecture that would be more appropriate than the one actually screened. In communicating information through pictures it has the further disadvantages of its inability to abstract, to generalize, or to sample properly from complex populations of events. It possesses no analytic capabilities other than those provided by the commentator.

To point to these severe deficiencies of television as a source of politically relevant information is not to deny its effects on the political system. The most obvious of these effects is its power to focus the attention of an entire society for a period of time on a particular set of events—whether these be trips to the moon, riots, or summit conferences. In general, television *informs* very little about such events, but it may succeed in evoking strong emotions simultaneously from millions of viewers, and consequently in rearranging the public agenda.

POLITICS AS INFORMATION PROCESSING

This last example, as well as the earlier example of energy policy, are illustrative of a broader point: that our political institutions are organizations, and that what we have said about the design of information-processing systems for organizations applies fully to the design of the decision-making components of the political system. Nowhere is the problem of attention management and the conservation of attention of greater importance than in the political process.

The themes of alienation of the electorate and the need to "return government to the people" that have been prominent in recent public discussion of our institutions are, of course, not new to the American political scene. Cynicism about the political process is deeply ingrained in the American culture. For the most part, proposals for political reform have focused on strengthening controls over the professional full-time participants in the system, elected or appointed (e.g., recall elections, presidential primary), or on creating new channels of direct popular participation in decision-making (e.g., the initiative and referendum, official provision for citizen participation in program administration).

As high technology has come to play a larger role in our society, and in the provision of governmental services in particular, the growing difficulties of assuring that participation will be informed participation have not gone unnoticed. Informed participation in decision-making is a problem not only for the part-time contributors to the system—the voters—but for elected representatives and high-level administrators as well. It is at the core of the familiar organizational problem of the relation of experts to laymen.

An Example of Poorly Informed Participation

The phosphate detergent fiasco is only one of the most recent of innumerable instances of the difficulties of settling technical issues with wide public involvement. A problem existed: excessive algal bloom in lakes. It was known that this condition occurred only in waters having a high level of organic nutrients; phosphate, in particular, was highly suspect as culprit. (Clear scientific evidence on the precise mechanisms of eutrophication, and the precise conditions under which it will or won't occur is nearly nonexistent.) A substantial fraction of the phosphate in water is contributed by household detergents. There exist nonphosphate or low-phosphate detergents. Therefore—but the "therefore," however obvious it may seem, left unanswered most of the critical questions: Would removal of phosphate from household detergents do any good if other phosphate sources remained? Was phosphate, in fact, the principal culprit? What are the alternative methods, other than changing detergents, for eliminating phosphate from lakes? What are the properties of the alternative detergents, and what consequences would their use have? What would be the relative costs of various courses of action?

As our previous analysis should lead us to predict, the mass media had a large impact in focusing public attention on the eutrophication problem and in creating insistent demands for forceful action. There is no difficulty in picturing on television a dead fish or (at least on color television) an algae-green lake. What the mass media could not do was to remove the scientific unknowns from the problem or provide a systems analysis of alternatives. As a result of the pressure for action, the federal government came close to banning phosphate from detergents, but fortunately had not done so by the time some of the difficulties and dangers of the alternatives had become known.

My intent here is not to suggest what the solution of the problem should have been but to use these events to point to the weaknesses of our current decision-making processes in political matters where complex technical issues are involved. Most of the current proposals to remedy these weaknesses are of a traditional kind: Create new organizations to provide the technical expertise that is now lacking. The two most prominent proposals are the creation or strengthening of organizations that would represent the consumer and the creation of organizations for technology assessment, these latter to be responsible to the legislative body.

So far as these proposals go, they seem to me sound, but I

would warn that we should not expect too much from them. In particular, in talking about "consumer organizations," we must remember that that is precisely what a government is created to be, and thus new organizations of this kind are no more exempt from the iron law of bureaucracy than are existing institutions (as experience with trade unions, political parties, and the American Medical Association should have taught us).

The Contribution of Systems Analysis

If magic is to be performed, it will not come through the mere creation of new organizations. The problem is not primarily one of control but of information—not one of enforcing virtue but of discovering the path of virtue. We do not need new organizations so much as we need new decision processes. To illustrate my meaning, let me cite some happier examples than the phosphate debate of recent public discussion.

The struggles over the anti-ballistic missile and the supersonic transport are, to my mind, examples of what we may hope for in the way of informed discussion of highly technical and complex issues. This does not mean that the correct decisions were necessarily reached. I have no more infallible means for deciding that than did the disputants at the time of the debate. Honest and reasonable men could and did take either side of either question. But what distinguished these particular debates was that both sides were armed with sophisticated analyses based on man-years of careful study supported by quantitative models. For this reason, it was possible for the layman, with a reasonable expenditure of time, to understand where the differences lay—which disagreements about assumptions were responsible for the divergent conclusions reached. Moreover, for each of the decisions there was not a single analysis but several, prepared by protagonists who had different sets of interests and different viewpoints.

Thus, the ABM and SST decision processes were informed by analyses that met three essential criteria: comprehensiveness, technical sophistication, and pluralism. Satisfaction of these criteria does not guarantee that correct decisions are reached—in a world of uncertainty and conflict of interest, that guarantee can seldom be provided. It does tend to assure that the decisions reached are such as reasonable men of good will could arrive at. And it is the guarantee of due process, not the guarantee of infallibility, that democratic institutions require.

In making this plea for more and better systems analyses and more and better institutional arrangements for carrying them out, I should not want to be thought to be urging centralization of any and all decisions. An equally important direction for improvement of decision processes is to instill new vigor into market mechanisms as an essential component of a decentralized society. Our growing awareness of the externalities, particularly environmental costs, that the price system has ignored in the past has caused something of a crisis of confidence in market mechanisms as social regulators and decision-makers. Where externalities are present, there is an alternative, however, to centralization: incorporating the externalities in the pricing process. A tax on oxides of sulphur emitted into the atmosphere is an example of such a measure. To attack such a proposal as "a license to pollute" is to substitute sloganizing for problem solving. We need not only to solve the problems we perceive, but, in solving them, to minimize the drain on our scarce resources. Using the price system as motivator, where it is applicable, is one of the most powerful means available to us for enlisting a multitude of energies and minds into the search for least-cost solutions to our problems.

CONCLUSION

The major problems of governmental (and corporate and educational) organization today are not problems of departmentalization and coordination of operating units. Instead, they are problems of organizing information storage and information processing—not problems of the division of labor, but problems of the factorization of decision-making. These organizational problems are best attacked, at least to a first approximation, by examining the information system in abstraction from agency and department structure.

With the rapid development of information-processing technology, the corporate and public decision-making processes are becoming immensely more sophisticated and rational than they were in past eras. If we require any proof for this, we need only compare the ABM debate (regardless of whether we like its outcome) with any debate on the Acropolis reported by Thucydides —or, for that matter, with any debate in the U.S. Congress in the first half of this century.

With the development of information-processing technology, we have a growing capacity to consider interactions and tradeoffs among alternatives and consequences; to cumulate our understanding of fragments of the whole problem by embedding these fragments in comprehensive models.

Barbara Ward and others have pointed out to us that the largest crises in our world today are crises of aspirations. The population problem is as old as Man. What is new about it today is that we are resolved not to accept a gloomy outcome but to deal with it. For centuries, Man's actions have been creating all kinds of unintended and unexpected consequences. He could live in good conscience with his actions to the extent that he was unaware of these consequences. Today, we can trace minute and indirect effects of our behavior: the relation of smoking to cancer, the relation of the brittleness of eagles' eggs to the presence of DDT in the environment. With this new ability to trace effects, we feel responsible for them in a way we previously did not. The intellectual awakening is also a moral awakening.

The new problems created (or made visible) by our new scientific knowledge are symptoms of progress, not omens of doom. They demonstrate that Man now possesses the analytic tools that are basic to understanding his problems—basic to understanding the human condition.

Of course, to understand problems is not necessarily to solve them. But it *is* the essential first step. The new information technology that we are creating enables us to take that step.

Chapter XV

SELECTIVE PERCEPTION:

THE IDENTIFICATIONS OF EXECUTIVES[1]
(with DeWitt C. Dearborn)

An important proposition in organization theory asserts that each executive will perceive those aspects of the situation that relate specifically to the activities and goals of his department (See Chapter X, above). The proposition is frequently supported by anecdotes of executives and observers in organizations, but little evidence of a systematic kind is available to test it. It is the purpose of this chapter to supply some such evidence.

The proposition we are considering is not peculiarly organizational. It is simply an application to organizational phenomena of a generalization that is central to any explanation of selective perception: Presented with a complex stimulus, the subject perceives in it what he is "ready" to perceive; the more complex or ambiguous the stimulus, the more the perception is determined by what is already "in" the subject and the less by what is "in" the stimulus.[2]

Motivational and cognitive mechanisms mingle in the selective process, and it may be of some use to assess their relative contributions. We might suppose either: (1) selective attention to a part of a stimulus reflects a deliberate ignoring of the remainder as irrelevant to the subject's goals and motives, or (2) selective

[1] This chapter is taken, with minor revisions, from *Sociometry*, 21:140–144 (1958), reprinted with permission.
[2] J. S. Bruner, "On Perceptual Readiness," *Psychological Review*, 64:123–152 (1957).

attention is a learned response stemming from some past history of reinforcement. In the latter case we might still be at some pains to determine the nature of the reinforcement, but by creating a situation from which any immediate motivation for selectivity is removed, we should be able to separate the second mechanism from the first. The situation in which we obtained our evidence meets this condition, and hence our data provide evidence for internalization of the selective processes.

METHOD OF THE STUDY

A group of twenty-three executives, all employed by a single large manufacturing concern and enrolled in a company-sponsored executive training program, was asked to read a standard case that is widely used in instruction in business policy in business schools. The case, Castengo Steel Company, described the organization and activities of a company of moderate size specializing in the manufacture of seamless steel tubes, as of the end of World War II. The case, which is about 10,000 words in length, contains a wealth of descriptive material about the company and its industry and the recent history of both (up to 1945), but little evaluation. It is deliberately written to hold closely to concrete facts and to leave as much as possible of the burden of interpretation to the reader.

When the executives appeared at a class session to discuss the case, but before they had discussed it, they were asked by the instructor to write a brief statement of what they considered to be the most important problem facing the Castengo Steel Company —the problem a new company president should deal with first. Prior to this session, the group had discussed other cases, being reminded from time to time by the instructor that they were to assume the role of the top executive of the company in considering its problems.

The executives were a relatively homogeneous group in terms of status, being drawn from perhaps three levels of the company organization. They were in the range usually called "middle management," representing such positions as superintendent of a department in a large factory, product manager responsible for profitability of one of the ten product groups manufactured by the company, and works physician for a large factory. In terms of departmental affiliation, they fell in four groups:

Sales (6): Five product managers or assistant product managers, and one field sales supervisor.

Production (5): Three department superintendents, one assistant factory manager, and one construction engineer.

Accounting (4): An assistant chief accountant, and three accounting supervisors—for a budget division and two factory departments.

Miscellaneous (8): Two members of the legal department, two in research and development, and one each from public relations, industrial relations, medical and purchasing.

THE DATA

Since the statements these executives wrote are relatively brief, they are reproduced in full in the appendix. We tested our hypothesis by determining whether there was a significant relation between the "most important problem" mentioned and the departmental affiliation of the mentioner. In the cases of executives who mentioned more than one problem, we counted all those they mentioned. We compared (1) the executives who mentioned "sales," "marketing," or "distribution" with those who did not; (2) the executives who mentioned "clarifying the organization" or some equivalent with those who did not; (3) the executives who mentioned "human relations," "employee relations" or "teamwork" with those who did not. The findings are summarized in the table on p. 312.

The difference between the percentages of sales executives (83%) and other executives (29%) who mentioned sales as the most important problem is significant at the 5 per cent level. Three of the five nonsales executives, moreover, who mentioned sales were in the accounting department, and all of these were in positions that involved analysis of product profitability. This accounting activity was, in fact, receiving considerable emphasis in the company at the time of the case discussion, and the accounting executives had frequent and close contacts with the product man-

| | | Number who mentioned | | |
Department	Total number of executives	Sales	"Clarify organization"	Human relations
Sales	6	5	1	0
Production	5	1	4	0
Accounting	4	3	0	0
Miscellaneous	8	1	3	3
Totals	23	10	8	3

agers in the sales department. If we combine sales and accounting executives, we find that eight out of ten of these mentioned sales as the most important problem; while only two of the remaining thirteen executives did.

Organization problems (other than marketing organization) were mentioned by four out of five production executives, the two executives in research and development, and the factory physician, but by only one sales executive and no accounting executives. The difference between the percentage for production executives (80%) and other executives (22%) is also significant at the 5 per cent level. Examination of the Castengo case shows that the main issue discussed in the case that relates to manufacturing is the problem of poorly defined relations among the factory manager, the metallurgist, and the company president. The presence of the metallurgist in the situation may help to explain the sensitivity of the two research and development executives (both of whom were concerned with metallurgy) to this particular problem area.

It is easy to conjecture why the public relations, industrial relations, and medical executives should all have mentioned some aspect of human relations, and why one of the two legal department executives should have mentioned the board of directors.

CONCLUSION

We have presented data on the selective perceptions of industrial executives exposed to case material that support the hypothesis that each executive will perceive those aspects of a situation that relate specifically to the activities and goals of his department. Since the situation is one in which the executives were motivated to look at the problem from a company-wide rather than a departmental viewpoint, the data indicate further that the criteria of selection have become internalized. Finally, the method for obtaining data that we have used holds considerable promise as a projective device for eliciting the attitudes and perceptions of executives.

APPENDIX

Executive	SALES
4.	Apparent need for direct knowledge of their sales potential.
	Apparent need for exploitation of their technical potential to achieve a broader market and higher priced market.
	Apparent need for unit and operation cost data.
5.	How to best organize the company so as to be able to take full advantage of the specialized market available.
6.	Appointment of Production Manager familiar with business.
	Analysis of market conditions with regard to expansion in plastic market.
12.	Develop a sales organization which would include market research.
20.	Lack of organization to plan and cope with postwar manufacturing and sales problems.
25.	The President's choice of executive officers.

	PRODUCTION
1.	Policy pertaining to distribution of product should be reviewed with more emphasis on new customers and concern for old.
15.	Lack of clear-cut lines of responsibility.
16.	Determine who the top executive was to be and have this information passed on to subordinate executives.

18.   Review the organization.

Why so many changes in some of the offices such as works manager.

24.   Absence of policy—should be set forth by company head.

ACCOUNTING

7.   Standards brought up to date and related to incentives. (Incentives evidently do not exist.)

9.   Future of the company as to marketability of products —product specification—growth or containment or retirement (i.e., from product).

10.   Distribution problems. Not necessarily their present problems in distribution, but those that undoubtedly will arise in the near future—plastics, larger companies, etc.

11.   Reorganization of the company to save its lost market for its product and to look for an additional market is the prime problem.

OTHER

3.   (Legal) Manufacture of one product which (a) competes against many larger manufacturers with greater facilities in competitive market, and (b) is perhaps due to lose to a related product much of its market.

14.   (Legal) Board of Directors.

8.   (Public relations) The handling of employee relations —particularly the company-union relationship.

17.   (Industrial relations) Can we get the various departments together to form a team in communications and cooperation.

19.   (Medical) 1. Reorganization of corporate structure
                 2. Lines of authority and command
                 3. Personnel relations.

21.   (Purchasing) We should start to think and organize for our peacetime economy.

22.   (Research and development) Overcentralized control by the president.

23.   (Research and development) No formal organization with duties defined.

Chapter XVI

THE BIRTH OF AN ORGANIZATION[1]

ON APRIL 3, 1948, the United States Congress approved the Economic Cooperation Act, implementing the so-called "Marshall Plan." Some four months later, by the end of July, the Economic Cooperation Administration was a going concern, complete with organization chart, and had already accumulated a considerable body of experience in the administration of its foreign aid program. The following pages are concerned with some of the events that took place in the creation of the ECA and some of the lessons for organization theory that can be drawn from these events.

The account is not a "case" in the usual sense, much less an administrative history. In fact, it comes closer to being administrative autobiography than administrative history, since what I know of these events was gained largely from the vantage point of a position in the Organization and Management Division of the agency. While I have had some small opportunity to check the objectivity of my observations with persons who held positions in other parts of the agency at the same time, I am sure that they never saw exactly the same things that I saw, nor do I have any reason to believe that what I saw was the "reality." Indeed, one of the morals of the story I am about to tell is that in its formative stages the organization consisted largely of a series of pictures in the minds of different people. These several pictures were far from congruent with each other, and the process of organizing consisted in considerable measure in arriving at a single picture that was held more or less in common.[2]

[1] This chapter is taken, with minor revisions, from *Public Administration Review*, 13:227–236 (1953), reprinted with permission.
[2] The principal published sources against which my observations have been checked are:

FIRST STEPS

A good deal of the history of the agency during its period of mushroom growth can be read in the phone directories that were issued at frequent intervals, at first almost daily. The first directory, issued about April 13, lists fifteen names. Since it does not include clerical personnel, we may assume that the total number of persons who arrived on the scene in the first week and a half was about thirty. By April 22, the list contained 138 names including clerical personnel; by July 26, it contained 741 names, and the period of rapid growth was over.

The growth process was clearly one of cell-splitting. Within a few days after his appointment as administrator, Paul Hoffman had appointed to the agency, in addition to two personal assistants, a director of operations, Wayne C. Taylor; an acting controller, soon replaced by E. L. Kohler as controller; and a director of administration, Donald C. Stone. He also brought in three economists to review for him the substantive programs that had been developed before the agency was formally created. The senior member of this group was Richard H. Bissell, who had served as executive secretary to the President's Committee on Foreign Aid.

At this stage in the proceedings, on the program side of the agency the cell-splitting process was very slow; on the side of the machinery of organization, it was very rapid. There are two reasons for this discrepancy. First, there was already in existence in the State Department an "interim aid" unit that was administering the earlier assistance funds granted to Austria, France, Greece,

---

PCFA.   President's Committee on Foreign Aid (Harriman Committee). *European Recovery and American Aid.* November 7, 1947.

HSC.   80th Congress, Second Session. House Select Committee on Foreign Aid (Herter Committee). *Final Report.* H.R. 1845. May 1, 1948.

ECA1.   Economic Cooperation Administration. *First Report to Congress,* for the Quarter Ended June 30, 1948.

ECA2.   Economic Cooperation Administration. *Second Report to Congress,* for the Quarter Ended September 30, 1948.

These reports will be referred to by the initials indicated. The first two relate to the period prior to the enactment of the act, the second two to the first six months of ECA's existence.

Italy, and Trieste, that kept the supply "pipeline" filled in the early organizing period, and that was soon absorbed as a Procurement Transactions unit in ECA.[3]

Second, in this stage questions of mechanics were much clearer than questions of substance. It was clear that the agency would need rooms, telephone service, and other housekeeping services, and that it would have to be prepared to hire large numbers of personnel. Even the press relations function was not overlooked. It was much less clear how the agency would go about performing its function of administering foreign aid.

By the middle of April the director of administration had appointed a budget director, an organization and methods director, a personnel director, and an office services director. By the third week in April 63 per cent of the personnel were in these units and another 13 per cent in the Controller's Office, leaving 24 per cent (not including the State Department group) for all the activities associated with the substantive program. By July 26 the personnel in the program units had increased from one-quarter of the total staff of the Washington office to one-half.

In mid-April, ECA resembled nothing so much as a manufacturing concern without a factory. An office desk or a telephone could be obtained in a matter of hours. In the new, partially finished building the agency occupied, interior partitions were being erected with amazing rapidity. But whatever product was emerging was being produced by the State Department group, which was operating with a minimum of contact and almost no direction from the new agency.

These observations are not intended critically. The course of events is completely understandable. Since there existed in Washington a clear conception of what an administrative agency looked like—that is to say, the skeleton of an abstract administrative agency—the framework could be erected. But since no conception existed, or at least no consensus, of ECA as an agency with a program to administer, the skeleton was not yet ready to be covered with flesh, blood, and nerves.

[3] For a description of the interim aid organization, see HSC, pp. 758–763.

THE ALTERNATIVE APPROACHES

How then, did the program of the ECA and the organization to implement that program, emerge? ECA like all organisms, had a prenatal history. In fact, as it turned out, it had a large number of claimants to parenthood—more than could be accommodated.

It is possible to identify at least six important approaches to the organization of ECA. To an important extent, the early administrative history of the agency can be written in terms of the rise and fall of these approaches and of the administrative units with which they were associated. Since they are not wholly mutually incompatible, and since no single one was clearly espoused by the statute creating ECA, the final structure that emerged made room for several of them. In the next paragraphs these six approaches are characterized.

The Commodity-Screening Approach

Considerable experience had been gained in the administration of foreign assistance through wartime aid programs, notably the FEA, and subsequently in the interim-aid programs. Here the chief human repositories of administrative memory were to be found in the export licensing unit in the Office of International Trade of the Commerce Department and in the interim-aid group in the State Department. In addition, there were in the Departments of Agriculture and Interior, among other places, a number of persons who had played important roles in these earlier programs.

The conception of foreign assistance inherited from this tradition was one of determining specific commodity needs of foreign countries and approving or disapproving individual shipments of specified quantities of commodities. The decisions involved were those needed for screening these individual transactions against program criteria—for example, the need of the country for the commodity to sustain its war effort or nutritional levels and the availability of commodities in scarce supply.[4] Such a screening

---

[4] A discussion of conceptions involved in commodity screening for export control will be found in HSC, pp. 638–43, 646–87.

process called for two kinds of specialized knowledge: knowledge of needs or requirements and knowledge of availabilities. The former suggested some combination of commodity and area specialization in the agency; the latter pointed primarily toward commodity specialization.

The Balance of Trade Approach

The enactment of the Marshall Plan legislation had been preceded by considerable research activity both in Europe and in the United States. This research had been concerned primarily with the question of determining the magnitude of Europe's needs for American assistance.

The Committee of European Economic Cooperation, in response to Secretary Marshall's original proposal, had drawn up such an estimate in the fall of 1947. Starting with estimates of the consumption requirements of the participating countries, the committee compared these with projected production levels and arrived at estimates of the bill of goods that would have to be imported to maintain the proposed consumption levels, and then of the balance of payments picture that would result from the import program. The "dollar gap" thus arrived at provided a basis for the amount of American assistance requested. The CEEC report was reviewed and scaled down by a group of committees in this country. These revised estimates provided the basis for the ECA legislation and the subsequent appropriations.[5]

In this picture of the foreign assistance program, individual commodity purchases played a very subordinate role. Once the aggregate figure for aid to each country was arrived at, it was of little importance whether a particular import was financed with ECA dollars or with dollars from the export trade.

This approach clearly derives from economic theory. The analysis of consumption needs and productive capacities follows the so-called "national income approach" that has had wide currency among professional economists in the last decade. The notion that the foreign assistance problem was one of making up

[5] The estimating procedures of PCFA and HSC are based squarely on the balance of trade approach.

a "dollar deficit" follows from the traditional balance of payments concept that has been central to international trade theory.

What both of these conceptions suggested from an organizational point of view, although in slightly variant forms, was the need for an agency that could arrive by economic analysis at over-all decisions on dollar amounts of foreign assistance to individual countries.

The European Cooperation Approach

Another set of organizational preconceptions was obtained by viewing the Marshall Plan as a means for bringing about a greater measure of international trade, economic cooperation, and rationalization of industry in Western Europe. This approach to the program was an essential element in the studies already mentioned and an integral part of State Department and congressional policy.[6] Its organizational implications were: first, that the initiative for programming should rest upon the European countries acting cooperatively; second, that our relations with them under the program should be multilateral rather than bilateral, and that these relations should be channeled primarily through the Paris rather than the Washington office of ECA.

The Bilateral Pledge Approach

Somewhat different from the idea that the central aim of the program was to foster European cooperation was the idea that assistance should be conditioned on bilateral pledges between the individual participating countries and the United States.[7] Since one element in the required agreement was the willingness of the participating country to engage in cooperative arrangements with the other countries, the two conceptions were certainly not in direct contradiction. Nevertheless, the bilateral agreements created the necessity for direct negotiation in cooperation with the State Department with individual countries, and, from an organizational

[6] HSC, pp. 21–56, 603–4; PCFA, pp. 4–6, 31–2.
[7] HSC, pp. 869–77; PCFA, pp. 108, 273–7; ECA1, Appendix I.

point of view, weakened CEEC and the Paris office of ECA as the primary channels of contact. The bilateral agreements also emphasized certain specifically American goals such as securing the continued availability of strategic materials.

The Investment Bank Approach

The American government had also had experience, through the Export-Import Bank, in granting loans to other countries for capital improvements. The Economic Cooperation Act specifically provided that, of the $5.3 billions in aid to be extended in the first year, $1 billion be in the form of loans, and the Export-Import Bank be used as the machinery through which these loans were to be handled. This led to the conception that, at least with respect to the loan portion of the program, the problem was to determine whether individual projects for plant construction or other capital improvements were economically sound in the sense of having a good prospect of earning a return on the investment. The Congress itself was ambiguous (and probably intentionally so) in stating the criteria for approval of loans. Both the earning power of the investment and the ability of the country to repay, from a balance of payments point of view, were to be considered.[8] The facts that the stated intention of Congress included the investment banking criteria, and perhaps more important that Mr. Taylor, the director of operations originally appointed by Mr. Hoffman, came to ECA from the Export-Import Bank, had important consequences for the organization of ECA during the first months.

The Policy-Administration Approach

Along with the extensive substantive planning that had been going on prior to the enactment of the law in April, thought had also been given, particularly in the Bureau of the Budget (predecessor of the OMB), to the way in which the program would be administered if it were enacted. Some of the broad issues were

[8] HSC, pp. 634–6, 718–9.

whether to put the activity in the State Department or to establish a new agency, and whether, if a new agency were established, it should be a corporation. These issues were decided by the Congress and not by the organizational planners, and we shall not consider them further here.

The Budget Bureau, however, had also constructed some tentative plans for the internal organization of the agency if one were created. Because the Budget Bureau did not have, and probably could not have had, a clear conception of the program, its plans shared many of the characteristics of the organization that developed early in April—great emphasis on machinery and little on production. If the name of the agency had been taken off the bureau's proposed organization chart, it would have been extremely difficult to determine whether the organization was to engage in foreign assistance, salt mining, or the practice of law. Provision was made for a bureau of policy coordination, a program bureau, a bureau of operations, and a controller. The first would be concerned with the broader aspects of European recovery, the second with the review of commodities lists, the third with actual procurement, and the fourth with documentation and accounting for funds.

The idea that one should deal with a complex problem—any problem—by first making broad decisions, then implementing these with more specific decisions, and then implementing these in turn is a familiar one in the literature of administration—and in books on "how to think." This plan mistook an analytic description of the governmental process for a list of the administrative units needed in carrying out a specific governmental program.

As a matter of fact certain elements that later emerged in the ECA organization can be identified with the units proposed by the Budget Bureau. But except in the case of the controller, this was a matter of coincidence and not planning, and as the organization was modified by gradual adaptation, the unit corresponding to policy coordination absorbed more and more of the functions of the program bureau, and the program bureau absorbed completely the bureau of operations. The reasons will perhaps become clear in the sequel.

THE DEVELOPMENT OF PROGRAM ORGANIZATION

Having surveyed some of the principal conceptions of the foreign assistance program that could be identified in Washington in April of 1948, we are ready to resume our story of the actual process of organization. As the process of cell division continued, each of the program conceptions we have described found a concrete embodiment in one or more of the emerging organizational units.

The fate that each unit suffered tended to depend upon two things. Its fate depended, first, upon how simply and clearly its underlying conception of the program could actually be implemented. Each program conception provided a basis for an administrative organization only as it was further elaborated and spelled out in terms of concrete administrative activities, and as it led to a workable allocation of decision-making responsibilities. In the case of ECA, for example, a program conception could not be regarded as workable unless it could be elaborated into a decision-making process for allocating $5 billion among the Western European nations and for translating these allocations into authorizations for the purchase of specific goods and services. Not all the approaches were capable of being implemented in this sense —several of them were simply not workable.

A unit's fate depended, second, on the natural alliances it found with powerful Washington agencies surrounding the ECA that shared its conception of the agency program.[9] To the extent that more than one program conception could be made workable, in the sense just described, such alliances might decide the outcome as between competing approaches.

What we are about to describe, then, is a power struggle in which ideas—in particular the conception of the program— played a major role both as *weapons* and as *motives* for empire-building. The conceptions were weapons because they could be used by the particular administrative units that represented them to advance their claims to a larger place in the program. They

[9] HSC, pp. 698–730, 755–78; ECA1, pp. 42–5.

were motives for empire-building because the administrators of these units saw the broadening of the functions of their units as the principal means for implementing their conceptions of the program. I do not believe that this kind of power struggle was a peculiarity of ECA but rather that a deeper analysis of the phenomenon of empire-building in government and in business would show that these elements are always present and very often are of central importance. Because of the fluidity of the organization it is easier to identify them in the early history of ECA than in an agency that has already gone through a process of "natural selection."

The *commodity screening* view of ECA's program prevailed in the Procurement Transactions Division (the new name of the State Department interim-aid group) and in two program units that were set up on a commodity basis: the Foods Division and the Industry Division. The Foods Division was largely under Agriculture Department influence, and all three of the units had close working relations with the Office of International Trade in the Department of Commerce. Commodity screening was also the prevalent conception in the ECA Controller's Office.

The *origins* of the commodity screening approach have been traced back to the wartime aid programs. The *workability* of the conception rested largely on several provisions of the act itself. One of these required that the aid should not impair the fulfillment of vital needs of the American people. Crude oil was to be purchased, as far as possible, outside the United States; no meat was to be purchased in this country except horsemeat. Other clauses for the protection of the American economy related to wheat flour, farm machinery, fertilizers, agricultural commodities in ample supply, and surplus war assets. Private trade channels were to be used as far as possible in the procurement of supplies, and at least half the goods were to be shipped in American bottoms. Finally, it was required that commodities not be purchased outside the United States at prices higher (with certain adjustments) than the American price.

The effect of all these provisions was to require scrutiny of individual transactions. Within ECA, these clauses were administered largely by the Procurement Transactions group and (particularly the price provisions) by the Controller's Office. Outside ECA, the Commerce, Agriculture, and Interior Departments were vitally concerned with these same provisions.

Paradoxically, these provisions also created a basic weakness in the commodity screening approach. The crucial decision in screening scarce commodities was not whether their purchase was financed from ECA funds, but whether they were to be exported from the United States. Hence, quotas of total shipments of each commodity had to be established, and these quotas had to be enforced through export licenses rather than through the approval of financing. As a consequence, the main responsibility had to devolve upon the Commerce and Agriculture Departments rather than upon ECA.[10]

The same weakness undermined the more naïve, but strongly held, conception that the purpose of screening individual transactions was to conserve the American taxpayer's money by making sure that the European nations were using the funds only for "needed" items. Since 50 per cent of total European export dollars was being earned in the course of regular international trade and only 50 per cent was provided by ECA, if a transaction were disapproved, the particular item in question could be procured instead with earned dollars and another item substituted on the ECA list. However desirable the conservation of American funds, this goal could not be secured by decisions on individual transactions.

In the end, then, the ECA organization had to adapt itself to the facts that export licensing, not procurement transaction screening, was the effective means of control over individual transactions, and that screening could not be employed effectively to control the over-all European import program. The Controller's Office, with its auditing responsibilities and interest in the pricing provision, remained as the only center of power for the commodity screening approach. This approach gradually disappeared from the conceptions of the programming divisions.

The *balance of trade* conception found its base—at first a very unstable base—in the economists who began to be brought into

[10] PCFA, p. 113; HSC, pp. 672–86; ECA1, pp. 14–18, 44.

the agency, largely by Bissell and largely on a consulting basis. Mr. Hoffman and most of the senior personnel immediately associated with him were preoccupied in the early days with external problems. They had to work out relations with the State Department and negotiate the bilateral agreements: they had to develop instructions for the Paris office that was just coming into existence: and they had to prepare for the appropriations hearings on the Hill. (The appropriation bill was approved only on June 28.)

This left the task of developing the programming procedures and of reviewing the second- and third-quarter programs of foreign assistance to the economists. And indeed, as nearly as I could observe, the actual program revision was the work of a few very able and energetic, very young, and very inconspicuous men who had participated in the interdepartmental committees reviewing the original CEEC proposal and who were now operating under Mr. Bissell. The exact size or identity of this group was not easy to determine, but it could not have consisted of more than a half-dozen professionals.

The *European cooperation* approach was easier to describe than to implement.[11] In essence it required the strengthening of the organization through which this cooperation was to be planned by the European nations themselves—the OEEC (Organization for European Economic Cooperation). Because the Paris office was clearly the appropriate unit for dealing with OEEC, and because the cooperation goals had little relevance for the day-to-day tasks of programming and financing assistance, this approach never had a strong organizational embodiment in the Washington office. The Fiscal and Trade Policy Division that later emerged had most concern with it, but the center of gravity was in its Paris counterpart.

The cooperation approach had, however, a negative implication that influenced thinking about the Washington office. There was great temptation to establish "country desks" to specialize in the problems of the individual countries. Indeed, area units of this kind were contemplated in the Budget Bureau organization plan.

[11] ECA1, pp. 6–13, 46.

They were to be located in the program bureau, which was to be a replica of the FEA organization—with an "areas" division and a "commodities" division. This conception was vulnerable to the attack, however, that it would foster bilateral relations with the individual countries rather than cooperation among them. These objections prevented country desks from sprouting as rapidly as they might have in the agency. They did not, in the long run, altogether prevent them from developing in subunits where specialized knowledge of the individual countries was needed for programming and arriving at balance of trade estimates.

As already mentioned, *bilateral agreements* with the cooperating nations were required by the act. Negotiation of the pledges was a high-level matter involving State Department leadership. In the ECA Washington office, only the Office of the General Counsel was deeply involved. Once the pledges had been signed, their implementation of necessity devolved largely on the Paris office and the ECA Special Missions in the cooperating countries. Hence the agreements never exerted an important influence upon the organization of the Washington office. (Again the Fiscal and Trade Policy Division, operating in close liaison with the Treasury Department, is a partial and minor exception.)

The *investment bank* approach found its main internal support in the Director of Operations, Mr. Taylor, and its external support in the Export-Import Bank. The conception was applicable, if at all, only to a small part of the agency's total program. Mr. Taylor's unit soon became isolated from the flow of day-to-day transactions in the agency and gradually withered on the vine. The rapid decline of this unit was easily visible in terms of size of staff, changes in titles (Mr. Taylor became "the assistant to the administrator"), and actual office locations.

The unit early established its claim as the loan-approving authority in the agency, but a growing conflict developed between the investment criteria and the balance of payments criteria for loans. A crisis in the fall of 1948, resulting from the fact that a large proportion of the loan funds were still uncommitted, gave convincing evidence of the unworkability of the investment bank approach and led to a resolution of the conflict in favor of the balance of trade approach. Since I was not an eyewitness to these events, I cannot describe them in detail.

What this all adds up to is that during the first two or even three months the entire operating portion of ECA consisted of three groups. The first, comprised of Mr. Hoffman and a few high-level aides, conducted the "international relations" of the agency, so to speak, with the Congress, with the State Department, with other federal departments, and with the participating nations. During this period they negotiated the bilateral agreements and saw the appropriation bill through the Congress. A second group, in Mr. Bissell's office, worked up a quarterly aid program and shaped up the programming procedures that were later accepted. A third group, inherited from the State Department, actually processed the requests for aid and kept the pipelines full. These three groups, together with their clerical support, could not have consisted of more than 75 persons, and probably fewer. During this period the rest of the agency was not so much "doing" as getting ready to do.

THE ORGANIZATION AND MANAGEMENT DIVISION

We have been describing an organization that grew and assumed a reasonably coherent form without apparently ever having been planned. I think this is a reasonable description of what happened, or at least a first approximation to such a description. What was the Organization and Management Division doing during this period to justify its existence?

During the early days it was extremely difficult to get more than a very fragmentary picture of what was going on or who was doing what. The operating personnel, each of whom conceived that he had a job to do and little time in which to get it done, did not want to spend their time talking to procedures specialists or reading organizational announcements. The O & M Division made a valiant effort to find out what the procedures actually were, and to record them, and I think they partly succeeded. If the division had any influence on the form that the organization took, it was by means of techniques that are not usually described in handbooks on methods work.

A small staff brought into the division early in April for the purpose of making organizational plans spent two feverish weeks trying to arrive at their own conceptions of the foreign assistance program and the organizational implications of those conceptions. For better or worse, the two conceptions that found greatest acceptance in the division were the balance of trade approach and the European cooperation approach.

The first important attempt, made in the third week of April, to influence the organization in the direction of implementing these notions consisted of a mimeographed memorandum—"Basic Principles of ECA Organization"—circulated in draft form by the division on April 30. This memorandum largely ignored the proposed Budget Bureau plan, emphasized the balance of trade approach, and pointed to the weaknesses in the commodity screening and investment bank approaches. It stressed the need for strengthening the Paris office in order to foster multilateral rather than bilateral negotiations and warned against the dangers of "country desks."

No attempt was made to secure formal approval of the principles embodied in the memorandum, thus avoiding a tedious and probably interminable process of obtaining agreement. The memorandum was formulated as a set of underlying assumptions and their organizational implications, rather than as an organizational blueprint or a compendium of functional descriptions.

The idea behind the document was that a relatively brief draft memorandum of some two thousand words *might* gain some circulation in the agency, that it *might* actually be read by a few influential people, and that a few of the central concepts *might* be absorbed and influence future thinking about organization. I found some evidence in later contacts around the agency that the document did not pass unobserved, but it would be impossible to assess precisely what influence it had.

At about the same time, the O & M Division found that the Personnel Division was depending upon it to provide descriptions of positions so that jobs could be classified and appointments authorized in the various units. This put the O & M Division in a highly strategic position to influence the rate of growth of the units. Until a unit could describe its functions to O & M and get some measure of agreement as to the role it was to play in the structure, it found itself up against an impenetrable wall of red tape (or perhaps "red feathers" would be a better metaphor) in attempting to secure approval of its appointments. To be sure, personnel could be retained by a determined unit chief on a consulting basis, but the lack of a table of organization made a unit's position very uncertain and exercised a definite check on expansion. This procedure made possible in the early weeks an effective delaying action against the establishment of country desks and the multiplication of statistical units.

Undoubtedly the unit that fared worst in the situation was that under the director of operations, since the O & M analysts found themselves unable to reconcile Mr. Taylor's conception of his task with the over-all pattern that was emerging in the agency. While I think the fate of that unit would have been the same in the long run in any event, the halt in its expansion during these critical weeks gave Mr. Bissell and his assistants time to organize their activities into some kind of coherent pattern.

A happy accident gave the O & M Division its third tool. In the appropriations hearings Mr. Hoffman was asked by Congressman Taber to state the maximum number of persons he would need in the Washington office of the agency. There was very little but air from which to draw the number, but Mr. Hoffman drew 600. I have always felt, although I know of no solid way of defending the figure, that this was a very good number. Good or bad, having stated the number, Mr. Hoffman had to live with it. He also had in his hands a means for countering the inevitable requests of the Washington units for more and still more personnel as the cell splitting process went on.

When, early in June, the personnel "needs" stated by the heads of individual units were added up, the total was found to exceed 600 by a considerable margin and a process of personnel allocation had to be undertaken. At this point the deputy administrator turned to the O & M Division for help in arriving at a balanced table of organization; a series of hearings were held with the heads of individual units to determine personnel ceilings; and staff from the O & M Division participated in those hearings.

Of course in the end the ceiling had to bulge. By the end of July, the Washington staff exceeded 700. But the agency as it finally evolved was certainly spectacularly smaller than any federal agency carrying out a task of comparable magnitude, and the sudden reduction in its rate of growth by the end of July can only be attributed to the ceilings.

On July 26 the first official organization chart of the Washington office of the ECA was reproduced. The chart did not create new organizational arrangements but ratified and gave solidity to the patterns that had tentatively emerged. From the beginning of August on, it provided a set of historical boundaries in terms of which new claims for territory had to be argued.

It should be reasonably clear from the recital of these events that the views of the O & M Division were by no means the predominant influence on the form that the ECA organization finally took. That final form embodied in large part the views expressed in the "Basic Principles" memorandum circulated on April 30, but the relationship was in only small part causal. The memorandum represented less an influence on organization than a rather accurate forecast of the mold into which the organization would be forced by the requirements of its tasks and goals—the conditions of "workability."

THE AFTERMATH

An organization chart reproduced in ECA's *Second Report to Congress* depicts the structure of the Washington office as it existed on December 1, 1948.[12] That chart shows the focus of program activities to lie in the office of the assistant deputy administrator for program, Mr. Bissell. Under him, the balance of trade approach was implemented by the Program Coordination Division, assisted by the Foods, Industry, and Fiscal and Trade

[12] ECA2, p. 85; also, ECA1, pp. 37–42.

Policy Divisions. Provisions of the law unrelated to the central programming functions were being handled by China, Korea, Strategic Materials, and Transportation Divisions and the Office of Labor Advisers. The Office of the Controller was performing auditing functions, and a Statistics and Reports Division was "auditing" the effect of the program on the European economy.

The other important boxes on the chart correspond to the usual housekeeping units—administrative services, personnel, O & M, budget, security, and information. Mr. Taylor had become assistant to the administrator, with a small staff. The Procurement Transactions Division had dwindled to a small Program Methods Control Staff attached to Mr. Bissell's office. A total of 770 persons was employed in the Washington office, 290 in the Paris office, and 1,127 in the country missions.

The initial July 26 organization chart differed in only minor details from the chart of December 1. In less than four months, during which it was already in operation, the agency had attained virtually its final form. That form was one dictated by and predictable from: (1) the relative political support for differing conceptions of the agency task; (2) the identifications and conceptions of the other government agencies surrounding ECA; and (3) the appropriateness of the structure for implementing that conception of the agency's task which prevailed.

But while the form was predictable it was certainly not planned. The processes of cell multiplication and the power struggles within and around the agency were the main processes through which this rapid adaptation and evolution of an effective organization took place.

What this suggests is an exceedingly close analogy between the development the agency went through in attaining an effective organization and the processes an individual goes through in solving a complex problem. (Cf. Chapters V and XI, above.) The world in all its complexity cannot be grasped in a single picture. Problem-solving involves the invention and testing of a whole series of simplified approximations, each of which provides a partial representation of the total complex problem. The problem is solved when a "picture" of the situation has been evolved which, though still a simplification of the real situation, is sufficiently realistic and sufficiently comprehensive to provide a reasonable approximation.

Each of the "approaches" I have described was such a simplified picture of the complex governmental problem with which ECA had to cope. The organization that evolved represented an oversimplification of the task—an overemphasis of certain of its aspects, a relative neglect of others. But it represented an oversimplification that did encompass the central features of the task and the requisite political emphases, and did so relatively effectively.

In this sense, the organization structure of ECA can be regarded as a reflection of the way in which the foreign assistance problem was structured by human minds endeavoring to grapple with its complexity. Each organizational unit can be roughly equated with some identifiable element in one of the competing conceptualizations of the problem. The Program Coordination Division and the other programming divisions under Mr. Bissell can be equated with the parts of the balance of trade conception. The gradually changing functions of the Foods and Industry Divisions, and their eventual subordination to program coordination and export licensing, can be equated with the gradual victory of balance of trade over commodity screening. The disappearance of Procurement Transactions was a disappearance of the policy-administration conception. No loan division emerged from Mr. Taylor's efforts because the investment bank concept could not be translated into a workable plan of organization. The examples can be multiplied, and several others have been cited earlier.

The proposition that an organization changes with changes in its task and its environment is not new. It has been verified in many instances—for example in the fine analysis by Gaus and Wolcott of the history of the United States Department of Agriculture.[13] When we see these processes in the large, however, we see them only in equilibrium. They are seemingly inexorable adap-

[13] John M. Gaus and Leon O. Wolcott, *Public Administration and the United States Department of Agriculture* (Chicago: Public Administration Service, 1940).

tations of an organization to its political and technological environment.

When we observe these same processes in the short run, and particularly at a moment of large and rapid shift, we recognize that environmental forces mold organizations through the mediation of human minds. The process is a learning process in which growing insights and successive restructurings of the problem as it appears to the humans dealing with it reflect themselves in the structural elements of the organization itself.

This view has important implications for the process of governmental reorganization. First, it adds weight to the proposition, if more weight is needed, that reorganization can seldom affect efficiency without affecting program goals. When we change the organization, we change the picture that the people in it have of the concrete tasks to be done and the concrete goals to be achieved—their concept of the program. When we change the concept of the program, we change the relative emphasis that the various parts of the complex whole will receive, we alter allocations of resources and relative priorities among goals.

Second, the view set forth here casts some light, perhaps, on the significance of formal organization. Plans of organization affect behavior in at least two ways. First, when they are officially approved, they draw force from the motivations of legitimacy—employees feel that they *ought* to observe the plans because they accept the system of authority that approved them. Second, we have seen here that plans may influence behavior because they provide employees with a conceptual scheme of the agency's program, a scheme that serves as a framework for decision and action. If the scheme is "workable"—if it translates the agency's complex problem into terms that are clear and understandable to the persons who have to solve it, if it leads to a relatively simple division of activities and is helpful as a guide to decision—then its workability will be a powerful force toward its acceptance.

Chapter XVII

THE BUSINESS SCHOOL:
A PROBLEM IN ORGANIZATIONAL DESIGN[1]

THE THEORY of organizations has become a standard topic for business school instruction and research. Business schools, of course, are organizations, generally associated with those larger organizations we call universities. It would seem appropriate, therefore, to ask whether business schools are not themselves interesting objects—or specimens—for organization theory. Does anything we know about the design of organizations apply to business schools? Can we use our knowledge of organization theory to improve our own institutions?

There are several approaches to organizational design, no one of which provides a complete basis for a finished plan. A way to begin that is frequently fruitful, however, is to investigate the information flows that are essental for accomplishing the organization's objectives, then to examine what these information patterns imply for organization structure.

BUSINESS SCHOOL GOALS

The tasks of a business school are to train men for the practice of management (or some special branch of management) as a profession and to develop new knowledge that may be relevant to improving the operation of business.[2] The training may take place in a variety of ways and at several levels: A business school may

[1] This chapter is taken, with minor revisions, from the *Journal of Management Studies,* 4:1-16 (1967), reprinted with permission.
[2] R. A. Gordon and J. E. Howell, *Higher Education for Business* (New York: Columbia University Press, 1959), chap. ii.

335

offer undergraduate or postgraduate courses for young men intending to enter business but who have not had much or any business experience; it may offer post-experience courses for managers at various levels of responsibility; it may offer research courses for men who want to train themselves for careers of teaching and research in business.

Research conducted in a business school may cover a wide spectrum from studies aimed at advancing fundamental knowledge about human behavior, economics, and even mathematics to studies aimed rather directly at improving business practice. Regardless of where the research lies on the spectrum, the fact that it is carried on in the environment of a business school presumably means that it has some relevance, direct or indirect, for business. I shall try later to specify the criteria of relevance.

THE INFORMATION BASE OF THE PROFESSIONAL SCHOOL

Business schools are a particular species in the genus known as professional schools. The objectives of all professional schools—engineering, medicine, law, education, business, architecture, or what not—can be stated in the same general terms: education and training for prospective or present practitioners in the profession and for persons wanting to do teaching and research in the professional school—research to advance knowledge relevant to the practice of the professions. We should expect, therefore, that at an appropriate level of generality, the organizational design problems of all professional schools will be essentially the same.[3] We will not be disappointed in this expectation, and we will find it instructive to compare business schools with some of the other kinds of professional schools mentioned above.

Information and skills relevant to the accomplishment of a professional school's teaching and research goals come from two

---

[3] N. B. Henry, ed., *Education for the Professions,* 61st Yearbook of the National Society for the Study of Education, Part II (Chicago: University of Chicago Press, 1962). *Education for Professional Responsibility.* Proceedings of the Inter-Professions Conference on Education for Professional Responsibility, Buck Hill Falls, 12th–14th April, 1948 (Pittsburgh: Carnegie Press, 1948).

main sources. First, they come from the world of practice: information about the institutional environment in which the profession is practiced, about the problems of the practitioner, the skills he needs, and the techniques that have been discovered for handling professional problems. Thus, the business school must understand the business environment, the nature of the manager's tasks and problems, and the skills and techniques employed by successful managers and successful business organizations. Comparable lists of the needs for information and skills from the world of practice can be drawn up for engineering schools, medical schools, schools of education, and the others.

Second, the professional school must have effective access to information and skills within the several sciences that are relevant to and contributing to the improvement of professional practice. In the case of the business school, the relevant sciences include at least economics, psychology, sociology, applied mathematics, and computing science. The business school must understand such things as the principle of marginalism, the theory of human motivation, political processes, linear programming theory, the structure of problem-oriented computer languages, and probability theory.

To speak of "the business school knowing" about the world of practice, and about the relevant sciences is, of course, a metaphor. Schools do not "know," people in them do. After I have spelled out the general lines of organization, I will ask in more detail who needs to know what in the business school. Meanwhile, I will continue to use the metaphor for brevity.[4]

In one-to-one correspondence with the two main bodies of information and skill the professional school needs to know are two sets of social systems that possess the knowledge: the social system of practitioners, on the one hand, and the social systems of scientists in the relevant disciplines, on the other. Those social systems themselves have elaborate institutions and procedures for storing, transmitting, developing, and applying knowledge. In

---

[4] I will also, for brevity, use "knowledge" to refer not simply to "knowledge about" (i.e., facts and principles of some phenomena), but also "knowledge how" (i.e., how to produce desired results, how to conduct inquiry, how to solve problems, and so on).

business, the institutions are business firms, trade associations, and professional management societies. In the sciences, the institutions are graduate schools, research institutes, and professional societies. Generally speaking, the main way in which an organization can get access to the information and skill that are stored and transmitted by a social system is to participate in that social system. If this is to be done by the business school, the school must participate effectively in the social and information system of business, on the one hand, and in the social and information systems of the sciences, on the other.

Liberal and Professional Education

To understand the organizational designs that are developed in this paper, it is essential not to confuse the distinction we are making between knowledge from the disciplines and knowledge from the profession with the distinction that is so often made between "liberal" and "utilitarian" knowledge. The former distinction refers to the sources of knowledge, the latter (if it is a meaningful distinction at all, which is questionable) refers to the uses to which knowledge is put.

Pierson, in his study of American business education, speaks of colleges and universities as being "the product of two distinct and sometimes conflicting traditions. According to the first . . . , knowledge is pursued for its own sake. . . . Most proponents of this view . . . would regard direct preparation for particular careers as basically alien to the purpose of academic work. . . . The other great tradition . . . would leave ample room for those students desiring to prepare for particular careers. According to this tradition, the search for truth is not impugned because it proves useful nor is education necessarily unworthy because it is pursued for its career value.[5]

The present chapter assumes that the goals of a university include both the pursuit of knowledge for its own sake, and the application of knowledge to practical pursuits. It does *not* assume

[5] F. C. Pierson, *The Education of American Businessmen* (New York: Mc-Graw-Hill, 1959), pp. 16–17.

that one of these goals is the sole possession of the disciplines, the other, the sole possession of the professions. On the contrary, there is no reason why knowledge about physics should be useless; and no more reason why knowledge about optimal inventory control or organization structure should not be intellectually and esthetically interesting.

The sometimes explicit premise that utility is the only touchstone of relevance for knowledge in the professional school, and the sometimes implicit premise that *in*utility is the only touchstone of relevance in the disciplines are mischievous doctrines that have caused untold harm to education in both professions and disciplines.

Even if, for purposes of argument, we were to accept utility as the primary criterion of ultimate professional relevance, a much broader criterion would have to be applied within the professional school to make of it a viable educational enterprise. Education cannot go on, at a satisfactory level, without intellectual challenge and excitement. The professional school must be vigorous in research as well as teaching and must provide a solid intellectual core to the professional as well as the disciplinary portion of its concerns. The next section discusses the conditions for generating successful research in the professional school; in a later section more will be said about the problem of intellectualizing the "art" of professional design.

Knowledge Requirements for Research

It will be useful for later discussion to spell out in a little more detail the knowledge required if the business school is to carry out successfully its research responsibilities—its task of creating new knowledge. One of the central difficulties in invention is that it calls on two quite different kinds of knowledge: knowledge about needs to be filled and knowledge about things that can be done (i.e., about the laws of nature and what they make possible).

Invention is easiest when it can operate at one extreme or the other of the range from end-use requirements to laws of nature. The effective sales engineer and product engineer, on one end of the range, immerse themselves in information from the end-use environment. They try to discover what products customers would like to have, and in what respects present products are less than fully satisfactory in use. Then they apply known technology to provide the new or improved products.

At the other end of the range, the pure scientist immerses himself in knowledge from the environment of natural science. He tries to discover what questions about natural phenomena have not been answered. Then he applies known research techniques to answer these questions.[6]

Research becomes much harder to do when it undertakes to answer several kinds of questions at once. Product engineering becomes more difficult when it seeks to go beyond the obvious information about customer needs that can be picked up from the end-use environment, and tries to conceive what needs the customer would have if only he knew he had them! One way to do this is to turn to the environment of scientific knowledge, seeking there materials and processes that have not had practical application; then asking what uses they might have. When it comes off, this kind of product invention is likely to have far larger impact than routine sales and product engineering.

In corresponding fashion, pure science becomes more difficult when it goes beyond the obvious unanswered questions to be found in the environment of science itself and looks to areas of application for new kinds of unanswered questions; then seeks to apply the methods of science to answer them. It is more difficult, because in the ordinary kind of pure science described earlier, if the scientist cannot answer the question he poses initially, he can modify and simplify it until it shows promise of being answerable. But if he is presented with a question from the area of end use, he does not have this option: He cannot substitute a simpler answerable question if it does not solve the real-life problem.

If science becomes more difficult when it undertakes to answer questions posed from outside science, it also acquires the potentiality of becoming more fruitful. Many of the very good

---

[6] The invention of new research techniques is, of course, another mode of pure science activity.

problems in science that have led to extraordinary developments in pure science have been posed from outside. Industrial chemistry provided much of the impetus for pure research in organic chemistry, and telegraphy, wireless, and telephone for pure research in electricity and magnetism. In the social sciences, the contacts during World War II of economics with military operating problems set off a major revolution in the theory of the firm, while the need to understand and deal with the Great Depression earlier performed a similar service for macroeconomics. Thus, necessity is indeed the mother of important inventions, including many that are important to the pure sciences.

These alternative ways of doing science have been spelled out because they disclose a whole range of opportunities for the business school. The business school is not simply an environment in which researchers with strongly applied interests can take known principles of economics or psychology, or known techniques of statistics, and use them to solve practical business problems. If this were the only kind of research for which the environment was favorable, the kinds of persons who could be attracted to business school faculties would be severly—almost fatally—restricted.

The business school *can* be an exceedingly productive and challenging environment for fundamental researchers who understand and can exploit the advantages of having access to the "real world" as a generator of basic research problems and a source of data. Later, I will show why the business school not only *can* be made attractive to such scientists but *must* be if it is to do its job.

Fundamental Research in Other Professional Schools

That the possibility of creating an attractive fundamental research environment in a professional school is not hypothetical but real can be demonstrated by the experiences of the better engineering and medical schools in the United States. (Perhaps elsewhere, as well, but I am familiar only with the American experience.)

Schools like California, Carnegie, and Massachusetts Institutes of Technology might almost better be described as schools of science than schools of engineering. An examination of doctoral theses in these and other strong engineering schools discloses that most of the research topics would be appropriate to physics, chemistry, or mathematics departments in the university. Few are specifically "engineering" topics in the sense of being aimed at design, or even in being highly applied.

Similarly, the medical schools at such universities as Chicago, Johns Hopkins, and Harvard have in many ways closer connections with research in biology and biochemistry than with medical practice. Much of the fundamental work in biochemistry today is being carried on in medical school environments.

As a matter of fact, the pure science emphasis both in the strong engineering schools and in the strong medical schools has reached a point of creating concern as to whether the needs of the practicing professions are being met. I will return later to this important problem of balance—or rather of synthesis. The issue before us just now is whether pure science can be done effectively in a professional school environment. The experience just cited constitutes a clear affirmative answer.

ACCESS TO THE KNOWLEDGE BASE: BUSINESS

We concluded earlier that the main way an organization gains access to the knowledge stored and transmitted by a social system is by participating in that system. How can business schools participate effectively in the business system?

Historically, the schools have tried to answer this question in several ways. They have sought faculty members with management experience; they have encouraged faculty consulting practice and have offered consulting and applied research services to business; they have brought in businessmen as occasional lecturers; they have offered post-experience courses as another route for bringing managers within their walls. The idea behind all these lines of action is to get as close to the actual practice and environment of business as possible. How well have these methods worked?

Faculty with Business Experience

Seeking faculty members with management experience has provided a number of outstanding successes and innumerable failures and mediocre outcomes. If we think hard about the conditions for success, we will be surprised less by the failures and struck more by the impressive exceptions. What might motivate a man to leave a business career, temporarily or permanently, for teaching in a business school?

He might have attained only a relatively low level in management, with modest prospects for further rise, so that the business school offers him financial and professional advancement. This man, unless he is quite young when he makes the choice, is unlikely—and experience bears this out—to shine more brightly in academia than he did in business. In the exceptional case, and there are exceptions, what he brings to the business school is ability, not business experience, for he has operated at too low levels for his experience to have much value.

He might be nearing retirement and feel that his energies no longer enable him to keep up the fast pace of management activity. Of course there is no evidence, and less experience, that low energy and the desire for semi-retirement produces professorial excellence. This man is likely to suffer from the further dangerous illusion that good business teaching consists in "telling the boys how I did it."

He might be looking for a new range of experiences, have an affinity for things intellectual, and catch the excitement of a first-rate university environment. He is the exception, the rare bird we must net at all costs.[7] And after we have netted him, we must provide the challenge he was looking for. We must help him learn to teach, to interact fruitfully with the more long-haired among

[7] Four (but not ten) outstanding examples of such exceptions come to my mind as I write this: three of these people came to Academia in their forties, one in his sixties. Two had previously had academic experience early in their careers.

his colleagues, and to keep the feeling of excitement that led him to make the change. If he finds that being a professor is just being a businessman at second hand and at a lower salary, we have lost him, and the sooner, the better for him. We will see so few of his species in a lifetime, that we must seek him at all ages and levels in business. We must not miss the man whose age suggests he is near retirement, but who is really eager to avoid it (its restfulness, that is; not just its status).

The "typical" business school faculty member, however, even on the applied end of the faculty, will not be a man with much or any experience as a manager. He will be a man who has followed an academic career. We must provide ways in which he can get access to the business environment. (We must provide these ways even for the man who has had business experience, for that experience will recede rapidly into the past.)

Consulting Practice and Field Research

Consulting practice is potentially an excellent route of access. Its potential will be realized only if there is a strong institutional tradition in favor of nonroutine consulting at a high professional level, and against routine consulting. If the school is to receive any benefit from the consulting practice of its faculty, that practice must also remain within reasonable limits of time—an average of one day a week is a rule of thumb many schools have found practical.

Research that brings the faculty member inside the business firm for many hours—while he gathers data by observation and interview, or while he collaborates in the research with management personnel—is probably at least as valuable as consulting. There need be no sharp line between the two, except:

1. The faculty member and the firm he is working with should both be crystal clear as to when he is doing the one, and when the other.

2. He should almost never receive payment when he is doing research, always when he is consulting.

3. The research agreement should never promise valuable results to the business firm, although such results should be welcomed if they arise as a by-product.

4. Research should generally be based on an agreement between the school and the business firm, consulting on a direct relation between the professor as an individual and the firm.

Research has an especially important part to play in gaining access to the business environment for the more junior faculty members and for those farthest from the applied end of the faculty spectrum. Participation in research is an important means, also, for their acquiring knowledge and skills that can gradually provide them with assets that can be marketed through consulting activity. It is not at all important whether the research is "applied" in intent or "pure;" it should be aimed at questions the faculty members think significant. What is important for the purpose under discussion is that the conduct of the research bring about massive exposure of the faculty members to actual behavior inside the business firm.

It is a mistake to think that contact with the environment of business calls for narrowly "applied" activities. The managers themselves are far more qualified than outsiders, whether professors or not, to handle the short-run, practical problems that require intimate knowledge of the business. The outsider is in a better position to learn something and to build a continuing relation if he has something to give as well as something to get from it. This usually means that he should be dealing with long-range, fundamental questions that draw on information from outside the business, as well as information in it—the kinds of questions that are likely to be neglected by the business itself in its preoccupation with immediate concerns. Even the consulting relation is most satisfactory when it relates to matters of a relatively long-range kind.

The other devices mentioned above for gaining access to the business environment—lectures by businessmen and post-experience courses—do not need extended comment. The outside lecturer is more often used than used well. Many of the comments above on research and consulting have implications for structuring the relation with post-experience students. I will leave these to the reader to spell out.

ACCESS TO THE KNOWLEDGE BASE: THE SCIENCES

If the faculty members of business schools are not recruited from business, then they will be recruited from among the men who take graduate work (1) in business schools, (2) in the scientific disciplines relevant to business. Provided that certain rather difficult conditions are met, the latter group will provide access to the bodies of scientific knowledge associated with their disciplines.

The difficult conditions arise because it is not enough just to recruit men from the scientific disciplines; the business schools must recruit *first-rate* men. If it is only rarely that a first-rate businessman will want to join a business school faculty, we must not suppose that first-rate scientists will have this urge much more often. In the value structures of almost all the scientific disciplines, the word "pure" carries positive connotations and the word "applied," negative connotations. Pure and fundamental research is high status research. Whether we like it or not, that is a fact, and a fact that business schools must take into account in their faculty planning.

The business school cannot assume, then, that the typical bright, well-trained economist, psychologist, or mathematician will want to join its faculty. It can assume, more realistically, that "business school" is a dirty word to him. It must find the positive reasons and must provide the conditions that will convince him that he can do significant, fundamental work in the business school environment, and do it *more* effectively there than in a traditional department of economics, psychology, or mathematics. High salaries will help in the persuasion, but they will not do the job unaided.

And what tenable arguments *can* the business school give a scientist that it will offer him a superior research environment? The main one was stated in a previous section: In the business school he will be confronted with problems of end use, arising from the environment of business, that he can transform into exciting, non-routine problems of fundamental research. Twenty years of success with this research formulation strategy at several business schools makes the argument more persuasive than it was a generation ago. But even today, it will appeal mostly to the adventuresome, to the maverick. There is no harm in that, except that people who are both bright and adventuresome are always in very short supply.

The business school does not stand a chance of recruiting first-rate scientists if it insists that all research done in its walls must have direct relevance to business. It will do better to demonstrate its respect for fundamental research by having, and valuing, in its faculty at least some members much of whose work does *not* have obvious relevance to business but does command high respect in its discipline. I will say more about that when I come to the topic of "synthesis." Equally important, when tests of relevance are applied, it is essential that they be applied by people who understand the tortuous, many-step process by which fundamental knowledge may gradually be brought to bear on problems of practice.

Since it has been done in business schools and in schools of medicine and engineering as well, it is clearly possible to recruit good scientists to the professional school faculty and to create an environment where they will be and feel productive. Where it has been done, it has been done by respecting the scientist's desire for identification with, and approval by, his scientific discipline. If an economist is not respected by economists, he is unlikely to achieve self-respect from his contributions to management science, or even his contributions to economics drawn from his contact with management science.

The price to be paid for keeping good scientists, if it is a price, is that a certain part of their activity will result simply in good science, not particularly relevant to the specific concerns of the business school. If *all* their activity is of this kind, then the point of their being in the business school has been lost. This brings us, finally, to the problem of synthesizing the knowledge brought into the business school from the two environments.

THE PROFESSIONAL SCHOOL IN THE UNIVERSITY

There is no single or simple answer to the question of how far the professional school should depend on other departments in the university for teaching in the disciplines, or how far it should be self-contained. Nor is there any point in repeating here the usual cautions against duplication of faculty and courses in the university.

Under any circumstances, however, a strong case can be made for not excluding the disciplines entirely from the professional school faculty. At a minimum, each of the relevant disciplines should have an effective beachhead within the professional school. The business school, for example, needs some social or organizational psychologists, some applied mathematicians and statisticians, and some economists, as well as its professionally oriented faculty. It needs them whether or not (perhaps one could almost say "especially if") those disciplines are represented elsewhere on the faculty.

If the university has a strong economics department or a strong psychology department, then the business school must have effective communication with members of those departments in order to have access to the corresponding part of its knowledge base. Having members of these disciplines in its own faculty, at least with joint appointments whose "jointness" is more than nominal, is almost essential to maintaining such communication. It goes without saying that faculty with joint appointments can perform their function only if they are *more* than minimally acceptable as colleagues to the members of the disciplinary departments. Second-class citizens cannot do the job.

Some of the psychologists and economists with joint appointments will need to be sufficiently strongly identified with their business school functions to take a vigorous role in staff and curriculum planning in the school. Arrangements under which the disciplines provide "service" courses to the professional school, without accepting major responsibility for what goes on in that school, are guaranteed gradually to destroy the intellectual foundations of the professional training.

One way in which the professional school can strengthen its ties with the disciplines is to provide funds for fundamental research in areas *broadly* relevant to its mission, and to make these funds available to appropriate scientists in the disciplines—and particularly to pairs or groups of faculty members who link the school with the disciplines. In fact, the practical steps for bringing about better communications between the profession and the disciplines are really very much the same, independently of whether the faculty in the disciplines are outside or inside the professional school. We shall therefore continue our discussion of these questions on the assumption that some, at least, of the disciplinary faculty are inside the school.

THE KNOWLEDGE BASE: SYNTHESIS

The business school envisaged in the last three sections would consist largely of one faculty cohort drawn from the scientific disciplines and a second, more "applied" cohort trained in the business schools themselves. The danger is that the barrier between these two sets of social systems will simply be transferred from the outside world to the interior of the business school itself. Hence the problem of designing the business school organization has only been half solved when the school finds that it has one foot firmly planted in each of these systems.

A social system left to itself gravitates toward a position of equilibrium—of maximum entropy, so to speak. The position of maximum entropy for a professional school is one in which the portion of the faculty that is trained in the profession is absorbed in the culture of the profession, while the portion that is trained in one of the underlying disciplines is absorbed in the culture of that discipline, leaving a deep gulf between them.

Unfortunately, this position of equilibrium does not permit the business school to perform its teaching and research functions effectively. The "practical" segment of the faculty becomes dependent on the world of business as its sole source of knowledge inputs. Instead of an innovator, it becomes a slightly out-of-date purveyor of almost-current business practice. Again, this outcome is not peculiar to business schools but has often been noted in engineering schools, schools of education, and other professional schools during periods when their orientation has been most "practical."

Similarly, under equilibrium conditions, the discipline-oriented segment of the professional school faculty becomes dependent upon its disciplines of origin for goals, values, and approval. Sealed off from the practitioner's environment, that environment becomes inaccessible and irrelevant to them as a source of data, of research problems, or of development and application of innovations. Two equally deleterious developments follow. On the one hand, the members of each discipline in the professional school demand increasing autonomy so that they can pursue the goals defined by their discipline without regard to the "irrelevant" professional schools goals. On the other hand, the professional school environment loses any special attraction it might have as a locus for research and teaching, and the group becomes less and less able to attract and retain first-class members.

Some of these dynamics can be seen in the historical development of American business schools. Originally spawned, in most cases, within economics departments, they gradually moved in the direction of the business environment, until the "pure" economists formed minority enclaves. Their minority status and their detachment from the professional orientation of the rest of the school led the economists, in turn, to seek autonomy, and often separation, from the business school.[8] A similar history can be traced in the relation of psychology departments to schools of education, and science departments to engineering schools.

A professional school administration—the dean and senior faculty—have an unceasing task of fighting the natural increase of entropy, of preventing the system from moving toward the

8 F. C. Pierson, *op. cit.,* chap. 3.

equilibrium it would otherwise seek. When the school is no longer able, by continual activity, to maintain the gradients that differentiate it from its environment, it reaches that equilibrium with the world that is death. In the professional school, "death" means mediocrity and inability to fulfill its special functions.

All efforts to prevent this equilibrium state of death must be aimed at lowering the barriers that impede communication between the discipline-oriented and the profession-oriented wings of the faculty. If the scientists in the professional school are to resist the claims and persuasions of their discipline in order to achieve the goals they can best achieve in the professional school environment, they must have access to the informational system of the profession. If the professionally oriented faculty are to be more than Monday-morning quarterbacks of the world of practice, they must have access to the new knowledge produced in the disciplines.

The specific measures that will best achieve this end will vary with time and place. They range from the simple and concrete to the sophisticated and subtle. Such a trivial matter as office locations may be important. Homogeneous office grouping of faculty —almost guaranteeing homogeneous luncheon groupings and the restriction of casual conversation to homogeneous clusters—is the worst possible arrangement; but it is the arrangement that will normally emerge unless it is deliberately avoided.

Departmental structures must not be allowed to develop within the professional school, or, if they are unavoidable, their importance must be minimized. It may be necessary to give specialized subgroups some particular responsibilities for the recruitment and evaluation of faculty within their specialties—but under no circumstances exclusive responsibility.

Curricular planning, too, can best be done by groups that cut across disciplinary boundaries. Marketing is an aspect of business institutions, but influence processes are an important topic in social psychology, and the theory of consumer choice a topic in economics. They are all concerned with the same human behavior, hence need to be brought together, not separated, in the curriculum. Inventory control has been an area of fruitful application of modern quantitative techniques, which in turn involve the economists' basic principles of marginal analysis.

In the same way, almost every curricular area can be organized so that practical management problems are rubbed up against economic and psychological theories and mathematical techniques —and conversely. These kinds of joint planning activities may, in time, lead also to some collaboration in the teaching itself, and to an interest of disciplinary specialists to extend their teaching into applications, and *vice versa*.

Parallel opportunities to encourage communication across boundaries can be sought in research. There is no guaranteed magic in "inter-disciplinary research." Attempts to apply this formula mechanically and without realistic appraisal of the appropriateness and feasibility of a particular form of collaboration have produced thumping failures. But if faculty members from different disciplines find themselves in frequent contact with each other, a pair or triad will occasionally discover an area of common interest where they want to undertake joint work. The task of the school's administration is not to establish artificial and sterile formal plans for interdisciplinary work but to encourage the contacts that will cause projects to develop spontaneously and to support them when they do emerge.

Encouragement of doctoral thesis problems that require the student to work with faculty members from several disciplines is often a useful device for acquainting the faculty with each other's work. Advanced graduate students can provide a valuable leaven, if they are not allowed to specialize too soon or too narrowly in their own training.

I am sure that these examples do not exhaust the possibilities for lowering the barriers to communication between disciplines. It is not important what particular techniques come into play in any particular case. What is important is that the administration of the professional school take the lowering of barriers as a major goal of its policy. Practices that strengthen the bonds of specialization existing in the scholarly or business world are to be avoided or accepted with the utmost reluctance. Practices that have the opposite effect are to be sought for, encouraged, and abetted untiringly. To do this, the organization must be willing to expend energy continually to oppose the social forces that would otherwise push it toward equilibrium with its environment.

ART AND SCIENCE

One of the deep sources of communication difficulty between the discipline-oriented and the practice-oriented members of a professional school faculty stems from the difference between science and art, between analysis and synthesis, between explanation and design. The goal of the pure scientist is to explain phenomena in nature: the laws of physics, of physiology, or of consumer behavior, as the case may be. The goal of the practitioner is to devise actions, or processes, or physical structures that work—that serve some specified purpose.

The techniques the scientist uses toward his goals are usually called "analytic." To explain phenomena, he dissects them, pulls them apart into simpler, familiar elements. The techniques of the practitioner are usually called "synthetic." He designs by organizing known principles and devices into larger systems.

Analysis leading to explanation is generally thought to be itself susceptible of analysis and systemization. It is thought to be teachable because explicitly stateable. Explicitness and lawfulness are characteristics attributed to science. Synthesis aimed at design is generally thought to be intuitive, judgmental, not fully explicit. Design cannot be fully systemized, hence is an art, so it is said. Medicine is an art, engineering is an art, management is an art, teaching is an art.

The character of the professions as arts has in modern times created a barrier to their full acceptance as proper inhabitants of a university. (Historically, of course, the medieval universities *were* professional schools.) It has not been thought that synthesis and design could be the subjects of systematic instruction in the same sense that analysis and explanation could. The former were not fully "intellectual" subjects, hence only marginally appropriate for university, and especially graduate, training. A major reason why applied science has almost driven engineering from the research and graduate programs of engineering schools, and modern biology and biochemistry have almost driven medicine from the medical schools, is that the former subjects, in each case, have had a quality of intellectual "toughness" and explicitness that the latter have lacked.

A full solution, therefore, of the organizational problem of the professional schools hinges on the prospect of developing an explicit, abstract, intellectual *theory* of the processes of synthesis and design, a theory that can be analyzed and taught in the same way that the laws of chemistry, physiology, and economics can be analyzed and taught. The bases for such a development cannot be discussed at length here, but I will simply assert with little elaboration that the prospects are exceedingly good at the present time.

The primary reason why the prospects are good is that in several fields of professional practice (notably engineering and business), the decision-making process underlying design is now sufficiently well understood so that computer programs have been written that automate it in significant instances. Since these programs for synthesis could not have been written without an understanding of the design process, they provide tangible examples, open to inspection for purposes of research and instruction, of the internal cognitive structure of design and synthesis. We no longer have to apply the label of "art" to these kinds of design activities, to conceal our ignorance of the processes they involve.

Our increasing ability to approach synthesis and design as rigorous intellectual disciplines—to make these processes the proper objects of teaching and research—supplies a missing component in the construction of an effective professional school organization. For these new disciplines provide a focus for the profession-oriented part of the faculty, and a set of tasks more challenging than merely monitoring and interpreting the information system of the business environment, or even applying existing knowledge to business problems. They give us, therefore, means for increasing the intellectual attractiveness of the school's practitioner-oriented concerns, and making it easier thereby to establish meaningful communication between the faculty dealing with these concerns, on the one hand, and the discipline-oriented faculty, on the other. We can hope for a gradual reduction in the university's distrust of the "applied" character of the professional school's task, and a consequent rise in the respect accorded to faculty members oriented toward the profession.

A PARALLEL PROBLEM: RESEARCH AND DEVELOPMENT

I have emphasized throughout that the organizational problem facing business schools is not peculiar to them but is shared with all the other professional schools as well. All have the common problem of bridging the gap between the social system that produces scientific knowledge, on the one hand, and the social system where professional practice takes place, on the other.

If this is a correct characterization of the central organizational problem, then it is a problem common not only to professional schools but is present in all kinds of research and development organizations. For the fundamental task of a research and development activity is to use basic scientific knowledge to create and improve industrial products and processes, and to use information about the needs of industry and its customers as a source of good research problems for scientists. R & D activity is successful when it accomplishes these goals; it fails when a gap appears somewhere in the communications chain between pure scientists on the one end and production and sales engineers on the other.

The natural equilibrium of an R & D organization, like the natural equilibrium of a professional school is mediocrity and futility. R & D management, like professional school administration, must take as a central task lowering the cross-disciplinary communications barriers. The particular techniques appropriate to the industrial and university environments may differ, but the pattern of organization they are seeking to achieve is fundain the one case will certainly carry valuable lessons for the other.

mentally the same. What we learn about successful organization

CONCLUSION

The central thesis of this paper is sufficiently simple so that no lengthy conclusion is needed. Organizing a professional school or an R & D department is very much like mixing oil with water: It is easy to describe the intended product, less easy to produce it. And the task is not finished when the goal has been achieved. Left to themselves, the oil and water will separate again. So also will the disciplines and the professions. Organizing, in these situations, is not a once-and-for-all activity. It is a continuing administrative responsibility, vital for the sustained success of the enterprise.

INDEX